Analyzing

Opera

Verdi and Wagner

California Studies in

19TH CENTURY MUSIC

Joseph Kerman, General Editor

Analyzing

Opera

Verdi and Wagner

EDITED BY
CAROLYN ABBATE
AND ROGER PARKER

University of California Press
Berkeley, Los Angeles, London

The publication of this book
was made possible in part by a grant
from the American Musicological Society.

University of California Press
Berkeley and Los Angeles, California

University of California Press, Ltd.
London, England

LIBRARY OF CONGRESS
Library of Congress Cataloging-in-Publication Data

Analyzing opera: Verdi and Wagner / edited by Carolyn Abbate
and Roger Parker.
p.   cm.—(California studies in 19th century music ; 6)
Papers originally presented at the Cornell Verdi-Wagner
Conference, Cornell University, October 1984.
Includes index.
ISBN 0-520-06157-8 (alk. paper)
1. Verdi, Giuseppe, 1813–1901. Operas—Congresses.
2. Wagner, Richard, 1813–1883. Operas—Congresses.
3. Operas—Analysis, appreciation—Congresses.   I. Abbate,
Carolyn.   II. Parker, Roger, 1951–   .   III. Cornell University.
IV. Cornell Verdi-Wagner Conference (1984).   V. Series.
MT95.A59 1989
782.1′092′2— dc 19   88-21072
                                                                          CIP
                                                                          MN

Printed in the United States of America
1   2   3   4   5   6   7   8   9

Contents

Acknowledgments

It is customary for the editors to compliment contributors on their courtesy and promptness, virtues indispensable for the completion of a volume such as this. We are indeed happy to do so: all our contributors were courteous; most were prompt; we are grateful to them all.

The present collection evolved from a conference devoted to Verdi and Wagner that took place at Cornell University in the autumn of 1984. (For a detailed account of the papers given there, see the present writers' "Osservatorio: The Cornell Verdi-Wagner Conference, October 1984," *Studi verdiani* III [1985], 131–37.) The conference could not have taken place without generous funding from the National Endowment for the Humanities,[1] from Princeton University, and from many sources at Cornell; nor would it have been so smooth-running (in the circumstances, one fears, only a relative term) without the assistance and support of Lenore Coral, Joanna Greenwood, Don Randel, and James Webster. We should also like to acknowledge with thanks and no small regret a group of further contributors to the conference, whose excellent papers could not, for one reason or another, fit into the somewhat restricted focus of the present volume. These contributors included William Ashbrook, Robert Bailey, Will Crutchfield, Arthur Groos, Ursula Günther, Harold Powers, Gary Tomlinson, and James Webster. Ashbrook's paper has since appeared as "The First Singers of *Tristan und Isolde*," *Opera Quarterly* III, no. 4 (1985/86), 11–23; Günther's as "Wagnerismen in Verdi's *Don Carlos* von 1867?" in Carl Dahlhaus and Egon Voss, eds., *Wagnerliteratur— Wagnerforschung* (Mainz, 1985), 101–8; Tomlinson's as "Italian Romanticism and Italian Opera: An Essay in Their Affinities," *19th-Century Music* X (1986), 43–60; Webster's as "To Understand Verdi and Wagner We Must Understand Mozart," *19th-Century Music* XI (1987), 175–93; and Groos's as "Wagner's *Tristan und Isolde:* In Defense of the Libretto," *Music and Letters* 69 (1978), 465–81.

As the book took shape, others gave much-needed help: Diana Waltman typed the editors' introduction more times than we care to remember; Adelyn Peck and Alice Clark were invaluable editorial assistants; Doris Kretschmer

---

1. The opinions set forth do not necessarily reflect those of the Endowment.

represented the University of California Press with tact and good humor. Joseph Kerman was an exemplary series editor. He advised in numerous ways from a very early stage, and his interventions have saved the editors many embarrassments, both large and small. Finally we want to thank Harold Powers, who first suggested the idea of a conference on Verdi and Wagner, and who, from that time onward, encouraged, assisted, and admonished us at regular periods.

A Note on Citations

Wagnerian passages are cited either by text cues ("Hagen, was tatest du?"), or, where greater precision is demanded, by measure numbers or reference to the Schirmer vocal scores (using page/system/measure within system: 50/3/1–4). This method of citation allows readers to find their way without undue difficulty in any one of the many full-score editions rather than requiring them to use one particular edition.

The Verdi scores available present, if anything, an even more chaotic situation than that for Wagner. The articles on *Ernani* and *Rigoletto,* which grew out of work on the Complete Verdi edition, make direct reference to the relevant volumes of that edition. The remainder of the Verdi citations refer to the standard Ricordi vocal scores (again using page/system/measure within system) unless the nature of the discussion requires another method.

Needless to say, reference to vocal scores is solely for the convenience of readers and is not meant to suggest that consultation of the full orchestral scores is anything less than indispensable for those who wish to analyze this repertoire.

Introduction
On Analyzing Opera

CAROLYN ABBATE AND ROGER PARKER

A commonsense definition of "analyzing opera" would impute no esoteric meaning to the phrase. For most people "analyzing an opera" would mean "interpreting an opera" or "explaining an opera," to contribute to a richer understanding of the work. Classic books such as Ernest Newman's *The Wagner Operas* or Edward J. Dent's *The Mozart Operas,* both highly literate commentaries on matters such as background, plot, and music, are analyses of opera in this sense. Both volumes tell the story in familiar and friendly words.

For some purposes, analyzing opera need go no further than this, but for the musician, music historian, or theorist, the idea of analyzing opera—indeed, of analyzing any musical genre—will evoke something different. Analysis, broadly defined, is a detailed and complex investigation into the substance of a musical work, one taking the musical text as its primary object. At its best, musical analysis nourishes what Joseph Kerman has called a "comprehensive, 'humane,' criticism of music,"[1] an interpretation of text guided by the musicality and intellect of a gifted writer. Theodor Adorno has written bluntly that "all criticism of any value is founded in analysis; to the extent that this is not the case, criticism remains stuck with disconnected impressions," for "analysis has to do with *das Mehr* [the above-and-beyond] in art; it is concerned with that abundance which unfolds itself only by means of analysis, . . . the truly 'poetic' in poetry; and the truly poetic in poetry is that which defies translation."[2]

The analysis that merely describes musical events is like the translation that passes over all meaning, that passes over the "truly poetic." To go beyond me-

---

1. Joseph Kerman, "Academic Music Criticism," in Kingsley Price, ed., *On Criticizing Music* (Baltimore, 1981), 53.

2. Theodor W. Adorno, "On the Problem of Musical Analysis," trans. Max Paddison, *Music Analysis* I, no. 2 (1982), 176–77.

chanical conversions of musical notation into written words, analysis must uncover something beyond or behind the mere sonic surface.[3] That "beyond and behind" might be the relation of the critic's stance toward the piece and his knowledge of its reception. It might be the connection of the piece to other musical works, its intertextuality. It might be the unveiling of relationships between different musical gestures in the piece and a demonstration of how these relationships define the unique universe within which the piece unwinds on its own special terms. Such an analysis, even if couched in language that may be abstruse and intricate, may reward the reader with insight into both the marvelous and the shocking in a familiar work.

Given our broad definition of the term and our generous characterization of the art, it seems that analysis can only enrich our conceptions of a musical work. Why, then, should the notion of analyzing music seem to many a less than lively pursuit?

> The word "analysis" easily associates itself in music with the idea of all that is dead, sterile, and farthest removed from the living work of art. One can well say that the general underlying feeling towards musical analysis is not exactly friendly. . . . One will encounter this antipathy again and again, above all in the rationalization represented by that absurd though utterly inextinguishable question: "Yes, everything you say is all very well and good, but did *the composer himself* know all this—was the composer *conscious* of all these things?"[4]

Adorno here implies that hostility toward analysis grows out of a kind of philosophical immaturity, a childish hankering after irrelevant biographical legends. Concern for the human composer and his foibles can, he argued, be kept separate from the work as an object of scrutiny, even though this detachment may seem hard-hearted and win for analysis little sympathy.[5]

Are the flaws of analysis, however, only in the eyes of Adorno's unsophisticated beholder? The kind of analysis we attempted to characterize above is an ideal, and one that fully merits the respect Adorno accorded it. That ideal, sadly, is rarely attained; critics of analysis have a point. For one thing, too much analytical writing is overlaid with a protective sheen of technical jargon and couched in inexpressive prose.[6] Style, of course, should not in itself deter us from evaluating substance, yet the critical reader may feel justified in doubting

---

3. "Beyond and behind" will have a familiar ring. The words are taken from two well-known essays on the proper spheres of analysis, theory, and criticism: Edward T. Cone's "Beyond Analysis," *Perspectives of New Music* 5 (1967), 33–51, reprinted in Benjamin Boretz and Edward T. Cone, eds., *Perspectives on Contemporary Music Theory* (New York, 1972), 72–90; and David Lewin's "Behind the Beyond," *Perspectives of New Music* 7 (1969), 59–69. See also Edward T. Cone, "Mr. Cone Replies," ibid., 70–72.

4. Adorno, "On the Problem of Musical Analysis," 171.

5. Joseph Kerman, *Contemplating Music* (Cambridge, Mass., 1985), 72–73.

6. This objection is raised by Peter Kivy, *The Corded Shell: Reflections on Musical Expression* (Princeton, 1980), 8–9, 67–68.

the sensitivity of a writer whose means of communication is unthinking, inelegant, or imprecise. More substantive criticisms can also be made. All too often, practitioners of musical analysis labor doggedly to discover the hallmarks of autonomous structure, or coherence, or organic unity in a work. By doing so, they may ignore a hundred rich contexts for their object, including those we might regard as historical: the conditions of its invention, its intertextuality. Perhaps betraying an atavistic urge toward the calmer waters of earlier generations' critical battles, they end up producing a kind of New Criticism writ small.

But the point runs deeper, touches more directly the focus of the present volume. Many critics assume a priori that the musical object, to be of value, *must* be unified in certain conventional ways. This assumption is, of course, related to a naive insistence that interpretation can and ought to be wholly detached from its context. But analysis is at its worst when trapped in a tautological cage of value judgments predicated on musical unity, for then it has no devices for coping with music that is ambiguous, with musical disasters within the piece analyzed, with the enigmatic. Indeed, a critical passage such as the following suggests that the myth of definable unity thrives unchallenged in certain circles:

> The lack of a comprehensive theoretical model sometimes leads the author into equivocal expressions, as if to say: Well, it could be heard this way, but then, it *could* be heard this other way. The inescapable conclusion is that the passage is rich in ambiguity. Of course, ambiguity in music does not really exist. Some musical phenomena can be understood in several ways . . . but surely one of the functions of analytical insight is to show how all but one of the apparent or "theoretical" possibilities are artistically untenable in a given context.[7]

The reviewer's implication is that Beethoven wrote music that is unambiguous (and *therefore* good), music whose structure is limpid, whose workings are transparent. This does Beethoven a grave disservice. Furthermore, the notion reflects a kind of interpretive positivism that would surprise scholars and critics who work in related fields, and perhaps partially explains the dearth of dialogue between music analysts and those who deal in other arts.

In such an atmosphere, it is hardly surprising that opera has fared rather badly as an object of "detailed and complex investigation" into matters musical.[8] For opera is not music alone; it lives in association with poetry and dramatic action, an association that has made it idiosyncratic and special, certainly different in fundamental ways from instrumental music. Those whose analytic

---

7. Bruce B. Campbell, review of Janet M. Levy's *Beethoven's Compositional Choices* in the *Journal of Music Theory* XXIX, no. 1 (1985), 193.

8. Twentieth-century opera has fared rather well in this respect; George Perle's work on *Wozzeck* and *Lulu,* and Milton Babbitt's essay on *Moses und Aron* (in Benjamin Boretz and Edward T. Cone, eds., *Perspectives on Schoenberg and Stravinsky* [Princeton, 1968], 55–60) are exemplary. Yet perhaps the operas at issue have something to do with this. All three may be said to be both artworks and, on some level, musical analyses of themselves. Put another way: they were operas created for musical analysis and incomplete without it.

staple is nonoperatic music may feel baffled by opera and may deal with it in inappropriate ways; they may be limited by their preoccupation with analytic modes whose criteria of value run to organic unity or Hanslickian virtues of formal perfection. At worst they may feel obliged to cram the music into a shell of coherence far too small to encompass it.[9] Perhaps more often, they simply recoil, as Heinrich Schenker did. Schenker's comments on Wagner seem to echo Nietzsche's castigation of Wagner as "musical miniaturist." Wagner's music, Schenker wrote more than once, was unable to maintain its tonal syntax (hence, logic and structure) except in very brief patches.[10] Made uneasy by such music, Schenker did not otherwise venture into the brackish waters of opera, not even as far as the illusory purity of the Mozartean set-piece.

Of course, any writer who, like Schenker, chooses to regard opera as music alone is seeing only one of the three primary colors. "Analyzing opera" should mean not only "analyzing music" but simultaneously engaging, with equal sophistication, the poetry and the drama. Analysis of opera might also attempt to characterize the ways that music in opera is unique; that is, to address the idiosyncrasies that set operatic music apart from the instrumental music that has shaped our notions of analysis.

These are, very broadly, the goals set by the essays presented here. The notion of juxtaposing those two operatic lions of the nineteenth century, Verdi and Wagner, is, of course, hardly new.[11] But comparative studies have tended to assume that the two are radically dissimilar as musicians and music dramatists. Wagner and his "symphonic opera" set against Verdi "the melodist" is only the hoariest of many familiar antitheses, but it serves to highlight the particular terms according to which comparisons are usually made, and it reminds us of the potency of the instrumental norm. By bringing together writers whose critical stances could be expected to be contradictory, we hoped for highly charged exchanges, but also, more optimistically, for an emerging sense of common purpose.

In certain respects, the cumulative force of these essays is revisionist; fondly held views of the composers are refashioned. One example: the issue of "words

9. This fault mars, for instance, Robert Donington's essay on global thematic cross-reference in *Orfeo*. Donington assumed that the opera *en tout* had to be "unified" on some level. See "Monteverdi's First Opera," in Denis Arnold and Nigel Fortune, eds., *The Monteverdi Companion* (New York, 1968), 261–66. Charles Rosen's view of the Mozart finale as a largish sonata form is another case in point. It is surely too comfortable to understand Mozart's multipartite, thematically varied, and loosely organized sequences of theatrical-musical moments as having the same degree of coherence as a sonata first movement; see *The Classical Style* (New York, 1972), 301–5. This is not to say that the sections in a Mozart finale are not in certain ways related to one another, simply that the evocation of sonata form gives a misleading impression of the nature and intimacy of those relationships.

10. See, for instance, *Harmony,* trans. Elizabeth Mann Borghese (Chicago, 1954), 174, or the well-known passage in *Das Meisterwerk in der Musik* II (reprinted Hildesheim, 1974), 28–30.

11. The most notable publication of recent years has been Friedrich Lippmann, ed., *Colloquium "Verdi-Wagner" Rom 1969* (Cologne, 1972).

and music," with all it involves, lurks near the edges of some essays, while in others it takes on all the force of a dramatic *Hauptmotiv*. Traditional juxtapositions have tended to stress as the difference between Verdi and Wagner in this respect that Wagner, as author of his own libretti, must necessarily have subjugated the text to the music more effectively than did his Italian contemporary.[12] But Verdi emerges here as the more absolute musician, and Wagner—in part—as an artist whose poetry controlled, and even fought against, his musical decisions.

Our larger purpose was that suggested in the title of this volume: to consider the analysis, and the criticism, of opera, the assumptions of such analysis, and the preoccupations of writers engaged in it. It was our view (though not necessarily that of all our colleagues) that if analysis deals with musical substance, then analysis of opera should confront nonmusical elements that may inform that substance. As Pierluigi Petrobelli has recently put it: "In opera, various 'systems' work together, each according to its own nature and laws, and the result of the combination is much greater than the sum of the individual forces."[13] Certain essays in the present volume embrace this clash of systems with some enthusiasm; others take the nonmusical systems as given; still others—with a certain self-consciousness—avoid interpreting them altogether. Even in the last case, however, the status of opera as a hybrid medium is tacitly acknowledged. This status seems bound to become an increasingly important aspect of our reaction to the medium.

Our focus on Verdi and Wagner resulted in part from the wealth of interpretive writings that has, since the nineteenth century, been accruing to the accounts of both. Verdi and Wagner both had questionable reputations among musical purists and were accused of musical ineptitude by conservative (usually German) critics. Writers in the nineteenth century who were well or ill disposed toward one or the other were therefore nudged into closer consideration of musical matters in order to support their value judgments. Many preoccupations in late-twentieth-century analytical writings on the two composers can be traced to the preoccupations, and the conclusions, of this earlier tradition. The essays collected here are no exception. Some edge toward new analytic modes appropriate to opera while others react to canonic interpretations of specific works, but all should be viewed in light of their ancestry, through a review of the traditions against which they stand.

---

12. A point which Verdi himself alluded to in an interview for the *Neue Freie Presse* in 1875: "When our conversation turned to Wagner, Verdi remarked that this great genius had done opera an incalculable service, because he had had the the courage to free himself from the tradition of the aria-opera. 'I too have attempted to blend music and drama in my *Macbeth*,' he added, 'but unlike Wagner I was not able to write my own libretti.' " Quoted in Marcello Conati, *Encounters with Verdi* (Ithaca, N.Y., 1984), 109.

13. Pierluigi Petrobelli, "Music in the Theatre (à propos of *Aida*, Act III)," in James Redmond, ed., *Themes in Drama 3: Drama, Dance and Music* (Cambridge, England, 1981), 129.

*   *   *

Analysis of operatic music on a grand scale began with the nineteenth-century interpretations of Wagner. For better or worse, changing fashions in Wagnerian interpretation have left imprints in critical writing on all other nineteenth-century opera. In Verdians' debates concerning tonality and drama we hear vague echoes of Alfred Lorenz's interpretation of *Tristan*; the idea of "reminiscence motive" inevitably, if wrongly, evokes the leitmotive. The difficulties in surveying the Wagnerian field of play reside not in locating participants but in sorting out the crowd, and complaints about the mass of verbiage that has attached itself to Wagner's life and work are by now an obligatory opening gambit in any book on the subject. Yet it seems worth emphasizing that a surprising amount of that mass is devoted not to Wagner's personality but to his music and his music-theoretical writings. We may choose to disregard much of this literature on the grounds that it is not analytical after our mock-technological fashion, but to do so is to risk overlooking work that is both rich and provoking.

In the broadest sense, the tradition of analyzing Wagner goes back to the 1850s, when a number of book-length studies of his music had already appeared, along with many critical articles in the German musical press. These earliest essays, when not puzzling over the prose in *Oper und Drama,* tended to measure his four published operas—*Rienzi* to *Lohengrin*—against the traditional and contemporary repertory then most popular: Mozart, Weber, Bellini, Donizetti, Halévy, Meyerbeer. Warm approval of the conventional elements in Wagner's early operas was commonplace and was invariably accompanied by vehement rejection of any device not codifiable within the usual—generally Italianate—constraints for "numbers."[14] Wagner's use of reminiscence themes was often belittled as mere rhetorical effect, heavy-handed at that, and was criticized for creating musical illogicalities by allowing music to symbolize poetry with too great an intimacy.[15]

From the outset, then, Wagner's early critics distinguished between a self-sufficient musical logic and an intrusive text-generated gesture. It is a distinction that has been maintained ever since, albeit in many different forms. In 1893 critic Christian von Ehrenfels extended the argument to Wagner's later works; from him the dialectic of "form-defining" and "referential" passed to Lorenz, and has been often invoked since then.[16] Wagner's early partisans took the opposite position. Espousing the novel as a matter of pride, they fastened on just those rhetorical motivic and orchestral effects as a powerful means of new and specifically musical inventiveness, as well as an aid to dramatic expres-

---

14. See, for example, Hanslick's 1846 essay "Richard Wagner und seine neuste Oper *Tannhäuser,*" reprinted in Helmut Kirchmeyer, *Das zeitgenössiche Wagner Bild* III (Regensburg, 1968), cols. 147–83.

15. Otto Jahn, "Tannhäuser," in *Aufsätze über Musik* (Leipzig, 1866), 73–74.

16. Christian von Ehrenfels, "Die musikalische Architektonik," in *Bayreuther Blätter* XX (1893), 267; Alfred Lorenz, *Das Geheimnis der Form bei Richard Wagner* I (Berlin, 1924), 73–74.

sion. Liszt's 1851 essay on *Tannhäuser* and *Lohengrin* is a locus classicus, singling out the symbolic motives for particular praise and discussing their function as musical commentaries on the drama.

The performance and publication of Wagner's music dramas in 1859–1876 created a Wagnerian analytic industry of considerable proportions. Like the criticism of the 1850s, this second wave included both critics and partisans, but the writers ill-disposed toward Wagner continued to measure his work against conservative musical precepts and traditional operatic models. If Eduard Hanslick had found *Tannhäuser* daring, he could hardly help experiencing *Tristan* as an amorphous chain of musical moments, each called up in reaction to a dramatic point; "formlessness" and "harmonic illogicality" were the catchwords of the opposition.[17] What may seem puzzling is that the partisans—even those most intoxicated by Wagner's music—also heard long stretches in the later works as extended ariosi of no particular coherence. They had been prodded to this perception by Wagner himself, for both his familiar formula of "unendliche Melodie" and his image of the "symphonic web" were calculated to capture an experience of music as narrative fabric. Wagner, of course, in response to his critics' accusations had pointed to constant motivic repetition in his works as proof of their purely musical coherence. His explanation was specious, for "coherence" in this sense is so vague and fundamental that it might be applied to any music. But the partisans took their tone from the master. They felt no need to interpret his music as logical or structured by the standards of contemporary *Formenlehre*; instead they merely appealed to vaguer aesthetic criteria to argue for its power and beauty. It was not until the end of the nineteenth century that Wagner's defense was conducted in the same terms as the attacks against his music.

Hans von Wolzogen's *Ring* analysis of 1877 stands at the turning point; it was the first systematic musical exegesis of Wagner's later work, a map of thematic eddies in the *Ring* whose substance and method are heavily marked by Wagner's image of the symphonic web. The book (along with Wolzogen's essays on the other operas) is one source all Wagnerian analyses—indeed, all analyses of opera—must still confront. Wolzogen's description of the *Ring* is cast solely in terms of motivic recurrences across all four operas. But more important, of course, he interpreted the motives as signs representing objects, characters, concepts in the drama—as leitmotives. Every time we make an apology for continuing to use Wolzogen's labels we acknowledge the unshaken force of his example. More than this: by using the verbal tags, even if only as a convenience, we underline for any reader all the referential connotations of the motives, whether self-evident or ridiculous and whether or not we ourselves believe in them.

17. See, for example, Hanslick's essay "Die Meistersinger von Richard Wagner," in *Die moderne Oper: Kritiken und Studien* (Berlin, 1875), especially 310–12.

The misuses to which leitmotivic exegesis has been put encourage us to bemoan Wolzogen's example. But regret may be tempered by other considerations. First, Wolzogen's essay on the *Ring* was a product of discussions with Wagner and preserves something of Wagner's view of his own work.[18] Second, the referential connections are real, at least in the *Ring*. Finally, Wolzogen's guide made no claim to expose a last secret of Wagner's musical thought; it indexed a single phenomenon. The concept of form, for instance, is not ignored; it is, quite simply, passed over, rather casually at that. Wolzogen did make offhand references to "Lenzlied" or "Isoldes Erzählung," to the passages we also regard as the more shaped and self-contained of Wagner's "web"; it seems, then, that Wolzogen was not only well aware of but actually took for granted a distinction between closely structured and more diffuse music. But, unlike later generations, he was uninterested in examining or rationalizing his intuitions about form; Wagner's motivic symbolism had absorbed him entirely.

A vast number of later publications were to replicate, translate, and expand Wolzogen's basic guides, and, in a certain class of writings, taxonomy of motives became a sufficient explanation of Wagner's music and, in part, an excuse for avoiding further inquiry into its workings. The labeling of motives prevails to this day as the most common popular mode of Wagnerian "analysis," having been widely disseminated to an English-speaking audience in the work of Ernest Newman and Deryck Cooke. Both men accepted without hesitation the notion that finding, describing, and naming thematic fragments constituted a sufficient account of Wagner's musical language. Indeed, the process of deciphering alleged musical symbols mutated in their hands into an exercise with a momentum all its own, pursued with comical doggedness.

For example, Newman puzzled long over recurrences of what Wolzogen called the "Flight" motive in parts of the *Ring* where flight is furthest from anyone's mind.[19] The "Flight" motive had in fact been badly named; Wolzogen had attached the label carelessly when he noted the figure in *Rheingold*, as it accompanied Freia's flight from the Giants. Newman took Wolzogen's casual label literally, and in doing so was forced to the absurdity of scolding Wagner for misapplying the "Flight" motive when no one was fleeing, for making an error in a musical dictionary whose existence was merely assumed.[20] Wolzogen's misnomer was later rightly cited by Cooke as a piece of blatantly bungled labeling, one that went unquestioned for almost a hundred years. But Cooke drew the wrong moral from the story. It should have served as warning that motives, even in the *Ring,* are hardly as precisely lexical as the hundreds of labels

---

18. The point is made by John Deathridge in his review of *The Wagner Companion* (London, 1979), in *19th-Century Music* V, no. 1 (1981), 84.

19. Ernest Newman, *The Wagner Operas* (New York, 1949), 459–60.

20. Ibid., 510.

suggest. Instead, Cooke merely preached a rewriting of the dictionary, with truer identifications provided for every thematic scrap.[21]

*   *   *

The Verdians of the nineteenth century were, initially, not dissimilar to their Wagnerian counterparts; they were critics whose principal forum was the daily feuilleton or the weekly musical journal. Until Verdi's death in 1901, the best writing about his music appeared in the press, often combining critical matters with the expository and the descriptive.

Especially in the first decade of his career, Verdi found himself the object of much polemical exchange. From the advent of Rossini on, Italian critical opinion became increasingly distant from popular taste, and Verdi's success was often seen as an extreme celebration of Italy's brash musical insularity, a symptom of the public's demand for noise and effect over subtlety and adventure. Though most observers recognized immediately that a new force had arrived, not all approved of the novelty. "Poco canto e molto rumore" ("little melody and much noise") was the leitmotive—with some even the idée fixe—of the opposition and, particularly in Germany, Verdi underwent frequent attack as a mangler of larynxes, an arch cabalettista, the man who changed bel canto into con belto.[22] Even at the beginning, however, there were some surprisingly astute reactions, ones that pierced what must have seemed an uncomfortably forthright compositional exterior. As early as 1840, the *Allgemeine musikalische Zeitung* carried a long account of *Oberto* that recognized the appearance of an important new voice.[23] By the mid to late 1840s, each new opera rallied a host of belletrists.

The recently collected journalistic reactions to *Macbeth*'s premiere in 1847 form a representative group. Value judgments appear by the barrow-load— the shorter the acquaintance, it seems, the easier it was to make up one's mind; there are also interesting comments on Verdi's relationship to his predecessors and contemporaries; some challenging attempts to discuss aesthetic questions—opera's responsibility toward naturalism, its compatibility with the supernatural—but virtually nothing that we would call analysis. L. F. Casamorata's extended critique might seem an exception: it contains "technical" remarks and even some musical examples. Not so. The detailed comments are the least convincing and imaginative section of this valuable essay, their substance remorselessly Procrustean. Verdi sometimes places musical accents on unac-

21. Deryck Cooke, *I Saw the World End* (Oxford, 1979), 39–73.

22. For an account of some early German reactions, see Marcello Conati, "Saggio di critiche e cronache verdiane dalla *Allgemeine musikalische Zeitung* di Lipsia (1840–48)," in *Il melodramma italiano dell'ottocento: Studi e ricerche per Massimo Mila* (Turin, 1977), 13–43.

23. See Marcello Conati, "*L'Oberto conte di San Bonifacio* in due recensioni straniere poco note e in una lettera inedita di Verdi," in *Atti del 1° congresso internazionale di studi verdiani* (Parma, 1969), 83–87.

cented syllables. At one point he has a D♭ in the melody against a C in the bass. With just a little more care, Casamorata suggests, such errors could have been put right.[24]

As we move to the second half of the nineteenth century and to the well-nigh universal acceptance of Verdi as Italy's leading composer, it becomes clear that the Italian cultural scene will furnish no Wolzogens, no systematic attempts at description. But if Wagner's seeming radicalism encouraged his commentators to explore new exegetical methods, the best Italian critics benefited from the other side of the coin, using Verdi's persistence with traditional formal models as a point on which to sharpen their perceptions of his originality and power. The representative Verdian critic of the period is Abramo Basevi, whose 1859 monograph on the composer is frequently cited in the modern literature and has recently been reprinted.[25]

Reasons for our continuing interest in Basevi are not hard to find. Basevi knew thoroughly the repertoire against which Verdi was writing; his division of Verdi's work (up to *Aroldo*) into four manners and two broad stylistic periods, with *Luisa Miller* as the dividing line, is in tune with modern-day views; and his lively discrimination about the comparative successes and failures of Verdi's works, though occasionally rather *de haut en bas,* is refreshing when compared with the relentless hagiography of the later nineteenth century. Basevi's most valuable contribution lies in his taxonomies of traditional forms (in general more systematic than we find elsewhere) and in the acuteness with which he measures Verdi's achievement against them. On a few occasions, his tone with Verdi is rather like Hanslick's or Ludwig Bischoff's with the young Wagner—approving of conformity and the artful execution of known conventions, often disdainful of stylistic novelty. The "Salve Maria" from *I Lombardi,* for example, one of Verdi's most radical formal experiments, went too far: "The first two periods . . . are a simple succession of notes, and nothing more, which do not bind together to form a musical *concept*; for this reason they lack one fundamental of musical composition." On the other hand, Basevi was no die-hard: the Sparafucile-Rigoletto Duet in Act I of *Rigoletto* met with his approval, even though it departs so completely from "la solita forma de' duetti."[26]

Despite all this, Basevi, like Hanslick, has probably absorbed too generous a share of attention from today's scholars. The more we explore mid-nineteenth-century music criticism, the more it becomes clear that Basevi's uniqueness is in scope—he deals with all Verdi's operas from *Nabucco* to *Aroldo*—rather than in method or critical prejudices; and, of course, he collected his essays (originally written for a weekly journal) into a book. In fact, a body of Italian criticism

24. In David Rosen and Andrew Porter, eds., *Verdi's Macbeth: A Sourcebook* (New York, 1984), 368–412.

25. Abramo Basevi, *Studio sulle opere di Giuseppe Verdi* (Florence, 1859; rpt. Bologna, Biblioteca storico giuridica e artistico letteraria, 1978).

26. Ibid., 24, 191.

contemporary with and later than Basevi is equally acute but almost totally un-known. An assemblage of the best of this writing, by such figures as Francesco Regli and, later, Filippo Filippi, might transform our views of nineteenth-century interpretations of Verdi.

*   *   *

It is during the mid-nineteenth century that our two composers first become entangled. Near the end of his monograph, discussing *Simon Boccanegra,* Basevi sounds a note that will occasionally reappear in later nineteenth-century discus-sions of Verdi: "At least judging from the Prologue, I would say that it seems as though Verdi was following in the steps of the famous *Wagner*—from afar, but none the less following."[27] Basevi had by that time already written some of the first articles on Wagner to be published in Italy.[28] Soon the Wagnerian cause was taken up by Boito and the *scapigliatura,* although their impressions were arguably less than profound: the first Italian performances of Wagner (a run of *Lohengrin* in Bologna) did not occur until 1871, and knowledge of the Master's work would have been through his theoretical writings or, at best, vocal scores. Burgeoning *wagnerismo* came to a crisis, perhaps not surprisingly, at Verdi's operatic home of La Scala, Milan, where the 1873 performances of *Lohengrin* inspired some lively displays of cultural xenophobia. But the Wagnerian vogue, at least as it affected creative musicians, was rather short-lived in Italy (especially when compared to the situation in France); rationalism prevailed, as we can see from the fact that some of Verdi's most sympathetic and intelligent critics (Ar-rigo Boito, Filippi) were also knowledgeable and enthusiastic Wagnerians. In spite of Verdi's periodic complaints, his later operas were only occasionally tarred with the Wagnerian brush.

Verdian analysis, like critical writings on Wagner, emerged slowly from the feuilleton, and certainly did so much later—some would say, not until the mid-dle of the twentieth century. Critical and analytical works lagged behind the indispensable series of biographical and epistolary publications that appeared from 1900 to the 1960s: the *Copialettere* of 1913, and works of Carlo Gatti, Alessandro Luzio, Franco Abbiati, and Frank Walker. The turn of the century also saw the decisive emergence of what Gabriele Baldini would later term the "exclamatory" type of criticism, much of it inextricably bound up with the at-mosphere of bombastic chauvinism that had engulfed Italy. It was hardly fortu-itous that this period also saw the enshrinement of Verdi as the "vate del

---

27. Ibid., 264.

28. For information about these and other early writings on Wagner in Italy, see Marcello De Angelis, *La musica del Granduca: Vita musicale e correnti critiche a Firenze 1800–1855* (Florence, 1978), in particular vi–vii and 197–98. For a recent account of Wagnerism in nineteenth-century Italy, see Marion S. Miller, "Wag-nerism, Wagnerians, and Italian Identity," in David C. Large and William Weber, eds., *Wagnerism in Euro-pean Culture and Politics* (Ithaca, N.Y., 1984), 167–97.

Risorgimento," the bard of Italy's drive toward national unity. This easy identification of art with politics was arguably a far more serious obstacle to genuine understanding of the music than any lingering Wagnerism, and it certainly accelerated the laying down of critical arms; the fact that the myth continues to be accepted today proves its potency and perhaps also shows that many informed musicians are still nervous of confronting Verdi entirely on his own terms. The matter is illustrated to perfection by Alfredo Soffredini's 1901 monograph on Verdi. Up until *Rigoletto* he keeps himself reasonably in check, but then, "Confronted by genius in all its magnificence, in all the magic of its splendor, one can no longer speak, even to mouth praises; and in the words of Giosuè Carducci, *one worships!*"[29]

There were, of course, exceptions. Massimo Mila's two reasoned and balanced monographs deserve more attention than they at present receive.[30] Dyneley Hussey's 1940 book, though of course sympathetic to its subject, exhibits a peculiarly English attitude toward opera. Between the lines we read of a cultural tradition in which the primacy of spoken drama as a yardstick of dramatic truth and effectiveness had never seriously been challenged. When Hussey criticizes Boito's *Falstaff* libretto for losing "much that gives the play its immortal quality—the tang of the English character and of the English countryside that makes Shakespeare's hand unmistakeable,"[31] the remark carries deep resonance. The few studies that could properly be called analytical tend inevitably to betray a Wagnerian perspective: it is difficult to account in any other way for the continuing interest in Verdi's use of recurring themes. As we said earlier, during this period analyzing opera was geared almost exclusively to the Wagner industry; specifically, to the concern for labeling leitmotives. No wonder Verdi seemed an unlikely target. In the 1950s, Joseph Kerman wrote a convincing and fairly thorough account of Verdi's use of recurring themes. The article runs to sixteen pages.[32] To the Wagnerians, it must have seemed like clutching at straws.

Recent motivic studies have of course not restricted themselves to those few recurring themes. Roman Vlad, Peter Pal Varnai, and, most thoroughly, Frits Noske have all made attempts to consider Verdi's treatment of motive as form-building, unifying, and, above all, as capable of dramatic articulation. Noske has gone further, his studies of semiotics leading him to the notion of a "musico-dramatic sign." This is "a musical unit which stresses, clarifies, invalidates, contradicts, or supplies an element of the libretto. The sign is semanti-

29. Alfredo Soffredini, *Le opere di Verdi* (Milan, 1901), 145; quoted from Gabriele Baldini, *The Story of Giuseppe Verdi* (Cambridge, England, 1980), 171–72.

30. Massimo Mila, *Il melodramma di Verdi* (Bari, 1933); *Giuseppe Verdi* (Bari, 1958).

31. Dyneley Hussey, *Verdi* (London, 1940), 21.

32. For an early study of recurring themes, see Gino Roncaglia, "Il 'tema-cardine' nell'opera di Giuseppe Verdi," *Rivista musicale italiana* XLVII (1943), 220; Kerman's essay is "Verdi's Use of Recurring Themes," in Harold S. Powers, ed., *Studies in Music History: Essays for Oliver Strunk* (Princeton, 1968), 495–510.

cally interpretable and discloses dramatic truth."[33] This last sentence is crucial, and with it Noske drifts perilously close to Wolzogen. As with the leitmotive, the "sign" is deemed to exist only if it can be given an appropriate label, a semantic interpretation. In spite of the fresh theoretical terms, the old Wagnerian perspective is still in sharp focus.

But twentieth-century commentators on Verdi have had one advantage over Wagnerians of the same period: they can take for granted Verdi's deployment of certain conventions. The nature of the most basic musical shapes in an opera like *Il trovatore* is self-evident, for common musical and operatic sense tells us that they are the individual numbers. Because this ground was at least solid the Verdians were, potentially, freer to speculate about musical subtleties within scenes, about tonal structures or motivic cross-references. Not so the Wagnerians after Wolzogen. If they began to reject the nineteenth-century image of *Musikdrama* as text-generated sonic tapestry, they desired in its place an explanation of Wagner's works as masterworks, whose design was as logical and artful as a Mozartean ensemble. But on what scale? Only around the turn of the century was a search begun for definitions of form in works that seemed on the surface to owe nothing to the formal conventions of traditional opera.[34] The endeavor was to reach its culmination in the 1920s, in the work of Alfred Lorenz.

This most notorious of Wagner's champions was, of course, reacting with some violence to the old view of Wagner's music as a web of momentary symbolic effects. His declared intent was to expose the secret of form in Wagner's later music. Lorenz was by no means the first to bring the discourse of Wagnerian analysis back into the purely musical sphere and to write about designs rather than motives. The first appendix of his *Ring* study—entitled "Behandlung des Formproblems bei Wagner in der bisherigen Literatur"—still stands as the most exhaustive published bibliography of Wagnerian *Formenlehre*. Indeed, pursuit of Lorenz's citations to earlier literature can be a sobering exercise, effective against premature assumptions that one has oneself discovered some new *Geheimnis*. But Lorenz outdid all of his mentors, including even Karl Grunsky; he was more systematic, more emphatic, more insistent. He engaged a scale of musical time that was vast, as evinced in the black, boldface sentences familiar to all who habitually consult his work, those that begin "I do not hesitate" and end by informing us that all of *Rheingold* is a monstrous *Bogen* in D♭.

33. Frits Noske, *The Signifier and the Signified: Studies in the Operas of Mozart and Verdi* (The Hague, 1977), 316.

34. Guido Adler made the provocative (if self-evident) suggestion that even in *Musikdrama* might be traced the lineaments of number opera; see *Richard Wagner* (2d ed., Munich, 1923), 222–30. The notion has been discussed by Rudolf Stephan, "Gibt es ein Geheimnis der Form bei Richard Wagner?" in Carl Dahlhaus, ed., *Das Drama Richard Wagners als musikalisches Kunstwerk* (Regensburg, 1970), 9–12; and by Dahlhaus, "Formprinzipien in Wagners *Ring des Nibelungen*," in Heinz Becker, ed., *Beiträge zur Geschichte der Oper* (Regensburg, 1969), 100–102.

In coming to grips with Lorenz, we might well recall the assumptions upon which his analyses were built. He took Wagner's description of the "poetic-musical period" in *Oper und Drama,* part III, as a prescription for interpreting all the later operas, arguing that such "periods" were extended musical passages oriented to a single tonic. He envisaged the tonic as a force that controlled all harmonic events within each period. The other analytical decisions he made were subordinate to this parsing of each work into tonal periods; only after borders were established did he explore foreground articulations. The smaller divisions depended on thematic recurrences and local harmonic syntax. The inflexible bars and *Bogen,* the improbable strophes, and the other "forms" that became his stock-in-trade were thus triumphantly exposed within musical articulations established a priori by tonal considerations. Small wonder, then, that considerable cunning and an occasional blithe disregard for the aural surface were necessary for their creation.

Any critic whose appetite for ridicule is keen will find Lorenz's writings a rich source; but substantive objections to Lorenz's work, though weighty, are actually rather few in number. His claim that a single tonic might be maintained across long stretches of Wagner's music (to say nothing of a whole opera) is unfortunate: nothing seems to be gained but the false comfort of an illusory unity. His belief that all musical substance might be understood in terms of a few formal or procedural paradigms led him to find form where none exists, or even should exist. But more important: by forcing all of Wagner's music to seem organized to the same degree he ignored self-evident distinctions between more ordered and less ordered music, between loosely rhythmic prose and periodic phrasing, between clear diatonicism and deliberate harmonic obfuscation.

To these objections we can reply with at least one compliment. Lorenz maintained that Wagner's music was not simply leitmotivic chitchat; he insisted stubbornly and loudly that it was ordered into patterns and controlled by musical procedures that had nothing to do with the unavoidable referential obligations of all operatic music. He saw long-range cohesiveness residing in tonal recurrence and (on a smaller scale) in repetition and transformation of motives and in the sequence of musical events created by this procedure. Setting out his basic ideas in these perhaps excessively vague and neutral terms, we see that they might well be extracts from more modern analytical manifestos.[35] The ritual slap upon Lorenz's hand—that weary and inevitable feature of all Wagnerian analyses in the past few decades—has by now become superfluous. Lorenz should be read not because he discovered a last secret but within the context of

---

35. As David Lewin has put it: "Lorenz was the first to provide solid ground for our intuitions that Wagner's mature music dramas are organic unities. Even more important, he was the first to sense and claim that these dramas could be *analyzed* in that connection." See "Amfortas's Prayer to Titurel and the Role of D in *Parsifal,*" *19th-Century Music* VII, no. 3 (1984), 337, n.1.

his training and time. If we can thus make *Das Geheimnis der Form* an artifact, we can free ourselves from anxiety about its influence.

That influence has been immense. It is possible to see much of later-twentieth-century analysis of Wagner as Lorenzian fallout, whether through judicious adaptation of his thought or through critical reaction to it. Writers such as Robert Bailey, Nors Josephson, Reinhold Brinkmann, and Patrick Mc-Creless, who posit sustained tonics or pitch-complexes as background to long musical spans, adopt one of Lorenz's fundamental precepts, though they often disagree with his more peculiar analytical decisions when it comes down to cases.[36] Their rereadings of long-range tonal connections in Wagner's later operas have given us synoptic maps more sensitive to musical subtleties than some of Lorenz's. They have clarified and expanded Lorenz's nebulous (and occasionally farcical) notions about iconic keys or, as Bailey calls them, "associative tonalities." They have emphasized the profound consequences that tonal symbolism may have for the basic organization of an opera, suggesting that text-generated quotations of tonalities determine the emergence of certain keys at certain dramatic foci, whether those keys are in any sense logical in their local context or not.

But even writers who have been attracted by Lorenz's belief in sustained tonal spans may balk at Lorenz's Riemannesque arches: his insistence that the harmonic digressiveness of Wagner's more prosy music be forced into relationships with those intermittent plateaus of tonal stability that may punctuate each set. One could push the objection to Lorenz's background tonics much further, by suggesting that even these plateaus are deceptive, slyly contrived to create an illusion. With their loud cadential gestures, orchestral reinforcements, and local nods at diatonicism they mimic the aura of a structural tonic arrival, and yet the status of these moments as tonic is not necessarily substantiated by their larger harmonic context.

Lorenz's most articulate critic has been Carl Dahlhaus, whose essays on Wagnerian form have called into question not only the details of Lorenz's interpretations but the spirit of his theoretical stance. Dahlhaus's writings have become touchstones for many recent Wagnerian analyses and are, along with Lorenz's, the most influential Wagnerian commentaries to appear in this century. The number of citations to them in the present volume is only one indication of the central position they occupy.

Already in the 1960s, Dahlhaus had pointed out that Lorenz's principal assumption concerning the tonal unity of "periods" was derived from a misread-

---

36. Robert Bailey, "The Structure of the *Ring* and Its Evolution," *19th-Century Music* I (1977–1978), 48–61; Nors Josephson, "Tonale Strukturen im musikdramatischen Schaffen Richard Wagners," *Die Musikforschung* XXXII (1979), 141–49; Reinhold Brinkmann, " 'Drei der Fragen stell' ich mir frei': Zur Wanderer-Szene im 1. Akt von Wagners 'Siegfried,' " *Jahrbuch des Staatlichen Instituts für Musikforschung* V (Berlin, 1972), 120–62; Patrick McCreless, *Wagner's* Siegfried: *Its Drama, History, and Music* (Ann Arbor, 1982).

ing of Wagner's definition of "poetic-musical period," that Wagner was describing only the setting of perhaps sixteen or fewer text lines and not the vast (up to 900-odd measures) stretches Lorenz had conceived.[37] He argued that the logic of Wagner's form was better understood on a rather small scale, basing his conclusion not only on a careful interpretation of *Oper und Drama* but on his own musical intuitions. Form on such a small scale could be seen as mutable and dynamic, rather than closed and static. Dahlhaus has suggested that we perceive Wagner's music as evoking conventional procedures—rondo, ritornello, strophic repetition, variation, sequence—by means of motivic and harmonic gestures, but that these conventions may be thrown awry or implied anew with each passing moment; invariably such manipulations serve a musico-dramatic end.[38] Unlike the neo-Lorenzians, Dahlhaus has explained referential evocations of tonalities as *Einfälle,* unpredictable events that, like leitmotivic quotations, take place at the command of the text and have no long-range or deep musical consequences. His separation of rhetorical gesture from purely musical development is, of course, not absolute. Wagner's genius may reside in his ability to accommodate both at will.

✳   ✳   ✳

The notion that characters, objects, or dramatic *topoi* may have tonal as well as motivic identity has come to be a central issue in the analysis of opera other than Wagner's, and it is not surprising that the role of tonal symbolism and of other musical factors that operate across an entire opera became one of the *points d'appui* in analysis of Verdi's music when the tide finally turned to musical issues. This turn came in the 1960s and was fostered from the first by the Italian Institute for Verdi Studies. From 1960 onward, the Institute published a series of *Bollettini, Quaderni,* and *Atti* which, in scope and scholarly precision, soon outweighed the critical and analytical work of the previous sixty years. Much of this work was brought to a larger audience, and magnificently synthesized, in Julian Budden's three-volume commentary on the operas. In its sophistication and

---

37. Carl Dahlhaus, "Wagners Begriff der 'dichterisch-musikalischen Periode,'" in Walter Salmen, ed., *Beiträge zur Geschichte der Musikanschauung im neunzehnten Jahrhundert* (Regensburg, 1965), 179–87. An excellent English précis of Dahlhaus's work, and that of other contemporary German Wagnerians, may be found in Anthony Newcomb, "The Birth of Music out of the Spirit of Drama," *19th-Century Music* V (1981–1982), 38–54.

38. This thought is most concisely expressed in "Formprinzipien," 119–21, especially 120: "überlieferte Satztypen wie die Lied-, die Sonaten- und die Rondoform bildeten für Wagner zwar Voraussetzungen, auf die er sich auch dann noch stütze, wenn er über sie hinausging, verloren jedoch die normative Bedeutung, die ihnen in der musikalischen Formenlehre zugeschrieben worden war. Statt sie als Muster zu respektieren, benutzte Wagner sie als Mittel oder Gerüste, die manchmal, aber nicht immer, tauglich waren . . . und so sind im *Ring*—und zwar je nach den Forderungen des musikalischen dramatischen Augenblicks— nicht selten verschiedene Formtypen miteinander verschränkt, so dass in einer Analyze . . . versucht werden muss, einerseits die Formen, die in eine Szene oder einen Szenenteil eingeschmolzen sind, zu rekonstruieren und andererseits die Veränderungen zu beobachten, denen sie durch die Verquickung miteinander ausgesetzt sind."

scope, this work goes far beyond the analogous Wagnerian tome, Newman's *The Wagner Operas*.[39] True, two documentary projects of immense importance are now in progress: the Italian Institute's complete edition of Verdi's correspondence, and the University of Chicago Press and Casa Ricordi critical edition. But, while Wagnerian analysis exists alongside a great mass of biography and quasi-political (or philosophical) interpretive writing, much of the literature on Verdi is now analytical, or at least seeks to combine analysis with source studies.

What of this present-day industry in Verdian analysis? Can it be characterized in any useful manner? Certainly in one respect the ghost of Wagner seems to have been laid: motive is seldom studied as a "form-building" unit. But has a new—for some, more sinister—spectre from across the Alps taken his place? The issue of tonality and drama remains highly contentious. It may even be that Verdian critics can most clearly be categorized by their attitudes toward this topic, and few can raise the issue without invoking, for good or ill, the theories of Heinrich Schenker.[40] The matter was, by and large, left alone by earlier critics, the assumption usually being that Verdi was primarily a "melodist" (as we mentioned earlier, the comparison with Wagner the "symphonist" being more or less explicit). Indeed, this attitude retains some currency today. David Kimbell, at the analytical outset of his recent monograph on Verdi's early operas, states baldly:

> Opera is song—dramatic, lyrical, declamatory, virtuoso, as varied and as resourceful as may be, but always song—and the pre-eminent musical values are therefore those that can be most fully expressed in this one-dimensional medium. *The elements of melody and rhythm are of more significance than those of harmony, counterpoint and colour.* Moreover, the greater emphasis placed upon these elements of style dictates a manner of treating the harmony and orchestration that is difficult to reconcile with more Romantic and modern practice.[41]

The italics are ours, and the emphasis they give is perhaps sufficient to expose the problem: such statements can be made (and accepted) only in the heat of polemic. To separate "melody" from "harmony" and "counterpoint" may be defensible in certain repertoires, but for one such as Verdi the notion creates severe theoretical problems. Nor, of course, does Kimbell's subsequent analysis of the operas attempt any such separation.

In this respect, the other extreme of opinion is more radical. Those who wish to see Verdi's operas *à l'allemande,* as large-scale "symphonic" movements (or

---

39. Julian Budden, *The Operas of Verdi*, 3 vols. (London, 1973, 1978, 1981).

40. During one session of the Cornell conference from which the present collection of essays evolved, every chair seemed submerged in photocopies of voice-leading graphs. Quipped one irreverent delegate, "Ist hier ein freier Sitz?"

41. David Kimbell, *Verdi and the Age of Italian Romanticism* (Cambridge, England, 1981), 307–8.

as perceptible articulations of a tonic) seem quite willing to advance structural postulates that ignore all but the overall "harmonic motion," and on occasion make Lorenz on Wagner seem a model of caution. The locus classicus of this approach must remain Siegmund Levarie's assertion that *Il trovatore* "begins in E major and ends in E flat minor, so that the tonal flow of the entire work amounts to an enharmonically reinterpreted Neapolitan cadence."[42] The lively polemic that followed Levarie's article on *Un ballo in maschera,* from which the above is an extract, clarified few specific issues in that opera, but set many to thinking about the problem and the extent of their own commitment. In one sense, of course, Levarie's argument is easy to refute. Some characteristically wise words from E. T. Cone:

> What does it mean to say that an opera is "in" a certain key? Not, to be sure, merely that it ends in that key, or even that it begins and ends in the key. If the former were a sufficient condition, then it would be trivially possible to assign a key to all operas except atonal ones. If the latter were sufficient, any opera could be tonally unified by supplying it with a prelude in the key of its finale. Surely, if the designation of a single key as the tonality of an opera is to have more than superficial relevance, it must refer somehow to the progress of the entire opera.[43]

However, soon after this, Cone offered remarks about the later Verdi that many would find more provocative. He saw it as "useful and illuminating to consider *Falstaff* as rooted in C major" and considered that "*Otello* can profitably be ana-lyzed as developing a single key."[44]

Perhaps matters have focused a little since these stands were made; certainly only one of the papers collected here shows anything so extreme even as Cone's remarks on the late Verdi, though all would take the business of tonality more seriously than Kimbell. However, this middle ground is still broad enough to offer a considerable range of opinion, even within the present volume. Though in different ways, David Lawton and Martin Chusid each see the opera he is discussing as an architectural tonal construct, even though the keys both cite are, typically, presented as "blocks" rather than as moments of particular articu-lation within modulatory flux. The question of whether we perceive relation-ships between these "blocks" in quite the same way as we would between, say, the beginning and end of a symphonic movement still nags; as does, perhaps even more importantly, that of the status of intermediary passages: are they, tonally speaking, functionless? Timbre and vocal sonority may, as Lawton sug-gests, be important elements in bridging the gaps, and so, of course, will be the various dramatic articulations. However, if one argues for perceived *functional*

---

42. Siegmund Levarie, "Key Relations in Verdi's *Un ballo in maschera,*" *19th-Century Music* II (1978–1979), 143.

43. E. T. Cone, "On the Road to *Otello*: Tonality and Structure in *Simon Boccanegra,*" *Studi verdiani* I (1982), 72–73.

44. Ibid., 74, 75.

relationships between large forms (large-scale dominant-to-tonic relationships, for example), then the problems of small-scale functionality seem vitally relevant.

On the other side of the field, an increasing number of Verdians feel that tonality has now been done to death, that we must look to a "multivalent" analysis based on an accumulation of the various systems in play. Vital to this argument is the continuing presence of traditional formal models in the later operas, models which, as we know from earlier in the century, can readily be perceived as units regardless of whether they coincidentally act as closed tonal motions. The interaction of text forms and musical forms, and the work done in this area by Robert Moreen, by Harold Powers, and, later, by Peter Ross becomes an integral part of the analysis. Given his approach and the formal models he deals with, the fact that much of Powers's recent work has been based on *Otello* might at first seem deliberately provocative. As we see from Cone's statements, it is an opera even the conservatives allow to have some degree of large-scale tonal planning. But perhaps this is not really the case. It has long been tacitly assumed that Verdi's operas must necessarily move toward greater tonal unity as they become more continuous (again, we can guess that implicit Wagnerian comparisons are being made). There is of course no reason why this should be so. A glance at the mainstream musical tradition of the nineteenth century would suggest quite the opposite. A work written in 1890 is far less likely to boast firm tonal unity than one from 1840. Perhaps it is no accident that some of the most persistent arguments for large-scale tonal planning in Verdi are based on works such as *Macbeth* (1847) and *Rigoletto* (1851).

Some salutory reflections on the topic of tonal relations come from those who combine sketch studies with analysis. Not that this topic is without its own theoretical problems, of course, particularly concerning the extent to which sketches can be advanced as evidence for value judgments or analytical observations. But in Verdi's case, and especially with the earlier operas, the composer was clearly willing to make important additions and alterations to the structure of his work at a comparatively late stage of composition; this fact may call into question many of our assumptions about why his operas work so well as they do. Nearer home, there is the continuing problem of transposition. In his study of the *Ernani* autograph, for example, Philip Gossett points out that Verdi originally wrote Elvira's Act I Cantabile "Ernani! . . . Ernani involami" a half-step lower, a fact that is particularly striking because in its definitive form (in B♭ major) the aria is flanked by pieces in the same tonality. At the other end of his career, in *Otello,* Verdi continued to transpose, perhaps even more radically: the Act II Quartet from *Otello* underwent a late change down a half-step from B major to B♭ major. In both cases powerful circumstantial evidence suggests that Verdi made the alteration to suit a particular singer. As James Hepokoski gently advises, such evidence is, at the very least, likely to place on the defensive those who concern themselves with large-scale tonal matters.

True, the composer's priorities as his work neared performance may not necessarily have been the same as his initial, more purely creative ones; he may even
have felt obliged to do violence to his opera simply to ensure an adequate first
performance. But, so far as we know, Verdi never considered revising such matters, and we can only assume that he was indifferent to the whole business. As
yet, no one has confronted this problem head on, and it may be some time before we arrive at an aesthetic of Verdian opera that can accept some aspects of
tonal planning while fully accounting for the randomness of others.

✳   ✳   ✳

"Random," "diffuse," "illogical," "inexplicable": hardly the words we associate
with analyzing Wagner. Watchwords culled from this volume's Wagnerian
opening paragraphs have a different ring, masculine, familiar, perhaps a bit
stolid: "coherence," "organic unity," "structure," "form." It seems we have inherited part of Lorenz's analytic ideology, even as we labor to expose the rag-
gedness of Lorenz's technique. This faintly shopworn litany—"coherence,
unity, form"—has sonorous effect, but can by no means summarize or define
the stances taken by present-day interpreters of Wagner. With Dahlhaus, most
contemporary Wagnerians are seeking to elude Lorenz's shadow and have ex-
hibited considerable ingenuity in devising new ways to read a Wagnerian opera. Not only do they depart along different methodological paths, but—as in
several cases in the present volume—they reach neatly opposing conclusions
about the most basic issues. The collection of Wagnerians here assembled do,
however, have one point in common. Except for John Deathridge, with his essay on the *Lohengrin* composition draft, all concern themselves with *Musikdra-
men*. Put another way, they are attracted to those of Wagner's works most unlike those of his Italian rival.

Conscious or unconscious, this is an evasion, albeit a hallowed one. Wagner's
work before *Rheingold* has, with few exceptions, been disdained by writers of
analysis greedy to confront the musical delights of *Tristan* or the *Ring*. At best,
the "operas" are subjected to cursory rough handling in teleological arguments
seeking the ancestry of Wagner's musical maturity. How many leitmotives are
there in *Der fliegende Holländer*? When did Wagner start soldering single numbers into a superficially seamless whole? Set against the solemn and difficult
questions we ask of the later music, these inquiries seem trivial. As Deathridge
and Arnold Whittall have pointed out, we may get closer to an apprehension of
Wagner's musical culture, and of *Tristan*, in scrutinizing *Lohengrin*—perhaps
even *La Reine de Chypre*—with the intelligence routinely accorded to the later
work.[45] Clarion calls for solutions to the "problem" of Wagner after 1850 have
not been muter of late, but resolution of the problem may yet have to wait upon
an understanding of *Lohengrin* in its own context.

45. Arnold Whittall, "Wagner's Great Transition? From *Lohengrin* to *Das Rheingold*," *Music Analysis* II,
no. 3 (1983), 268–69.

Of course when Wagnerians writing serious critical studies of the music overlook everything before Zurich, they are to some extent guided by Wagner into a maze of his own making. His constructed history of music bypassed, on the whole, his own early "operatic" works, spinning instead thick threads between Wagner and Beethoven, Wagner and the great tradition of German instrumental music, the great tradition and Wagner's later works. Even the innocent might suspect that those threads, while not necessarily illusory, were calculated to distract, to direct the eye away from cords that bound Wagner to Weber, Bellini, Meyerbeer, and a far less ennobled musical tradition. The evocations in this collection of essays—of symphonies, instrumental conventions and procedures, Beethoven, and Schenker—may thus owe some of their color to Wagner's own history of nineteenth-century music, a faintly mythic history now deeply embedded in our own music-historical culture.

One of the small ironies exposed by a juxtaposition of contemporary Verdians and Wagnerians lies in their differing attitudes toward musical scale. While many Verdians are now focusing on global phenomena—Chusid and Lawton on long-range gesture are present examples—the Wagnerians have lately circumscribed their fields of inquiry to single scenes or parts of them (Amfortas's Prayer, Loge's Narrative, Fricka's Aria).[46] They strive to define the marks of self-containment in what Newcomb, citing Dahlhaus, calls "forms of intermediate size."[47] We may be dazzled by Wagner's claims to a stepfather in Beethoven, but we evidently find unsatisfying his vision of musical logic as a simple consequence of thematic repetition and variation across five or six hours. We restrict our perception. We make elaborate descriptions of musical devices deemed more intriguing than mere motivic repetition. Perhaps we are secretly intimidated by Schoenberg's mordant remarks concerning those who imagine they understand music if they recognize a recurring theme.[48] But more than this, our constraint may betray a secret nostalgia for operatic numbers, or for small, sedate instrumental movements whose identity and self-containment can at least be taken much more for granted.

The fine detail of Wagner's harmonic and tonal languages is complex, their workings enigmatic and elusive, fascinating theorists from the late nineteenth century, through Schoenberg and Ernst Kurth, to the present. Patrick McCreless and Matthew Brown have dealt with the issue here, employing Schenkerian theory to dissimilar ends. Brown's description of "tonal models" at work in Isolde's narrative suggests that Schenker's (and not merely Schenkerish) theory is fully able to account for the harmonic choreography of the piece. McCreless, considering the Norns' Scene, plays two interpretations against each other.

46. David Lewin, "Amfortas's Prayer"; Dahlhaus, "Formprinzipien," 99; Newcomb, "The Birth of Music," 55–56.

47. See p. 202, below.

48. Cited in Carl Dahlhaus, *Arnold Schoenberg: Variationen für Orchester* (Munich, 1968), 9.

One is an intentionally prim Schenkerian reading; the other is more ad hoc. What falls out of his comparison are two kinds of music: harmonic and contrapuntal orthodoxy for the first two Norns, for the third an odder, chromatic—if not atonal—idiom. "Multivalent" analysis in this case seeks to reveal opposed or dissimilar musical forces and even to hint at allegorical meanings for them. A most delightful Wagnerian analysis, David Lewin's account (in *19th-Century Music*) of the tonally *zauberisch* in Amfortas's Prayer in *Parsifal*, also finds allegories in Wagner's metamorphoses of harmonic systems; these metamorphoses are, however, exposed only by striking not one but two analytical-theoretical attitudes.

The question of tonality as cohesive force has shaped Newcomb's explorations of Wagnerian form, but in a very different fashion, for he believes that long-range tonal connections play at most a subordinate role. Indeed, Newcomb has deliberately and provocatively banished considerations of "large-scale tonal motion" from his interpretation of formal gestures in *Tristan* and *Siegfried,* though he does not question their very existence, as Dahlhaus does.[49] Newcomb instead concentrates on the form-building kinesis inherent in the opposition and transformation of thematic "sentences" and their melodic-harmonic properties. This thematic interaction, immediately perceptible, is the listener's first way of "structuring his experience" of the music through time. Newcomb slips this procedure into a historical context by arguing that Baroque ritornello conventions and Wagner's interest in Bach may have played a part in this compositional technique.

*   *   *

By adducing an instrumental genre as a compositional model, Newcomb has entered tangentially into another vexatious debate. What of the drama, the text, the role they play while the music is *in statu componendi*? What of opera's "interplay of systems"? It is not by coincidence that we are returning to a motive of our *Vorspiel.* Reading libretti as poetry may well generate an interpretation at odds with the reading imposed by the music. Music can misread words; it can ignore them; its view is not always literate. If we are insensitive to the literary text, we are not in a position to know when music corresponds to words, or responds to words, and when it does not.

The uneasy, elusive symbiosis between opera's various systems was a subject on which, in the end, Wagner was ambivalent and Verdi (typically) pragmatic. Wagner's ambivalence may surprise those accustomed to thinking of grandiose and confident abstractions like the *Gesamtkunstwerk.* His prose writings on instrumental music—in particular, the symphony—expose conflicting ideas, born of a desire to legitimize his work in the eyes of conservative critics, and,

49. Carl Dahlhaus, "Tonalität und Form in Wagners *Ring des Nibelungen*," *Archiv für Musikwissenschaft* XL, no. 3 (1983), 165–73.

ultimately, to explain the workings of his creative imagination. The significance of any absolute conception of music in his compositional psychology remains unclear. For the moment, however, we may simply wish to make an addition to our catalogues of Klingsor's magic. We know of harmonic intricacies, the tonal plans, the turnings of a motivic kaleidoscope, the unfolding formal gestures. But what of the energy of an antagonistic interplay: how a text ruffles music (a thing only the unsophisticated will limit to leitmotivic citation); how music overwhelms the drama's meaning. There is no need, in the end, to appeal to the tautology of a perfect union of drama and music as an ultimate explanation. Verdi, of course, hardly ever theorized. But in his interminable wrangles with librettists, he more than once let slip an awareness that neither the words nor the music of opera should be considered self-sufficient or independent. In a famous passage about the "parola scenica" in *Aida,* for example, he warns Antonio Ghislanzoni that "in the theater it is sometimes necessary for poets and composers to have the talent *not* to write either poetry or music."[50] We would do well to nurture such ambiguities.

The inevitable eclecticism in analyzing opera is paralleled, it seems, by contention over what musical insights we may have produced. On the role of tonality at all levels, the assumptions of formal convention, the scale of musical time on which we can begin to discuss musical connections, no consensus has been struck. Yet this lack of agreement is not a signal to search for the truth amid the contradictions. Instead, we should find in the contradictions the strength to jettison, at last, the *Geheimnis,* the idea that Verdi or Wagner (even within one opera or one scene) always wrote one kind of music, with only one set of tonal properties, always appealing to the same expectations of formal conventions, manipulating symbolic motives, ever reverent to the drama, ever perfect in the music. The contradictions may even enable us to confront the idea of analysis, or analyzing opera, with less militance or exasperation.

It should be no news that "analysis" aiming to reveal only absolutes of coherence or unity is sterile; the idea needs no further belaboring here. In the *Versuch über Wagner* Adorno dismissed Wagnerian (specifically, Lorenzian) analysis with the unflattering phrase "a graphic game, without power over the actual music."[51] And who among us, faced with long, droning passages of analytic prose or unstylish diagrams, has not thought something of the sort?

But if such words make us uneasy, they may make us less draconian in our assertions about how operatic music must work, more measured in our confrontation of its great figures, slower to put music through deductive systems or ideological matrices. Perhaps we can find interpretations that have, if not power "over the music" (for that implies diminishing music by translating it into prose), then at least power to illuminate it more warmly. Opera is peculiar; its

---

50. Gaetano Cesari and Alessandro Luzio, eds., *I copialettere di Giuseppe Verdi* (Milan, 1913), 641.
51. Theodor W. Adorno, *In Search of Wagner,* trans. Rodney Livingstone (Manchester, 1981), 42.

clash of systems can produce incongruities and extravagant miscalculations. At a time when organicism is no longer an adequate interpretive metaphor and when musical scholars tend more and more to reject positivism in criticism as well as history, opera is becoming a central area of investigation. This is hardly a surprise. Analysis of opera often reveals the imperfect, the ambiguous, the illogical. If it shows us how to recognize such qualities, perhaps it can also teach us to face them without uneasiness or fear.

Part 1

Sources and Interpretations

Chapter 1

The Composition of *Ernani*

PHILIP GOSSETT

The only known surviving music manuscript of significance for the original version of *Ernani* is its complete autograph score. This document reveals a great deal about the compositional history of the opera.[1] Moreover, careful examination of the structure of the autograph manuscript compels us to reconsider the more general question of Verdi's work methods during the 1840s.

The past fifteen years have seen numerous studies of Verdi's compositional process based on sources preserved in accessible collections or published in facsimile. These studies have had to construct hypotheses from limited evidence, despite the certain knowledge that extensive additional material is extant; the present essay is no exception. This unavailable material includes manuscripts, languishing in private collections, that have been described or even partially reproduced in catalogues issued by auction houses or antiquarian manuscript dealers. More significant, we have only a shadowy knowledge of the musical treasures unquestionably present at S. Agata in 1941, when Angiolo Carrara-Verdi allowed Carlo Gatti to print in facsimile the entire autograph sketch of *Rigoletto* (1851) and to include in his *Verdi nelle immagini* selections from other manuscripts of Verdi's sketches.[2]

---

1. Much of the material presented here, including the musical examples and description of the Verdi autograph, grows out of work done in collaboration with Claudio Gallico during the preparation of the critical edition of *Ernani* edited by Professor Gallico (*The Works of Giuseppe Verdi,* Series I, Vol. V [Chicago, 1985]). Let me thank Professor Gallico for his permission to cite freely material first published in the Introduction and Critical Commentary of his edition.

Apart from the complete autograph score of *Ernani,* several autograph album leaves of favorite themes from the opera exist, penned by the composer after its premiere, but these are not relevant to the issues raised in this study.

2. Carlo Gatti, *L'abbozzo del Rigoletto di Giuseppe Verdi* (Milan, 1941), and Gatti, *Verdi nelle immagini* (Milan, 1941).

No list of the musical manuscripts at S. Agata has ever been made public, if indeed such a list exists, but Gatti did remark that complete sketches survived there for all Verdi's operas beginning with *Luisa Miller* (1849).[3] These manuscripts are generally assumed to be similar to the *abbozzo* for *Rigoletto*, a largely complete and continuous draft of the entire opera in reduced score, in which the composer notated most of the vocal parts and gave occasional indications of orchestral solos or accompaniment. But the *Rigoletto* facsimile also contains sketch fragments: some predate the draft, some were worked out during the preparation of the draft, and at least one was made after the draft was completed.[4] The few available facsimiles of sketches in Verdi's hand, whether reproduced from sources at S. Agata or other collections, reinforce this suggestion of Verdi's methods: exemplifying different stages in the history of the operas, they indicate that the composer's compositional process involved many layers of activity.[5]

There is every reason to believe that Verdi's musical legacy at S. Agata contained more than the sketches attested by Gatti. Several other kinds of musical manuscripts must be there. To begin with, some complete compositions surely exist: the autograph of the withdrawn *Aida* "Overture" is known to survive at S. Agata;[6] other complete music may also be preserved, including juvenilia.

An even more extensive series of manuscripts, rarely mentioned, needs to be considered: pages removed by Verdi from the complete autographs and replaced with new music, either before the operas had been orchestrated, when these pages still represented skeleton scores, or after the orchestration was finished. Such rejected passages or earlier versions can be precisely documented for almost all of Verdi's operas. Everything we know of Verdi's habits, at least after he established himself at S. Agata with Giuseppina Strepponi in 1851, speaks against his having destroyed these rejected autograph manuscript leaves, which are of considerable significance. In some cases we know precisely what autograph materials are lacking, for example, in the original versions of *Stiffelio*,

3. In his introductory remarks to *L'abbozzo del Rigoletto*, Gatti wrote: "The sketch is preserved with the others of the Maestro's operas, from *Luisa Miller* to *Falstaff* and the *Pezzi Sacri*, in the Villa at Sant'Agata, in which the great man lived and composed for more than fifty years." Furthermore, on p. 182 of his *Verdi nelle immagini*, Gatti provided the following caption for the photograph of a room at Sant'Agata: "The small room in which are preserved the sketches of the operas from 'Luisa Miller' to 'Falstaff' and the 'Pezzi Sacri.' "

4. The sketch is described by Martin Chusid in his Commentary to the critical edition of *Rigoletto*, Series I, Vol. XVII of *The Works of Giuseppe Verdi* (Chicago, 1983), 5–9. No complete analysis or transcription of the sketch exists. The most important commentaries are those by Gino Roncaglia, "L'abbozzo' del *Rigoletto*," in *Galleria verdiana (studi e figure)* (Milan, 1959), 87–100, first printed in the *Rivista musicale italiana* XLVIII (1946), 112–29; Pierluigi Petrobelli, "Osservazioni sul processo compositivo in Verdi," *Acta Musicologica* XLIII (1971), 125–42, in particular 132–42; and David Lawton, "Tonality and Drama in Verdi's Early Operas," diss. University of California, Berkeley, 1973, 212–78.

5. I intend to discuss these sources more fully in a parallel study that analyzes more generally the problem of Verdi's compositional process during the first fifteen years of his operatic career.

6. The Verdi heirs made a copy of the autograph available to Arturo Toscanini. Recently the Sinfonia was recorded under the direction of Claudio Abbado. See the peculiar discussion of the piece's twentieth-century history in Julian Budden, *The Operas of Verdi*, 3 vols. (London, 1973, 1978, 1981), III, 191.

La traviata, Simon Boccanegra, and *La forza del destino,* all of which can be reconstructed from secondary sources. In other cases, close analysis of the autograph
scores suggests the existence of previous layers of music and allows us to guess
at the nature and even the character of the missing music.

Because of the limited accessibility of documents pertaining to Verdi's compositional process, scholars concerned with the roots of his art have studied in
detail those few sources currently available. For the early operas, where Gatti
mentioned no sketches, several types of documentation exist: numerous pages
of real sketches, including one for *Alzira* in the Gesellschaft der Musikfreunde
in Vienna;[7] rejected bifolios from various autographs, including those from the
autograph of *Attila* in Paris;[8] and compositional emendations, to use James
Hepokoski's term, in various autograph scores.[9] Our examples from *Ernani* belong to this last category.

Hepokoski has defined three types of emendation in Verdi's autographs:
simple erasures and rewritings, crossed-out measures or staves, and radical revisions signaled by the presence of replacement folios. Analysis of Verdi's autographs suggests a fourth category, related to Hepokoski's third: revisions that
can be inferred from structural irregularities in the manuscripts. To understand
these, we must recognize how Verdi's manner of writing his manuscripts differs
from that of many of his predecessors, a question with broad implications.

Let us begin by considering a few simple revisions in the vocal lines of
Ernani. Though an analytically meaningful treatment of such emendations
would require either a more general consideration of this single opera than is
possible in the present study, or the comparative study of a wide number of
emendations over many works, these examples from *Ernani* are significant in
their own right. When the melodies involved are among those we consider
characteristic of the composer at this period, their genesis helps us understand
the particular nature of his achievement.

7. See Pierluigi Petrobelli, "Pensieri per 'Alzira,' " in *Nuove prospettive nella ricerca verdiana (Atti del con-
vegno internazionale in occasione della prima del "Rigoletto" in edizione critica, Vienna, 12/13 marzo 1983* (Parma,
1987), 110–24. At least one other sketch for the opera is extant.

8. The manuscript, Ms. 2208 of the Bibliothèque Nationale, Paris, was first mentioned by Budden, *The
Operas of Verdi,* I, 249n. A fuller description and analysis are given by Michel Noiray and Roger Parker, "La
Composition d'*Attila*: Etude de quelques variantes," *Revue de Musicologie* LXII (1976), 104–24. A facsimile
of the first folio of the manuscript is given facing p. 122. William Weaver, in *Verdi: A Documentary Study*
(London, 1977), provides a caption for his plate 88 describing the opening pages of this manuscript, but the
manuscript reproduced to accompany the caption has nothing to do with *Attila*. It seems to be in Donizetti's
hand and is a canceled folio from the autograph of a father-daughter duet, to which the composer added
elaborate and unrelated sketches on empty staves.

9. Let me thank Professor Hepokoski for sharing with me several of his studies prior to their publication, including "Compositional Emendations in Verdi's Autograph Scores: *Il trovatore, Un ballo in maschera,*
and *Aida*" (forthcoming in *Studi verdiani* IV) and "An Early Version of Violetta's 'Addio del passato' (*La
traviata,* Act III)." An important study that provides detailed consideration of compositional emendations in
a single opera is David Lawton's treatment of *Macbeth,* "Observations on the Autograph of *Macbeth I*," in
David Rosen and Andrew Porter, eds., *Verdi's Macbeth: A Sourcebook* (New York, 1984), 210–26.

EXAMPLE 1.1.   First version of the cabaletta from Ernani's first-act
cavatina: flute and bass lines.

The theme of the cabaletta "O tu, che l'alma adora," from Ernani's first-act
Cavatina, a characteristic example of Verdi's early style, was achieved through
compositional revisions undertaken directly in the autograph manuscript. The
layers in which Verdi notated the score can be uncovered by differentiating
places where a previous version was corrected from those where only the final
version appears. The composer first wrote the flute and bass lines in the orchestral ritornello (Ex. 1.1). To correct them, he scraped away the original version
and substituted the definitive one. Oboe, clarinet, and violin parts doubling the
melody in the ritornello, on the other hand, have only the final version.

The entire vocal line and its accompanying bass originally continued with the
earlier version (Ex. 1.2). When he decided to alter the melody, Verdi crossed
out this music for Ernani at mm. 87–88 and 91–92, writing the revised version
on the staff above; at 103–4, he scraped away the original layer and wrote the
definitive one on the same staff. In each case he also corrected the bass. Only
after settling on the final version did he add doubling instrumental parts.[10]

The original version has rhythmic, melodic, and harmonic problems. Rhythmically the opening is limp: an upbeat to an accented downbeat, immediately
copied with the same upbeat to the third beat of the measure, the two gestures
separated only by an interpolated rest. Melodically the vocal line follows a
single-minded linear path to the high F and G, without gathering force for the
melodic peak. The dominant sonority accompanying the C on the fourth beat

10.   Since there is no upbeat in the revised theme, Verdi inserted a measure of orchestral vamp before the
reprise, by dividing the original first measure of the reprise into two bars, scraping away the initial version of
the vocal line, and entering the new one over it. Throughout this reprise, only the vocal line is present in the
autograph. In his rush to prepare the score, Verdi neglected to correct the remainder of Ernani's melody in the
reprise.

EXAMPLE 1.2.   Ernani's first-act cabaletta: original vocal line.

EXAMPLE 1.3.   Cabaletta: revised vocal line.

creates a premature cadential arrival in the second measure. Occurring twice within the first two phrases, this casual cadence weakens the true cadence at the end of the period.

The revision, the first part of which is found in Example 1.3, resolves each of these problems. Verdi avoided the double upbeat and rest by syncopating the opening rhythm. The line ascends quickly through E♭, then returns to D before continuing forcefully to F and G. Although the dominant harmony could undergird the melodic E♭ in m. 88, Verdi preferred the subdominant, reserving the dominant for the end of the antecedent phrase. Each of these changes helps transform the initial draft into a more powerful expression of Ernani's feelings.

EXAMPLE 1.4. Original cadence.

EXAMPLE 1.5. Revised cadence.

EXAMPLE 1.6. *Oppure* for high B♭.

Another vocal revision is worth considering. After the repeat of the cabaletta theme, the original cadential phrase (Ex. 1.4), sung twice, forcefully ascended to high B♭. This version is distinctly stronger than Verdi's revision (Ex. 1.5). Though the register of doubling instrumental parts may have been a factor in suggesting the change, problems inherent to Ernani's range were surely decisive. The highest note demanded of him in the opera is A, except for a single acciaccatura on B♭ in the largo of the first-act Finale. Verdi also wrote a B♭ in the third-act Finale but provided a lower, distinctly less satisfactory *oppure* (Ex. 1.6). The composer simply did not expect B♭ to be within Ernani's range, although he clearly would have preferred the singer to use the note in Act III.[11] Yet woe betide the modern Ernani who cannot bellow a high B♭ at the close of his Cavatina. It is another case (Manrico's part in *Il trovatore* is even more notorious) where inauthentic high notes have become for modern performers not merely alternative readings but the touchstone of a role.

Sensitive to the electrifying appeal of a well-placed high note, Verdi was equally aware that shameless repetition robs the effect of its glamor. We can even watch him eliminate high notes certainly falling within a singer's compass. A striking example is in the first-act Terzetto for Elvira, Ernani, and Carlo. The cabaletta theme concludes *a 3,* with Elvira ascending to and holding a high C

11. Whether it would be legitimate for a tenor to restore Verdi's original cadential phrase in the cabaletta is more questionable.

EXAMPLE 1.7. Transitional phrase, original version.

EXAMPLE 1.8. Transitional phrase, revised version.

before the cadence. The transition to the partial reprise of the cabaletta theme begins with a C-major phrase, subsequently repeated with an internal modulation to A minor. Because Elvira originally sang the same melody in the C-major phrase as in its A-minor repetition, her line ascended to high C (Ex. 1.7). Only the vocal line existed in this form, and Verdi promptly scraped it away; all instrumental parts reflect the final version (Ex. 1.8). Considering that Verdi concluded the Terzetto with yet another ascent to high C for Elvira, his decision to alter the transition was wise. Such evidence of Verdi's sensitivity to the problem of stratospheric pitches should at least give us pause before we presume that interpolated high notes do no harm to the substance of his work.

✳   ✳   ✳

We can now turn our attention to more profound changes, those involving more elaborate rewriting or structural alterations; but, to do so, we must first consider certain aspects of the genesis of *Ernani*. Descriptions of Verdi's compositional procedure tend to draw unwarranted conclusions from Gatti's statement that complete sketches exist only after *Luisa Miller*. As Pierluigi Petrobelli has written: "For the preceding operas we know only a few sketches or annotations for separate parts, individual scenes, or isolated vocal phrases."[12] This is true, but there is evidence that what we "know" may not be representative of what once existed.

Perhaps we have been unduly influenced by the example of previous composers. Rossini, Bellini, and Donizetti wrote operas using either a series of bifolios (with adjacent ones often derived from a single sheet) or a succession of gathered sheets (that is, gatherings of two bifolios). The composer did not need to predict the precise dimensions of each piece. The most that could remain blank

12. Petrobelli, "Osservazioni sul processo compositivo in Verdi," 128. In the subsequent discussion (pp. 142–204), Petrobelli suggests that the existence of extensive sketches from *Luisa Miller* on "goes hand in hand with the change in Verdi's musical style" (p. 162).

would be a single folio, easily eliminated. While typical of early-nine-teenth-century operatic autographs, these procedures were not used for the cop-ies in which operas circulated; there, each number was commonly written in a single gathering of multiple bifolios. Knowing the precise length of a compo-sition, the copyist could anticipate the necessary size of its gathering. Advan-tages of single gatherings are obvious: it was simpler to handle sections of the manuscript and be sure they remained in order.

The structure of the autograph of Verdi's *Ernani* is summarized in Chart 1.1. We see that, in general, Verdi used single gatherings of nested bifolios for indi-vidual numbers. The largest unit is made up of 13 bifolios (in N. 8); most fall between 6 and 10. Longer pieces are divided into multiple gatherings (N. 7, for

CHART 1.1. The structure of the autograph of *Ernani*.

NUMBER	FASCICLE STRUCTURE
Preludio	1 of 2 nested bifolios
N. 1	1 of 7 nested bifolios
N. 2	1 of 9 nested bifolios
N. 3	1 of 10 nested bifolios
N. 4	1 of 8 nested bifolios, + 1 of 6
N. 5	1 of 8 nested bifolios, to which another 2 nested bifolios were added between the second and third folios, + 1 of 5, + 1 bifolio (*spartitino*)
N. 6	1 of 6 nested bifolios, to which 1 folio was added between the first 2 folios
N. 7	2 of 8 nested bifolios
N. 8	1 of 13 nested bifolios, + 1 of 3, of which the last folio was cut away
N. 9	1 of 10 nested bifolios
N. 10	1 of 6 nested bifolios
N. 11	1 of 8 nested bifolios
N. 12	1 of 7 nested bifolios, to which another bifolio was added between the last 2 folios, + 1 folio (*spartitino*)
N. 13	1 of 6 nested bifolios
N. 14	1 of 3 nested bifolios, within which are an additional 4 single folios, + 1 of 8, + 1 of 2

example, has two, each of 8 nested bifolios). The pieces by and large fill their gatherings precisely, without blank folios or disturbances in the manuscript structure. This procedure would have been impossible had Verdi been unable to estimate precisely the dimensions of each piece before preparing its skeleton score. The inescapable conclusion is that *Ernani* was thoroughly sketched before Verdi began writing his autograph. That Gatti does not mention sketches *alla Rigoletto* before *Luisa Miller* does not mean they never existed. Before the early 1850s the composer's relatively nomadic life may have interfered with his preserving such documents.[13]

Nor does this general procedure preclude the presence of uncertainties or alterations. At the end of the Duetto for Silva and Ernani (N. 9), for example, Verdi found himself with a single remaining leaf and an excess of music. He therefore squeezed 31 measures on a single page, fol. 212v, rendering the score almost illegible. In another case, the Act III Finale (N. 12), he added a bifolio between the last folios of the original gathering. The hypothesis that Verdi expanded the piece while transcribing from a presumptive sketch cannot be excluded, though a simpler explanation would be that he miscalculated the necessary quantity of manuscript paper.

The remaining instances of serious irregularities in manuscript structure, especially the first-act Finale (N. 5) and Terzetto Finale (N. 14), signal important musical alterations. Even where manuscript structure is not in question, however, many of the compositional emendations in *Ernani* address issues that are fundamental to the quality of the opera.

These emendations can be assigned to three distinct periods: (1) while Verdi was writing the skeleton score, before vocal parts had been extracted by copyists—documentary evidence places this period from 1 through 27 January 1844; (2) between the copying of the vocal parts and the completion of the orchestration, from early February through 27 February, when Verdi consigned the completed autograph to the theater so that orchestral parts could be copied; (3) after orchestration, mid-February through the premiere on 9 March. Theoretically, changes could postdate the premiere, but secondary sources agree unanimously with Verdi's latest revisions, implying these revisions had been made before any copies were derived from the autograph.

The most interesting changes are from the first two periods, and we shall be primarily concerned with them. But it is worth mentioning two cuts the composer made in the Scena ed Aria for Carlo, N. 8, after he completed the orchestration. The first omission involves a two-measure orchestral *tutti* on the note C, *fortissimo,* that provided a curtain-raiser for the entire number as well as serving as a modest transition between the B♭-major conclusion of the previous Terzetto and the C-major chord with which the ensuing orchestral Scena be-

---

13. Further documentation pertaining to this issue will be given in the study mentioned above in footnote 5.

EXAMPLE 1.9. Omitted transitional passage in N. 8 (piano reduction).

gins. (The passage is given in a piano reduction in Example 1.9.) It is a purely
formal gesture, and Verdi later decided that the direct juxtaposition of the B♭-
major conclusion for full orchestra and the C-major string sonority introducing
Don Carlo was more effective.[14]

A similar motive impelled the other cut Verdi made after orchestration was
complete. Elvira first appears on stage in the *tempo di mezzo,* just after Carlo,
frustrated at being unable to find the hidden Ernani, threatens to torture Silva
and his guards. Followed by her attendants and Giovanna, Elvira enters precipi-
tately, singing:

> Deh! cessate . . . in regal core
> Non sia muta la pietà.

What makes her entrance so dramatically effective is its directness, its lack of
precisely the artificial symmetry Verdi had originally intended: Elvira's eight
measures were planned as two parallel eight-measure phrases, each ending on
the tonic, differentiated only in their approach to the cadence. (The entire passage is given in Example 1.10, reduced for piano and voice.) Ultimately, the
composer omitted mm. 151a–h. To conceive such a phrase symmetrically is
consonant with the stylistic traditions of Italian opera. But, as with Donizetti at
his best, Verdi's understanding of the dramatic situation led him to abandon
musical symmetry in favor of dramatic immediacy in moments where the two
forces were at odds.

Verdi made few significant alterations in *Ernani* after the orchestration was
completed, but he did recast many passages in the skeleton score. In the next
two examples, these changes caused no disturbances in the structure of the
manuscript. In the first case, Elvira's Cavatina (N. 3), and particularly its Scena,
the changes reflect both the composer's effort to intensify the dramatic declamation and his attention to vocal range and detail. In the second case, the introductory section of Carlo's Scena (N. 10), his desire to establish an effective
opening instrumental sonority drove him to undertake a major revision.

14. I have discussed Donizetti's efforts to free his style of similar formal gestures in my *"Anna Bolena" and
the Artistic Maturity of Gaetano Donizetti* (Oxford, 1985), 46–58.

EXAMPLE 1.10. Elvira's entrance in N. 8, original version (piano/vocal reduction).

The Scena preceding Elvira's Cavatina originally began in E major, and its vocal part was quite different throughout. Moreover, the *primo tempo* of the Cavatina was conceived in A major, with both the vocal line and the bass written in that key. Verdi later transposed "Ernani! . . . Ernani involami" a half-step higher, without altering his notation. Instead, he provided a peculiar tenor clef for Elvira (which gets the pitches right but places the notes an octave too low) as well as the verbal instruction "mezzo tono sopra."[15] As the orchestration was prepared directly in B♭ major, the transposition must have preceded that stage.

Why did Verdi alter the key of the *primo tempo*? With a B♭-major *primo tempo*, he achieved tonal unity in the Cavatina, whose cabaletta is also in that key. But in the preceding Ernani Cavatina, the *primo tempo* is in C major and the cabaletta in B♭, while in Carlo's Act II Aria the *primo tempo* is in A major and the cabaletta in B♭. Tonal unity of the aria does not appear to have been an overriding consideration for Verdi in 1844. Indeed, the only other multipartite number in *Ernani* with tonal unity is the Duetto for Ernani and Silva concluding the second act, a piece with a short and episodic first section leading to a main stretta movement, *prestissimo*. Verdi's attitude toward tonal closure in multipartite numbers was already very cavalier: freedom from that convention of an earlier generation facilitated tonal thinking that extended beyond the limits of individual numbers. Nonetheless, there is no evidence that this transposition is related to questions of large-scale tonal organization in *Ernani*. It seems more likely that in his change of key Verdi was seeking to exploit the range and qualities of Sofia Loewe's voice more fully. The new key slightly raises the tessitura of the music (much of which sits rather low), without moving beyond the range defined for Elvira elsewhere in *Ernani*.

Although the transformation of the opening Scena is more complete, decisions concerning its tonality were probably also occasioned by the change of key in the *primo tempo*. An E-major ritornello in the Scena could not properly introduce a B♭-major *primo tempo*, nor could E♭ major gracefully prepare one in A.[16] In any event, Verdi transposed the orchestral ritornello down a half-step and significantly changed Elvira's vocal line. (The earlier version, which exists only in skeleton score, is shown in Example 1.11, part *a*; the final version, in part *b*.) The original is less expressive in its intervals and harmonies, and more lyrical at its conclusion. Compare the opening phrases. The earlier vocal line remained within the compass of a fourth, while in the revision, Elvira immediately ascends a fourth, then mounts to high G and arpeggiates rapidly down to low E♭. Her "Oh! non tornasse ei più!" outlined an octave, even if the note F♯ was reharmonized from F♯ minor at 16a to D major at 17a. In the revision, the

---

15. He corrected the bass line by scraping away the original notes and writing the new part on the same staff.

16. There is no problem in the other direction. The *tempo di mezzo* begins in D minor, which can be approached without strain either through its dominant (A major), as in the original version, or through its submediant (B♭ major), as in the revision.

continued

EXAMPLE 1.11. The original (*a*) and final (*b*) versions of the Scena
from Elvira's first-act cavatina.

EXAMPLE 1.11. *continued.*

EXAMPLE 1.11. *continued.*

melody outlines a diminished seventh. Compare also her description of Silva as
"quale immondo spettro." In the original it is one of three successive appoggiatura figures; in the revision Verdi singles it out for expressive ornamental treatment, arpeggiating the diminished seventh chord on F♯ over a D orchestral
pedal.

Elvira's description of Silva's words of love, sung "con grazia" in the original,
gives them an unambiguous lyricism. Expanding the range, forcing the leap of a
minor third to F, and pressing the figuration higher render the meaning more
equivocal. Verdi's original conclusion of the Scena, with its "dolce" marking
and anticipation of the orchestral coda, provides a lyrical tone. This is reduced
in the angular final version, with its octave leaps, harmonization of the name
"Ernani" to a diminished seventh chord, and concise diction. Throughout these
revisions, Verdi was aiming at a rhetorically more dramatic and forceful presentation of the woman of Aragonese blood. Watching Verdi's self-criticism helps
us approach his music with greater sensitivity to its expressive language.[17]

17. Notice that the four-note turn figure Roger Parker has called a unifying feature throughout the Scena
e Cavatina of Elvira is present three times in the vocal line of the original version (at mm. 21a, 24a, and 26a);
in the final version it appears only twice. More is not necessarily better: I point this out simply to support
Parker's analysis. Verdi surely had these figures in mind as he composed the piece. See Roger Parker, "Levels
of Motivic Definition in Verdi's *Ernani,*" *19th-Century Music* VI (1982), 141–50, particularly 146–48.

EXAMPLE 1.12. Carlo's Scena, opening ritornello, original version for trumpet.

Just as concern for dramatic values and vocal detail were becoming essential to the young Verdi, so was awareness of instrumental sonority crucial to his developing art. A striking indication of this in *Ernani* is the presence of the bass clarinet, introduced prominently at the ritornello preceding Carlo's Scena in Act III and recurring at an important moment near the close of the opera. The normal orchestra at the Teatro La Fenice did not include a bass clarinet, and examination of Verdi's autograph reveals that he did not at first expect to have such an instrument available.[18] We shall examine the final Terzetto in a moment; let us here concentrate on Carlo's Scena.

From the beginning, Verdi wanted this Scena to open with a striking sonority, using a reduced orchestral texture.[19] His original plan was to begin the piece with brass choir: an ensemble of horns, trumpets, trombones, and cimbasso, with the solo melody assigned to a trumpet. This configuration was to be contrasted with the reduced group of lower strings accompanying Carlo's lyrical solo "Oh de' verd'anni miei," a solo cello pitted against an ensemble of three cellos and one double bass playing pizzicato. Verdi wrote out the entire opening ritornello for trumpet (Ex. 1.12), presumably to be accompanied by massed brass chords.[20] Let us not denigrate this version: had Verdi completed it, we would praise the sonorous majesty of the melodic line and the way it prepares Don Carlo's transformation into Emperor Charles V.

18. See Gallico, ed., *Ernani,* Introduction, xxvii–xxviii. Donizetti had used a bass clarinet to full advantage a few years earlier, in his *Maria de Rudenz,* which had its premiere at the Teatro La Fenice of Venice on 30 January 1838. My thanks are due to William Ashbrook, who brought this to my attention.

19. Julian Budden has pointed out that "in every early Verdi opera there are some extra-ordinary moments. Usually there is one number in which the orchestration is reduced to three to five instruments: a chamber music conception of scoring." See his remarks in "A propos du développement de l'instrumentation au début du XIXe siècle," *Acta Musicologica* XLIII (1971), 247. One might add that similar passages for reduced sets of instruments are equally typical of Rossini's operas. Desdemona's prayer in *Otello* (for wind choir) and the Duettino for Zelmira and Emma in *Zelmira* (for English horn and harp) are two obvious examples.

20. He must have proceeded through most if not all of the Scena before changing his mind, since another intervention for solo trumpet was included near the end of the Scena.

EXAMPLE 1.13. Carlo's Scena, opening ritornello, final version for bass clarinet.

During January, as he composed *Ernani* in Venice, Verdi determined that it would be possible to engage a bass clarinetist. He therefore completely altered the instrumentation, adding to the new solo bass clarinet an accompaniment for two regular clarinets and two bassoons. The atmospheric shading and expressive character thereby achieved make this one of the most memorable moments of the opera. The color darkens. Instead of proclaiming the majesty that is to be, it reflects the ambiguity and torment of Carlo's soul. Italian opera may be unable to reproduce, in Budden's words, "some two-hundred Alexandrines such as Hugo here puts into the mouth of Carlo,"[21] but it can create an instrumental equivalent for his state of mind. The trumpet line is not abandoned; Verdi prepared instead a variation for bass clarinet (Ex. 1.13), chromatic and "serpentine" (Budden's term) in character. The effectiveness of the revised version does not result simply from the new orchestral sonority. The structural transparency of the original trumpet line is excessively schematic. Notice its opening antecedent–consequent phrase, each half of the phrase beginning with the same music, as well as the exactly repeating one-measure figure that follows. While the underlying structure remains unchanged in the revision, the melody develops more freely, so as both to disguise the exact equivalences of the original and to give the musical surface a richer color.

Nor is the choice of figuration haphazard. The revision is marked by a series of sixteenth-note patterns with referents elsewhere in *Ernani*. They are similar to the figuration Verdi employed in Elvira's Scena, discussed above (compare, for example, m. 6 of Example 1.13 and m. 15 of Example 1.11, either part *a* or part *b*), and recur prominently in the vocal line of Carlo's "Oh de' verd'anni

21. Budden, *The Operas of Verdi,* I, 161.

miei." Indeed, the extent to which these referents seem crucial to the final version leads one to speculate whether it was the instrumentation that led Verdi to develop new musical materials or whether his search for a richer field of melodic referents led him to the new instrumentation.

∗   ∗   ∗

The final two examples to be discussed here are the result of more extreme compositional emendations, in which alterations to the basic structure of the autograph of *Ernani* were necessary. The first example helps us to understand the history of a particularly problematic moment in the opera, the opening of the first-act Finale. The second provides new information about the opera's ending Terzetto, a composition of great significance to Verdi's developing art.

The outline of *Ernani* prepared by Francesco Maria Piave and Count Alvise Francesco Mocenigo in mid-September made no provision for a solo composition for Silva. When he learned that the part was to be assigned to the baritone Antonio Superchi, Verdi wrote to the secretary of the Teatro La Fenice on 22 September asking Piave to "try to give the baritone something *cantabile,* for I am told he sings beautifully."[22] He repeated this request in a letter of 2 October: "Please find a place for a nice *cantabile* at the moment Ruy enters, particularly since Superchi sings very well and since the moment is propitious, and Victor Hugo himself has his character speak these words: 'Take and trample beneath your feet this sign of my honor . . . tear out my white hairs etc.' "[23] On 10 October he continued the discussion with Piave, remarking: "Following a few expressions of surprise, [Don Ruy] himself would begin the *adagio* of the concerted finale, and I would like him here to be the dominant figure in the vast canvas."[24] This suggests a solo introduction to an ensemble, much like the one Verdi had written for the baritone in the first-act Finale of *Nabucco,* "Tremin gl'insani."

After deciding to recast the vocal parts (assigning Ernani to a tenor rather than the originally projected contralto), Verdi moved Superchi to the role of Don Carlo. He made Silva a bass, but no appropriate singer was available for the role. A certain Rosi is mentioned by Count Mocenigo, who adds in a letter to Verdi: "You did not find him good enough to sustain a principal part."[25] Unable to offer an alternative, Verdi was willing to compromise on Rosi as Silva, "since this part involves only the finale of the first act, some short solo

---

22. "Di dare qualche cosa di cantabile al baritono che mi si assicura che canta angelicamente." Marcello Conati, *La bottega della musica: Verdi e La Fenice* (Milan, 1983), 85. All quotations from Verdi's correspondence are taken from this exemplary study. The translations are my own.

23. "Lo pregherei poi nel momento che sorte Ruy di lasciar luogo a fare un bel cantabile tanto più che Superchi canta benissimo, e poi il momento si presta, ed anche Victor Hugo fa dire queste parole: 'Prendete, schiacciate co' vostri piedi quest'onorevole segno . . . strappate i miei bianchi capelli etc.,' " 91.

24. "Dopo poche parole di sorpresa, farei che egli stesso cominciasse l'adagio del finale concertato, e vorrei che in questo punto fosse la prima figura del gran quadro," 95.

25. "Ma Ella non lo trovò da tanto da sostenere una parte principale," 100.

phrases in other pieces, and a duet in the second act, but a very forceful one with chorus. In the third act, Gomez sings only in ensembles. In the fourth act there will be the final trio, but if the poet bears with me we could focus attention on the two lovers. On the other hand, Rosi's impressive presence and deep register will be appropriate for this piece."[26] In Piave's original libretto, prepared during the autumn and still entitled *L'onore castigliano,* the poet had planned a full Cavatina for Silva, "Prodi invero vi mostrate," with cabaletta.[27] But in Piave's manuscript these stanzas were crossed out and a different hand wrote: "Questo pezzo si omette." The omission probably reflected the decision to assign the part to Rosi.

With Rosi still intended for the part of Silva, or with no acceptable alternative, Verdi projected the first-act Finale as given in Example 1.14.[28] In this state, the manuscript of the entire Finale consisted of one gathering of eight bifolios followed by another of five. Reconstructing this version requires reading between the lines and under scratched-away pitches, but the basic meaning is secure. When Verdi laid out this Finale in skeleton form, it did not include a solo movement for Silva. Since Verdi wrote the dates of 1 and 2 January 1844 on the autograph manuscripts of the first and third numbers of Act I, we can presume that the Finale existed in this form early in January. The music is entirely in recitative through the revelation of the identity of the King. Verdi shaped the scene by the use of recurring orchestral motives, such as those in measures 8 (G minor) and 17a (B♭ major) or the *fortissimo* figure at 13 (E♭ major), later picked up at 24a in F minor and repeated during the course of the recitative in the same key.

At some point, however, Rosi vanished, and another singer, Vincenzo Meini, was chosen by Verdi himself to portray Silva. By 18 February Meini in turn had abandoned the part, perhaps because its register was too low for the singer's more baritonal voice. (Indeed, Marcello Conati points out that in the next year Meini did sing in a revival of *Ernani* at Madrid, but he took the part of Don Carlo.)[29] It seems logical to suppose that Verdi's decision to provide Silva with a *cantabile* movement, as he had originally intended, coincided with his decision, presumably in January, to assign the role to Meini. To accomplish this, the composer scratched out several bars in the skeleton score and inserted a new gathering of two bifolios between the second and third folios of the original gathering. On this inserted gathering, late in the history of the composition,

---

26. "Poiché in questa parte non c'è che il finale nel 1.° atto: alcuni pertichini, ed un duetto nel 2.ᵈᵒ atto, e questo duetto di molta forza e con cori. Nel terz atto non vi sono per Gomez che pezzi d'assieme. Nel 4.° atto vi sarà il terzetto finale, ma se il poeta avrà pazienza potremo dare quasi tutto l'interesse ai due amanti: d'altronde poi la figura imponente, e la voce grave di Rosi in questo pezzo farà assai bene," 100–101.

27. The text is reproduced in Gallico, ed., *Ernani,* xix.

28. The sections that persisted into the final version, 1–15 and 58–61, are given in a reduction for voices and piano; the connecting measures (16a–24a), which were ultimately replaced, are reproduced as in the autograph, with the vocal line and bass.

29. Conati, *La bottega della musica,* 122.

EXAMPLE 1.14. First-act Finale, original version of Silva's entrance.

EXAMPLE 1.14. *continued*.

Verdi added "Infelice, e tu credevi." Though Meini then disappeared from the cast, to be replaced in turn by the young bass Antonio Selva, no further alterations or *puntature* in the part are evident in the autograph. Orchestration was completed only after the Finale had taken its final shape.

Most puzzles concerning the cabaletta added by Ignazio Marini to this *cantabile,* at the time of the revival of the opera at the Teatro alla Scala of Milan on 3 September 1844, have been resolved by Roger Parker.[30] "Infin che un brando vindice" was written by Verdi, but not for *Ernani.* It is part of a Cavatina in-

30. See Roger Parker, " 'Infin che un brando vindice': From *Ernani* to *Oberto*," in *AIVS Newsletter* XII (1984), 5–7.

serted into Act I of *Oberto,* at Marini's request, for performances in Barcelona during Carnival 1842.[31] We have no evidence yet of whether Verdi authorized its presence in *Ernani,* nor do we know who made the small changes in the music of *Ernani* preceding the new cabaletta in order to accommodate the insertion. Furthermore, although the *Oberto* music has not been found, examination of its libretto reveals a significant difference between the two cabalettas: there is no chorus in *Oberto.* The choral interventions in *Ernani* are simple; still, someone had to prepare them.

The strangest aspect of the story is the fate of Verdi's version with the *cantabile* alone. By about 1850, Ricordi had altered the printed string parts in order to include the cabaletta.[32] Henceforth, when the latter was omitted (and it was rarely performed during the nineteenth century), it was simply cut from the revised version. There was no way to perform the original text, since it no longer existed in the parts. Instead, the inauthentic version given in Example 1.15 was usually heard. The prolonged dominant of F minor has the weight necessary to prepare the cabaletta, which is in the relative major, a harmonic technique common in Italian opera of the period, but it seems too auspicious for the recitative continuation. Verdi's original, far from prolonging the dominant, resolved it to F minor before continuing with "Uscite!" as in Example 1.16, a more balanced musical gesture. The critical edition makes it possible to perform *Ernani* either as Verdi originally intended it or, should it seem appropriate, with the cabaletta he prepared for *Oberto.* Let us hope it clears away forever the erroneous hybrid version that held the stage for over a hundred years.

*   *   *

Whatever his uncertainties concerning Silva's appearance in Act I, Verdi had no doubts about the conclusion of *Ernani.* In his first letter to Count Mocenigo he remarked that the opera should conclude "with the magnificent trio in which Hernani dies etc."[33] To Piave's suggestion of a different ending, he wrote on 2 October: "For God's sake do not finish with a Rondò, but make the trio: and this trio must be the best piece in the opera."[34] To the idea that the trio might

---

31. After the publication of Parker's article, the letter from Verdi to Ignazio Marini that accompanied the Cavatina was auctioned by Sotheby's, London, on 9 May 1985, as lot 218; a full page is provided in facsimile in their catalogue. From the letter, dated 15 November 1841, we learn that the text of the new Cavatina was by Temistocle Solera. Of the cabaletta, Verdi wrote: "The cabaletta is bold and I think it will be right for your voice, just like the Aria of the second act [of *Oberto*]. Make sure that in the cadences of the cabaletta, where the syncopated notes begin, there is a gradual crescendo, even in the orchestra, and then you will see what an effect it will make." ("La cabaletta è ardita e credo starà bene per la tua voce, come quella dell'Aria del secondo atto. Bada che nelle cadenze della cabaletta dove incominciano le note sincopate che sia un crescendo ben grado anche dell'orchestra ed allora vedrai che vi sarà effetto.")

32. The history of the printed performing materials for *Ernani* is told by Gallico in his Critical Commentary to the edition, *Ernani,* 11–16.

33. "Col magnifico terzetto in cui muore Hernani et[c].," 74.

34. "Per l'amor di Dio non finisca col Rondò ma faccia il terzetto: e questo terzetto anzi deve essere il miglior pezzo del'opera," 91.

* In the revised version, the interpolated cabaletta follows here.

EXAMPLE 1.15. Nineteenth-century performing version of passage
from first-act Finale (inauthentic).

EXAMPLE 1.16. Passage from first-act Finale, original version.

conclude "with a solo for Hernani, sung as he dies, or of another character,"[35] Verdi responded: "[Piave] can finish the trio as he likes, but I think a solo by Ernani would be dull. What will the other two be doing?"[36] Even when Sofia Loewe pressured Piave into writing text for a Rondò, Verdi held fast to his conviction.

Though this background is well known, the final trio was, in fact, extensively revised by the composer. Only small elements of the original can be reconstructed, but they reveal Verdi's growing mastery of his art. Problematic areas fall at the beginning and the end of the composition. The first is hinted at in the title: not "Scena e Terzetto Finale," as one might suppose, but "Scena, Duetto e Terzetto Finale," implying a substantial section for two voices, like the Elvira-Carlo duet in the first-act "Scena, Duetto indi Terzetto." But the word *Duetto* is neatly crossed out, and no formal duet exists in the score.

The structure of the autograph and a later notation by Verdi clarify this cancellation. The manuscript at present consists of a gathering of three nested bifolios, inside which are four additional single folios, followed by gatherings of eight and then two nested bifolios. The abnormally small size of the first gathering and the presence of four single folios bear witness to a textual problem just before the first single folio. On the previous verso Verdi changed two measures and crossed out a third, over which he wrote, "Levare il Duettino alle parti di canto." These canceled measures are given in Example 1.17. Though we cannot reconstruct its entire history, Verdi had clearly written a Duettino; indeed, he may even have orchestrated it, for the remaining measures of recitative were fully scored for the strings. It was present in the manuscript at the end of January when copyists prepared vocal parts, and they entered it into the *particelle* of Ernani and Elvira. From Verdi's autograph copy of the *Ernani* libretto we can even discover the lyrical verses he probably employed for this duet:[37]

> ELV.: Oh quante amare lacrime
> Compensa tale istante!
> Converso è il duolo in giubilo
> Per questo core amante.
> Mi sembra un sogno, un'estasi
> Che l'anima confonde.
> Il cielo di due miseri
> Sentiva alfin pietà.

35. "Con un principale, di Hernani, che lo canterebbe morendo; ovvero di un'altro attore," 102.

36. "Il terzetto lo finisca come vuole, mi pare però che un solo assoluto d'Ernani sarebbe una seccatura. Cosa faranno gli altri due?" 102.

37. This libretto, also auctioned at Sotheby's in London on 9 and 10 May 1985, is now on deposit at the Pierpont Morgan Library in New York. The source is described and analyzed in the unpaginated Afterword in the introduction to the critical edition of *Ernani*, immediately before the Index of Numbers.

ERN.:   Cessato, o cara, è il turbine
Che ottenebrò mia stella.
Essa ritorna a splendere
Più limpida, più bella,
Or che il tuo sguardo angelico
Luce di amor le infonde.
Il cielo di due miseri
Sentiva alfin pietà.

A 2.:   Fino all'estremo palpito
T'adorerà il mio cor;
Eterno, pari all'anima
Per te vivrà il mio amor.

In the absence of evidence to the contrary, there is reason to presume that this was the text Verdi set to music.

When the composer decided to omit the Duettino, he replaced the canceled pages with the first of the four single folios which at present form part of the first gathering in the Finale. A rhythmic alteration in the first bar of the second single folio and extensive ink blots on that leaf from the new one both support this hypothesis. The final version, in a reduction for piano and voices, is given in Example 1.18.

EXAMPLE 1.17. Canceled measures from the fourth-act Finale, early version.

EXAMPLE 1.18. Fourth-act Finale, final version (piano/vocal reduction).

What did *Ernani* lose from this interchange, and what did it gain? We have no further direct information about the Duettino, but the piece filled at least three folios, the missing halves of the last three single folios in this gathering. That most compositions with multiple gatherings begin (or originally began) with eight nested bifolios might suggest a similar structure for the Finale, in which case the missing Duettino would have filled seven folios, the length of the Duetto movement for Elvira and Carlo in the Scena, Duetto indi Terzetto of Act I, "Da quel dì che t'ho veduta." Both alternatives point to a significant formal movement for Elvira and Ernani. The scope of the verses in Verdi's autograph copy of the libretto provides further support for this hypothesis.

Verdi replaced this movement with three measures of lyrical outpouring in octaves, a musical apotheosis of the passion of Elvira and Ernani that is all the more poignant because the orchestra disappears before the cadence; only Silva's horn accompanies the final note. These three measures, with their alternation of major and minor inflections, refer back significantly to other moments in the opera: the orchestral figure at the end of the Scena immediately preceding Elvira's Cavatina, "Ernani! . . . Ernani involami"; the soaring ensemble phrase in the third-act Finale, "A Carlo Quinto sia gloria ed onor," with its alternation of D♮ and D♭; the oath for Ernani and Silva in the Duetto Finale of the second act, which moves from B♭ major to B♭ minor and back. This last reference is particularly important, because it serves to intensify the dramatic irony: the love that Ernani and Elvira swear in these three measures is doomed precisely because of the earlier oath.

This is the first musical gesture in Verdi that succinctly yet completely summarizes a complex web of emotions.[38] Its heirs are well known: "Amami Alfredo," sings Violetta in the Scena from Act II of *La traviata,* and no aria has the impact of those few measures; the "Bacio" theme in *Otello,* however we analyze its tonal and melodic associations, is profoundly affecting. Verdi believed in "parole sceniche" because his music could transform and illuminate them. These three measures replacing the Duettino in the *Ernani* Finale mark a crucial stage in Verdi's development.

The three measures recur at the end of the opera. The concluding gathering of the Terzetto consists of only two bifolios. There are reasons to believe that the internal bifolio replaces an earlier layer. Only on this bifolio does the bass clarinet, previously used in Carlo's Scena alone, return. But the bass clarinet was a late addition to Carlo's Scena, and it is inconceivable that its presence in the Finale, where it lends color to a melody it shares with the flute and clarinet, could have preceded its soloistic use in the Scena. Furthermore, the bifolio concludes with a reprise of the new three-measure phrase. It is unlikely that these measures originally preceded the final leaf of the opera, which begins with the three heavily canceled measures in skeleton score given in Example 1.19. The syllable "-tar" concludes the verses "Per noi d'amore il talamo di morte fu l'altar," the words ultimately sung to our three-measure phrase.

The crucial evidence is the single note on the downbeat in the clarinet. This pitch must have followed an instrumental solo on the previous page. As the manuscript now stands, however, there is no such solo. Indeed, the clarinets are verbally instructed to play in unison with the oboes. Thus, the preceding bifolio must be a substitute for one or more bifolios originally present within this final gathering. What might this version have been? It seems unlikely that the "dolcissimo" tune for two clarinets in these canceled measures, though it bears a generic relationship to other musical ideas of the trio, would have surfaced first in the final moments of the opera; rather, it is treated as the continuation or reprise of an earlier idea. Indeed, in this brief melody we may catch a glimpse of

---

38. The possibility cannot be excluded that this phrase, or one much like it, formed part of the canceled Duettino, perhaps for the section *a 2,* whose text, "Fino all'estremo palpito," begins similarly to the "Fino al sospiro estremo" of the final version.

EXAMPLE 1.19. Canceled measures from final leaf of *Ernani* autograph.

the substituted passage from the end of the Finale or even of the missing Duettino for Elvira and Ernani.

✳   ✳   ✳

Although we cannot be certain that Verdi sketched *Ernani* elaborately before he began writing the skeleton score which became the complete autograph, the structure of the autograph points strongly in that direction. Was this hypothetical draft similar to the *Rigoletto* sketch? Might such a sketch or any of the canceled pages from the autograph—such as the omitted Duettino—still exist at S.

Agata? At present we cannot know. That Verdi must already at the time of *Ernani* have been working with extensive sketches is striking, however, and immediately differentiates him from Rossini, Bellini, and Donizetti, none of whom appears to have worked regularly in this fashion.[39] The emendations we have traced here are therefore late alterations during the course of composition, and yet their importance is fundamental to the artistic quality of *Ernani*.

Think of the ending of *Ernani* with a formal duet movement instead of the three-measure ecstatic phrase and without the reappearance of the bass clarinet. Think of Carlo's Scena with a very different instrumental introduction. Think of the first-act Finale without "Infelice, e tu credevi." Think of the extraordinary changes of detail in Ernani's cabaletta and Elvira's Scena e Cavatina. Composers make changes in their scores as they work; that is hardly surprising. But the compositional emendations in the autograph of Verdi's *Ernani* touch on matters crucial to the nature of the work: its melodic character, expressive declamation, instrumental timbre, and musical structure. By studying these emendations, we study what made Verdi the composer he was becoming.

39. According to Francesco Degrada, however, it appears that Saverio Mercadante regularly sketched his later operas. See his preface to Carla Moreni, *Vita musicale a Milano 1837–1866: Gustavo Adolfo Noseda collezionista e compositore,* Musica e Teatro, Quaderni degli Amici della Scala I (Milan, 1985), 13.

Chapter 2

Through the Looking Glass
Some Remarks on the First Complete Draft of Lohengrin

JOHN DEATHRIDGE

Readers of recent Wagner studies may have noticed the striking imbalance between the number of analyses of Wagner's works on the one hand and the relatively few examinations of manuscript sources on the other.[1] This is not the place to elaborate on the peculiar dynamic of the field that has given rise to this situation.[2] Nor do I want to dwell on the limitations analysts have necessarily imposed on themselves in order to come to terms with the agglomeration of classical symphonic formulas, operatic devices, and resurrections of the ritualistic origins of music and theater that lie at the core of Wagner's art. Rather, with one intensive example I want to make the simple point that, despite occasional studies of the genesis of individual works,[3] Wagner's sketches have not received the critical attention they deserve.

This is a greatly expanded version of an earlier paper, "Zur Kompositionsskizze des 'Lohengrin,' " in Siegrid Wiesman and Christoph Mahling, eds., *Bericht über den internationalen musikwissenschaftlichen Kongress Bayreuth 1981* (Kassel, 1984), 420–24, and will form part of a larger study of *Lohengrin* now in preparation. The inventory of the first complete draft of *Lohengrin* appended to the earlier paper is now incorporated in John Deathridge, Martin Geck, and Egon Voss, *Verzeichnis der musikalischen Werke Richard Wagners und ihrer Quellen* (Mainz, 1986) hereafter WWV. To facilitate cross-references, the catalogue uses an internal numbering system for both works and sources. The first complete draft of *Lohengrin* is designated WWV 75, Musik II.

1. See, e.g., Susanna Gozzi, "Nuovi orientamenti della critica wagneriana," *Rivista italiana di musicologia* XIX (1984), 147. Gozzi devotes twenty-three pages to an in-depth survey of analytical and critical works and only three to manuscript studies.

2. See John Deathridge, "Grundzüge der Wagner-Forschung," in U. Müller and P. Wapnewski, eds., *Richard-Wagner-Handbuch* (Stuttgart, 1986), 803–30.

3. Studies not mentioned by Gozzi, "Nuovi orientamenti," include C. von Westerhagen, *Die Entstehung des "Ring", dargestellt an den Kompositionsskizzen Richard Wagners* (Zurich, 1973; Eng. trans. Cambridge, England, 1976); W. Breig, "Studien zur Entstehungsgeschichte von Wagners *Ring des Nibelungen*," diss. University of Freiburg, 1973; John Deathridge, "Wagner's Sketches for the 'Ring,' " *Musical Times* CXVIII (1977), 383; John Deathridge, *Wagner's* Rienzi: *A Reappraisal Based on a Study of the Sketches and Drafts*

The point perhaps seems too obvious. Yet even in the realm of Wagner biography—the most overworked area of research into this composer, which, in a sense, is also the most neglected (Wagner's biographers have not been overconcerned with documentable facts)—there is still much to say about his working methods. Cosima Wagner, for instance, in her diaries frequently mentions Wagner's preoccupation with composition, but she is seldom, if ever, illuminating about it, usually preferring to describe it on virtually every page with the single lapidary sentence *Richard arbeitet,* "Richard is working." It is a striking fact, too, that while Wagner presented his friends and benefactors with cleanly written orchestral drafts, fair copies, and innumerable album leaves, he hardly ever parted with his more spontaneous, and hence more revealing, sketches that show the complexities of his music in a fragile and raw condition. Certainly, Wagner had a sure instinct for the voyeurism that was part of the flattering attention of his admirers, most of whom were less interested in gaining insight into the composition of a work than in the thrill of peeping into something that had the appearance of privacy within a finished masterpiece. Wagner was nonetheless highly sensitive about the intimate subject of how he composed, almost as if he were afraid that his rough sketches could show too much that was unmasterly and reveal an important secret of his music: the camouflaging of its technical processes.

If Wagner was careful with his more intimate manuscripts, posterity has tended to treat them roughly and often downright irresponsibly. Few have been able to distinguish between the valuable and the irrelevant, with the result that important documents have been thoughtlessly given away as gifts and sold back and forth on the market so that copies are often impossible to obtain. One manuscript particularly affected by this is the first complete draft, or so-called composition sketch,[4] of *Lohengrin* written between May and July 1846. Originally it consisted of twenty-one sheets, of which, largely owing to the unthinking generosity of the Wagner family, only fourteen survive. Among the recipients of single sheets extracted from the document were at least one institution and a number of individuals, including Adolf Hitler and Richard Strauss, so that even its fragmentary condition can be said to reflect something of the history of Wagner's fame. It is obvious, too, that a rigorous scholarly analysis of the music of *Lohengrin* cannot ignore this extraordinary document entirely, mirroring as it does, in varying degrees, the creative fantasies and the often paradoxical relation between theory and practice that are part and parcel of this key work and its complex history. The remoteness of many musicologists from mundane extra-

---

(Oxford, 1977); I. Vetter, *"Der fliegende Holländer* von Richard Wagner: Entstehung, Bearbeitung, Überlieferung," diss. Technische Universität Berlin, 1982; C. Abbate, "The 'Parisian' Tannhäuser," diss. Princeton University, 1984.

4. See John Deathridge, "The Nomenclature of Wagner's Sketches," *Proceedings of the Royal Musical Association* CI (1974–1975), 75, and cf. the Foreword of WWV. The terms used in this paper are translations of those used in WWV.

musical concerns—among which I include even Wagner's libretti[5]—has resulted in perhaps too narrow a view of the sketches of opera composers in general. One cause of this situation is a too stringent attitude toward the role in sketch studies of "purely musical analysis."[6] The deliberately wide-ranging remarks that follow, then, are intended not only as a preliminary investigation of the first complete draft of *Lohengrin,* but also as a stimulus to further discussion of Wagner's sketches in the broader context that the extramusical ambition behind his works demands.

I

On 17 December 1845, Wagner read the first draft of the text of *Lohengrin* to a group of artists in Dresden, the so-called *Engelklub,* who met regularly to discuss each other's work. Among those present was Robert Schumann who, as we know from his letter to Mendelssohn written the next day,[7] was also thinking of turning the subject of Lohengrin into an opera. Over twenty years later Wagner dictated the following passage in his autobiography *Mein Leben*:

> [I] had completed the poem for *Lohengrin.* As early as November [*sic*] I read this poem to my close friends, and shortly afterwards to Hiller's circle [the *Engelklub*] as well. It was praised and deemed "effective." Schumann also liked it, yet couldn't figure out the musical form I had in mind for it, as he couldn't find any passages suitable for traditional musical numbers. I then had some fun reading him different parts of my poem just as if they were in aria and cavatina form, so that in the end he smilingly conceded the point.[8]

The comment is intended as a somewhat snide reference to Schumann's conservatism as Wagner saw it. But it is an unwitting confession, too, of a conservative element in *Lohengrin*: if there were no trace of traditional operatic forms in

---

5. Notable exceptions are K. G. Just, "Richard Wagner—ein Dichter? Marginalien zum Opernlibretto des 19. Jahrhunderts," in S. Kunze, ed., *Richard Wagner: Von der Oper zum Musikdrama* (Bern, 1978), 79–94; and C. Abbate, "The Parisian 'Venus' and the 'Paris' Tannhäuser," *Journal of the American Musicological Society* XXXVI (1983), 73.

6. Douglas Johnson's review of my *Wagner's* Rienzi in *19th-Century Music* III (1979–1980), 269. See my reply in the same journal, V (1981–1982), 278.

7. The letter is wrongly dated 18 November [1846] in F. Gustav Jansen, ed., *Robert Schumann's Briefe: Neue Folge* (Leipzig, 1904). See also WWV, 323.

8. "[Ich] führte . . . das vollständige Gedicht des 'Lohengrin' aus. Bereits im November las ich dieses Gedicht meinen Hausfreunden, bald auch dem Hillerschen Kränzchen vor. Es wurde gelobt und 'effektvoll' gefunden, auch Schumann war damit ganz einverstanden; nur begriff er die musikalische Form nicht, in welcher ich es ausführen wollte, da er keinerlei Anhalt zu eigentlichen Musiknummern ersah. Ich machte mir den Spass, ihm verschiedenes aus meinem Gedicht in der Form von Arien und Kavatinen vorzulesen, worüber er sich lächelnd befriedigt erklärte." Richard Wagner, *Mein Leben,* M. Gregor-Dellin ed. (Munich, 1969), 339 (Eng. trans. by Andrew Gray [Cambridge, England, 1983], 326).

its libretto, Wagner could hardly have transformed parts of it on the spur of the moment into a conventional number opera. Also, Wagner decided later to arrange concert versions of several highlights and to publish his own arrangements, with piano accompaniment, of "a number of the most attractive vocal pieces" from the opera.[9] These were not only among his greatest hits in the nineteenth century, but also a puzzling complement to the aura of through-composed music drama with which he liked to surround the work in later life.

If the form of the number opera is not far beneath the surface of *Lohengrin,* the first complete draft—with the exception of the prelude and the transition between the second and third scenes in the third act—is probably Wagner's first attempt to compose the music of an opera systematically from beginning to end. This is vividly demonstrated by Wagner's clear numbering of each sheet. Unlike the first drafts of earlier works, up to and including *Tannhäuser,* which are provided with autograph numbering referring at most to single scenes not necessarily written in chronological order, the consecutive numbering of the sheets of the first draft of *Lohengrin* embraces virtually the entire work. Of course, it would be a mistake to assume that the ordering of a document automatically reflects the compositional process of the music it contains. Nonetheless, Wagner's open ambition to distance *Lohengrin* from the traditional number opera by creating the impression of virtually seamless musical continuity, and the striking absence of sketches prior to the first complete draft that are significantly more than preliminary attempts to shape central motivic material, together suggest that the first draft reflects a conscious attempt to compose the music of the entire work through to the finish and to give it a formal rhythm that transcends its operatic roots.[10]

One of the most striking advances of *Lohengrin* over Wagner's previous operas is the more sophisticated dovetailing of musical transitions with striking visual events, particularly at or during changes of scene. (Not for nothing did Schumann stress in his letter to Mendelssohn that the painters belonging to the *Engelklub* had been more impressed than anyone else with Wagner's libretto.) Wagner certainly became aware of this after having finished *Lohengrin,* as a letter to Theodor Uhlig written in December 1851 proves.[11] But while writing the first complete draft of the opera he was less certain about these transitions, most of which greatly add to the feeling of seamless continuity through entire acts in the finished opera, effectively disguising as they do more conventional divisions beneath the surface of the work. The unforgettable arrival of the swan

9. "Eine Anzahl der ansprechendsten Gesangsstücke." See Erich Kloss, ed., *Briefwechsel zwischen Wagner und Liszt* (Leipzig, 1912), I, 282. See also WWV 75, Musik X, XIVa, and Erläuterungen, 318, 320, 325–26. For details of the concert arrangements, which played a key role in the reception history of *Lohengrin,* see WWV, 325–26.

10. Few musical sketches prior to the first complete draft have survived and perhaps few ever existed. But see WWV 75, Musik Ih and Ij, 314–15.

11. Richard Wagner, *Sämtliche Briefe,* Gertrud Strobel and Werner Wolf, eds. (Leipzig, 1967–), IV, 241.

on the famous $^6_4$ chord marking the beginning of Scene 3 in the first act was originally presaged by some inaccurate gauging of the formal rhythm of the music (Fig. 2.1, bottom two braces of sheet 3 recto), and the beginning of Scene 3 arrived sixteen measures too early (Fig. 2.2, at the words *Scene 3* squeezed between the top two braces of sheet 3 verso). The transition from the first to the second scene in the second act, when Elsa appears on the balcony—a dramatic moment mentioned by Wagner in his letter to Uhlig—was originally more tenuous and marked an abrupt division between scenes.[12] The striking harmonic progression that disguises the division in the finished work was penciled in only later, while another memorable transition, between the second and third scenes of the third act, is even less well defined in the first complete draft, consisting simply of a blank space on the verso of sheet 17, and a short verbal description that had to be elaborated subsequently by two supplementary musical sketches.[13]

II

The fourth sheet of the composition sketch is lost. Yet missing documents can be eloquent precisely because they are absent, even though the suggestive gaps they leave must be handled with the greatest caution. We know what happened to the fourth sheet, from a note in the National Archive of the Richard Wagner Foundation in Bayreuth: "I gave sheet 4 on 20 April 1932 to Adolf Hitler for his forty-third birthday. Winifred Wagner."[14]

Hitler's enthusiasm for *Lohengrin* has been vividly described by Winifred Wagner in Hans Jürgen Syberberg's film devoted to her; she claimed that Hitler knew the opera sufficiently well to hear immediately, during a performance in Bayreuth in 1936, that Furtwängler had opened the cut authorized by Wagner in Lohengrin's narration in the third act.[15] Even if Winifred Wagner's account

12. The original transition on the verso of sheet 7 of the first complete draft consisted simply of an F♯-major chord reduced to a tremolo on F♯ followed, after a double bar, by a straightforward B♭-major arpeggio which starts on a new stave, probably to emphasize the division between the scenes. The striking change in the final work from an F♯-minor chord to B♭ with added seventh (A♭) in second inversion and an outline of the subsequent harmonic progression were later penciled into the draft.

13. WWV 75, Musik Ig and Ii, 314.

14. "Blatt 4 habe ich am 20. April 1932 Adolf Hitler zum 43. Geburtstag geschenkt. Winifred Wagner." Other parts of the draft given away as souvenirs by the Wagner family are sheet 8 (presented by Wieland and Wolfgang Wagner to Richard Strauss on his eighty-fifth birthday on 11 June 1949) and sheet 17 (presented by Siegfried Wagner to Adolf Zinsstag around 1920). Fortunately, both sheets survive. Nothing is known about the missing sheets 9, 10, 13, 14, and 15. On the fate of the last sheet, 21, see the final paragraph of the present essay.

15. The cut was authorized shortly before the first performance of *Lohengrin,* which took place on 28 August 1850. See Wagner's letter to Liszt dated 1 August 1850 in *Sämtliche Briefe,* III, 373. The missing fifty-six measures were first published in full score in Michael Balling's edition of the opera in 1914 and then in

is to be taken more as anecdote than fact, her birthday present to Hitler just nine months before his final seizure of power in Germany (the so-called *Machter-greifung*) nonetheless casts a sombre cloud over the history of the *Lohengrin* draft. It is certainly ironic, although probably a coincidence, that the fourth sheet must have begun with the musical setting of the last word of King Henry's two lines in the first act: "Hab' Dank! Erkenn' ich recht die Macht, die dich in dieses Land gebracht." I am no more suggesting, of course, that this has any significance than that—considering that the sketch must have also contained Lohengrin's words to Elsa, "Wenn ich im Kampfe für dich siege, willst du, dass ich dein Gatte sei?"—Winifred Wagner's present of the sketch to her powerful friend was in any way hinting at matrimony. It is nevertheless one of those faintly ominous moments in the history of the reception of *Lohengrin* which, in view of the unhappy union of art and politics brought about by Hitler and Winifred Wagner in the 1930s, cannot easily be forgotten.

III

Wagner's almost complete avoidance of triple meter in *Lohengrin* is commonly regarded—wrongly, in my opinion—as one of its central flaws.[16] The critique, which amounts to little more than the well-known fact that *Lohengrin* is in regular 4/4, 2/4, or 2/2 time except for ninety-seven measures in the first act (from King Henry's prayer "Mein Herr und Gott"), has a tradition dating back to the first performances in 1850. The trouble with the critique is that it ignores possible variations of accent within the measure, or within a larger formal rhythm which, even though the measures it contains may be regular, can itself be asymmetrical and complex. Arnold Whittall has turned the criticism on its head: instead of taking issue with Wagner's predominant use of duple and quadruple meter, he asks whether any features in the ninety-seven measures in 3/4 time justify the existence of this metrical oasis. Rightly, he finds nothing in the text to imply triple rather than duple or quadruple meter in the musical setting of it. Nor does he see that the choice of triple meter has anything to do with the regularity and balance of this songlike passage. The only conclusion he comes to is that the "choice may well have come about simply because Wagner felt that a solemn music like that of the Pilgrims' Hymn in *Tannhäuser* was appropriate here: there are indeed similarities."[17]

---

vocal score in Richard Wagner, *Sämtliche Lieder,* ed. Emil Liepe (Leipzig, 1916). See WWV 75, Musik XIVe, 320, and XVIf, 321.

16. See, e.g., Robert Bailey, "Wagner's Musical Sketches for 'Siegfrieds Tod,' " in H. Powers, ed., *Studies in Music History: Essays for Oliver Strunk* (Princeton, 1968), 478.

17. Arnold Whittall, "Wagner's Great Transition? From *Lohengrin* to *Das Rheingold,*" *Music Analysis* II (1983), 273.

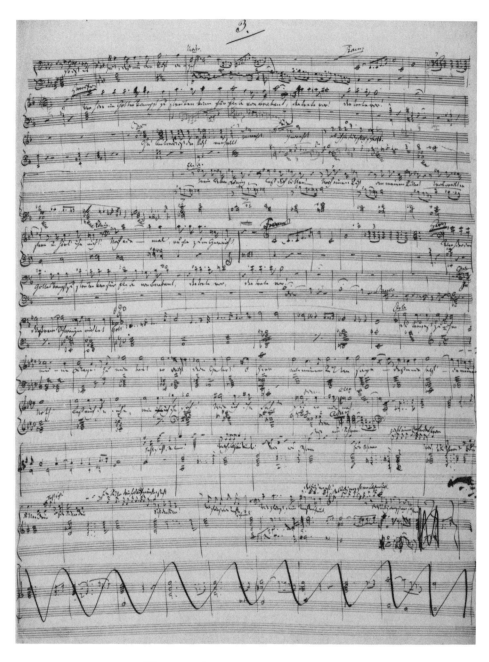

FIGURE 2.1. First complete draft, sheet 3 recto (NA - A II b 2).

FIGURE 2.2. First complete draft, sheet 3 verso (NA - A II b 2).

At the beginning of the recto of the fifth sheet of the *Lohengrin* draft (Fig. 2.3), we can see that Wagner originally composed the ensemble following the King's prayer, "Du kündest nun dein wahr Gericht," in 4/4 time. Since the prayer and the ensemble are closely linked and in triple meter in the finished work, it is not unreasonable to suppose that the King's prayer, the sketch of which was almost certainly part of the sheet Winifred Wagner presented to Hitler, was in quadruple meter too. It seems probable, then, that all of *Lohengrin* was first conceived in duple or quadruple meter. This makes the metrical oasis in the first act of the finished work even more enigmatic. Why did Wagner transform the music of the ensemble, and in all likelihood the entire passage of ninety-seven bars including the King's prayer, from quadruple into triple meter? It is unlikely that the transformation had much to do with Wagner's need for solemn music like the Pilgrims' Hymn in *Tannhäuser,* since the passage sounds just as solemn, if not more so, with four beats to the measure.[18] One remotely conceivable reason for the alteration might have been to facilitate smoother performance. The enharmonic changes in the vocal ensemble are unaccompanied and difficult to keep in tune, especially when combined with flagging tempo. Yet if Wagner wanted to avoid out-of-tune singing, his solution—if it is one—rarely cures the malaise. Certainly, I have never heard a performance of these ninety-seven bars in the theater that, even with the greater "swing" of triple meter, has not had to be saved by the man with perfect pitch (or a tuning-fork) planted in the chorus specifically for the entry of all the men and the King's herald at "Des Reinen Arm gib Heldenkraft," who sing at the correct pitch—usually a semitone and often a tone higher than the previous unaccompanied and invariably ever-flattening enharmonic changes. An entirely convincing answer to the question posed by Whittall, then, is probably impossible.

IV

The recto of the fifth sheet is also interesting with respect to a prominent red herring in Wagner research: the question of whether it was Wagner's music or his texts that occurred to him first. The sheet shows that Wagner wrote down the final chorus of the first act without text (Figure 2.3, bottom two braces). At a glance, the first draft of the chorus corroborates the following statement by Wagner recorded in Cosima's diaries (25 March 1878): "In *Lohengrin* (1st finale) he [tells me] he thought of the music first and then worked out a text for

---

18. The Pilgrims' Hymn was in triple meter from the start. See the transcription of Wagner's first sketch in C. Kinsky, ed., *Manuskripte, Briefe, Dokumente von Scarlatti bis Strawinsky: Katalog der Musikautographen-Sammlung Louis Koch* (Stuttgart, 1953), 246–47.

FIGURE 2.3. First complete draft, sheet 5 recto (NA - A II b 2).

the chorus."[19] On closer inspection this statement looks more problematic. Wagner did invent a new text after writing the music; what he does not say is that the original text of the passage already existed in the verse draft of the libretto completed on 27 November 1845,[20] that is, some months before the finale to the first act was composed. Wagner had clearly forgotten that when he came to put music and text together at the end of the first act he decided to write a new text for the chorus—a more complex process recorded by a supplementary sketch to the first draft (Fig. 2.4) in which parts of the old text ("Ertönet Jubelweisen / Dem Helden, Gottgesandt!") are crossed out at the end of the second and the beginning of the third brace and some of the new text is inserted, notably at the top of the page and in the second brace. In no way does the document prove the primacy of music over text in chronological terms, nor is the question important. Yet Wagner's insistence that he thought of his music first does raise some interesting biographical points. He probably did distort the facts a little to counteract the notion prevailing in some quarters that he relied not on musical instinct but on dubious extramusical stimuli. And, of course, like most other opera composers he sometimes invented musical ideas independent of scenic and verbal associations. The statement to Cosima and others like it in the same period also reflect the preoccupations of the composer of *Parsifal,* who had become disenchanted with the theater and whose ambition to write purely instrumental music without texts of any sort was increasingly dominating his thinking.

V

Despite the number of missing sheets in the first complete draft of *Lohengrin* there is enough material to explode a prominent legend in the Wagner literature: the idea that Wagner composed the last act of the opera first. Ernest Newman, for example, writes as follows: "In the third act, the first of the three to be set to music, we get a hint of the line along which his [Wagner's] development as a musician might have proceeded had not that deep inner change taken place in him that was to result in an entirely new synthesis of the factors of opera."[21] Newman saw a progressive development in Wagner's style from the third act, through the first, and culminating in the second. "It is not to be wondered at

---

19. "Im *Lohengrin* (ltes Finale) habe er zuerst die Musik auch gehabt und dann den Text der Chöre ausgearbeitet."

20. For details of the manuscript, see WWV 75, Text II. Otto Strobel's assumption that the date at the end of the draft referred to a revision of the ending and not to the completion of the manuscript was based on an incorrect dating of a letter from Schumann to Mendelssohn. See footnote 7 above and Otto Strobel, *Richard Wagner, Leben und Schaffen: Eine Zeittafel* (Bayreuth, 1952).

21. Ernest Newman, *Wagner Nights* (London, 1949), 166.

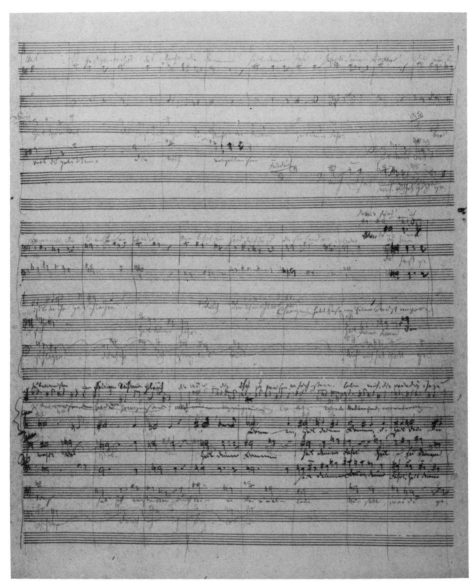

FIGURE 2.4. Supplementary sketch, Act I conclusion (NA-A II b 3 [(1)]).

that Wagner left the composition of the second act to the last," he writes, "for psychologically and musically it confronted him with the most difficulties."[22]

Newman's interpretation is based on a misunderstanding of one of those relatively rare sentences in *Mein Leben* that is entirely accurate. Referring to the

22. Ibid.

musical composition of *Lohengrin,* Wagner states: "I adopted a course of action I was never to repeat: I completed the third act first."[23] In the original German text Wagner uses the word *ausführen,* which means to work something out in detail. Thus he is not likely to be referring to the continuous outline sketches in the first complete draft, quite apart from the fact that the complete paragraph in *Mein Leben* makes it abundantly clear that Wagner has in mind a second and more solid draft of *Lohengrin*—the so-called orchestral sketch[24]—which he completed much later, on 2 August 1847. The situation was actually the reverse of Newman's assertion: Wagner was not confronted with the most psychological and musical difficulties in the second act, but in the third. The first complete draft shows that he began by composing the first act and worked through to the end of the opera. It was only after friends had criticized the ending as it appears in the first draft of the libretto that he realized he was going to have trouble with it, and the problems became more evident after he had set a revised version of the last scene in the first complete draft of the music. As we shall see in a moment, his difficulties were not inconsiderable. It was therefore perfectly logical for him to fix the final form of the opera in the second complete draft by starting with the third act.

VI

On 12 May 1852 the composer and conductor Julius Schaeffer began a series of articles in the *Neue Berliner Musikzeitung* on Wagner's *Lohengrin* "in relation to his treatise *Oper und Drama.*"[25] While the series was still being published, a short reply appeared in the *Neue Zeitschrift für Musik* for 18 June 1852; it was written by Wagner's friend and aide Theodor Uhlig. Amid the partisan polemics about Wagner that appeared almost weekly during this period in newspapers and journals all over Germany, Uhlig's "small protest" seems insignificant.[26] Yet it encapsulates a central paradox of Wagner's theory and practice and attempts to interpret it, albeit somewhat ideologically, for a public confused by a composer whose ideas seemed more advanced than his works. While recommending Schaeffer's article, Uhlig claimed that its author was nonetheless guilty of a "chronological mistake" by reading too much of *Oper und Drama* into *Lohengrin.*[27] According to Uhlig, Schaeffer was judging *Lohengrin*

---

23. "Hierbei geriet ich auf ein sonst nie wieder von mir befolgtes Verfahren: ich führte nämlich den dritten Akt zuerst aus." Wagner, *Mein Leben,* 350 (trans., 337).

24. For a detailed explanation of this term, see Deathridge, "The Nomenclature of Wagner's Sketches," 75.

25. Julius Schaeffer, "Über Richard Wagner's Lohengrin, mit Bezug auf seine Schrift: 'Oper und Drama,' " *Neue Berliner Musikzeitung* VI (1852), 153ff.

26. Theodor Uhlig, "Ein kleiner Protest in Sachen Wagner's," *Neue Zeitschrift für Musik* XXXVI (1852), 277–78.

27. Ibid., 277, "Nur eines chronologischen Irrthumes macht Hr. Schaeffer sich schuldig."

by a theoretical standard which, although created by Wagner himself, should be applied less to existing than to future works. The absence in *Lohengrin* of *Stabreim*—the alliterative verse form that is the theoretical core of the third part of *Oper und Drama*—should have made Schaeffer aware of his "mistake," Uhlig writes. The theories in the treatise do embrace Wagner's practice up to that time, Uhlig admits. But the theories "go much further than what has been presented to the public in *Lohengrin*."[28]

Uhlig was taking his cue from Wagner. In a letter dated 31 May 1852, Wagner had written to Uhlig in glowing terms about Schaeffer's article and two months later even considered giving Schaeffer, as a token of gratitude, one of six presentation copies of the first edition of the full score of *Lohengrin*.[29] Wagner was particularly struck by Schaeffer's remarks on the way identities of keys are "dissolved" in *Lohengrin*.[30] This prompted Wagner to say that key characteristics cannot be separated from instrumentation: to see a key as an absolute apart from other parameters, he told Uhlig, was an "uncritical half-measure."[31] He then launched into a discourse about harmony and orchestration that has become famous among analysts, even though they have rarely paid more than lip service to it.[32] But Schaeffer's public statement about the absence of *Stabreim* in *Lohengrin* irritated Wagner. The accuracy of the statement was not at issue; he simply felt that Schaeffer was diminishing the importance of a major technical innovation.

Schaeffer's article is only one of a number of attempts made in the early 1850s to compare *Lohengrin* with Wagner's theoretical writings of the Zurich years. The most famous, though least interesting, is a book by Joachim Raff on the Wagner "question." Raff is aware of the correct "line" of the Wagner party and repeats Uhlig's assertion that the theories of *Oper und Drama* cannot be completely read into *Lohengrin*. Yet in his critique of the opera he reverts to the critical standard set by *Oper und Drama* as if there were no chronological distance at all between opera and treatise.[33] Schaeffer, on the other hand—

28. Ibid., 278, "Denn die Theorien, welche Wagner allerdings nicht aus der Luft gegriffen, sondern aus den Ideen zu seinen erst noch zu erwartenden Kunstwerken geschöpft hat, gehen weit über Das hinaus, was im 'Lohengrin' der Öffentlichkeit vorliegt."

29. *Sämtliche Briefe* IV, 447. Only one presentation copy survives (dedicated to Robert Franz) and is now at Carnegie-Mellon University, Pittsburgh. See J. L. Hunt, "Music in the Rosenbloom Collection of Hunt Library at Carnegie-Mellon University," *Notes* XXXIII (1976–1977), 553.

30. *Sämtliche Briefe* IV, 385: " 'zerfliessen der individualität der tonarten.' " Despite the quotation marks, Schaeffer actually wrote: "Das Zugeständniß wird ihm [Wagner] aber Jeder machen, . . . dass es ihm nämlich gelungen ist, alle Individualität der Tonarten aufzuheben." Schaeffer, "Über Richard Wagner's Lohengrin," 162.

31. *Sämtliche Briefe* IV, 386: "eine kritiklose Halbheit."

32. A notable exception is Carl Dahlhaus, "Zur Theorie der Instrumentation," *Die Musikforschung* XXXVIII (1985), 161.

33. Joachim Raff, *Die Wagnerfrage. Erster Theil: Wagner's letzte künstlerische Kundgebung im "Lohengrin"* (Braunschweig, 1854), particularly 202–12.

notwithstanding Uhlig's slight misreading of his article[34]—avoids the pitfall. He makes some convincing points about the choruses in *Lohengrin,* for instance, while quite aware that Wagner suggested the abolition of choruses altogether in *Oper und Drama.*[35] And he chooses just those "elements of musical expression" discussed in the treatise—the harmonization of verse melody and the "announcement of gesture, reminiscence and premonition"[36]—that were not simply abstract ideas belonging to an "Artwork of the Future" but a real part of *Lohengrin,* Wagner's most advanced opera known at the time.

Uhlig was nonetheless right to say that what had been presented to the public in *Lohengrin* was only a part of Wagner's rethinking of the state of opera. Uhlig did not know, however, that Wagner's sketches for the work—out of public view, of course—show signs of a deeper confrontation. If Wagner and Uhlig tended to see *Lohengrin* as a step on the ladder to the utopian drama of the future, Schaeffer's more intuitive and less ideological response is actually more in tune with the opera's ambiguities, some of which can be sharply focused if Wagner's handling of them in the sketches is taken into account. Despite the mixture of old and new ideas in the finished work, the sketches show that Wagner's struggle with technical innovation, especially in the third act, was more involved and contradictory than it is usually taken to be. Indeed, the sketches make Newman's image of stylistic progress in *Lohengrin* seem simplistic at best, for Wagner was not only reaching out to what he himself in his Zurich writings, including *Oper und Drama,* called "the labyrinth of theoretical speculation,"[37] but he also returned swiftly from this looking-glass world of new forms and ideas when his pragmatic instincts got the better of his intellectual fantasies.

34. Although Uhlig claims that the absence of *Stabreim* in *Lohengrin* should have made Schaeffer notice his "mistake" (see footnote 27 above), not only is Schaeffer fully aware of the almost complete absence of *Stabreim* in *Lohengrin* but he also insists that Wagner's preoccupation with iambic pentameter scarcely hinders "the complete emancipation of the poet from the tyranny of the musician" ("die vollständige Emanzipation des Dichters von der Zwingherrschaft des Musikers"). Schaeffer, "Über Richard Wagner's Lohengrin," 161.

35. Schaeffer (ibid., 169) observes: "Unmotivated display [of the chorus] is avoided with the greatest stringency" ("Unmotiviertes Parademachen [des Chores] ist mit der grössten Strenge vermieden") and points out Wagner's unusually resourceful voice-leading in double-choir and six-part writing that creates timbres which, Schaeffer claims, were possible until then only in the subtlest orchestral music. Schaeffer is already scotching the idea (which has persisted to this day) that the choruses in *Lohengrin* are somehow "reactionary." In view of Wagner's call in *Oper und Drama* for clear motivation and logic and the substitution of the chorus for a heightened use of the orchestra as commentator on the action, the choruses in *Lohengrin* are, if studied closely, perhaps more progressive than they are usually taken to be.

36. Ibid., 170–71: "Resumiren wir kurz die Elemente der musikalischen Ausdrucksmittel im Wagnerschen Drama, so haben wir die Versmelodie—deren Harmonisierung—die Kundgebung der Gebärde, der Erinnerung und der Ahnung. Auf diese Elemente werden wir denn auch bei der speziellen Betrachtung der Oper 'Lohengrin' . . . ganz besonders Rücksicht zu nehmen haben."

37. *Sämtliche Schriften und Dichtungen,* 16 vols. (Leipzig, n.d.), VII, 88: "das Labyrinth theoretischer Spekulation."

VII

The first and second complete drafts of the third act of *Lohengrin* are a veritable battlefield of revisions, some of them quite drastic. This is not the place to give a full overview of Wagner's reworking of the act, but I have selected three examples that give some idea of what was involved.

We all know that too much dialogue and narration are recipes for certain boredom in the opera house. Yet it was clearly Wagner's ambition to introduce these anti-operatic elements into *Lohengrin* (and the later music dramas too) in order to create a more "closed" form of musical theater, that is, less like the "open" form of traditional opera with its largely arbitrary selection of events for the sake of outward display, and nearer the logical coherence of classicist drama with its formal balance and continuity achieved by the integration into the dialogue of events external to the action.[38] And many contemporary commentators did praise the text of *Lohengrin* as an opera libretto unusual in being able to stand on its own, apart from the music. Adolf Stahr, one of the most perceptive critics of the first performances, even called the work a "practical critique" of opera, a "creative negation" which, not only on account of the artistic autonomy of its libretto but also because of the rhythmic uniformity and deliberately anti-virtuosic character of the music, acted as a "real polemic" against modern opera.[39]

In a letter to Stahr dated 31 May 1851, Wagner protested that the polemic had not been "intentional." Rather, his identification with the subject had allowed him to indulge in a full and rich, that is to say, operatic setting of the libretto while overlooking those aspects that had turned *Lohengrin* into a "protest."[40] Wagner was not being entirely frank. Into the structure of the third act he had consciously inserted at least two narrations and an extended dialogue that introduced events external to the action which he must have known were strong, if not openly "polemical," elements undermining one of the decisive aesthetic traits of opera: its scenic and musical immediacy. What he did not say to Stahr was that he had deliberately negated some of these anti-operatic traits in his sketches for *Lohengrin* when he realized that, in this opera at least, they were not going to work musically in the theater.

38. See Carl Dahlhaus, *Wagners Konzeption des musikalischen Dramas* (Regensburg, 1971), 15–21, and Reinhard Strohm, "Dramatic Time and Operatic Form in Wagner's 'Tannhäuser,' " *Proceedings of the Royal Musical Association* CIV (1977–1978), 1. Both authors base their observations on the theory of "open" and "closed" dramatic forms elaborated in Volker Klotz, *Geschlossene und offene Form im Drama* (Munich, 1960).

39. Adolf Stahr, *Weimar und Jena* (Leipzig, n.d.), 79: "Seine Schöpfung erschien mir wesentlich als eine praktische Kritik, als eine thatsächliche Polemik, eine schöpferische Negation."

40. *Sämtliche Briefe*, IV, 59–60: "In *Einem* thun Sie mir vielleicht Unrecht: Sie nennen meinen 'Lohengrin' eine thatsächliche Polemik gegen die moderne Oper; Sie weisen mir in ihm puritanischen Eifer nach. Gut! aber nennen Sie es nicht eine absichtliche Polemik: ich war, als ich diese Oper schrieb, von dem Gegenstande auf eine Weise eingenommen, dass er mich zu keiner andern Absicht kommen liess, als ihn recht voll und üppig, recht tönend zu Tage zu bringen."

It seems odd to point out classical features in *Lohengrin*, of all operas. Yet the version of the third act in the first complete draft shows that Wagner wanted to introduce more formal symmetry, dialogue, and narration than the operatic tendency of the work could stand. Since all three of our examples have to do with the shaping of the ending of the opera, it is appropriate to begin with a lengthy passage in Wagner's autobiography (dictated between 28 March and 15 April 1867) outlining his reaction to a criticism by the writer Hermann Franck of the ending as it appears in the first draft of the libretto:

> [Franck] considered the punishment of Elsa by Lohengrin's departure unseemly: he understood perfectly well that it was precisely the most characteristic element in the legend that was expressed in this highly poetic event, but he doubted whether it did full justice to the sense of tragedy when allowance was also made for dramatic realism. He would have preferred to see Lohengrin die before our eyes as a result of Elsa's betrayal. At any rate, as this did not seem permissible, he wanted to see him riveted to the spot by some powerful motivating force and prevented from leaving. As I naturally wouldn't even think of such a thing, I nevertheless began considering whether the cruel separation could not be eliminated, while still retaining Lohengrin's indispensable departure for distant realms. I tried to find a means of permitting Elsa to depart with him, to do some sort of penance which would require her too to withdraw from the world; this struck my friend as more hopeful. While I was languishing in uncertainty about this, I gave my poem to Frau von Lüttichau for perusal and for consideration of the objections Franck had raised. In a little note expressing her delight with my poem, she stated flatly on this particular matter that Franck had to be utterly devoid of poetic sense if he thought *Lohengrin* could end in any other way than my text depicted. I heaved a sigh of relief; I triumphantly showed this letter to Franck; extremely embarrassed and hoping to excuse himself, he at once initiated an exchange of correspondence on the subject with Frau von Lüttichau, which certainly cannot have been uninteresting, though I never got to see any of it. But the result was that *Lohengrin* remained the way it had been.[41]

---

41. Wagner, *Mein Leben*, 339–40 (trans., 326f.): "[Franck] fand die Bestrafung Elsas durch Lohengrins Scheiden verletzend: er begriff zwar sehr wohl, dass eben das Charakteristische der Sage in diesem hochpoetischen Zuge ausgedrückt sei, blieb aber im Zweifel, ob dieser Zug den Anforderungen des tragischen Gefühles mit Berücksichtigung der dramatischen Wirklichkeit entsprechen könne. Er hatte lieber den Lohengrin durch Elsas liebevollen Verrat vor unseren Augen umkommen sehen. Jedenfalls, da diese nicht statthaft erschien, wünschte er ihn durch irgendein gewaltiges Motiv festgebannt und am Fortgehen verhindert zu sehen. Da ich natürlich von all dem nichts wissen wollte, kam ich doch darauf, mir zu überlegen, ob die grausame Trennung nicht erspart, das unerlässliche Fortziehen in die Ferne aber doch erhalten werden könnte. Ich suchte ein Mittel auf, Elsa mit Lohengrin fortziehen zu lassen, zu irgendwelcher Busse, welche sie ebenfalls der Welt entrückte; das schien meinem geistvollen Freunde schon hoffnungsreich.—Während ich hierüber in Unsicherheit versetzt war, gab ich mein Gedicht auch Frau v. Lüttichau zur Durchsicht und Prüfung des von Franck angeregten Dilemmas. In einem kleinen Briefchen, worin sie mir ihre Freude an meinem Gedichte ausdrückte, äusserte sie sich über den schwierigen Punkt mit grösster Bestimmtheit kurz dahin, dass Franck ja aller Poesie bar sein müsse, wenn er nicht begriffe, dass der 'Lohengrin' gerade so und auf keine andere Weise ausgehen könne. Mir war ein Stein vom Herzen; ich zeigte Franck triumphierend den Brief; dieser, mit äusserster Beschämung, setzte zu seiner Entschuldigung sich sofort mit Frau v. Lüttichau in einen gewiss nicht uninteressanten Briefwechsel, den ich selber nicht zur Einsicht bekam, dessen Ergebnis es jedoch war, dass es im Betreff des Lohengrin beim alten verblieb."

But *Lohengrin* did not remain the way it had been. The accuracy of Wagner's other statements is difficult to test, for the relevant letters are lost. Yet the suspicion that Wagner, with the benefit of hindsight, is deliberately trying to make Franck look faintly ridiculous and ineffective as a critic is supported not only by the *Lohengrin* sketches but also by a letter to Franck, written during work on the opera, containing spontaneous and grateful remarks that are probably a more accurate reflection of Wagner's true reaction to Franck's criticism. "Your doubts have been very useful to me," he wrote on 30 May 1846, adding at the end of the letter, "I think I have learned a great deal."[42]

What had Wagner learned? He tells Franck that the crux of the latter's criticism is not its call for alternative solutions to the opera's ending but its focusing of a potential lack of "taut dramatic effectiveness."[43] Having set the libretto aside for a few months, he could now read his own work, as far as that was ever possible, like an "unprejudiced outsider." Its "poetic intention" seems to be that the atonement for Elsa's betrayal can only be an inevitable punishment brought about by her "separation" from Lohengrin.[44] It is not enough, however, to let Lohengrin reproach Elsa and simply leave: the moment of separation must be more palpable if it is to avoid confusion about the fate of both Lohengrin and Elsa. Thus Lohengrin's participation in the tragic outcome of the opera, Wagner tells Franck, has to be made much clearer.[45]

Wagner then altered Lohengrin's dialogue with Elsa "O Elsa! Was hast du mir angetan," quoting some altered and additional lines in his letter to Franck. Instead of reproaching Elsa sadly, Lohengrin now gives the reason for his departure. Loving her warmly, he felt his heart "turning away from the chaste service of the Grail." He must therefore pay eternal penance since he had mistakenly thought that "a woman's love could be of heavenly purity."[46] A little later in the dialogue, Wagner added eight lines emphasizing the punishment of

42. *Sämtliche Briefe,* II, 512, 514: "Hier hat mir nun Ihr Zweifel sehr viel genützt . . . ich glaube, wieder Viel gelernt zu haben."

43. Ibid., 512: "der dramatischen geschlossenen Wirksamkeit."

44. Ibid., 511: "Ich habe mein Gedicht nach einiger Unterbrechung, soviel dies möglich ist, als unbefangener Fremder angesehen, und seine poetische Absicht spricht mir so aus: Die Sühne für Elsa's Vergehen kann nur in ihrer Bestrafung liegen, und selten kann ein Vergehen eine consequentere und somit unerlässlichere Strafe nach sich ziehen, als sie hier in der Trennung ausgesprochen ist."

45. Ibid., 512: "[Ihr Zweifel hat] mich dringend darauf hingewiesen . . . *Lohengrin's* Betheiligung an dem tragischen Ausgange deutlicher zu machen, als dies der Fall war." A detail not mentioned by Robert Bailey in his valuable transcription and discussion of the passage in the first complete draft preceding Lohengrin's narration in the third act is that in the revised final version Wagner cut Lohengrin's four lines "O halte ein, so hart ihn zu verdammen" to "doch schuld'ger nicht mag er als Elsa sein." Lohengrin reproaches Elsa harshly by resorting to an unlikely defense of Friedrich who, he says, is hardly more guilty than Elsa. The omission of the lines corresponds to Wagner's admission to Franck, in the letter quoted here, that Lohengrin's reproach of Elsa, his sole personal response to the situation in which he finds himself, is dramatically inadequate. See Robert Bailey, "The Method of Composition," in Peter Burbridge and Richard Sutton, eds., *The Wagner Companion* (London and Boston, 1979), 278–86.

46. See Chart 2.1, alternative text, bottom of first column: "Fühlt' ich zu dir" to "keuschem Dienst entwandt!" In the verse draft the alternative text is pasted over the original version.

separation to be inflicted on Elsa.[47] Neither "punishment" (*Strafe*) nor "separation" (*Trennung*) is mentioned in the text of the original libretto at this point, yet they become key words in the revised version, since they both motivate Lohengrin's actions and reflect his fate. If Elsa is to suffer for her transgression in asking the forbidden question, Lohengrin is to be punished too for having longed for Elsa "more than for God."

In the first complete draft of the music Wagner dropped the idea of the "chaste service of the Grail" while retaining the added eight lines about "punishment" and "separation." Thus the motivation for Lohengrin's departure, already weakened, is put further out of focus by the position of the added lines at the end of an already overlong dialogue. A comparison of the three versions of the dialogue in the original libretto, the first draft of the music, and the final work respectively (Chart 2.1) shows that Ernest Newman's assertion that "virtually none of the alterations [Wagner] had outlined in his letter to Franck were carried over into the poem" is misleading.[48] Only four of the added lines remain in the final version (beginning "Nur eine Strafe"); but they still contain the ideas of punishment and separation that Wagner introduced after considering Franck's criticism. Furthermore, Wagner gave greater emphasis to two of the lines in the finished opera by preceding them with an operatic ensemble that climaxes just at the point where Lohengrin declaims the two key works "Getrennt, geschieden." There is no trace of the ensemble in the first sketches of the opera, as Wagner's setting of the last part of the dialogue in the first complete draft shows (Fig. 2.5 and Ex. 2.1). Wagner recomposed this passage at a surprisingly late stage, replacing its bland, foursquare vocal gestures—Stahr would have surely called them "puritanical" and a polemical "creative negation"—with the mounting tension of what is in effect a traditional "set piece."[49] Franck's criticism, then, left its mark not only on the text of the opera but on the music. The first draft of the libretto lacked "taut dramatic effectiveness," as Franck felt (at least according to Wagner). If the first complete draft of the music compounded the fault with aimless phrase and harmonic structure, Wagner's final version is another, more successful attempt to realize in musical terms what he had learned: the necessity of heightening Lohengrin's participation and of inventing a clear motivation for his departure. This time, however, he abandoned all trace of experiment and turned instead to a robust operatic formula.

47. Ibid., bottom of second column: "Nur eine Strafe gibt's" to "der Trennung Noth!"

48. Newman, *Wagner Nights,* 179.

49. Cf. Example 2.1 with *Lohengrin,* Eulenburg score, pp. 780–99. Significantly perhaps, Wagner broke off work on the second complete draft just after Lohengrin's words "Nun muss ich ach! von dir geschieden [sein]." After a two-month break Wagner continued, on 11 February 1847, on a new brace with the recomposed "Mein Gatte, nein!" Two drafts of the new music, then, were possibly written down in this period (WWV 75, Musik Ic and Ii, 314). If this hypothesis is correct, Newman's idea of stylistic progress in *Lohengrin* looks more problematic than ever, since the ensemble—one of the most conservative passages in the opera—would have been the last part of the work to be composed.

CHART 2.1. Three versions of the Elsa-Lohengrin Duet, Act III, Scene 3.

VERSE DRAFT	FIRST COMPLETE DRAFT (19 verso, 20 recto)	FINAL VERSION
*Lohengrin (mit schmerzlichster Ergriffenheit):	Lohengrin:	Lohengrin (mit schmerzlichster Ergriffenheit):
O Elsa! Was hast du mir angethan?	O Elsa! Was hast du mir angethan?	O Elsa! Was hast du mir angethan?
Als meine Augen dich zuerst ersahn,	Als meine Augen dich zuerst ersahn,	Als meine Augen dich zuerst ersah'n,
Zu dir fühlt' ich in Liebe mich entbrannt,	Zu dir fühlt' ich in Liebe mich entbrannt,	Zu dir fühlt' ich in Liebe mich entbrannt,
Und schnell hatt' ich ein neues Glück erkannt.	Und schnell hatt' ich ein neues Glück erkannt.	Und schnell hatt' ich ein neues Glück erkannt:
Die hohe Macht, die Wunder meiner Art,	Die hohe Macht, die Wunder meiner Art,	Die hohe Macht, die Wunder meiner Art,
Die Kraft, die mein Geheimnis mir bewahrt,	Die Kraft, die mein Geheimnis mir bewahrt,	Die Kraft, die mein Geheimnis mir bewahrt,
Wollt' ich dem Dienst des reinsten Herzen's weihn:	Wollt' ich dem Dienst des reinsten Herzen's weihn!	Wollt' ich dem Dienst des reinsten Herzen's weih'n:
Was rissest nun du mein Geheimnis ein?	Was rissest nun du mein Geheimnis ein!	Was rissest nun du mein Geheimnis ein?
		Jetzt muß ich, ach! von dir geschieden sein!
Elsa (zu seinen Füßen):	Elsa:	Elsa:
O mein Erlöser! Sieh mich hier vergeh'n,	O mein Erlöser! Sieh mich hier vergeh'n!	Mein Gatte, nein!
Aus tiefster Schuld für mich um Gnade flehn!	Aus tiefster Schuld für mich um Gnade flehn!	Ich lass' dich nicht von hinnen!
Bist du so göttlich, als ich dich erkannt,	Bist du so göttlich, als ich dich erkannt,	Als Zeuge meiner Busse bleibe hier!
Sei Gottes Gnade nicht aus dir verbannt:	Sei Gottes Gnade nicht aus dir verbannt:	
Der Sünderin in bittrer Reue Zähren,	Der Sünderin in bittrer Reue Zähren	
Sollst du wie er Verzeihung auch gewähren!	Sollst du, wie er Verzeihung auch gewähren!	
Lohengrin:	Lohengrin:	Lohengrin:
O ich verzeih! Dir Tugendhaften, Reinen	O ich verzeih! Dir Tugendhaften Reinen	Ich muß, ich muß! mein süsses Weib!
Erkennt mein Herz den Preis entzuckungs-voll!	Erkennt mein Herz den Preis entzückungs-voll,	

continued

CHART 2.1. *continued.*

VERSE DRAFT	FIRST COMPLETE DRAFT (19 verso, 20 recto)	FINAL VERSION
Doch jammernd muß der Menschheit Loos ich weinen, Der Gnade nur, nie Glück erspriessen soll! Wie lange noch sollt ihr des Heil's entbehren, Da wahres Glück dem Zweifel ferne bleibt, Konnt' ihm dies keusche, reinste Herz nicht wehren, Das unstet nun ich weit von dannen treibt!	Doch jammernd muß der Menschheit Loos ich weinen, Der Gnade nur, nie Glück erspriessen soll! Wie lange noch sollt ihr des Heil's entbehren Da wahres Glück dem Zweifel ferne bleibt, Konnt' ihm dies keusche, reinste Herz nicht wehren, Das unstet nun ich weit von dannen treibt!	*Männer und Frauen:* Weh! *Elsa:* Nicht darfst du meiner bittern Reu' entrinnen: daß du mich strafest, liege ich vor dir! *Die Frauen:* Weh, nun muß er von dir ziehn!
D[er] König. Alle Edlen: Weh! Wehe! Mußt du von uns zieh'n, Du hehrer, Gottgesandter Mann! Soll uns des Himmels Segen fliehn? Wo fänden dein wir Tröstung dann!	*Chor:* [?]	*Lohengrin:* Ich muß, ich muß, mein süsses Weib! *König, Männer und Frauen:* Weh! Weh! Weh! Mußt du von uns ziehn, du hehrer, gottgesandter Mann! Soll uns des Himmels Segen fliehn, wo fänden dein wir Tröstung dann? O bleib! O bleib!
Elsa: Mein Gatte, nein! Ich lass dich nicht von hinnen! Als Zeuge meiner Buße bleibe hier! Nicht darfst du meiner bittern Reu'	*Elsa:* Mein Gatte, nein! ich laß' dich nicht von hinnen! Als Zeuge meiner Buße bleibe hier! Nicht darfst du meiner bittern Reu'	*Elsa:* Bist du so göttlich, als ich dich erkannt, sei Gottes Gnade nicht aus dir verbannt! Büßt sie in Jammer ihre schwere Schuld, nicht flieh' die Ärmste deiner Nähe Huld!

entrinnen!
Daß du mich züchtigst, liege ich vor dir!

Lohengrin:
Ich muß! Ich muß, mein süßes, reines Weib!
Schon zürnt der Gral, daß ich ihm ferne bleib'!

Elsa (sich an ihn hängend):
Verstoß mich nicht! Wie groß auch mein Verbrechen!

Lohengrin:
O schweig! An mir ja selber muß ich's rächen.

Elsa:
Weh' mir! Fand' einst durch Haß ich Schmach
u. Noth,
Durch Liebe nun soll finden ich den Tod!

entrinnen,
Daß du mich züchtigst lieg' ich hier!

Lohengrin:
Nur eine Strafe giebt's für dein Vergehn,
Ach, mich wie dich trifft ihre herbe Pein!
Getrennt, geschieden sollen wir uns sehn,
Dies muß die Strafe, dies die Buße sein!

Elsa:
Weh' mir, wie soll es härr're Strafe geben,
getrennt von dir bleibt einzig mir der Tod!

Lohengrin:
Muß Göttlich fern des Grales Ritter leben,
Dein Gatte ach! erlag der Trennung Noth!

Verstoß mich nicht, wie groß auch mein
Verbrechen!
Verlaß, ach verlaß mich Ärmste nicht!

Lohengrin:
Schon zürnt der Gral, daß ich ihm ferne bleib!
Ich muß, ich muß!
Nur eine Strafe gibts für dein Vergehn!
Ach! mich wie dich trifft ihre herbe Pein!
Getrennt, geschieden sollen wir uns sehn:
dies muß die Strafe, dies die Sühne sein!

*Alternative text
Lohengrin (in schmerzlichster Ergriffenheit.):*
O Elsa! Was hast du mir angethan!
Als meine Augen dich zuerst ersahn,
Fühlt' ich zu dir in Liebe schnell entbrannt,

Mein Herz des Grales keuschem Dienst entwandt!
Nun muß ich ewig Reu' u. Buße tragen,
Weil ich von Gott zu dir mich hingesehnt,—
Denn ach! Der Sünde muß ich mich verklagen,
Daß Weibeslieb' ich göttlich rein gewähnt!

FIGURE 2.5. First complete draft, sheet 20 recto (NA - A II b 2).

continued

EXAMPLE 2.1. First complete draft, sheet 20 recto (extract).

EXAMPLE 2.1. *continued*.

VIII

Nothing shows Wagner's penchant for classical symmetry in *Lohengrin* better than the two narrations he planned for the final scene. Not only do they relate details essential to an understanding of the opera as a whole, but Wagner used them as the pivots of a quasi-symphonic structure that was to recapitulate key musical passages and themes heard during the course of the work. Lohengrin's narration "In fernem Land" has often been described as a powerful formal gesture that returns to the Grail music heard at the beginning of the prelude. But the role of the second narration by Ortrud has received little comment, largely because in the final work it has been reduced to a shadow of itself. Yet the first drafts of both libretto and music (Chart 2.2, Ex. 2.2, Fig. 2.6) show that Wagner intended Ortrud not only to give us a more detailed account of her past misdemeanors (and thus explain a number of perplexing moments in the plot of the opera) but also to recapitulate some important musical moments from the second act, including a thematic reminiscence of the opening (Ex. 2.2, mm. 45–52), numerous vocal allusions to Ortrud's "Entweihte Götter," and a specific orchestral reference to Ortrud's calling on Wodan and Freia (compare Example 2.2, m. 96, especially the words *Gestopft* [muted] and *Tremo*[*lo*], with the orchestration of the passage accompanying Ortrud's words "Wodan! Dich Starken rufe ich!" in the final version of the score). This attempt at long-range recapitulation is virtually nonexistent in the final version. Ortrud's narration in F♯ minor, too, was clearly intended to balance Lohengrin's in A major—a symmetry still noticeable but far less emphatic in the finished work.

Wagner's original setting of Ortrud's narration is modeled on Eglantine's final outburst in Weber's *Euryanthe* (see Chart 2.2). Not only are there resemblances in the wording of the text—Ortrud's "Sieg! Sieg! Willkommen Rächerstunde," for instance, is strikingly reminiscent of Eglantine's first line, "Triumph! Gerochen ist meine Schmach"—the vocal writing is also similar (Ex. 2.3). The two pieces have virtually identical dramatic functions. Eglantine recounts a misdeed perpetrated by herself but blamed on Euryanthe. Ortrud also tells us about her bad behavior—her machinations in getting rid of Elsa's brother by putting around his neck a magic chain that turned him into a swan—and makes it clear to the assembled company that Elsa is innocent of her brother's disappearance. Weber and Wagner are forced to lower the temperature of the music while Eglantine and Ortrud relate their past deeds. Here again the vocal lines are remarkably similar (Ex. 2.4). Eglantine tells us that it was she who stole the ring that made Euryanthe appear to be guilty of betrayal, while Ortrud sarcastically asks the assembled company whether they know who brought their proud hero to them. Ortrud clears Elsa, unjustly accused of murdering her brother, but points out with heavy irony that Elsa will lose her brother anyway since Gottfried, having brought Lohengrin to save his sister, will now have to carry Lohengrin back again.

CHART 2.2. Comparison of Eglantine's and Ortrud's speeches.

EURYANTHE, Act III Finale	LOHENGRIN, Act III, Scene 3 (First Complete Draft, 20 verso)	LOHENGRIN, Act III Scene 3 (Final version)
		(Ortrud tritt im Vordergrund rechts auf und stellt sich mit wild jubelnden Gebärde vor Elsa hin.)
	Ortrud:	*Ortrud:*
	Sieg! Sieg! Willkommen, Rächerstunde!	Fahr' Heim! Fahr' Heim, du stolzer Helde,
	Nun nenn' ich herrenlos dies Land!	daß jubelnd ich der Törin melde,
	Gepriesen deines Herzen's Wunde,	wer dich gezogen in dem Kahn!
	durch die ich meine Rache fand!	Das Kettlein hab' ich wohl erkannt,
	Weißt du, wer deinen stolzen Helden	mit dem das Kind ich schuf zum Schwan:
	dahergeführt an diesen Strand?	das war der Erbe von Brabant!
	Nun laß mich jubelnd dir es melden,	
	es war der Erbe von Brabant!	
Eglantine (in teuflischer Lust auffahrend):		
Triumph! Gerochen ist meine Schmach!		
Der Feindin Herz gebrochen!		
Es stürmt der Tod durch deine Brust!		
Betrogner! war dir meine Glut bewußt,		
wie legtest sorglos und vermessen		
die Schlange du an der Geliebten Brust?		
So hattest du mein Flehn vergessen?		
Vergessen meinen Todesschmerz?		
Vergessen deines Kaltsinns Hohn?		
Vergessen meines Zornes Drohn?		
	Chor:	*Alle:*
Adolar:	Ha!	Ha!
Abscheuliche!		
	Ortrud:	*Ortrud:*
Eglantine:	Ihn sollt' allein erreicht ich haben,	
Grausamer Adolar!	Er mußte meinem Zauber nahn!	
Verzweifle, da sie schuldlos war!	Ein Kettlein legt' ich um den Knaben,	
Ich war's, von deren Hand den Ring	Da ward das Kind zum wilden Schwan!	
der kühne Räuber dort empfing;	Hin schwamm er auf des Wasser's Fluthen,	
ich war's, die ihn der Gruft entwandte,	von dem er Hülfe wollt' empfahn,	
rein, wie das Licht, war Euryanthe!	den Ritter sucht' er auf, den Guten,	
	und zog zum Strand ihn hier heran.	

Dank, daß den Ritter du vertrieben,
nun giebt der Schwan ihm Heimgeleit!
Der Held, wär' länger er geblieben,
den Bruder hätt' er auch befreit!

Alle:
O höllischer Verrat! O herb Geschick!

Lysiart:
Wahnsinn'ge!

Eglantine:
Schnödes Werkzeug meiner Rache,
dich schleudr' ich in dein Nichts zurück!

Alle:
Abscheulich Weib, was kündest du?
Wo fänd' nun unser Jammer Ruh?

Ortrud:
Erkennt Verweg'ne, das Verbrechen,
das ihr verübt an diesem Land!
Lernt [so, wie sich die Götter rächen
Von deren Huld ihr euch gewandt!]

Dank, daß den Ritter du vertrieben!
Nun giebt der Schwan ihm Heimgeleit:
der Held, wär' länger er geblieben,
den Bruder hätt' er auch befreit.

Alle:
Abscheulich Weib! Ha, welch' Verbrechen
hast du in frechem Hohn bekannt!

Ortrud:
Erfahrt, wie sich die Götter rächen
von deren Huld ihr euch gewandt!

EXAMPLE 2.2. First complete draft, sheet 20 verso (extract).

EXAMPLE 2.2. *continued*.

continued

EXAMPLE 2.2. *continued.*

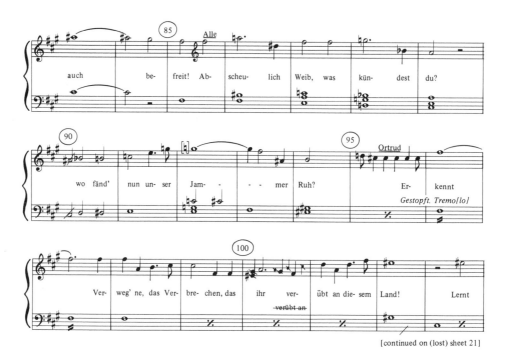

[continued on (lost) sheet 21]

Unlike Weber, Wagner realized that dramatic subtleties like these, relying as they do on a clear understanding of past events, are precarious when placed at the end of an opera racing toward its denouement with little time for facts that are distant from the intensity of the immediate present. Indeed, we are now in a position to see that the last-minute cut in Lohengrin's narration just before the first performance of the opera (see footnote 15 above) was the corollary of a revision Wagner had already made to Ortrud's narration in the sketches. In fact he both shortened the narration and recomposed it. The vocal line is lengthened (see Ex. 2.3) and the dissipated musical energy of the first setting is concentrated into a wild and highly effective philippic against Lohengrin in which the ironic point of the original text is lost in the increased excitement of the music. Wagner not only moved away from the *Euryanthe* model, he curtailed the narrative structure and the quasi-symphonic recapitulatory scheme of the last scene of the work by relying instead solely on a virtuoso display of "vengeance"—a gesture which, though it hardly sounds conventional here, has a sound pedigree in operatic tradition.

Wagner's return to opera in the last stages of composing *Lohengrin* is also suggested by his revision of the ending. As Chart 2.3 makes clear, he originally wanted Lohengrin to answer Ortrud's philippic with a prayer that was sung. In addition, he wrote a song for the swan ("Leb' wohl, Du wilde Wasserflut").

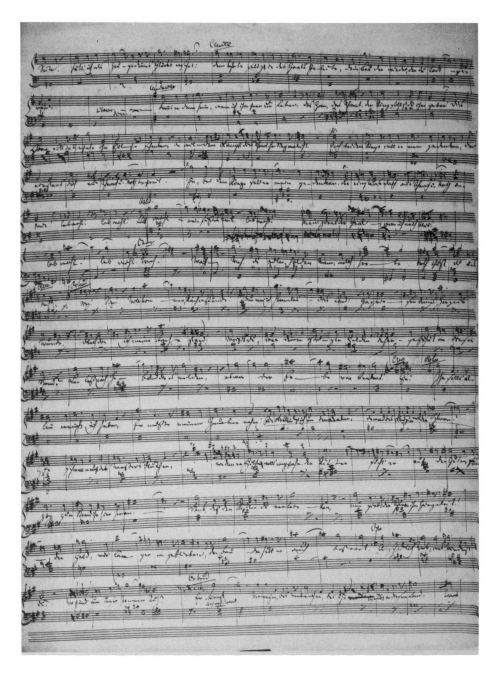

FIGURE 2.6. First complete draft, sheet 20 verso (NÀ - A II b 2).

First complete draft, *Lohengrin,* Act III

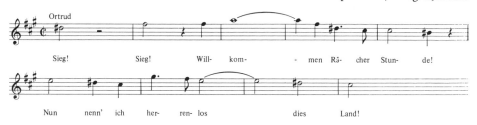

Final version, *Lohengrin,* Act III

EXAMPLE 2.3. Comparison of vocal lines in Eglantine's and Ortrud's speeches.

Euryanthe, Act III finale

First complete draft, *Lohengrin,* Act III
(omitted from final version)

EXAMPLE 2.4. Eglantine's and Ortrud's narration of misdeeds.

CHART 2.3. *Lohengrin*, Act III, Scene 3 (end) in preliminary and final versions.

VERSE DRAFT	FINAL VERSION
(presumably the text set to music on the lost sheet 21 of the first complete draft)	

Ortrud:

   [Lernt] so, wie sich die Götter rächen
   Von deren Huld ihr euch gewandt!

Lohengrin:

(der schon bereit in den Nachen zu steigen, hat, Ortruds Stimme vernehmend, eingehalten und ihr vom Ufer aus aufmerksam zugehört. Jetzt senkt er sich dicht am Strande feierlich auf die Knie.):

Ein Zeichen gib zu dieser Stunde,
Zu Dir ruf' ich, allew'ger Gott,
Daß nicht das Laster frech gesunde,
Mit Deinen Gnaden treibe Spott!
Als Balsam leg' es auf die Wunde,
Die Zweifel reinstem Herzen schlug!
Daß sich Dein hoher Will' bekunde,
Vernichte der Treulosen Trug!
Hör' mich in Demut zu Dir flehen,
Ein hohes Zeichen laß mich sehen!

(Seine Stimme wird hier völlig unvernehmbar, er betet mit gen Himmel gerichteten Augen stumm weiter. Während alle im äußersten gespanntesten Schweigen verharren, vernimmt man einen zarten Gesang, wie von der Stimme des Schwans gesungen.)

(Lohengrin, schon bereit in den Nachen zu steigen, hat, Ortruds Stimme vernehmend, eingehalten, und ihr vom Ufer aus aufmerksam zugehört. Jetzt senkt er sich, dicht am Strande, zu einer stummen Gebet feierlich auf die Knie.)

continued

CHART 2.3. *continued.*

VERSE DRAFT	FINAL VERSION
(presumably the text set to music on the lost sheet 21 of the first complete draft)	

VERSE DRAFT

Leb' wohl, Du wilde Wasserflut,
Die mich so weit getragen hat!
Leb' wohl, Du Welle blank und rein,
Durch die mein weiß Gefieder glitt!
Am Ufer harrt mein Schwesterlein,
Das soll von mir getröstet sein!

(Lohengrin erblickt plötzlich die weiße Gralstaube über dem Nachen schweben; mit einem dankenden Blick gen Himmel springt er auf und löst dem Schwan die Kette, worauf dieser sogleich untertaucht. Daraufhebt er einen schönen Jüngling [Gottfried] aus dem Wasser an das Ufer.)

Lohengrin:

Seht da den Herzog von Brabant!
Zum Führer sei er euch ernannt!

(Er springt schnell in den Nachen, welchen die Taube an der Kette faßt und fortzieht.—Ortrud ist mit einem Schrei zusammengesunken. Elsa blickt mit letzter freudiger Verklärung auf Gottfried, welcher nach vorn geschritten ist und sich vor ihm auf die Knie.—Da wendet Elsa ihren Blick nach dem Fluß.)

Elsa:

Mein Gatte! Mein Gatte!

FINAL VERSION

(Plötzlich erblickt er eine weiße Taube sich über dem Nachen senken: mit lebhafter Freude springt er auf, und löst dem Schwane die Kette, worauf dieser sogleich untertaucht: an seiner Stelle erscheint ein Jüngling—Gottfried.)

Lohengrin:

Seht da den Herzog von Brabant!
Zum Führer sei er auch ernannt!

(Er springt schnell in den Nachen, welchen die Taube an der Kette faßt und sogleich fortführt.—Ortrud ist beim Anblick der Entzauberung Gottfrieds mit einem Schrei zusammengesunken.—Elsa blickt mit letzter freudiger Verklärung auf Gottfried, welcher nach vorn geschritten ist und sich vor dem König verneigt. Alle brabantischen Edlen senken sich vor ihm auf die Knie.—Dann wendet Elsa ihren Blick wieder nach dem Flusse.)

Elsa:

Mein Gatte! Mein Gatte!

Both pieces were intended to stretch dramatic time, as it were, in order to delay the catastrophe with a long moment of premonition that was presumably intended as a significant preparation for the key mythical and symbolical events of the appearance of the white dove of the Grail, the release of the swan from Ortrud's magic chain, and the transformation of the swan into Gottfried. But this piece of interesting dramaturgy moved the work too far from its operatic impulses. Wagner cut it out, leaving what is fundamentally a purely scenic, more immediate conclusion.

Unfortunately, the last sheet of the first complete draft of the music is missing. It was given by Siegfried Wagner to the Deutsches Sängermuseum in Nuremberg on 8 December 1927. Despite extensive inquiries I have been unable to trace either the manuscript or a copy of it. The loss is considerable, since it is precisely Wagner's musical setting of the original ending of *Lohengrin* that would complete the vivid picture of Wagner's attempted escape from opera in the rest of the draft, especially in the last scene. True to his usual habits, Wagner kept the draft to himself while transcribing the song of the swan on the final page of it as an album leaf. In August 1853 he gave the leaf to an admirer, the singer Lydia Steche, with an accompanying remark to the effect that he had been forced to cut the song from the opera for reasons of what he called "the necessity of dramatic house-keeping"—"Die Notwendigkeit dramatischer Haushaltung." It is the only surviving fragment of the music cut in the final version that the last sheet of the draft contained.[50]

50. According to Otto Strobel ("Die Urgestalt des 'Lohengrin': Wagners erster dichterischer Entwurf," *Bayreuther Festspielführer* [1937], 158–67), Wagner sketched the dedication to Lydia Steche on the final sheet of the draft. The song "as if sung by the voice of the swan" (see Chart 2.3) was first published by A. Naubert in *Allgemeine musikalische Zeitung* XX (1893), 72. See also Carl Friedrich Glasenapp, *Das Leben Richard Wagners* II (5th ed. Leipzig, 1910), 186.

Figures 2.1–2.6 are reproduced by the kind permission of the Nationalarchiv der Richard-Wagner-Stiftung, Bayreuth.

Since this chapter went to press, sheet 15, one of the missing parts of the first complete draft (see footnote 14 above), has appeared. It contains the first draft of the Bridal Chorus in Act III (recto) and the opening of the ensuing Lohengrin-Elsa Duet (verso). The recto is reproduced on page 206 of Sotheby's catalogue for their auction held in London on 17 and 18 November 1988. In a letter (Beyreuth, 14 April 1923) sold with the sketch, Siegfried Wagner tells an Italian friend ("Signor Zamboni") that he is sending the sketch to him as a gift.

Chapter 3

Opera as Symphony, a Wagnerian Myth

CAROLYN ABBATE

I

Wagner saw himself as Beethoven's only legitimate son, the symphonic opera composer born of the last great symphonist. Out of this vision he created the literary-biographical myth that haunts his later writings, just as an obsession with symphonies haunted the last years of his life. The myth can be interpreted both psychologically and philosophically.[1] The obsession was intense and ultimately unfruitful; we have its physical remains in a puzzling handful of autograph fragments for "symphonic themes" (most from 1877 to 1883) and some cryptic remarks recorded in Cosima's diaries.[2] Seeking an interpretation of the fragments, John Deathridge has suggested that Wagner's own polemic concerning the symphony may, in the end, have been responsible for his inability to write one. He could not, in the 1860s and 1870s, wholly abandon the Hegelian stance of *Oper und Drama,* with its confident assertions concerning the inferiority of instrumental music. Wagner, taking on Schopenhauerian coloration, took another look at the virtues of "pure" instrumental music and attempted to modify his position in *"Zukunftsmusik"* (1860) and to emend that position further in later essays, especially in *Beethoven* (1870). This tangle of polemic could only become an encumbrance to Wagner in his tardy impulses toward symphonic, rather than operatic, writing; Deathridge's image is that of an aging Wagner struck compositionally silent by his own past philosophizing.[3]

---

1. Summaries of Wagner's writings on the symphony are given in Egon Voss, *Richard Wagner und die Instrumentalmusik: Wagners symphonischer Ehrgeiz* (Wilhelmshaven, 1977), 154–81; idem, "Richard Wagner und die Symphonie," in Carl Dahlhaus, ed., *Richard Wagner: Werk und Wirkung* (Regensburg, 1971), 207–19; and Klaus Kropfinger, *Wagner und Beethoven* (Regensburg, 1975).

2. See John Deathridge, "Wagner's Unfinished Symphonies" (forthcoming).

3. Ibid.

The subtler view of Wagner's preoccupation with the symphony suggests that the equation between Wagner and Beethoven and the notion that Wagner's operas are "symphonic" cannot simply be taken at face value. Both are specious, yet both are widely accepted. Later generations have found them convenient and comfortable: convenient because they provide a neat strand of music-historical continuity through a century of musical dislocations, and comfortable because they place a mantle of absolute-musical respectability—Beethoven's mantle—on Wagner's doubtful theatrical shoulders. So "opera as symphony" has become a commonplace of Wagnerian lore, an unremarkable truism:

> On closer inspection, the affinity between Wagner and Beethoven becomes clear. Despite the fact that Wagner wrote operas, his focus was centered on what was played by the orchestra—not what was sung on stage. . . . His musical fabric is a complex one, held together by *leitmotifs* which not only identify particular characters and situations, but unify the purely musical texture in the way the thematic material unifies a symphony or a chamber work. Wagner recognized the essentially abstract nature of his music. He claimed he was not continuing the tradition of Gluck, Mozart, or Carl Maria von Weber.[4]

Joan Peyser's paragraph stands here for hundreds that take the same line. Sophisticated critical writing has adorned statements concerning the "abstract nature" of Wagner's music with complicated analyses and lofty language, but has not questioned the many categorical and questionable assumptions that are implicit in such statements: that Wagner's music is always "unified" as "pure music"; that he himself always claimed this was so; that we should take Wagner's words as a reliable guide in our own interpretations of his work.

The meanings that have accrued to the word symphonic are at the heart of the problem. For Wagner, *symphonic* referred to certain specific musical qualities, the most important of which was a continuous network of interrelated thematic ideas, which he regarded as characteristic both of Beethoven's symphonies and of his own operas.[5] For us, *symphonic* may mean many other things. The word may merely pay a compliment to Wagner's orchestra and suggest elaborate instrumentation, or a large brass complement, or complexity of orchestral counterpoint. When we say Wagner's operas are "symphonic," we may even wish to imply that their formal designs are rooted in conventions for symphonic form. Alfred Lorenz made an astounding statement to this effect, declaring that "the . . . forms I have discovered in the Wagnerian *Musikdrama* were rooted

4. Joan Peyser, *The New Music: The Sense behind the Sound* (New York, 1971), 5.

5. This authentically Wagnerian understanding of *symphonic* has been applied to interpretation of Wagner's music in numerous analytical essays. One recent example is Wolfram Steinbeck, "Die Idee des Symphonischen bei Richard Wagner: Zur Leitmotivtechnik in 'Tristan und Isolde,' " in Siegrid Wiesman and Christoph Mahling, eds., *Bericht über den internationalen musikwissenschaftlichen Kongress Bayreuth 1981* (Kassel, 1984), 424–36.

not in traditions of opera that preceded Wagner, but in the symphonies of Beethoven." With this proclamation he anticipated a fanatic and rather silly strain of Wagnerian analysis, in which sonatas, adagios, and rondos are discovered lurking within *Tristan* or the *Ring*.[6]

But *symphonic* may mean something even more than this. When the word *symphonic* is used to describe Wagner's operas, it is used metaphorically, to convey an aesthetic judgment. What is meant is that these "symphonic" operas are as musically logical, as "unified," as German instrumental music of the accepted canon.[7]

This metaphorical use of *symphonic* involves both loose thinking and unstated assumptions, but it is most troubling on ideological grounds. The vague equation of something like the *Eroica's* first movement with an act from *Götterdämmerung* is ludicrous: the two simply do not possess the same kinds of musical formalities, the same degree of coherence, the same treatment of rhythmic gesture, the same proportions. When Carl Dahlhaus suggested a similarity between Brahms's symphonies and Wagnerian dramatic music, he was referring only to the composers' shared taste for constant transformation of small motivic fragments; he intended no formal comparison and imputed no Brahmsian musical tidiness to Wagner.[8] Wagner's post-*Lohengrin* operas indeed contain certain passages that hark back to formal devices of an earlier time, but others simply cannot be understood in those terms; the music is sometimes tightly knit and sometimes rather vague and digressive. As Joseph Kerman pointed out in *Opera as Drama,*

> The grief that Wagner causes many listeners is caused, or at least amplified, by a feeling that in being "symphonic" Wagner sets up purely musical conditions which then indeed he does not fill. . . . As purely musical forms, Wagner's operas succeed as well as any romantic symphonic poems of their length might be expected to succeed; which is to say, not too well.[9]

---

6. Alfred Lorenz, "Worauf beruht die bekannte Wirkung der Durchführung im I. Eroica Satze," *Neues Beethoven-Jahrbuch* I (1924), 183: "Die von mir im Wagnerschen Musikdrama gefundenen . . . Formen sind nicht in der ihm vorgegangenen Oper, sondern in der *Symphonie Beethovens* verwurzelt." Another locus classicus is Hermann Grunsky's "*Tristan und Isolde:* Der symphonische Aufbau des dritten Aufzuges," *Zeitschrift für Musik* CXIII (1952), 390–94, in which Act III is discussed in terms of sonata-allegro, "slow movement," scherzo, and the like.

7. This is the main thrust of Karl Grunsky's apologia in "Wagner als Symphoniker," *Richard Wagner Jahrbuch* I (1906), 227–44. The essay is one spiritual ancestor to an extensive body of later writings that take the same general line, such as Alfred Lorenz's *Das Geheimnis der Form bei Richard Wagner* (see especially I [Berlin, 1924], 73–74). Faint echoes of the idea crop up in works as diverse as Jack Stein's *Richard Wagner and the Synthesis of the Arts* (Detroit, 1960), 157–66; Josef Mainka's "Sonatenform, Leitmotiv, und Charakterbegleitung," *Beiträge zur Musikwissenschaft* V (1963), 11–15; Carl Dahlhaus, "Formprinzipien in Wagners 'Ring des Nibelungen,' " in Heinz Becker, ed., *Beiträge zur Geschichte der Oper* (Regensburg, 1969), 102; William Kinderman, "Dramatic Recapitulation in Wagner's *Götterdämmerung*," *19th-Century Music* IV, no. 2 (1980–1981), 108. For the counter-argument see Joseph Kerman, "Opera as Symphonic Poem," in his *Opera as Drama* (New York, 1956), 205–8.

8. John Deathridge and Carl Dahlhaus, *The New Grove Wagner* (New York, 1984), 99.

9. Kerman, *Opera as Drama,* 206–7. Guido Adler, in *Richard Wagner* (Munich, 1904), 173ff., bruited

Perhaps most troubling are the aspersions that use of the phrase *symphonic opera* casts upon opera itself. The phrase passes judgment on the relationship of music to the poem and the drama with which the music must coexist, belittling both the poetic and the dramatic component.

The expression *symphonic opera* might suggest that Wagner wrote his music, and that we must understand it, independently of any particular concern for symbolizing text, or (less radically) might appeal to the commonplace that Wagner's genius expressed itself in both musical and dramatic ideas, each completely satisfying, the two woven together into a perfect whole.[10] *Symphonic opera* might even imply that Wagner invented the music before the text, or that the music is more satisfying without the drama than with it (Debussy's opinion of *Parsifal*), or that both drama and music were modeled on instrumental genres and their compositional conventions.[11]

But music can be generated by poetry, and thereby transgress limits set upon instrumental (symphonic) music, and pass beyond what is comprehensible in the symphonic world. This is an image of music pulled awry by a text with which it cannot be at peace, of music driven to transcendence. And this was Wagner's own image of his works, one that coexisted, paradoxically, with his Beethoven myth. In the web of Wagner's words lies a fundamental contradiction, a contradiction largely ignored when modern proponents of "symphonic opera" appeal to Wagner's authority.

If we are to apply Wagner's words to the task of interpreting his music, then his peculiar use of *symphonic* needs to be set apart as entangled in paradox and contradiction. The single Wagnerian scene considered here, *Götterdämmerung,* Act II, Scene 5, is put into this context and interpreted quite deliberately, even exaggeratedly, in the light of words: what Wagner wrote on "symphonic opera," modern tropes upon his words, what Wagner wrote on operatic text, the text for the scene itself, its sound and its meaning. But the scene is also envisaged as a musical parable that comments on the matter at hand: a representation of the conflicting aesthetics of the operatic and the symphonic, in which a discursive music that takes its shape and voice from words becomes a symphonic music that pursues its own sonorous logic.

---

the idea that Wagner's shifts from loose recitative-like discourse to more formally knit units derived from the number convention of traditional opera.

10. See, for instance, Kinderman, "Dramatic Recapitulation," 112: "a more reasonable basis for analysis of Wagner's works would regard the *music* as the basis for the dramatic progression. . . . In works such as the last acts of *Siegfried* and *Götterdämmerung,* the manifold interrelationships in the tonal structure of the whole are regulated by a musical hierarchy, and this hierarchy coincides with and reinforces a hierarchy of dramatic values."

11. Anthony Newcomb, following Dahlhaus in viewing Wagner's music as adaptation of or self-conscious play on traditional formal conventions, argued that these musical conventions shaped Wagner's creation of dramatic situations; that is, that scenes might be deliberately calculated as analogies to the musical shapes and procedures; see "The Birth of Music out of the Spirit of Drama," *19th-Century Music* V, no. 1 (1981–1982), 41–42; also "Ritornello Ritornato: A Variety of Wagnerian Refrain Form," in this volume, pp. 202–21.

II

In *Oper und Drama,* as in the writings of the late 1840s, Wagner took a radical position on the symphony. He downgraded the status of symphonic music and exalted in its place his own dramatic music, a music deemed richer and fundamentally different in reflecting poetic meaning. One catchword employed in *Oper und Drama* for this enriched, symbolic music was *Versmelodie,* a musical setting of text in which that text's meaning would be mirrored by musical gestures. Such a procedure would bend the very fabric of music beyond what would be conceivable in the merely symphonic universe.[12] In short, Wagner wrote of a musical substance whose progress through time, whose essence, is not merely coordinated with but determined by the text; he insisted that such music will involve elements that are unthinkable in instrumental music.[13]

This is the point of the famous simile in *Oper und Drama* in which Wagner likened music to an ocean of endless harmonic possibilities. The *Musiker*—the instrumental composer—is terrified of this ocean and always swims close to the harbor, fearing musical incomprehensibility if he ventures too far from the calm waters of convention: "The Composer who wishes to express himself to us solely by means of notes is able to do so only by shrinking his endless [harmonic] possibilities to a very limited number."[14] Beethoven in this context is called the "kühnster Schwimmer" in a generally cowardly lot. But the Composer whose music is directed by poetry can dare the deeper waters.[15]

"*Zukunftsmusik*" may be seen as a crucial way-station in Wagner's metamorphosis from champion of symbolic music to defender of absolute music.[16] The essay was in part a revision of *Oper und Drama*; Wagner described it as a general outline of the earlier book, designed for a Parisian public suspicious of both his

12. See *Oper und Drama* III, in *Gesammelte Schriften* IV, 190–92; *Versmelodie* was discussed in Kropfinger, *Wagner und Beethoven,* 111–12, 165–72; and in Carl Dahlhaus, *Wagners Konzeption des musikalischen Dramas* (Regensburg, 1971), 98–110.

13. See, for example, the discussion of modulation in *Oper und Drama* III, *Gesammelte Schriften* IV, 190–92, in which the composer is shown how he can juxtapose remotely related keys in creating a tonal symbol for poetic meaning; Wagner wrote that "die Rechtfertigung für sein [the Composer's] Verfahren, das als ein unbedingtes uns willkürlich und unverständlich erscheinen würde, enthält der Musiker daher aus der Absicht des Dichters," ibid., 192.

14. Ibid., 188: "der Musiker, der sich nur in Tönen klar verständlich dem Gefühle mitteilen will, kann dieses nur durch Herabstimmung seines unendlichen Vermögens zu einem sehr beschränkten Masse."

15. Ibid., 187–88.

16. "*Zukunftsmusik*" was an ironic title for the German edition; the essay was written as a preface to the French edition of four of his libretti, *Quatre Poèmes d'opéras,* "précédés d'une lettre sur la musique" (Paris, 1861). The four operas were *Holländer, Tannhäuser, Lohengrin,* and *Tristan,* and the translations were prose renditions done by Frédéric Villot, the "ami" to whom the "lettre sur la musique" was addressed.

The "lettre sur la musique" was published simultaneously in Germany with its familiar German title. The word *Zukunftsmusik* had been coined by Ludwig Bischoff, the conservative editor of the *Niederrheinische Musikzeitung* and a prominent anti-Wagnerian. Bischoff meant the word as a mocking reference to Wagner's 1849 essay *Das Kunstwerk der Zukunft,* an essay he had patently misread. See Ernest Newman, *The Life of Richard Wagner* III (New York, 1941), 19–20; for an account of Bischoff's reply to Wagner's "*Zukunftsmusik*" see Kropfinger, *Wagner und Beethoven,* 178–79. In bringing out the *Quatre Poèmes* Wagner decided not

music and his ideas. It was, of course, much more: it was an account of Wagner's compositional experiences with the *Ring* and with *Tristan*. Robert Bailey has called it a retraction of *Oper und Drama,* consequent on Wagner's realization with *Tristan* that music *qua* music (and *sine* poetry) was central to his art.[17] Dahlhaus put it even more strongly, writing that "the continuity upon which Wagner insisted was . . . illusory. The very differences, the additions, the omissions, the shifts in emphasis which distinguish the theoretical precepts in '*Zukunftsmusik*' from those in *Oper und Drama* . . . are striking."[18] Dahlhaus viewed these revisions as in some sense unconscious, made in reaction to the musical and dramatic problems posed by the *Ring,* and made despite the declared intention of "outlining" the earlier treatise. The new aesthetic posture of "*Zukunftsmusik*" undoubtedly mirrored Wagner's philosophical education as well. There are Schopenhauerian winds rattling about in the later treatise; given Wagner's preoccupation with Schopenhauer in the mid-1850s, it is hardly surprising that purely instrumental music should be treated more gently in 1860 than it was in 1851.

If "*Zukunftsmusik*" was not a wholesale rejection of *Oper und Drama,* it was at least a thoroughgoing reexamination of the earlier book. In "*Zukunftsmusik*" Wagner confronted a dilemma. He wanted, for obvious reasons, to affirm one stance taken in *Oper und Drama,* that his own music is richer than any "pure" music because daring musical analogies for poetry extend his music's possibilities. At the same time, his absorption of Schopenhauer's musical *ethos,* and his own compositional experiences over the decade of the 1850s, led him to attach greater value to "pure" music, and in particular to the symphony; thus Wagner's revisionism in "*Zukunftsmusik*" centered on thoughts about Beethoven's symphonies in relation to his own musical language.[19] If the escape

to ask Villot to attempt verse translations; his miserable experiences with the verse translation of *Tannhäuser* for the Opéra had made him wary of the procedure. Villot's translation of the *Tannhäuser* poem for *Quatre Poèmes* was in fact an independent effort, completed in the autumn of 1860, and had nothing to do with the Opéra translation done in the spring and summer of 1860 by Wagner, his first collaborators Edmond Roche and Richard Lindau, and his final collaborator Charles Nuitter.

17. Robert Bailey, "The Genesis of *Tristan und Isolde,*" diss. Princeton University, 1969, 7, argued that Wagner wholly rejected the *ethos* of *Oper und Drama* not only in writing "*Zukunftsmusik*" but in composing *Tristan,* Acts II and III, and in all his post-*Tristan* works.

18. Dahlhaus, *Wagners Konzeption des musikalischen Dramas,* 100: "Die Kontinuität, auf der Wagner beharrte . . . ist bloßer Schein. Und gerade die Differenzen, die Zusätze, Auslassungen und Akzentverschiebungen, durch die sich Theoreme in 'Zukunftsmusik' von denen in *Oper und Drama* unterschieden, sind . . . ausschlaggebend." Dahlhaus considered Wagner's emphasis on symphony in "*Zukunftsmusik*" as one sign of this profound aesthetic revisionism, of a discontinuity between *Oper und Drama* and "*Zukunftsmusik*." By dwelling on the symphonic in his work, Wagner had in Dahlhaus's view shifted from an emphasis on the vocal part, deemed in *Oper und Drama* the chief carrier of musical symbolization of poetry, to the orchestral fabric as a bearer of musical meaning; Dahlhaus argued that this volte-face reflected Wagner's composition of the *Ring,* in which motivic action is centered in the orchestra; see ibid., 103.

19. Kropfinger wrote of "Wagners Ausführungen in *Zukunftsmusik,* mit denen er die Anwendung des von Beethoven entwickelten Verfahrens melodischer Ausspinnung thematisch-motivischen Materials aufs Drama propagierte": *Wagner und Beethoven,* 180; see also Dahlhaus, *Wagners Konzeption des musikalischen Dramas,* 106.

from this dilemma was sophistic, the paths taken in flight reveal an attempt to explain the composition of the *Tristan* poem and its musical realization, in terms essential to an understanding of Wagner's notions of *symphonic opera.*

"*Zukunftsmusik*" begins with a review not of musical issues, but of operatic poetry in general. Wagner wrote that his own early opera texts—*Holländer* and *Tannhäuser* included—had the typical failings of ordinary opera libretti; they were written too much with the "conventional form for operatic music [the number] in mind."[20] This meant that their texts were distorted in the musical setting by "frequent repetitions of words or lines, so that they might serve as mere underpinning for the operatic *Melodie,* that is, so that the text might be stretched out to fill up the proper broad proportions of the *Melodie* [musical fabric]."[21] However, "in the final musical execution of *Tristan,* there are no longer any repetitions of words; rather, the entire expanse [*Ausdehnung*] of the musical fabric [*Melodie*] is already prefigured by the web of words and poetic lines; that is, this musical fabric was already predetermined by the poem itself."[22] The remark that the "musical fabric is already predetermined by the poem" is like a magic mirror; each reader will be tempted to see in it what he wishes to see. But the context of the citation is significant. This part of "*Zukunftsmusik*" is one of Wagner's tacit codicils to *Oper und Drama* Part III, a commentary on the earlier work that was preparatory to a more radical departure from it. "Predetermined by the poem" referred to the *ethos* of text-setting expounded in *Oper und Drama*: that the music's motion, its course through time, will in certain ways be shaped by the poem which that music sets.[23]

One shift in emphasis away from *Oper und Drama* is expressed as a sort of reciprocity, the idea that a preexistent musical conception of some sort can play a part in the genesis of the *poem*: "If, as I hope, you could regard *Tristan*'s poetry per se as superior to the kind of poetry I was capable of producing for my earlier works, then you would have to conclude that prefiguring the musical form

20. "*Zukunftsmusik*," *Sämtliche Schriften* VII, 121–22: "herkömmliche Form der Opernmusik im Auge."

21. Ibid., 123: "Phrase darauf berechnet werden, durch zahlreiche Wiederholungen der Phrasen und der Worte als Unterlage unter die Opernmelodie, zu der dieser Melodie nötigen Breite ausgedehnt zu werden." In this and subsequent passages, *Melodie* is translated as "musical fabric." The translation is free, even whimsical, but it catches more shades of Wagner's meaning than would a translation as "melody." Wagner was not writing merely of melody as the upper voice of the texture, but of a more complicated idea; *Melodie* encompasses not just one voice but in a sense the entire musical web, its shape and progress. Kropfinger, *Wagner und Beethoven,* 111–14, 118, discusses at length the implications of Wagner's use of the term *Melodie* (which often occurred in compound words such as *Orchestermelodie* or *Wortversmelodie*).

22. "*Zukunftsmusik*," 123: "in der musikalischen Ausführung des 'Tristan' gar keine Wortwiederholung mehr stattfindet, sondern im Gewebe der Worte und Verse bereits die ganze Ausdehnung der Melodie vorgezeichnet, nämlich diese Melodie dichterisch bereits konstruiert ist."

23. Kropfinger's interpretation (*Wagner und Beethoven,* 122–23) was different; for him Wagner's idea that the "Ausdehnung der Melodie" was prefigured by the poem referred not to an aesthetic stance (that musical execution is in abstract ways guided by the meaning of the text) but, rather, to a compositional idea, that the continuous "durchorganizierte" musical fabric of the Beethovenian symphony (or of Wagner's post-*Lohengrin* works) was paralleled in a "continuous" drama in a libretto poem like *Tristan.*

within the poem had a felicitous effect upon the creation of that poem."[24] Wagner implies that the very fact that there is going to be music for the poem and that this music will be directed by the poem has lent the poetry a unique quality. He does not stop there:

> If it follows from this that the complete prefiguration of the musical form gives the poem itself a special quality (and this specifically according to the spirit of the poetic Will), then only one more question remains to be asked: is not something of the purely musical form [*musikalische Form*] of the *Melodie* sacrificed through this [prefiguration of music by the poem], in that the music forfeits its own freedom of [purely musical] movement and development? The Composer replies that by this procedure the musical fabric and its form are accorded a richness and inexhaustibility that one can hardly imagine to be possible without it.[25]

The reference to the richness of music animated and shaped by poetry, set in opposition to the plainness of instrumental music, sends the argument drifting back once more to the earlier book.[26]

The real shift in emphasis in "*Zukunftsmusik*" can of course be measured in the extent of the discussion of the symphony, a topic approached by the proposition of parallels between operatic set piece and Beethovenian symphonic movement. Both are formally lucid, based on conventional patterns. More important, both symphonic movement and Italian opera number are in Wagner's view explicable as self-sufficient musical entities. That is, the text in the Italian opera number is viewed as essentially irrelevant; it is there as mere verbal matter in a precalculated musical piece. Wagner associated the two genres under the rubric *Tanzform,* an old concept from *Das Kunstwerk der Zukunft* (1849), evoking no specific formal pattern but, rather, musical periodicity and formality (characteristic of dance music) per se:

> Not that I want to say anything derogatory about this [*Tanzform*]. I believe I have demonstrated that it is the basis for the consummate art-form of the Beethovenian symphony, and for this reason alone it deserves enormous credit. But it must be borne in mind that in Italian opera this form is to be found in its most primitive and underdeveloped state, while in the symphony it is expanded and developed to such

---

24. "*Zukunftsmusik,*" 123–24: "Wenn ich zu gleicher Zeit hoffen dürfte, daß Sie meiner dichterischen Ausführung des *Tristan* an sich mehr Wert beilegen können, als der bei meinen früheren Arbeiten mir möglichen, so müßten Sie schon aus diesem Umstande schließen, daß die im Gedichte vollständig bereits vorgebildete musikalische Form zunächst mindestens eben der dichterischen Arbeit vorteilhaft gewesen wäre."

25. Ibid.: "Wenn demnach die vollständige Vorbildung der musikalischen Form dem Gedichte selbst bereits einen besonderen Wert und zwar ganz im Sinne des dichterischen Willens zu geben vermag, so früge es sich nur noch, ob hierdurch die musikalische Form der Melodie selbst nicht etwa einbüße, indem sie für ihre Bewegung und Entwicklung ihrer Freiheit verlustig ginge? Hierauf lassen Sie sich nun vom *Musiker* antworten . . . daß bei diesen Verfahren die Melodie und ihre Form einem Reichtum und einer Unerschöpflichkeit zugeführt werden, von denen man sich ohne dieses Verfahren gar keine Vorstellung machen konnte."

26. See, for instance, *Oper und Drama* III, *Gesammelte Schriften* IV, 187, 188–92.

an extent that its relationship to the primitive state is like that of the fully flowering plant to the mere seedling.[27]

Wagner interpreted traditional operatic numbers as essentially instrumental, animated by their own musical formality rather than by the text they might set. The profound difference between the operatic number and the symphonic movement was one of degree and not of kind.

Wagner was, in short, concocting an antithesis, one whose spirit echoes the aesthetic posture of *Oper und Drama*. On one side is instrumental music, from impoverished opera numbers to magnificent symphonic movements; all logical, tidy, formal, musically explicable without reference to any text. On the other side is *his* music, semantically generated, musically audacious, and *au fond* inexplicable in purely musical terms.

In the final pages of "*Zukunftsmusik*" he would make his real departure from *Oper und Drama,* by drawing a parallel between the Beethovenian symphony and his own musical thought. He attempted to press two antithetical poles close enough to create a spark between them: the metaphor of symphonic opera. The famous passage likening Beethoven's first movements to a continuous net of transformed and interrelated motives is the key to the metaphor's meaning. Wagner asked: if the purely formal is the basis for Beethoven's symphonic movements, as it is for all instrumental music, what sets Beethoven's symphonies apart?

> Beethoven's symphonic procedure produced an entirely new result: a broadening of the whole musical fabric [*Melodie*], accomplished by means of the richest possible transformations of all the musical motives it contained, to generate a continuous large-scale musical piece, a piece that is nothing less than a single, unified, completely coherent *Melodie*.[28]

To us, this understanding of Beethoven's music in terms of simple thematic interrelationships seems unsophisticated, even primitive. Wagner's idiosyncratic thematic orientation is vividly evinced in his infamous denigration of Mozart's symphonies as inferior, discontinuous, moving through long, empty stretches of harmonic motoring or transitional roughage during which no thematic substance is perceptible.[29] This idiosyncrasy is central to evaluating Wagner's *symphonic opera* correctly; as the vaguest of analogies between his operas with their webs of recurring and developing themes and Beethovenian symphonic movements with their densely motivic surfaces.

27. "*Zukunftsmusik*," 125–26; see also Kropfinger, *Wagner und Beethoven*, 101–6, 137.

28. "*Zukunftsmusik*," 127: "Der ganze neue Erfolg dieses Verfahrens war somit die Ausdehnung der Melodie durch reichste Entwicklung aller in ihr liegenden Motive zu einem großen, andauernden Musikstücke, welches nichts anderes als eine einzige, genau zusammenhängende Melodie war."

29. Ibid., 126.

Indeed, Wagner was ultimately more interested in this "symphonic procedure" for its literary than for its musical possibilities: he saw in it a repetition and transformation that could be translated into linguistic terms. He argued that Beethoven had used his symphonic procedure of motivic transformation in the *Missa Solemnis*. "In his great Mass, Beethoven treated chorus and orchestra almost as he had in symphonies; this was possible because the universally familiar sacred texts—with their now almost wholly symbolic meaning—provided him . . . with a literary form that he could . . . break apart and reassemble by dividing up, repeating, or reordering the words."[30] In other words, such sacred texts resemble traditional opera texts in that they may be repeated and distorted to provide verbal matter for a musical shape, in this case for Beethoven's continuous web of themes.

No opera composer, no matter how symphonically inclined he might be, could possibly submit a dramatic poem to such violence. The meaning of a dramatic text is not merely symbolic and negligible; it must be defended, and the meaning resides in the orderings and juxtapositions of words, in niceties of syntax that would be devastated by repetition and reassembly: "A reasonably sensitive Composer could not possibly deal in such a fashion with the text of a dramatic poem, since in this case the words no longer have a merely symbolic meaning, but, rather, must follow a specific and logical sequence."[31] For the opera composer with symphonic aspirations, there is only one recourse. "The possibility remained open to create a dramatic poem that is itself a dramatic counterpart to the symphonic form, that is obedient to the fundamental canons of drama, while at the same time completely matching the richness and complexity of symphonic form."[32]

This is a tantalizing proposition. Wagner referred, of course, to a possibility realized in his own post-*Lohengrin* poems. But what is the poetic counterpart to the symphony? The key to the allusion is, again, Wagner's understanding of Beethoven's symphonic movements as a musical web in which continual repetition of related motives generated an unceasing musical rhetoric of statement and transformation.

---

30. Ibid., 127: "Beethoven hat in seiner großen Messe Chor und Orchester fast ganz wieder wie in der Symphonie verwendet: es war ihm diese symphonische Behandlung möglich, weil in den kirchlichen, allgemein bekannten, fast nur noch symbolisch bedeutungsvollen Textworten ihm . . . eine Form gegeben war, die er durch Trennung, Wiederholung, neue Anreihung usw. . . . zerlegen und neu verbinden konnte." In a letter to Louis Köhler of 24 July 1853, Wagner wrote that it was "impossible" to translate a Beethovenian symphonic procedure into linguistic terms: Erwin Kloss, ed., *Richard Wagner an Freunde und Zeitgenossen* (Berlin, 1909), 125.

31. *"Zukunftsmusik,"* 127: "Unmöglich konnte ein sinnvoller Musiker ebenso mit den Textworten einer dramatischen Dichtung verfahren wollen, weil diese nicht mehr nur symbolische Bedeutung, sondern eine bestimmte logische Konsequenz enthalten sollen."

32. Ibid., 127–28: "Dagegen mußte die Möglichkeit offen bleiben, in der dramatischen Dichtung selbst ein poetisches Gegenstück zur symphonischen Form zu erhalten, welches, indem es diese reiche Form vollkommen erfüllte, zugleich den innersten Gesetzen der dramatischen Form am besten entsprach."

Such a procedure might well find an analogy in certain poetic devices and in a peculiarity of language shared by all the post-*Lohengrin* poems. Of course, all these poems satisfy Wagner's first criterion for a dramatic poem, that is to say, exposition of a dramatic plot that proceeds logically. The peculiarity they share, however, is that of highly repetitive language. Patterns of phonetic and, above all, semantic repetition are built into the poems. Some repetitions—such refrain texts as the Norns' "Singe, Schwester, dir werf ich's zu"—exist on the surface of the poem. Other verbal recurrences are less direct, involving single portentous words and their variants, or phrases, or even stories told and told again (such as the narratives in the *Ring*), or disguised and transformed reenactments of symbolic actions, such as the gesture of suicide that closes each act of *Tristan*. These verbal recurrences are a poetic-linguistic parallel to the workings of a symphony; they are constructed verbal opportunities for musical repetition and transformation.[33]

Wagner's entire discussion of Beethoven and symphonic procedure—his real departure from *Oper und Drama*—can be evaluated on many levels.[34] The statement that both he and Beethoven employ constant repetition, fragmentation, and metamorphosis of thematic material is too banal, too general, to provide sophisticated insights into the music of either. We might better take it as Wagner's way of expressing the mythic bond between two compositional giants. The value of the discussion of the symphonic procedure in "*Zukunftsmusik*" lies in its suggestion of how a musical vision of motivic repetition and transformation could be converted into verbal recurrence in poetry.

Wagner's description of the business of composing music for a completed dramatic poem alludes to the *ethos* of text-setting already discussed in *Oper und Drama* Part III and in part repeats the earlier essay. When the composer sets himself to create the music for a particular poem, he finds that certain aspects of it have been "dichterisch bereits konstruiert." The poem may indeed have been informed—nebulously—by a musical idea, by Wagner's vision of Beethoven's repeated and transformed themes. But he did recognize the part accorded to the finished text's meaning in shaping the musical reality of a given work. He affirmed in "*Zukunftsmusik*" that, "by observing the Composer, the Poet will discover a secret that is hidden from the Composer himself: that the musical

---

33. Carl Dahlhaus touched on the idea of the *Ring* narratives as text calculated to generate motivic recurrence and recapitulation: *Richard Wagner's Music Dramas*, trans. Mary Whittall (Cambridge, England, 1979), 86–87. Kropfinger's interpretation of "poetisches Gegenstück zur symphonischen Form" was different from that offered here. Kropfinger argued that Wagner saw the Beethovenian symphonic procedure *au fond* as a model of continuity (a single "unending" fabric wherein one thematic idea mutates into another). The "poetisches Gegenstück" to such a model would be an operatic poem, like *Tristan*, in which there are no breaks in action or dramatic development; *Wagner und Beethoven*, 123–24.

34. Kropfinger, *Wagner und Beethoven*, 181: "Die unterschiedlichen Kritiken zu Wagners Orientierung an Beethoven lassen unberücksichtigt, daß Wagner Beethovens Verfahren zwar als Vorbild pries, daß er dessenungeachtet aber auf die Unterschiede hinwies, die zwischen dem Verfahren des Dramatikers und dem des Instrumentalkomponisten bestehen."

fabric [*melodische Form*] is capable of being developed far more richly than the Composer, in writing his symphonies, could ever imagine to be possible."[35] Music directed by poetry is elevated above the symphonic. Once the poem is written, it profoundly affects the specific details of musical execution. Such an aesthetic enables a transcendence of the limits set on pure music. This is not metaphysical chatter, but a reconfirmation of a position taken in *Oper und Drama*, reinforced by a reference to Wagner's famous simile of the dangerous harmonic ocean and the daring aquatic feats of the Poet-Composer, who is freed from the constraints of instrumental composition.[36]

III

In "*Zukunftsmusik*" Wagner made an ingenious escape from a philosophical dilemma. He remained true to his earlier Hegelian polemic of texted music as richer and bolder than "pure" music. By shifting the grounds of his discourse, he was able at the same time to reveal his reading of Schopenhauer, celebrate "pure" music, and invoke a "symphonic opera" of ever-recurring themes whose text was haunted by this Beethovenian musical vision. Wagner set himself in the mainstream of a revered tradition and claimed his Beethovenian patrimony.

In one conventional image of Wagner's later evolution as polemicist, the anti-symphonic radical of *Oper und Drama* metamorphoses into a conservative musical tyrant who could declare in *Beethoven* that music was the progenitor of both poetry and drama, with "*Zukunftsmusik*" as a phase in this metamorphosis. But this image is too simple.[37] Wagner's polemic concerning pure music indeed grew more vehement in later years. Yet this was only one of the many masks he assumed as he clung to the elaborate dualistic universe he had created in "*Zukunftsmusik*." Schopenhauerian paeans to pure music as representation of Will, deeming music an "a priori qualification of mankind for the shaping of drama,"[38] jostle straightforward remarks to the contrary:

> At lunch R. explained how differently one must work in the symphony and in music drama, where all is [musically] permissible except stupidities, since the action explains everything.[39]

35. "*Zukunftsmusik*," 129: "Er [der Dichter] wird dem Musiker das diesem selbst verborgene Geheimnis ablauschen, daß die melodische Form noch zu unendlich *reichere* Entwicklung fähig ist, als ihm [dem Musiker] bisher in der Symphonie selbst möglich dünken durfte."

36. Ibid.

37. Stein, *Richard Wagner and the Synthesis of the Arts,* 167, 188; see Kropfinger, *Wagner und Beethoven,* 155–56, 164–65, for a commentary on Stein's interpretation.

38. *Beethoven,* in *Gesammelte Schriften* IX, 106: "die aprioristische Befähigung des Menschen zur Gestaltung des Dramas."

39. *Cosima Wagner's Diaries,* trans. Geoffrey Skelton, I (New York, 1977), 129 (entry of 25 July 1869).

R. says, . . . "In me the accent lies on the conjunction of poet and musician; as a pure musician I would not be of much significance."[40]

Yesterday R. earnestly advised Herr Svendsen to choose for his instrumental music motives and themes as serene as possible. . . . Musical eccentricities need the drama to explain them.[41]

Wagner, then, did not believe in the essentially abstract nature of his music. As late as 1879, he was insisting with some vehemence that his music could not be understood in terms of abstract musical canons. Far from imputing any great comprehensibility to his music *qua* music, he wrote of audacity and illogic, of trespassing the bounds of purely musical coherence. He saw *Reichtum* (not error or failure) in this kind of music. But he did not see this music as wholly understandable in abstract, or, if you will, symphonic, terms. This argument is made, for example, in the three late essays of 1879, "Über das Dichten und Componieren," "Über das Opern-Dichten und Componieren im Besonderen," and "Über die Anwendung der Musik auf das Drama."

We need not advocate a fanatic acceptance of any Wagnerian writings (even when we think we are certain what they mean) as canon for our interpretations of his operas or of musical history: to suggest, for instance, that Wagner had discovered the *Geheimnis der Form bei Mozart* would be, one feels, over-reverent to the Ricardian view. Wagnerian critics of many persuasions have argued that Wagner's scores possess symphonic hallmarks of the kind Wagner himself identified: the repetition, fragmentation, and transformation of recurring motives. But others have argued that Wagner's scores possess qualities Wagner never mentioned: adaptations of specific formal conventions, large-scale tonal plans, layers of structural levels. We are free to call all these symphonic, if we must. The lighthearted appeal to Wagner's authority to legitimize what we find symphonic about his music is, however, no better than trickery, and to evoke Wagner's authority for a modern view of the symphonic—based on formal designs, large-scale tonal coherence, and the like—is at best naive, at worst dishonest.

Hermeneutic rigor of the bleakest sort might insist that Wagner's writings on his work be banished from any interpretation of that work. Few of us would be attracted to such a proscription even if we thought its enforcement possible. But if we choose to distort Wagner's metaphor of the symphonic opera in order to create our own metaphor, to change his metaphorical meaning to suit our analytical purposes, we ought to say so.

More than this: if we evoke Wagner's views at all, we are bound to consider the antithesis, the dark side, of Wagner's symphonic metaphor: his insistence on musical anomaly, on the inexplicable and symphonically unattainable riches

---

40. Ibid., 137 (entry of 16 August 1869).
41. Ibid., 520 (entry of 7 August 1870); see also Voss, *Richard Wagner und die Instrumentalmusik,* 170.

of the peculiar music that reflects poetic meaning. It is in the light of Wagner's own metaphor of the symphonic opera, and of its antithesis, that we can reinterpret the last scene in Act II of *Götterdämmerung*.

IV

The circumstances of *Götterdämmerung*'s genesis are strange. Much of the text, including most of Act II, Scene 5, goes back to the first copy of the *Siegfrieds Tod* poem in 1848, while the music was not written until 1869–1872. In other words, by the time Wagner wrote the music for *Götterdämmerung*, the poetry had long grown cold. For this reason, the poem might be dismissed as mere verbal and dramatic chaff, an insignificant sonic carrier for a symphonic music Wagner could not have foreseen in 1848.[42] Like all Wagner's later operas, *Götterdämmerung* indeed contains symphonic stretches in which the musical idea overwhelms and subdues the meaning of the text.[43]

This does not hold true throughout, however: Act II, Scene 5, is a case in point. This is the Conspiracy Scene, the long discussion between Brünnhilde, Hagen, and Gunther that culminates in their vow to murder Siegfried. The scene is spun out by means of a familiar Wagnerian gambit, the repetition of musical refrains that act as a simple point of aural reorientation as the scene unfolds. The Norns' scene, with its reiterated refrains of "Singe, Schwester," and Tristan's delirium scene, articulated by the sound of the "alte Weise," are other instances of the type.

There is nothing occult about the refrain music in the Conspiracy Scene, a motivic congeries that superimposes the uneasy appoggiatura of Hagen's call to the vassals (from Act II, Scene 3) on a monotonous chromatic fragment first heard in Act I, Scene 4 (Ex. 3.1).[44] Alfred Lorenz saw the Conspiracy Scene as a single large "period" in which smaller subsections were defined by the recurrence of this "Rachebund" motive, which he called a "starrer Refrain."[45] The word *starr*, "frozen" or "unyielding," is felicitous: it expresses with some force the musical idiosyncrasies of this refrain complex. With few exceptions, the refrain does not drift off the pitch level of Example 3.1; it is not transformed rhythmically in any of its restatements; it is similarly orchestrated in all its appearances, "unyielding," unchanged over time.

In addition to the "Rachebund" mentioned by Lorenz, there is a second cyclic gesture in the scene. This second refrain is derived from a stretch of

---

42. See Patrick McCreless, *Wagner's* Siegfried: *Its Drama, History, and Music* (Ann Arbor, 1982), 187–88.

43. See Dahlhaus, *Richard Wagner's Music Dramas,* 135–36.

44. The motive first appears with a text at Brünnhilde's line, "Nun erseh' ich / der Strafe Sinn," in Scene 3; it is anticipated in the orchestra during Waltraute's narrative.

45. Lorenz, *Das Geheimnis der Form* I, 44, 272.

EXAMPLE 3.1. The "Rachebund" refrain from the Conspiracy Scene.

Siegfried and Gunther's Act I "Brotherhood Oath" and develops a motive Lorenz called "Sühnerecht," a five-note descending gesture, whose origins go back to Hunding's "Heilig ist mein Herd, heilig sei dir mein Haus" in *Walküre*, Act I.[46] The excerpt from the "Brotherhood Oath" is transformed three times, becoming a second refrain (called here "Sühnerecht") for the Conspiracy Scene (Ex. 3.2). The first two transformations (A, B) are based only on the opening gesture of the source passage, the "Sühnerecht" motive. The third transformation (C) takes up more material from the source passage, developing the major-key martial flourish. Lorenz gave a synoptic and superficial view of the scene, and any neo-Lorenzian list of the moments at which the two refrains recur would tell us nothing about the other parts of the scene, neither about the musical time between the refrains nor about the musical effect of those refrains in their context.

V

The two musical refrains are in fact associated with particular words and exist in a broader sense as symbols for a dramatic progression in the scene. The words in question are striking. The poem for the Conspiracy Scene, like most of Wagner's post-*Lohengrin* texts, is repetitive, but in the texts of the two refrains the density of repetition becomes tremendous, almost narcotic.

[1] BRÜNN.:	Wer bietet mir nun das Schwert		Who offers me a sword
	Mit dem ich die Bande zerschnitt?		With which I can cut the bond?

• • •

HAGEN:	Und dort trifft ihn mein Speer!		My spear shall strike him there!
	Auf Gunther, edler Gibichung,		Up, Gunther, noble Gibichung,
5	Hier steht dein starkes Weib,		Here stands a mighty woman,
	Was hängst du dort in Harm?		Why linger there in grief?
GUNTH.:	O Schmach! O Schande!		Oh shame! Oh anguish!

• • •

46. This descending motive is itself, of course, an inversion of the four opening notes of the Curse motive.

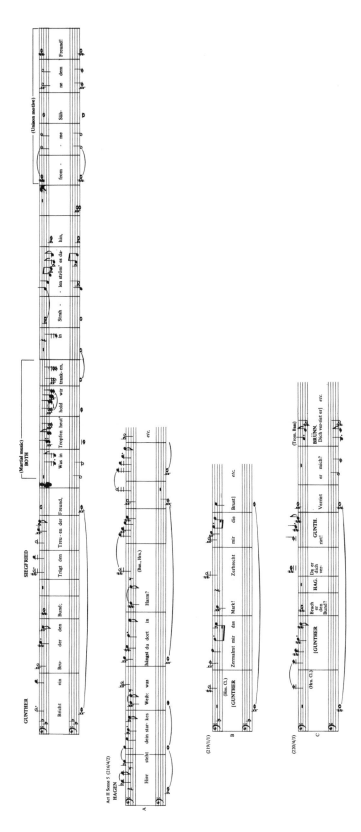

EXAMPLE 3.2. Three transformations of the "Brotherhood Oath."

HAGEN:	In Schande liegst du,	You lie there in shame,
	läugn' ich das?	That I don't deny.

      •   •   •

10 GUNTH.:	Betrüger ich, und betrogen!	Deceiver am I, and deceived!
	Verräter ich, und verraten!	A betrayer am I, and betrayed!
	Zermalmt mir das Mark,	Let my bones be crushed,
	Zerbrecht mir die Brust!	Let my heart break!

      •   •   •

HAGEN:	Dir hilft kein Hirn,	My mind cannot help you,
15	Dir hilft keine Hand,	My hand cannot help you,
	Dir hilft nur—	Only one thing can help you—
	Siegfrieds Tod.	*Siegfried's Death.*
GUNTH.:	Siegfrieds Tod?	Siegfried's Death?
HAGEN:	Nur der sühnt deine Schmach!	Only that can atone for your shame!

      •   •   •

20 HAGEN:	Des Bundes Bruch	For the broken bond,
	Sühne nun Blut!	Only blood can atone!
GUNTH.:	Brach er den Bund?	Did he break the bond?
HAGEN:	Da er dich verriet.	In that he betrayed you.
GUNTH.:	Verriet er mich?	Did he betray me?
25 BRÜNN.:	Dich verriet er,	He betrayed you,
	Und mich verrietet ihr alle!	And you have all betrayed me!
	Wär ich gerecht,	Had I my rights
	Alles Blut der Welt	All the blood of the world
	Büßte mir nicht eure Schuld.	Would not purge your guilt.
30	Doch des einen Tod	But the death of one
	Taugt mir für alle;	Shall serve for all;
	Siegfried falle,	Siegfried shall fall,
	Zur Sühne für sich, und euch!	In atonement for himself, and for you!

      •   •   •

HAGEN:	Uns allen frommt sein Tod!	His death will serve us all!

      •   •   •

³⁵ GUNTH.:	So soll es sein,	So be it,
BRÜNN.:	Siegfried falle!	Siegfried dies!
	Sühn' er die Schmach,	He shall atone for the shame
	Die er mir schuf,	That he has brought to me,
	Des Eides Treue	The faith of the oath
⁴⁰	Hat er getrogen,	He has betrayed,
	Mit seinem Blut	With his blood
	Büß er die Schuld!	He shall purge his guilt!

Repetition here has a specific dramatic import, as the obsessed, monotonous language of individuals suffering great emotional distress. Gunther and Brünnhilde are possessed by their memories of Siegfried's crimes. Should they stray from their obsession, Hagen is there to guide them. He whispers back to them their own cruel words, reminding them of their wounds and acting as agent provocateur in the conspiracy, to further his own secret cause.

The words associated with the refrains are for the most part transformations of the ominous sestet that closes the Act I "Brotherhood Oath":

> Bricht ein Bruder den Bund—
> Trügt den Treuen der Freund—
> Was in Tropfen heut'
> Hold wir tranken,
> In Strahlen ström' es dahin,
> Fromme Sühne dem Freund.

> If one brother breaks the Oath—
> If one friend betrays the other—
> What today only in drops
> Solemnly we drink,
> In streams shall it flow forth,
> As holy atonement to the faithful.

The variations on this sestet in the Conspiracy Scene's refrains form a semantic field that encompasses several ideas: a severed bond (line 2, "Bande zerschnitt"; line 20, "des Bundes Bruch"); betrayal and treachery (lines 10–11, "Betrüger ich, und betrogen!/Verräter ich, und verraten!"; lines 39–40, "des Eides Treue/ Hat er getrogen"); and finally, a bloody death required as atonement (line 19, "Nur der sühnt deine Schmach!"; lines 41–42, "Mit seinem Blut/Büß er die Schuld!").

The recurrences of these phrases have a phonetic as well as a semantic component. They belong to a constructed family of alliterative roots on *t, b,* and the sibilants *s, z,* and *sch.* The periodic return of dense clusters of these sounds produces a disturbing effect of recognition in the scene when Hagen speaks the gnomic words for the opera, the words "Siegfrieds Tod." As he says them, we realize that we have heard their *sounds* (*s, t*), though not the words themselves, many times before. It is as if Hagen's words had wandered for a long time below the surface of the poem, but until he speaks them they ripple that surface from beneath, disguised within other words and other meanings that share their sonorous envelope.

The underlying dramatic conceit to the musical-textual recurrences lends the scene its great force in the theater. We come to make an association between Hagen's incitements to murder—his repetitions of certain words—and intrusions of the unyielding refrains into the music around them. The many minutes that pass between the repeated refrains are, broadly speaking, musical digressions from those refrains, and dramatic digressions as well, as Hagen's victims wander away from the subjects he wishes to keep at hand. These associations between musical recurrences and textual recurrences, or between musical effect and dramatic effect, are hardly meant as subtle; Wagner was painting with bold colors and gesturing in plain view of his audience.

Considered abstractly, however, as a musical event lodged in the context of a continuous musical discourse, the refrains are distinctly odd, disjunct; they sound like alarming intrusions into the music around them. The "Rachebund" refrain, repeated many times, always occupying the same pitch space, seldom rhythmically altered, is flung into the musical fabric of the scene and is never allowed to seep into its surroundings or to be affected by them. Put more strongly: the refrains are as music in the abstract somehow illogical, a meaningless interruption of the surrounding texture.

In the grossest terms, this procedure is the very antithesis of that progressive motivic development and musical interaction Wagner had deemed the essence of Beethoven's symphonic procedure. Droning, intrusive recurrences of untransformed motivic cells force musical stasis, an eternal return to an initial point. So it seems that Wagner's treatment of the refrains, however effective as a musico-dramatic trick, is inimical to "symphonic" ideals.

VI

This characterization of the Conspiracy Scene is a deliberate exaggeration, a straw man presently to be unstuffed. But the interpretation encompasses certain smaller truths. The notion of intrusion—that the refrains are shot abruptly and without apology into their surroundings—is one of these truths. The music for the Sestet closing the Act I "Brotherhood Oath" exemplifies this kind of intrusion (Ex. 3.3). A bald volte-face occurs within the diatonic martial music in C major, at measure 13, as an inverted D♭ chord follows the IV of measure

EXAMPLE 3.3. The closing sestet of the "Brotherhood Oath."

12.[47] The harmonic abruptness of the D♭ sonority is in effect soothed in measure 16, in a brief reversion to V of C (the G in the bass). But a profounder disjunction follows. The bass G becomes a passing note to F♯; the C-major martial rhythms are deposed; the outburst collapses to a grave, slow unison motive colored by B minor for "Fromme Sühne dem Freund" (mm. 17–25), culminating in the Curse motive.[48] This shift from one musical thought to the next is unprepared, unmediated, and not subsequently bound up by any encompassing gesture of musical closure, tonal or otherwise.[49]

The same musical intrusiveness is characteristic of certain refrain recurrences in the Conspiracy Scene, such as the first statement of the "Rachebund" refrain at the end of Brünnhilde's long opening speech (Ex. 3.4). The speech ends with strong cadential posturing toward B♭ major, a typical Wagnerian mock-closing flourish, in which the actual statement of the tonic chord is avoided. Here, the cadence is swallowed by an orchestral outburst that ends almost atonally, in wholly disorienting, chromatic parallel sixths that glide to a jarring halt on F♯–C for the refrain. This refrain is abandoned as abruptly as it was approached, as F♯–C is opened into octave D for Hagen's speech. The refrain and the chromatic tumble that attains it are a prolonged dissonant caesura between two plateaus, and the three musical statements—Brünnhilde's peroration, the refrain, and Hagen's opening gambit—are unconnected except by mere seamlessness of surface. There is no dead stop, yet there is a profound disjunction.

Both the end of the "Brotherhood Oath" and the first "Rachebund" refrain involve certain harmonic, linear, tonal, rhythmic, and instrumental events that are musically unseemly, even incoherent. Music has been extended beyond its proper sphere—by acting as a symbol for poetry. The sense of intrusion, the layers of anomaly that set off that unison motive in the "Brotherhood Oath," are frankly a piece of word-painting of an old-fashioned kind, a black mark alluding for a few seconds to the "schwarze Tonart" of B minor. The mark is scored under the text "Fromme Sühne dem Freund," Siegfried's unwitting prediction of his own death. If the unison passage is as music mere illogical effect,

---

47. The sound of the D♭ triad in this inversion is, of course, a motivic element in *Götterdämmerung*; cf. the Second Norn's line, "der Weltesche / welkes Geäst," or Hagen's "Noth ist da" (Act II, Scene 3), or Brünnhilde's "weiset Loge nach Walhall, / Denn der Götter Ende dämmert nun auf" (in the Immolation Scene). The sound (though not the particular pitch level on D♭) goes back to Erda's prediction in *Rheingold*, "[Alles was ist, endet, /] Ein düstr'er Tag / Dämmert den Götter."

48. The Curse motive has had since *Rheingold* its own intimations of B minor, superimposing F♯ as the dominant degree on C major as the triad of the Neapolitan.

49. Violent juxtapositions of this sort may be tamed by repetition and familiarity if the juxtaposed elements—intruder and interrupted context—become themselves a single recurring thematic idea. Carl Dahlhaus, taking his direction from Schoenberg, has written on the phenomenon, citing a "bizarre" Wagnerian chord progression (from Fasolt's warning speech in *Rheingold*), inexplicable in conventional harmonic terms, whose illogical juxtapositions are treated as a self-sufficient thematic idea. See "Tonalität und Form in Wagners *Ring des Nibelungen*," *Archiv für Musikwissenschaft* XI, no. 2 (1983), 169–70.

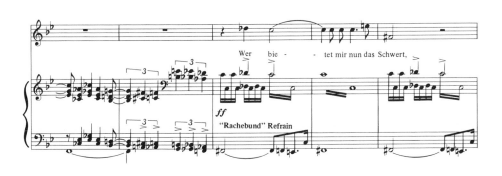

EXAMPLE 3.4. The "Rachebund" refrain in Brünnhilde's first speech (211/3/1–212/1/6).

as a poetic-musical gesture it draws on elaborate semiotic codes to shout its meaning. The abrupt intrusions of the "Rachebund" refrain are similarly calculated as complex musical responses to the words they accompany. By lodging the refrain at F♯–C, Wagner was reinforcing referential connections that extend back to *Rheingold* and continue to reverberate through the *Ring*: F♯–C is the structural interval of Alberich's Curse. The refrain's recurrences within the musical time of the scene (it is called up by the meaning and sound of certain words) and its pitch identity (suggested by older musico-dramatic associations within the *Ring*) are accorded greater importance than any principle of integration within the local tonal, linear, rhythmic, or thematic context. The refrain warps the music around it.

We cannot dismiss either example with the truism that all decent settings of dramatic poems involve "correspondences" of musical and dramatic events that maintain the integrity of both. These are not mere correspondences, and the music's integrity is not maintained. These are, to the contrary, instances of an *ethos* of musical symbolism; they are musical gestures, born of the text's meaning, that extend music's possibilities beyond what is plausible or explicable in any symphonic sphere. Analytical jargon generally reserved for "pure" music can certainly classify these gestures: the passage in Example 3.4 could be described as a "prolongation of a dissonant interval" or as a "transitional element mediating between B♭ and D." But such words do not explain musical anomaly or illogic; they simply retreat from it and so deny its tremendous force and its symbolic import.

In reply, of course, we could insist that Wagner's musical language had by the 1870s evolved to a point where such abruptness—whether of tonal juxtaposition, harmonic gesture, or rhythmic metamorphosis—is in fact no longer anomalous in the purely musical universe. But if we did so, we would be taking issue with Wagner himself, for he remained to the end of his life a passionate celebrant of his own musical eccentricities and illogicalities, devoting portions of essays such as the "Anwendung der Musik auf das Drama" (1879) to the subject. In the "Anwendung" Wagner illustrated musical anomaly with excerpts from his own work similar to the two from *Götterdämmerung* cited above. All Wagner's excerpts include harmonic transformations, dissonant simultaneities, tonal peculiarities. All are deemed inexplicable in terms of the normal rules of instrumental composition:

> If I had used a motivic shape like that employed in the second act of *Die Walküre,* as Wotan gives his lordship of the world over to the owner of the Nibelung hoard [i.e., the dissonant transformation of the Rheingold and Valhalla motives accompanying Wotan's "so nimm' meine Segen, Nibelungen-Sohn"], in, let us say, an overture, I would have done something more or less illogical, according to my view of comprehensibility in musical style. . . . With the help of a bizarrely [*fremdartig*] constructed harmony, I was able to present [the two motives] in such a fashion that this musical

phenomenon [*Tonerscheinung*], even more than Wotan's words themselves, made manifest for us an image of the terrible gloomy soul of the suffering god.[50]

Such "bizarrely constructed" music is not for the symphonic world, and Wagner reproached the younger generations of symphonic composers for pilfering his musical language to adorn an instrumental genre, in which that language cannot be understood.

We might, of course, take the more arrogant line that even Wagner could not truly comprehend the sense of his musical language, that twentieth-century theory with its sharp analytical tools explains away such bizarre constructions. This attitudinizing betrays considerable critical naiveté, to say nothing of an appalling parochialism. But such an attitude also shuts us off from the richness of Wagner's work, from a celebration of its disjointedness and an understanding of what Adorno called its anarchy, and the ends that anarchy served. With our focus refracted by one hundred years of later music and music-theoretical values, we tend to reject the idea of musical anomaly and illogic because we cannot recreate the force and significance the idea possessed in its original historical context.

VII

For Wagner, the symphonic was a continuous spinning-out of never-ceasing thematic webs. For us, the term *symphonic* might also mean periodic phrases, tonal coherence, rhythmic urgency. But for us "symphonic" has a metaphorical meaning as well: a symphonic work is one that is densely interconnected, that evolves organically to its final moments, that is comprehensible as pure music.

The Conspiracy Scene in *Götterdämmerung* is a musical argument broken and interrupted by text-incited intrusions of never-changing refrains: an antisymphonic scene. Or is it? Not entirely; this is the way the scene begins, but it is not how it ends. The music tells another story. It depicts a metamorphosis from anti-symphonic to symphonic, a balance tipped from an *ethos* of musical symbolization of poetry in the beginning, to music's genuine negligence toward the text in a "symphonic" end.

The Conspiracy Scene veers to the symphonic with the third statement of the two refrains. In their first appearances, these refrains seemed intrusive and unyielding: pitch, rhythm, instrumentation are invariable. Later in the scene the

---

50. "Die Anwendung der Musik auf das Drama," in *Sämtliche Schriften* X, 187–88: "Hätte ich ein Motivbildung, wie diejenige, welche im zweiten Aufzüge der 'Walküre' zu Wotans Übergabe der Weltherrschaft an den Besitzer des Nibelungenhortes sich vernehmen läßt: [here the essay reproduces a musical example] etwa in einer Ouvertüre vorgebracht, so würde ich, nach meinen Begriffen von Deutlichkeit des Stiles, etwas geradewegs Unsinniges gemacht haben . . . ich [konnte] sie, mit Hilfe einer fremdartig ableitenden Harmonisation, in der Weise verbunden vorführen, daß diese Tonerscheinung mehr als Wotans Worte uns ein Bild der furchtbar verdüsterten Seele des leidenden Gottes gewahren lassen sollte."

two refrains begin, gradually, to shift off their fixed pitch levels. But, more important, the refrains will no longer seem like stones dropped on marble; they begin to affect and be affected by the music around them.

This metamorphosis begins in Gunther's first speech, Hagen's pronouncement of the gnomic words "Siegfrieds Tod," and the subsequent exchange between the two (Ex. 3.5). The passage may be interpreted as three variations (in an exceedingly loose sense) of the same long phrase. Two elements are constant within all three. One is the deceptive cadence that introduces each variation (mm. 2, 19, 32). The other is a long-range bass motion from the initial note rising through a third: C–D–E in the first variation (mm. 2–15), C–D–E♭ in the second (mm. 19–26), and G♭–A♭–B♭ in the third (mm. 32–38).

In this third cycle Wagner created a disturbing mnemonic effect, a musical sibling to his anticipation of the words "Siegfrieds Tod" in the coruscations of *s* and *t* scattered through the poem. The sound of the rising third in the bass, the slow C–D–E and C–D–E♭ of the first two variations, is paralleled in the G♭–A♭–B♭ of the third. But in the third variation, this rising third begins to repeat, at progressively swifter pace and at other pitches, until it finally breaks to the surface of the music (m. 42) to become a sound heard only once before: the bizarre unison motive (F♯–D–E–F♯, "Fromme Sühne dem Freund") in the Act I "Brotherhood Oath." This is an extraordinary moment; we realize that apparently neutral sounds, the harmless ascending thirds twisting slowly beneath this passage, were not neutral at all, but known and sinister. Hagen's line here, "[Des Bundes Bruch] sühne nun Blut," indirectly echoes the words from the "Brotherhood Oath."

The discourse surrounding the refrains has changed. Now the two refrains appear as parallel incidents within a larger pattern of three variations. More than this, the refrains are no longer isolated from their surroundings; the music has begun to resonate beyond its boundaries. For instance, the characteristic F♯–C interval of the "Rachebund" is hidden in the cadences of measures 1–2 and 17–19. The interval has also crept into the middleground, for the bass line of measures 2–17 outlines it.

Just as the "Rachebund" refrain now seeps into the music around it, it is now integrated into a greater context and its musical meaning thereby changes; it is no longer an intrusion, but the turning point in a musical metamorphosis.

That metamorphosis involves the pitch-level shift within the three variations, from the pitch space around C–D–E/E♭ in the bass lines of the first two, to the G♭–A♭–B♭ bass of the third. The second variation begins very much like the first, but the bass C–D–(E) is deflected to E♭ at Hagen's words "Siegfrieds Tod." At that moment the "Rachebund" refrain sounds on E♭–A, then at G♭–C, its normal pitch level. The statement on G♭ is created, so to speak, as an epiphenomenon out of a "wrong" note, the inflected E♭. This "Rachebund" statement on G♭ is the turning point, establishing the G♭/B♭ minor tonal area of the third cycle in measures 32ff.

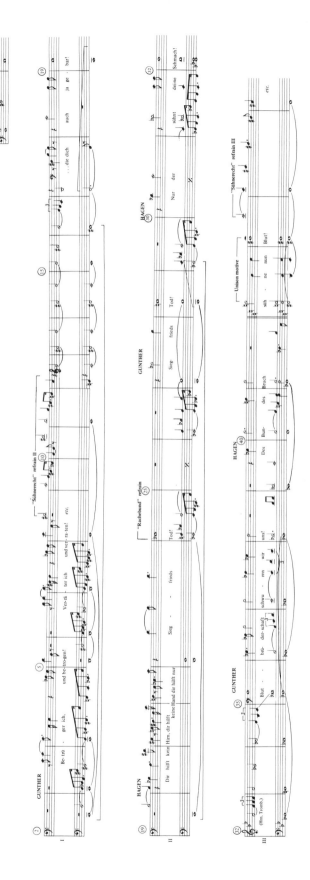

EXAMPLE 3.5.   The refrains, seeping into surrounding music.

When in this passage the "Rachebund" refrain is given on G♭–C (Ex. 3.4, mm. 29–32), it sounds the same as the initial statement on F♯–C. But the refrain now has new roles to play. It is one component in a developing cyclic pattern that is maintained both before and after the refrain is stated. It is a way station in a radical pitch inflection of that pattern from bass C to bass G♭; its characteristic interval controls the transposition of the pattern. Finally, this distinctive F♯–C intervallic color has begun to wash into music outside the refrain proper.

VIII

This new *musical* integration of the refrain with its surroundings represents a momentary victory of the symphonic principle. As the Conspiracy Scene draws to a close, in the hundred-odd measures of simultaneous singing that end the scene, the balance tips toward the symphonic. *Symphony* is here used loosely to evoke this finale's salient qualities: an instrumental periodicization of phrase, constant motivic development, tonal coherence and closure. Alone in the scene, the finale is cast in unvarying four- and eight-measure phrases, without change of tempo or meter; alone in the scene, the finale is unequivocally oriented to a single tonic, C major.

But the finale is more than this. It is also calculated as a last recapitulation of the refrain material, and one, moreover, that absorbs and transcends the many text-generated anomalies and abruptions those refrains had entailed. By this transcendence, the finale becomes Wagner's hidden commentary on the dialectic of symphony and *Musikdrama*. The finale inverts what Wagner saw as the symbolic progress of Beethoven's Ninth. In *Oper und Drama*, Wagner had written that Beethoven began the Ninth Symphony's finale with a melody that epitomizes the "symphonic" in its plainness and periodicity. But for Wagner, the finale of the Ninth goes on to transcend the symphonic and embrace the poetic, as that melody surpasses the bounds of absolute music and is transformed, in coming to hear and mirror Schiller's words.[51] If the Conspiracy Scene's finale is also a musical Credo, its message is very different: here, the symphonic overwhelms and defeats the poetic.

The finale is generated out of the refrains, beginning with a spinning out of the "Rachebund" refrain, followed by repetitions of the "Sühnerecht" refrain (Ex. 3.6). The two refrains have changed. They finally cede their once unyielding pitch identities, as the musical imperative of a motion toward the tonic C overshadows their individual identities. The "Rachebund" refrain has lost its fixed pitch space on F♯–C and shifts quickly upward in sequence. The "Sühnerecht" refrain had been fixed on bass E; in the course of the scene it

---

51. *Oper und Drama*, in *Gesammelte Schriften* IV, 188.

EXAMPLE 3.6. The two refrains in the finale of the Conspiracy Scene (225/3/1–226/3/2).

EXAMPLE 3.6. *continued*.

had moved once to F♯, and it converges here on G, becoming a thematic element within the dominant preparation for the final C-major flourish. The "Sühnerecht" refrain at last recapitulates most of its ancestor, the closing sestet of the "Brotherhood Oath." The sense of mnemonic closure thus created is tremendous; we realize we have heard the "Sühnerecht" refrain all along as mere commencement of a once-closed sequence; now that sequence has returned, closed once more.

The greatest change lies within this recapitulation of the final measures of the "Brotherhood Oath." It engenders one of Wagner's eeriest effects, one remembered by every listener: the moment in the finale when the voices of Brünnhilde and Gunther suddenly come together in parallel octaves with the orchestra. They sing the words "Mit seinem Blut/Büß er die Schuld," as Hagen sings in canon with them "D'rum sei der Reif ihm entrissen." Wagner here transformed the music clustered around a deliberate musical abruption in the "Brotherhood Oath," the odd unison motive (Ex. 3.7).

The raw matter of the transformation is slight: where the unison motive was stated once, it is now given twice, shifted down a half-step for the second statement. But the musical direction of the whole complex has been altered thereby. The original is a harmonically open-ended riddle of C major and B minor; the B-minor unison is an unhealed rift in its local context. The transformation reinterprets the riddle and closes the sequence. The harmony of measures 3–5 (toward C major) is twisted off its course; a D♭-minor chord is momentarily evoked and slips down to C and a tonic cadence. The unison motive is once again strange in its rhythmic languor. But what should have seemed strangest—the slip down a half-step and repetition—sounds instead familiar, like an echo of something once known and recognizable. The repetition of the unison motive and the slip from the color of D♭ to C is a gesture of resolution that works

EXAMPLE 3.7. Final transformation of the "Brotherhood Oath" in the Conspiracy Scene.

on many levels. The half-step slip, of course, creates a *tonal* resolution, a grasp at the cadence to C adumbrated in measures 3–5. But the half-step A♭–F♭–G♭–A♭ to G–E♭–F–G is a shadow in slow motion cast by D♭–C, the appoggiatura that has rung through the scene, the call of alarm in the "Rachebund" refrain. Once more, this unyielding refrain has seeped below the surface and into the fiber of Wagner's music.

IX

To speak of form in Wagner's music is sometimes to speak without meaning. The Conspiracy Scene is not a form or a structure in the sense of a musical shape that we can name (bar form, series of verses); its artfulness does not even reside in vague evocations of formal procedures. A formalist would be forced to view it as a loose assembly of "sections" punctuated by the refrains, and this view tells us next to nothing of its substance.

The musical dynamic of the scene does not reside in an evocation of form but in a metamorphosis over time. Gestures that at first are intrusive, illogical, un-reconciled with what precedes and follows them are gradually assimilated and finally consumed in engendering the "symphonic" musical juggernaut of the finale. In this metamorphosis is lodged whatever meaning the music may have. An anti-symphonic principle, one that twists music to serve the meaning of the words it accompanies, yields to a symphonic principle that addresses conventional musical canons of closure, coherence, motivic interrelationship. The Conspiracy Scene is an extended metaphor for the antithesis between two musical-aesthetic principles; it is an argument that gives the symphonic principle the final word.

But there is a great irony in the notion that a symphonic principle dominates the scene's end. To underscore this irony, we can look at a rara avis, one of the few sketch pages made for the later parts of the *Ring*, a sketch for this finale to the Conspiracy Scene (Figs. 3.1, 3.2). The sheet was Wagner's first attempt at drafting the finale; he removed it from its place in the composition draft for Act II and replaced it with the neater page now included in that draft.[52] The sketch begins with the "Sühnerecht" refrain, the music for Gunther's "Sühn' er die Schmach, die er mir schuf" (on page "22," first measure). In the final version, this is the moment at which Gunther, Brünnhilde, and Hagen begin to sing simultaneously. The sketch continues through the end of the act on page "22" verso.

Yet Wagner, as we see, drafted this entire final passage in the scene almost wholly *without* text or vocal lines, a method exceedingly rare not only in the

52. Both the sketch and the complete composition draft for *Götterdämmerung* are in Bayreuth, National-archiv der Richard-Wagner-Stiftung, Mss. A.II.a.4 (a miscellany of *Götterdämmerung* sketches) and A.II.f.1. I am grateful to the Richard-Wagner-Stiftung for permission to reproduce the sketch here.

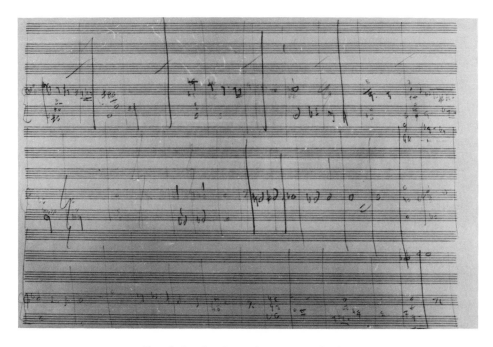

FIGURE 3.1. Sketch for the Conspiracy Scene finale, p. "22" recto.

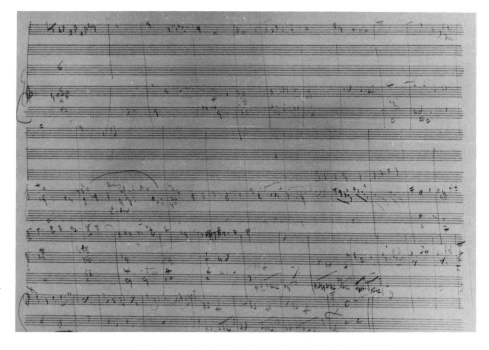

FIGURE 3.2. Sketch for the Conspiracy Scene finale, p. "22" verso.

composition draft for *Götterdämmerung* but in all the operas. The text and voice parts are present only on the new page "22" that replaced this leaf.

On the face of it, this glimpse into the sketching of the finale appears to confirm all I have said about the triumph of the symphonic principle: so pure and independent of poetry is its music that it could be executed in some early stage without text, without voices. Indeed, when Wagner got around to placing his poetic lines under this music (on the replacement page "22") he found that Hagen had not quite enough words, and so he repeated one of Hagen's lines ("Mir muss er gehören") to provide sufficient verbal volume for the abstractly conceived music.

But consider: the finale is dramatically static; the conspiracy is concluded, and the characters are merely reacting in the end to the decision for Siegfried's murder. The individual texts are actually incomprehensible, because three singers sing simultaneously. This is the only part of the entire *Ring* in which Wagner had to repeat lines mechanically, "that the text might be stretched out to fill up the proper broad proportions of the musical fabric." Those are Wagner's words, from "*Zukunftsmusik*," used to describe the textual-musical aesthetic of the conventional opera number. Dramatic stasis, simultaneous singing, repetition of text lines: the finale is not symphony, but opera.

Of course, it is a commonplace that the end of the Conspiracy Scene preserves some distant echo of a grand operatic stretta; for George Bernard Shaw, it was a "herculean trio, similar in conception to that of the three conspirators in *Un ballo in maschera*."[53] Shaw, as we recall, had no high opinion of *Ballo*. Dahlhaus put it less waspishly, writing that *Götterdämmerung* is operatic, not in any formal sense, but because its music, like that in conventional opera, overrides both drama and text.[54] Wagner himself had always recognized that the operatic number and the symphonic movement were in the end related more intimately to one another than to his own idiosyncratic, anti-formal *Musikdrama*. I have interpreted the music of the Conspiracy Scene as an extended metaphor, a representation of symphony's triumph over poetry and the singular music that only poetry engenders. But in the end, we can apply Occam's razor to my interpretation, for we need not explain as symphonic what Wagner readily understood as operatic: any musical passage comprehensible as pure music, one possessed of an abstractly musical coherence, one whose poem defers to music's stern and intricate demands.

---

53. George Bernard Shaw, *The Perfect Wagnerite* (4th ed., London, 1923), 76.

54. Carl Dahlhaus, "Entfremdung und Erinnerung: Zu Wagners *Götterdämmerung*," in *Bericht über den internationalen musikwissenschaftlichen Kongress Bayreuth 1981*, 419–20.

Chapter 4

Verdi's Composition of *Otello*
The Act II Quartet

JAMES A. HEPOKOSKI

The general outlines of the compositional history of *Otello* have been known for some time. In *The Man Verdi,* Frank Walker has provided a compact summary:

> [The music of] *Otello,* in essentials, was completed in three comparatively short bouts of composition: the first, very brief, was at Genoa in March 1884; the second, the principal one, at Genoa from December 1884 to April 1885; the third at Sant' Agata from the middle of September to early October 1885. The scoring of the opera occupied another year, with intervals, and during this time there was some revision, particularly of the first act, and working out of details left unsettled in the composition sketch.[1]

Filling in Walker's outline with specific details has been difficult for a number of reasons.[2] As is well known, the presumably extensive sketches for the opera, tantalizingly mentioned in 1941 by Carlo Gatti,[3] remain inaccessible. Moreover, during much of the time when the music was being composed, Verdi and Boito met frequently. Extensive correspondence between the two at this point would have been superfluous, and most of whatever "musical" discussion was necessary doubtless occurred face to face. (This situation contrasts markedly with that of the earlier creation and revision of the libretto, about which we

---

1. Frank Walker, *The Man Verdi* (1962; rpt. Chicago, 1982), 493.
2. Those details that were known through 1981 may be found summarized in Julian Budden, *The Operas of Verdi* III (London, 1981), 315–22; Walker, *The Man Verdi,* 488–94; and (the fundamental source) Mario Medici and Marcello Conati, eds., *Carteggio Verdi-Boito* (Parma, 1978), I, 69–119, and II, 318–59 passim (henceforth *Carteggio Verdi-Boito*).
3. Carlo Gatti, *L'abbozzo del Rigoletto di Giuseppe Verdi* (Milan, 1941), preface; Gatti, *Verdi nelle immagini* (Milan, 1941), xviii.

know a great deal.)[4] Similarly, until recently many of Verdi's letters to Giulio Ricordi during the *Otello* period were in private hands and not available for consultation. Except for a few lines here and there in scattered letters, typically revealing only those portions of the score with which Verdi was concerned at any given time,[5] one could find little concrete information about the composition of the music.

Fortunately, the situation is improving. The important new collection of Verdi-Ricordi letters, for instance, now located in the Biblioteca Palatina in Parma, illuminates the final stages of the composition of *Otello,* from August 1886 to January 1887: the conclusion of the orchestration and the preparation and revision of the vocal-score proofs. An enticing selection of these letters, also containing material bearing on the original staging, production, and selection of singers, has already appeared in print, the fruits of a 1981–1982 exhibition at the Museo teatrale alla Scala.[6] Still, many of the new letters remain unpublished, as do most of Giulio Ricordi's often lengthy responses, although plans to publish them as part of a comprehensive Verdi-Ricordi *carteggio,* under the editorship of Franca Cella and Pierluigi Petrobelli, are well under way.

Attention is also being turned to the early draft material: early versions of pieces altered before the *Otello* premiere. There is not a great deal of this material available, but there is more than one might perhaps have imagined. To the best of my knowledge, it consists of this:

1. Three separate sketches, or, better, excerpts from larger drafts.
    a. A one-page draft from the Act II Quartet, located in the Bibliothèque de l'Opéra in Paris. This document will be considered in some detail below.
    b. A single folio (with music written on both sides) from a draft of the Act III Trio, located in the Pierpont Morgan Library in New York.[7]

4. See *Carteggio Verdi-Boito* I, 1–6, 50–119, and II, 287–89, 305–59; Alessandro Luzio, "Il libretto di *Otello,*" in his *Carteggi verdiani* (Rome, 1935), II, 95–141; Budden, *The Operas of Verdi* III, 300–322; Walker, *The Man Verdi,* 473–79, 485–94.

5. Some of the most provocative are Emanuele Muzio's January–March 1886 letters to Giulio Ricordi (see *Carteggio Verdi-Boito,* II, 343–44) that mention Verdi's scoring of the concluding Act III concertato (28 January) and his revision of the Act I Love Duet (14 March), and the 14–16 May 1886 Verdi-Boito letters (*Carteggio Verdi-Boito* I, 105–7) that mention the revision of Otello's "Esultate!" entrance in Act I. See also footnote 2 above.

6. See Franca Cella and Pierluigi Petrobelli, eds., *Giuseppe Verdi–Giulio Ricordi: Corrispondenza e immagini 1881/1890* (Milan, 1982), 48–63. Petrobelli's preface, "Le lettere e la mostra," 5–6, provides an introduction to this new set of documents.

7. The draft has been reproduced in facsimile in Martin Chusid, *A Catalog of Verdi's Operas* (Hackensack, 1974), 136–37. One side of the folio is also reproduced in Andrew Porter's article on Verdi in *The New Grove Dictionary of Music and Musicians* XIX (London, 1980), 656; and in J. Rigbie Turner et al., *Four Centuries of Opera: Manuscripts and Printed Editions in the Pierpont Morgan Library* (New York, 1983), 90, where it is preceded (89) by a brief discussion. The sketch is the subject of a forthcoming study by Roger Parker and the present author.

c. A 1941 facsimile of a single page from the otherwise inaccessible S. Agata sketches (or draft?) of Act III, Desdemona's "Io prego il cielo per te con questo pianto," in Carlo Gatti's *Verdi nelle immagini,* 187.[8]

2. A manuscript reduction of the late August 1886 version of Act IV, prepared for the engravers of the first vocal score by Michele Saladino. (Verdi subsequently retouched the Willow Song twice, in mid-October 1886 and in early 1887.) The reduction, with corrections in Verdi's hand, is located in the Casa Ricordi Archives in Milan.[9]

3. Compositional emendations in the *Otello* autograph score itself (also in the Ricordi Archives): numerous erasures, corrections, and changes of "original" versions, particularly in the Love Duet, the Act II Quartet, and the Willow Song.

This paper grew out of a study of the Paris sketch of the Act II Quartet (a central concern of Sections I and III below),[10] but, in a broader sense, its principal concerns are analytical and deal both with the structure of the Quartet and its place within the broader canvas of Act II (issues dealt with primarily in Sections II and IV below). The sketch version bears directly on analytical matters because, as will be seen, it lacks three important measures found near the end of the Quartet, and, above all, because it is in a different key from the final version—B major instead of B♭.

I

The Quartet sketch, Paris, Bibliothèque de l'Opéra, Rés A 667 Suppl[t], is reproduced in Figure 4.1.[11] The actual document, much larger ($13\frac{7}{8}$ by $10\frac{1}{2}$

8. Budden, *The Operas of Verdi* III, 375n., comments about the sketch: "The melody is identical with that of the definitive score except for two E's in the second half of bar 21 ('Vede l'eterno') where the score has F's." In fact, the two notes mentioned are almost certainly both F's: Verdi, as so often, merged the ledger line with the note head, and E's make no sense with the given harmony. More significant, Verdi revised the melodic line on the sketch itself to conform with what we know as the "final version." It is clear that he originally conceived the two climactic measures, "lagrime che da me spreme il duol, le prime" (vocal score 220/1/1–2: see footnote 19 below) as four, proceeding in what we might consider doubled note-values and thus continuing the broad, striding quarter-notes of the sketch's beginning. The revision, an intensifying compression (a matter of adding a stem to the initial whole-note, flags to the ensuing quarter-notes, and so on), is visible on the sketch facsimile, but it occurs in the vocal part only; the original bass line is untouched. On the sketch itself a broader period (8 + 9) was telescoped into a more concise one (8 + 7).

9. The Saladino reduction (mentioned in Budden, *The Operas of Verdi* III, 391n.) and Verdi's later Willow Song revisions (the second of them datable only through access to some of the new—and still unpublished—Verdi-Ricordi letters in Parma) are the subjects of a study currently in progress by the present author.

10. I should like to thank Roger Parker for informing me several years ago about the existence of the sketch and providing me with a photocopy—one that ultimately sent me to study the sketch itself in June 1984. This work was made possible by an H. H. Powers Grant provided by Oberlin College.

11. The sketch is reproduced here through the kind permission of the Bibliothèque de l'Opéra in Paris.

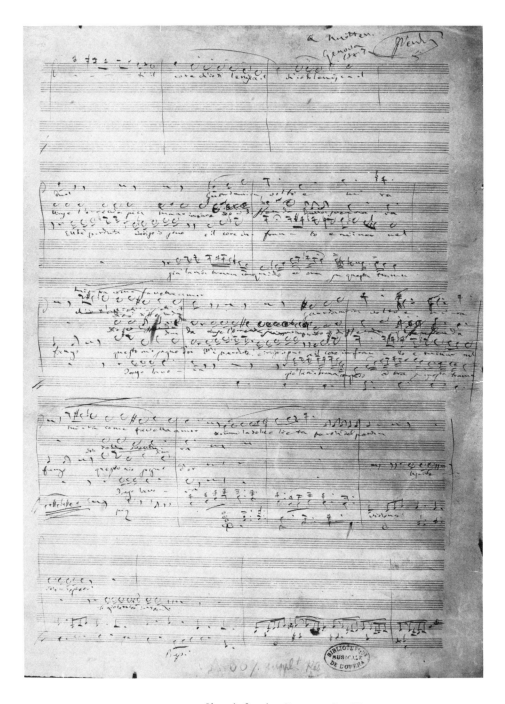

FIGURE 4.1. Sketch for the Quartet, Act II.

inches), is written on Verdi's usual 30-stave orchestral paper, manufactured by Lard-Esnault in Paris. The music consists of $15\frac{1}{4}$ measures, written in a moderately dark-brown ink, principally from the second half of the Act II Quartet. Only the recto bears music. The left edge of the recto suggests the work of a sharp blade: Verdi, that is, removed the other—probably blank—half of the original bifolio. The paper has never been folded, that is, it is unlikely that it was ever sent through the mail, as the Pierpont Morgan Act III Trio sketch seems to have been. A transcription is provided in Example 4.1.[12]

At the top of the sketch-page one finds Verdi's inscription, "A Nuitter / Genova 1887 [?]," followed by the composer's signature. This sketch, then, was a gift to Charles Nuitter, the archivist of the Paris Opéra and translator (often with collaborators) into French of several Verdi operas: *Macbeth* (1865), *Aida* (1872 and 1876), *La forza del destino* (1882), and *Simon Boccanegra* (1883). The composer may well have presented this page to Nuitter in 1887 (this was the year of the premiere of *Otello*—5 February, at La Scala), but the music on the page predates the inscription. Two features of this sketch bear on Verdi's selection of it as a gift. First, the music is written on only one side of the music paper: were this an extract from a continuity draft or at least some extensive draft (as the Pierpont Morgan Act III sketch seems to be), the music would continue on the verso. Second, at the end of the sketch, on the treble staff just after the last sixteenth-notes, Verdi has written "etc." This surely indicates that he meant to continue with music that had already been worked out in some way. The Paris sketch, therefore, appears to be a single page written to solve a contained problem encountered in some earlier draft: it revised something—or plugged a gap—and rejoined the prior draft (a larger, more continuous draft) at "etc." The composer probably decided to give this individual sketch-page to Nuitter because it was handy and separate.

In determining the sketch's date the most important clues are Iago's and Emilia's lines—two *quinario* quatrains—beginning in measure 4: Iago's "Già la mia brama / Conquido, ed ora / Su questa trama / Jago lavora!" and Emilia's "Vinse l'orrenda / Sua mano impura / Dio ci diffenda [*sic*] / Dalla sventura." These are "additional" lines that Verdi had requested from Boito on 9 December 1884, from Genoa:

---

12. At several points in the sketch Verdi entered two differing versions of the music, typically one on top of the other. This rendered the deciphering of portions of the sketch difficult: e.g., apart from the problem of determining the pitches, one cannot readily determine which layer is prior. In all cases except those that seemed to be errors or slips of the pen I have chosen the reading that differs most from the final version as being the principal—or first—sketch reading and have included the alternative reading on a smaller staff above the relevant part: Desdemona, m. 8; Emilia, mm. 4, 6, 7, and 8; bass accompaniment, m. 9. My guiding assumption has been that Verdi altered his first ideas in the direction of the final version. Similarly, in measure 6 Verdi first wrote (probably mistakenly) Desdemona's line as "Ch'io t'allieti il cor." He corrected the line by crossing out part of the text and rewriting the line properly, "Mira come favella amor," above Desdemona's staff.

EXAMPLE 4.1. *Otello,* Act II Quartet, Paris sketch: transcription.

EXAMPLE 4.1. *continued.*

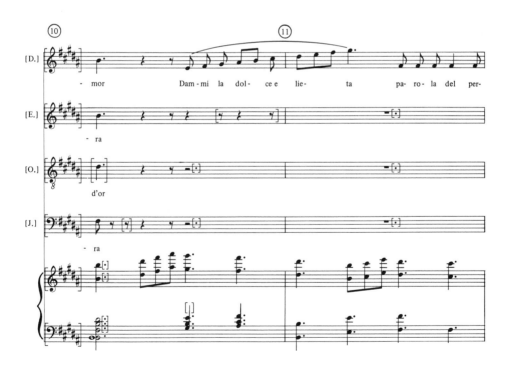

continued

EXAMPLE 4.1. *continued.*

In the Act II scene *a quattro* the dialogue between Iago and Emilia finishes too quickly. Desdemona is given the main musical phrase. Otello declaims in the intervals. The others almost speak (note and word): and thus these last mentioned finish too early. As I have already said, I would need four lines, asides, for each: Iago happy to have that handkerchief in his hands, and Emilia frightened that it is in his hands. The meter is *quinario*.[13]

13. *Carteggio Verdi-Boito,* I, 78–79.

It thus appears that during the early stages of the principal period of *Otello* composition Verdi had run out of lines at a moment that he had determined would constitute the dramatic midpoint, and the musical turning point, of the Quartet, Iago's wrenching of the handkerchief from Emilia after the words "A me quel vel!" Put another way, he needed additional *quinario* lines for the second half of the ensemble: simple repetition of the earlier lines would not do, for they preceded the pivotal dramatic act of the ensemble (and the opera), Iago's obtaining of the handkerchief. Boito responded in an undated, but surely immediate, letter with the lines for Iago and Emilia that one finds on the sketch: clearly, they had not been present in the original libretto.[14] At some (later?) point Boito rewrote Emilia's quatrain before Verdi entered this passage into the autograph score; her final text, that is, differs from that found on the Paris sketch.[15] Iago's corresponding verses, beginning "Già la mia brama / Conquido," remained unaltered.

This incident of the new lines explains why the sketch-page exists separately from the larger draft. While awaiting Boito's new text, Verdi had probably stopped drafting the Quartet at the point of Desdemona's medial solo and Iago's seizing of the handkerchief (where the Paris sketch begins)—or he could have separately sketched out some rough ideas for its continuation—and had continued his principal draft with the transition to the next section. Upon receiving the new lines sometime in mid-December, he doubtless drafted a separate sketch-page—the Paris sketch—to join up with what he had already written. This sketch, therefore, probably dates from mid-December 1884.

There are a number of small, "grammatical" differences between sketch and final version,[16] but two differences, as mentioned above, loom large and merit separate consideration here: for the final version Verdi interpolated an extra three measures (at the point of Ex. 4.1, m. 9); and the final version is a semitone lower than the sketch. Both are best considered within a broader discussion of the structural design of the ensemble.

14. For the letter see *Carteggio Verdi-Boito* I, 79–81; for the dating, II, 329. In the letter Boito also provided an additional quatrain in *quinario*, with the dialogue split between the two: [Iago:] "Già il laccio l'agile / Pensier trovò / [Emilia:] Muta ma vigile / Scorta sarò," which Verdi never used, and three more quatrains (also unused) which could have been inserted even earlier into the Quartet. For the revision of the "Vinse l'orrenda" quatrain, which is also contained in the letter, see footnote 15 below.

15. Emilia's final text ("Vinser gli artigli / Truci e codardi / Dio dai perigli / Sempre ci guardi") appears in Boito's hand in his post–9 December 1881 letter, immediately to the right of the "Vinse l'orrenda" quatrain, which has been crossed out (see *Carteggio Verdi-Boito* I, 80). Boito may have written this substitute quatrain in his original letter (in which case Verdi would have first selected the "Vinse l'orrenda" text for the sketch, then changed his mind) or added it later, perhaps during a subsequent visit to S. Agata or Genoa. In any event, the first layer that Verdi wrote into the *Otello* autograph score, the skeleton score, contains the final text, "Vinser gli artigli," etc.

16. See, for example, footnote 12 above and the preceding discussion in the text about Emilia's altered lines.

II

The Quartet itself, "Dammi la dolce e lieta / Parola del perdono," is the goal and central portion of a larger structure that Verdi shaped as a single piece: principally Act II, Scene 4, although it concludes with a few lines from the beginning of the following scene. The only "formal" designation of this larger structure is the one provided in a table of contents from the first vocal scores: a mere "Desdemona, Emilia, Otello, Jago."[17] It proceeds through three textual and musical phases that recall the Scena, slow set-piece (*adagio*), and, perhaps, *tempo di mezzo* structures of Verdi's earlier operas. In the first (beginning "D'un uom che geme sotto il tuo disdegno"), Desdemona and Otello share eighteen lines of dialogue that freely mix three types of *versi imparisillabi* (lines of odd-numbered syllables): *endecasillabo* (eleven syllables), *settenario* (seven syllables), and *quinario* (five syllables). The poetry differs from its earlier Verdian Scena models by including the *quinario* meter and avoiding the customary *versi sciolti* (unrhymed lines) in favor of rhyme. This section may be referred to as a "rhymed Scena," a characteristic (intensified) element of Boito's librettos for Verdi:[18] it functions, of course, as an entrance to the Quartet proper. The sec-

17. Verdi did not subdivide the *Otello* autograph score into the traditional separate "numbers" labeled by genre. The earliest issues of the vocal score and libretto, however, contain an "indice" that does specify subdivisions, and these are often but not always coextensive with those articulated by dramatic, that is, libretto, "scenes." Generally the subdivisions bear only the name of the relevant singers (for instance, in Act III, "Otello, Jago," "Desdemona, Otello," "Otello," "Otello, Jago, Cassio," "Otello, Jago," "FINALE"), but some are characterized by genre: in Act I, "URAGANO: Jago, Roderigo, Cassio, Montano, Coro—Otello," "CORO: *Fuoco di gioia*," and "BRINDISI: Jago, Cassio, Roderigo, Coro"; in Act II, "CORO: *Dove guardi splendono*, Desdemona"; in Act III, the above-mentioned "FINALE"; in Act IV, "CANZONE: Desdemona, Emilia," and "AVE MARIA: Desdemona."

It must be stressed that these subdivisions are not infallible guides to the actual internal workings and large-scale structure of the music. The Act II Quartet's designation in the "indice," for instance, refers the reader to p. 153 of the vocal score, that is to say, presumably to the moment of Desdemona's entrance, a measure or two after Otello's "Quel canto mi conquide," even though the music at this point clearly belongs to and rounds the preceding Homage Chorus. See footnote 19 below for another example. Indeed, the degree to which Verdi valued these "indice" titles—or even concerned himself at all with them—is unclear. Ricordi had asked Verdi about possible subdivision within the printed scores of the opera on 20 September 1886 (unpublished), but we know of no written reply; the subject might have reemerged, however, during Ricordi's four-day trip to S. Agata in the last days of that month. Conceivably, the subdivisions could be Ricordi's: the principal interest in explicit subdivision was his, not Verdi's, since the editor needed to think of extracting individual pieces from the score to sell separately as *pezzi staccati*. In sum, we are dealing with a subdivision-list prepared only at the editor's request in the very last stages of composition, and one whose eventual labeling was unreflected by catchwords or titles within either the autograph score or the printed score. Its presence in the early scores thus seems a mere concession made by Verdi to the customs of publishing. Similarly, in a letter of 9 November (also unpublished) Ricordi sought advice about and approval of his selection of *pezzi staccati*, which, as it turned out, were clearly related to the index-listing in the vocal score. Verdi's response of 11 November, a perfunctory "What you propose for the *pezzi staccati* is fine"—embedded within a much longer letter (incomplete in Franco Abbiati, *Giuseppe Verdi* [Milan, 1959], IV, 299)—does not suggest an intense concern over the issue. Under the circumstances, it appears that one need not alter an otherwise defensible analysis of a portion of *Otello* to fit the subdivisions implied either in the vocal-score index or in the *pezzi staccati*.

18. This type of rhymed-Scena verse occurs in fourteen passages of the *Otello* libretto. Its three most extensive occurrences are: forty-one lines (!) near the beginning of Act II ("Or t'è aperta la via di salvazione"),

ond phase shifts to the customary *versi lirici* (lyrical lines grouped into strophes, rhymed and metrically consistent) for the set-piece, but in this instance the two married couples are kept poetically separate by being assigned differing meters. Otello and Desdemona have parallel, ten-line *settenario* stanzas; Iago and Emilia sing eight quatrains of *quinario* (originally, of course, Boito had provided only six), some of them broken up into dialogue. An appended, modulatory transition or exit out of the Quartet, beginning with Otello's "Escite! Solo vo' restar" and lasting, it would seem, as far as Iago's "Non pensateci più," returns to the rhymed-Scena poetry that will also begin the next large-scale formal unit, "Tu?! Indietro! Fuggi!!" (172/1/1).[19] Verdi provides elegant musical transitions into and out of the three-phase structure; accordingly, the external boundaries—particularly the one at its end—are somewhat blurred. The first two of the major divisions merit more extensive consideration.

Rhymed Scena (46 measures, beginning 154/1/3). This is the more stylistically "progressive" of the two major sections, owing largely to the freedom provided by the irregularity and shifting accents of the poetry. Verdi, that is, encounters a poetry "lyrically" enhanced by rhyme, but one freed from a rhythmic predictability that would bias his musical thought into patterns of traditional, periodic syntax.[20] This loosely structured entrance section subdivides into four contrasting subsections. The first, Desdemona's intercession for Cassio, is relatively

---

including the Credo and proceeding up until Scene 3 (Otello-Iago: "Ciò m'accora"); twenty-two lines in Act III before the large concertato, beginning with Lodovico's "Ferma!"; and twenty lines in Act II immediately after the Quartet, beginning with Otello's "Escite! Solo vo' restar." For some of its occurrences in *Falstaff*, see the present author's *Giuseppe Verdi: Falstaff* (Cambridge, England, 1983), 32.

19. Page/system/measure references (00/00/0) have been made by consulting the currently available Italian-English vocal score published by G. Ricordi, ed. Mario Parenti (1964), pl. no. 52105. They are valid for all available Italian and Italian-English vocal scores.

The issue of where the exit Scena actually ends—that is, gives way to a Scena texture functioning clearly as an entrance into the next large-scale structural unit—is not our primary concern here. Exits and entrances are two phases of a single zone of transition from one set-piece to another, and Verdi often handles the phase-shift smoothly and almost imperceptibly. In the present instance, however, motivic echoes from the Quartet are heard in the orchestra until Iago's "Non pensateci più," and for this reason, despite the move away from the ensemble's B♭ major, the immediately preceding measures are more likely to be heard as belonging to the Quartet than as introducing something decisively new. The point of a logical structural and dramatic articulation at "Non pensateci più" is worth making, for Ricordi's *pezzo staccato* of the ensuing Otello-Iago scene (pl. no. 51146) began several measures earlier: its initial words, as well as those of the libretto scene ("scena quinta") and the vocal-score "indice," were "Desdemona rea!" (169/4/1). Although one readily admits that at this point we have entered a zone of transition that will continue for some time, it seems most accurate to recognize that, for the sake of plot clarification within its own narrow borders, the *pezzo staccato* began with the concluding music—the exit Scena—of the preceding structural unit. Similarly, the *pezzo staccato* that excerpted the Act II Quartet set-piece (pl. no. 51145) began with the words "Se inconscia, contro te, sposo, ho peccato," clearly the concluding portion only ("Subsection 4") of the preceding rhymed Scena.

20. Verdi, of course, had been calling for freer operatic poetry for decades. Some of his most telling remarks on this subject in the 1880s—the period of *Otello*—are found in letters to Charles Nuitter (and ultimately destined for Camille Du Locle) about new texts for the revised *Don Carlos* (published in Ursula Günther and Gabriella Carrara Verdi, eds., "Der Briefwechsel Verdi–Nuitter–Du Locle zur Revision des *Don*

slow at ♩ = 66 ("Lo stesso movimento"); the last three, bursting forth *fortissimo* with Desdemona's astonishment at Otello's angry refusal, are more rapidly paced at ♩ = 76 ("Allegro agitato," curiously also marked "lo stesso movimento"). The entire rhymed Scena modulates expressively with the shifting demands of the drama; it functions as a late-Verdian alternative to (or, better, "symphonic" enhancement of) recitative.[21]

The first subsection, Desdemona's intercession (pp. 154–55), illustrates the composer's masterly ability to spin a prolonged melodic idea from a generative motive without lapsing into "lyrical" or "static" periodicity. The entire subsection consists of a single sixteen-measure thematic sentence (moving from A minor to G major) whose eventual cadential formulation is repeated in the final five measures. Running through much of the sentence is the melodic interval of a fourth (bracketed in Exx. 4.2, 4.3, and 4.4), often stated in stepwise ascent or descent. Desdemona articulates the opening, middle, and close of her entreaty with similar vocal sonorities and melodic gestures, each with different harmonizations. Most prominently, the e^2-b^1 fourth-descent of "[disde]gno la preghiera" (Ex. 4.2) returns, varied, at "e il suo dolor" (Ex. 4.3) and "Intercedo per lui, per lui ti pre[go]" (Ex. 4.4). In each of these instances the "motivic" fourth wants to expand into a sixth: the e^2-b^1 is a highlighted segment of a larger more fundamental melodic motion, $\hat{6}$ (as upper neighbor)–$\hat{5}$–$\hat{4}$–$\hat{3}$–$\hat{2}$–($\hat{1}$) in a powerful gesture toward G major.[22] In addition, the upward motion of "[di]sdegno" (Ex. 4.2) reappears, intensified, at the word "prego" (Ex. 4.4), which initiates the cadence-gesture.

Moreover, the music proceeds largely by smooth parallelism and suave chromatic inflection—initially, at least, a correlative of Desdemona's grace—typically undergirded by a linear, descending bass. The parallelism of the $\frac{6}{3}$ gestures near the opening (154/2/1, the harmonies under Example 4.2, measure 2),

Carlos: Teil II," *Analecta Musicologica* XV [1975], 334–401). For example, from the letter of 28 October 1882, regarding the Philip-Posa duet (365): "I know the difficulties of your [French] rhyme, with its masculines and feminines, etc. etc. In a [spoken] tragedy one can quickly recite ten lines, and it doesn't much matter if there are a few superfluous words or phrases to serve the meter [*verso*] and the rhyme. But it's not like this in music, whose declamation, being slower, is chilled by a word or a phrase too many in the scenic points. I believe, as I said earlier, that for modern opera it would be necessary to adopt non-rhyming poetry—and more than this, *the word* [*le mot*], which strikes and sculpts, is sometimes drowned in a sentence because of the meter or the rhyme." Similarly, from 15 December 1882 (384): "The Act III variants in Elisabeth's *solo* still seem [*pajono*] weak to me. The fault is certainly one of the *rhyme,* of the *masculines* and *feminines* that have obliged Du Locle to write four lines merely to say, 'I was the fiancée of D. Carlos.' "

21. Cf. the remarks of Anthony Newcomb on Wagner's "musically loosely structured, recitative-like, illustrative unit[s]" in "The Birth of Music out of the Spirit of Drama," *19th-Century Music* V (1981–1982), 38–66.

22. The first two appearances of e^2-b^1 do not reach the ultimate tonic, but are deflected away and move upward. After the second appearance (and failure to reach her melodic goal), Desdemona's appeals intensify the drive to the melodic tonic. As she praises Cassio in stylized "anguished" sequences, she "supercharges" the ultimate resolution by rising to the high point of her melodic line, g^2 ("che di grazia è degno," 155/1/3), from which she floats downward (at last, successfully) to the tonic from $\hat{8}$, of course passing through the "motivic" $\hat{6}$–$\hat{5}$–$\hat{4}$–$\hat{3}$ on the way.

EXAMPLE 4.2. *Otello,* Act II Quartet, 154/1/3–154/2/3.

EXAMPLE 4.3. *Otello,* Act II Quartet, 155/1/1–3.

EXAMPLE 4.4. *Otello,* Act II Quartet, 155/2/2–3.

for instance, recurs in varied form near the end (155/2/1) with three parallel seventh chords in root position, D^7 (introduced by chromatic inflection from a root-position diminished seventh, $d\#^{o7}$), $C\#^7$, and "$C\#^7$," which is immediately interpreted, and spelled, as a German sixth in a fleetingly tonicized E minor. Tonally, subsection 1 begins in A minor, a consequence of the preceding Homage Chorus in E, and inflects almost at once toward G major (154/2/2), the key in which the thematic sentence ends. This G major is not decisively confirmed, however, until the final cadence. On the way one finds momentary pulls toward B minor (as III of G, 154/4/1–2) and E minor (as VI of G, 155/2/1–2). We also, of course, receive a powerful reminder of the underlying G-major control by the prominent sounding of V_4^6 in the eighth measure, 154/4/2.

The dramatic sense of all of this is clear. The unsuspecting Desdemona intends to make a simple request, which she clearly wishes to deliver as a graceful, embellished $\hat{6}$–$\hat{5}$–$\hat{4}$–$\hat{3}$–$\hat{2}$–$\hat{1}$ descent in G major. As if coyly testing Otello's mood, she makes two initial feints at her main point by stressing the "motivic" fourth (Exx. 4.2, 4.3), then finally moves more decisively with the fully revealed, by now properly intensified request (Ex. 4.4), whose precise point, "Tu gli perdona," she withholds until the moment of the G-major cadence (155/3/1–2). The psychology is perfect—or would have been perfect had not Otello had his prior conversation with Iago. Unexpectedly rebuffed, Desdemona immediately reactivates the cadence figure by touching on an embellishing chord, "$E\flat^6$," which, in the striking manner in which it is produced, that is to say, by double chromatic inflection from a G chord—followed by an immediate return to G—

is probably intended to carry with it an irresistible, if private, reminder of their love.[23] Otello's second, sterner refusal precipitates a radical change of texture and key.

Subsections 2, 3, and 4 may be dealt with briefly. The second subsection bursts forth largely "unprepared" (Desdemona's alarm, "Perchè torbida suona," 156/1/1) on a *fortissimo* E$^6_4$ chord, which retains only the implicit common-tone B of the preceding G major and shifts it to the bass. Its seven measures are harmonically static, a prolongation of the E$^6_4$, anxiously embellished with neighboring diminished sevenths. In subsection 3, the offer of the handkerchief ("Quell'ardor molesto," 156/4/2), Desdemona tries to appease Otello and returns—albeit with more urgency—to her language of chromatic quasi-parallelisms, now drifting toward E♭ minor ("se con questo / Morbido lino la mia man ti fascia," 157/1/2). In some senses, then, this music recalls that of subsection 1: notice also, for instance, the reappearance of insistent eighth-notes in the accompaniment, the presence of a linear, chromatically descending bass, and the ascending fourth on "morbido."[24] Otello's brutal response ("Non ho d'uopo di ciò," 157/2/1–2) blocks her suggestion of E♭ minor, and the music turns instead toward B♭ minor and ends with a tonic major chord in first inversion.[25] Subsection 4 ("Se inconscia," 157/4/1) is a simple seven-measure, B♭ transition into the ensemble. Its effect could not be more direct: Desdemona's earlier idea of melodic descent to the tonic, stressed in subsection 1, now becomes a stunned, virtually unadorned descent of a tenth, harmonized with fading glimmers of her chromatic, secondary dominant-oriented musical language of grace and charm, and sinking downward to her lowest note in the entire score, b♭, the beginning of the Quartet proper.

Set-Piece: Quartet (ca. 32 measures, beginning 158/1/4). The Quartet is divided into two main musical and dramatic subsections by Iago's central act of obtaining the handkerchief: drama and musical structure correspond perfectly. The first half, melodically led by Desdemona, may be termed the Exposition. The second half, initiated by the now dramatically doomed Otello in two "groundswell" phrases (belonging to the long-established type of vigorous,

23. The pattern of this embellishing motion ($^5_3$ ♭$^6_3$ ♮$^5_3$) is found frequently in positions of prominence in *Otello*. Its most characteristic and memorable occurrences (those that may well suggest an associative significance for the chordal motion) are stressed as head-motive ideas in the Act I Love Duet: its opening chords, under Otello's "Già nella notte densa" (95/1/1–2, in G♭); under Desdemona's first words of the opera, "Mio superbo guerrier!" (96/1/1); and without return to the ♭$^5_3$ under Otello's "Pingea dell'armi il fremito" (98/1/1). The same principle, double chromatic inflection, underlies the sudden appearance of the C$^6_4$ chord in an E-major cadential context at the climactic "ancora un bacio" (106/2/3–106/3/1–2).

24. As will emerge, the pitches of this "morbido" were originally conceived up a half-step, that is, as identical with those of "D'un uom che geme," further binding together subsections 1 and 3.

25. Notice also Desdemona's emphatic $\hat{6}$–$\hat{5}$–$\hat{4}$–$\hat{3}$–$\hat{2}$–$\hat{1}$ descent, now in B♭ minor, at "Tu sei crucciato, signor." And, again, considered up a half-step (see footnote 24 above), the sequentially rising pitches of the music at Otello's "Mi lascia!" (157/3/1–3) very nearly echo those of Desdemona's rising sequence (within a different key) on behalf of Cassio in subsection 1 (155/1/1–3).

formulaically repeated *crescendi* climaxing on cadential $^6_4$ chords that are so often found in the latter portions of Verdian ensembles), I shall, following Amintore Galli, refer to as the Peroration.[26]

The Exposition, "Dammi la dolce e lieta / Parola del perdono," is dominated by a single, expansive, periodic melody (eighteen measures for Desdemona) with dovetailed interpolations for the other singers, Otello in particular. This subsection is thus a telescoping of the more usual ensemble procedure—found, for example, in the Act III concertato—in which a solo exposition or group of expositions leads to a separate, later expansion into ensemble texture. It is important for the understanding of the drama—and of the larger structure of Act II—to realize that the head-motive of Desdemona's melody (Ex. 4.5*a*) is an easily recognizable variant of a melodic idea heard several times near the beginning of Act II, during the Iago-Cassio dialogue (see Ex. 4.5*b, c, d*). In Example 4.5*a–d*, the 12/8 rhythms and melodic shapes are virtually identical, and all of the corresponding "motives" involve a triadic climb though a B♭ chord on beat 2 (the arpeggiated chord is a tonic with seventh in the Quartet, a subdominant in the opening scene of Act II) and a quick return to the tonic through the two stepwise descending dotted quarter-notes on beats 3 and 4. At one point (Ex. 4.5*c*) the earlier fragment had set Iago's promise to Cassio, "e il tuo perdono è

26. Amintore Galli, closely associated artistically with Ricordi's rival publisher, Edoardo Sonzogno (and with the rival journal, *Il secolo*), was a professor of harmony, counterpoint, and music history at the Milan Conservatory from 1878 to 1903 and a prolific writer of books on musical forms and related topics (for example, his frequently reprinted—and massive—*Estetica della musica*). He wrote one of the earliest "analytical" discussions of *Otello* immediately after its premiere, "L'Otello di Verdi alla Scala di Milano," published in February 1887 both in *Il teatro illustrato e la musica popolare*, 19–26, and in *Il secolo*. The article was reprinted in Casa Ricordi's subsequent compilation, *Otello . . . Giudizî della stampa italiana e straniera* (2d ed. Milan, [1887]), 13–22. Galli referred to the second half of the Quartet as follows: "La perorazione colla frase d'Otello: . . . e il cor m'infrango [*sic*] / E ruinar nel fango / Vedo il mio sogno d'ôr . . . ' *imitata* liberamente poi dalle note di Desdemona, ha molta espressione ed effetto musicale, ma non offre esca al plauso: il componimento non fu sufficientemente compreso e forse non ha le qualità caratteristiche di tant'altri pezzi" (*Otello . . . Giudizî*, 19).

"Proper" Verdian structural terminology can be a rather difficult matter and has been much discussed in recent years. See, for example, Robert Anthony Moreen, "Integration of Text Forms and Musical Forms in Verdi's Early Operas," diss. Princeton University, 1975, in which the discussion centers on structural divisions within arias and duets through the 1850s. Structural units within ensembles present particularly vexing problems of taxonomy. Galli's rhetorical term *peroration*, although perhaps intended to refer only to this specific *Otello* ensemble, often seems an apt term for the repeated "groundswell" effects: a concertato intensifying and summing-up of the ensemble situation, usually preceding what is more obviously a coda. Cf. Filippo Filippi's humorous description of the standard Finale form that he insists is avoided by Verdi in *Otello*, the "*finali* soliti, di forma mercadantesca o petrelliana, colle proposte, risposte, quadratura e una interminabile cadenza finale: *partiam! partiam! partiam!* . . . e non partono mai" (*Otello . . . Guidizî*, 83). Here the "groundswell" or "peroration" seems to be referred to as the "quadratura"—or perhaps that technique can be considered a special type of "quadratura." Curiously, Verdi himself, in a 14 June 1857 letter to Tito Ricordi (describing a revision of the final quartet-with-chorus of *Simon Boccanegra* for a forthcoming performance in Reggio Emilia), once referred specifically to the practice of groundswell-repetitions (he was adding one): "Infine bisogna fare il ritornello alla frase del Quartetto finale come vedrai." (See Marcello Conati, *Il "Simon Boccanegra" di Verdi a Reggio Emilia [1857]: Storia documentata. Alcune varianti alla prima edizione dell'opera* [Reggio Emilia, 1984], 79.) But to introduce on these grounds yet another sense of *ritornello* into musical structure seems inadvisable.

EXAMPLE 4.5. Motives from *Otello,* Act II: *a,* Act II Quartet, 158/1/4–5; *b,* Act II, Scene 1, 109/5/1–3; *c,* Act II, Scene 1, 112/1/1–2; *d,* Act II, Scene 1, 112/4/1–2.

certo": by the time of the Quartet the person requesting pardon is no longer Cassio, but Desdemona.

Despite its evident antecedent-consequent ("double-period") construction (6 + 12), the Exposition melody is wide-ranging, with large, unpredictable leaps in its initial phrases, and its single eighteen-bar harmonic circle is traced very slowly. Indeed, the difficulty for the listener is that all eighteen measures must be grasped as a closed, periodic structure before the individual phrases take on their proper significance—no easy task, particularly since our ears are continually pulled away from Desdemona's lead to attend to the busy verbal overlay of the other three characters. Surely it is this factor that made the Quartet one of the most puzzling pieces in *Otello* at its premiere. "It was not understood" wrote Filippo Filippi in *La perseveranza,* "but it will please upon rehearings."[27] The sentiment was echoed in nearly all the journals: a certain Signor Gavazzi-Spech writing for the *Corriere di Roma,* for instance, commented, "The design of the piece is clear, but it is not easily grasped because of its [melodic?] curve. It will become one of the pieces most discussed by musicians, as one of the great pages of music that describes passions and situations."[28]

Within its periodic arch Desdemona's Exposition unfolds in broad phrase-pairs, in which the second member of each pair reworks rhythmic or melodic elements of the first, by no means a unique procedure for Verdi. Each phrase-pair sets four lines (2 + 2) of Desdemona's *settenario* text. Thus the "antecedent" of the Quartet consists of two parallel three-measure phrases, four lines of

27. *Otello . . . Giudizî,* 6.
28. Ibid., 47.

text. The next four lines ("Ma il labbro tuo sospira," 160/1/1, launching the "consequent" and beginning in the tonicized C minor) emerge in a pair of four-measure phrases, and each phrase divides into a 2 + 2 pair of subphrases: all nicely symmetrical. But the compositional "problem" of continuing this four-square phrase-pairing—with each unit consuming a quatrain of text—is that Desdemona's text is ten lines long, not a multiple of four. The stanza had been built by joining a quatrain in *rima incrociata* (*a-b-b-a*) with a very differently rhyming six-line group (*c-d-c-e-e-d*, where *d* represents lines with rhyming *tronco* endings). To mirror this poetic asymmetry of quatrain plus sestet, Verdi breaks the phrase-pairing after the eighth line ("Come favella amor") and moves directly into an unpaired four-measure extension (164/1/1) for the final two lines, which end with the *tronco* rhyme that seals off the stanza. The composer even repeats the *tronco* line ("Ch'io ti lenisca il duol") for emphasis— perhaps ironic emphasis, for it is precisely at this moment that Iago wrests the handkerchief from Emilia. The asymmetrical extension is a compositional response to textual structure. Verdi highlights it by bringing Desdemona up to a high $b\flat^2$, dropping out the other voices, and letting her float down to a cadence an octave below, once again relying on the texture of parallel $^6_3$ chords, which recall her musical "language" at the opening of the rhymed Scena. (The second measure of this extension is where the Paris sketch begins.)

Compared with what has preceded, the Peroration—or second subsection—is conventional, if vigorously compressed. Desdemona has already finished her ten-line stanza, but Verdi has permitted Otello, who also has ten lines, to have worked through only six: he has four left and, accordingly, it is he—the one with more "unexposed" poetic energy—who now leads this final subsection. Thus the Quartet, which had begun by focusing on Desdemona, now shifts its attention to Otello at exactly the moment when Iago takes possession of the handkerchief—a nice "kinetic" or dramatic tilt that may be the compositional idea from which the ensemble grew. Clearly, Verdi has reserved these final four lines in order that the standard groundswell repetitions of the Peroration, with their windups and releases onto the two cadential $^6_4$ chords, become the Moor's personal cries of humiliation: "Ella è perduta e irriso / Io sono"—a direct "commentary," even if he is unaware of it, on Iago's theft and a splendid employment of conventional devices to serve dramatic ends. (One might also notice the additional irony that Otello's *settenario* lines now take on the *quinario* accents of Iago's concomitant plotting.) Appropriately, in the first groundswell Otello darkens the established B♭ major with powerful mixtures from the parallel minor. The varied repetition, while not untinged with borrowings from the minor, is predominantly in the major mode.

Perhaps even more important, Otello's motive here, like Desdemona's at the beginning of the Exposition, varies and recalls music heard earlier. In this instance the rising fourth of his "Ella è perduta" motive (Ex. 4.6) is a varied reprise of Desdemona's first words in the rhymed Scena that preceded the Quar-

EXAMPLE 4.6. *Otello,* Act II Quartet, 165/1/1.

tet: the opening words, that is, of her intercession for Cassio, "D'un uom che geme" (Ex. 4.2).[29] In this manner the Quartet's Peroration is launched by important material that rounds with the initial idea of the preceding rhymed Scena. Scena and set-piece are drawn together, conceived as a single, larger unit. (Cf. the Scena references in the parallel ⁶₃ chords—164/2/1, mentioned above—that immediately precede the Peroration.) And, dramatically, it is at this point of "unmasking" that Otello, even more than Cassio, stands revealed as the real "uom che geme," the groaning man.

In the Paris sketch (Ex. 4.1, mm. 9–10) the phrase-pairs of the Peroration originally led directly, and perhaps too abruptly, to a coda-like reprise of the Exposition melody in the accompaniment,[30] but the final version interpolates another extension of three measures, one that includes the delicious surprises of the sudden G♭ ⁴₂ (V⁴₂ of the Neapolitan) and the unaccompanied singing (with the four singers largely undifferentiated in texture for the first time in the Quartet) that finds its way back to the tonic. In many respects this interpolation balances the only earlier unpaired phrase, the extension that had ended the Exposition. Both extensions are signaled by unexpected dominant-seventh sounds in last inversion (the second of them, of course, far the bolder); both initiate a change of texture—solo voice and parallel ⁶₃ chords in the first, unaccompanied singing in the second; both bring the soprano to a b♭²; both adopt the number of measures of their preceding phrase-pairs; both end with similar cadences. While the second extension is by no means structurally necessary—it exposes no new text and serves primarily to postpone a cadence through a delicious but decorative harmonic twist—its sonorous effect and subtle balance are welcome indeed.[31]

29. Frits Noske, in "Otello: Drama through Structure" [1971], reprinted in his *The Signifier and the Signified: Studies in the Operas of Mozart and Verdi* (The Hague, 1977), 161–62, argues that Otello's "Ella è perduta" motive refers to a "motif of Jago" earlier in the Quartet, his "Dammi quel vel!" (161/1/1). It is true that the underlying interval of a fourth also passes through Iago's part at that point, but those four fleeting notes for Iago are likely to go unnoticed in the density of the ensemble texture. It is difficult to imagine that Verdi considered them to be structurally decisive.

30. This section initiates a coda insofar as text is (once again) repeated and the harmonic function of the passage is to begin a strong, repeated grounding of the B♭ tonic. Its function as a reprise, of course, is obvious. With Otello's "Escite," the text leaves the Quartet proper and proceeds as a transitional exit in Boito's characteristic rhymed Scena texture. See footnote 19 above.

31. In the 1880s Verdi seems to have been fond of the practice of inserting an unaccompanied-ensemble passage near the end of the formal portion of an ensemble. He had included a similar, voice-only closing passage, five measures long, in his 1881 revision of the Terzetto from Act II of *Simon Boccanegra,* "Perdon, perdon, Amelia."

III

Of course the most striking difference between the Paris sketch and the final version is one of tonality: B major instead of B♭ major. Verdi's decision to transpose occurred quite late in the compositional process, during the last revisions and retouchings of the orchestration. In the autograph score the Quartet proper, "Dammi la dolce e lieta / Parola del perdono," begins on fol. 166^v.[32] There one may see the original five-sharp signature canceled and replaced by two flats—and all subsequent accidentals in all relevant instruments throughout the next few folios are altered to accomplish the transposition. Because a number of the variant readings in the sketch are visible as erasures in the vocal lines of the autograph score, it also seems likely that he copied the skeleton score of the Quartet's Peroration directly from the single sketch-page now located in Paris. The sketch settings, for instance, of Otello's two statements of "Questo mio sogno d'or" (Ex. 4.1, mm. 6, 9) differ from those in the final version (166/ 1/1 and 167/1/2; the final text reads "Vedo il mio sogno d'or"). The erasures in the autograph score at these points, fols. 170 and 170^v, agree with the sketch. Most significant, the skeleton score did not yet include the three measures later added to the end of the Peroration. These interpolated measures now appear on fol. 171, an inserted folio pasted in after the completion of the skeleton score. The first two measures of the early reading, the equivalent of Example 4.1, mm. 9–10, are clearly visible, but crossed out, as the original last two measures of fol. 170^v. They originally led directly to the first measure of fol. 172, now similarly crossed out.

The autograph score also reveals that the transposition began with the onset of subsection 2 of the rhymed Scena: some twenty-five measures prior to the Quartet proper, at the onset of the *allegro agitato* that follows Otello's second "Non ora." Example 4.7 shows the move into the *allegro agitato* as first written in the skeleton score of fol. 163^v (notice also the differing "Non ora"). Instead of changing all the accidentals of the explosive F$^6_4$, the original reading of the last measure of fol. 163^v, Verdi crossed it out, removed the next two folios (164–65), and replaced them with a new bifolio containing transposed music in fair copy. The next "original" folio is fol. 166, which contains the seven measures preceding the Quartet, Desdemona's "Se inconscia, contro te, sposo, ho peccato." Here, too, changed accidentals indicate that this passage was first entered a half-step higher.

The transposition ended only a few measures after the Quartet, with the words "s'asconda" in Iago's "Nella dimora / Di Cassio ciò s'asconda." Example 4.8 shows the relevant portions of the erased skeleton score of fols. 173^v and 174, with a slightly different vocal setting (over a C$^6_4$ for Iago, which Verdi rewrote to join up with his original music at "s'asconda." In summary, Verdi

32. I should like to thank G. Ricordi, Milan, for their kind permission to study the *Otello* autograph score and to transcribe some of my findings.

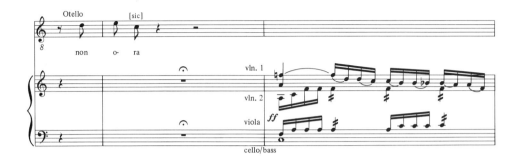

EXAMPLE 4.7. *Otello,* autograph score, fol. 163v
(original version, before erasures and corrections).

EXAMPLE 4.8. *Otello,* autograph score, fols. 173v–74
(original version, before erasures and corrections).

transposed a half-step lower a block of music some sixty-one measures long, beginning twenty-five measures before the Quartet (subsection 2 of the rhymed Scena "Perchè torbida suona"), including all of the Quartet, and ending with the transition at Iago's "ciò s'asconda."

With the knowledge of the new Verdi-Ricordi letters in the Parma Biblioteca Palatina (see footnote 6 above) one can now not only date precisely when the transposition was made but also suggest a reason for it. And the reason appears to be—no surprises here—a singer: Romilda Pantaleoni, the first Desdemona (with whom Franco Faccio was in love; he was one of her most ardent champions and, with others, had strongly urged the composer to consider her for the role). In the spring of 1886 Verdi had expressed fears, based on her recent success in Rome in Ponchielli's *Marion Delorme,* that her "passionate, ardent, [and] violent" artistry might prove too strong for the "calm and aristocratic passion of Desdemona."[33] In order to reassure the Maestro, Faccio examined Desdemona's part at S. Agata in the first week of August 1886. Ricordi himself brought Pantaleoni to S. Agata for a two-day visit—and, doubtless, a successful audition—on 29 August. It is likely that Ricordi brought back with him to Milan the manuscript score of Act IV, the first portion of *Otello* that Verdi deemed complete. Act I and the concluding part of Act III—probably the entire final scene, including the concertato—would be given to an assistant of Ricordi's on 11 September in Piacenza.[34] The composer delivered another installment of the *Otello* score, the remaining first part of Act III and, apparently, the first part of Act II, including at least the rhymed Scena preceding the Quartet, to Ricordi during a visit to Milan on 14–15 October. A few days later Pantaleoni returned to S. Agata for a far more extended visit, through 28 October, in order to study the role of Desdemona. (Thus only the second half of Act II remained to be orchestrated; for some time Verdi had also been correcting Michele Saladino's manuscript reduction of the portions that he had already submitted, and he had even started examining some of the printed proofs, particularly those of Act IV.)[35] Without a doubt, the Act II Quartet was still planned in B major.

On 23 October 1886, in the middle of Pantaleoni's visit, Ricordi, responding to a request now lost, wrote to Verdi: "Yesterday I sent [the] fascicle of the autograph score of the Quartet."[36] Another (as yet unpublished) letter from Verdi to Ricordi on the same date makes it explicit that the composer, already in possession of the Quartet proper, had just requested the return of the preceding fascicle of the autograph score, which contained the rhymed Scena, in order to

---

33. See Verdi to Ricordi, 29 June 1886, undated in Franco Abbiati, *Verdi,* 4 vols. (Milan, 1959), IV, 282.

34. See Verdi to Ricordi, 7 September 1886, in Cella and Petrobelli, eds., *Verdi–Ricordi,* 49.

35. See, for example, the evidence in the correspondence that has been already published, in Cella and Petrobelli, eds., *Verdi–Ricordi,* 49–59, and Abbiati, *Verdi,* IV, 290–307. Some of the above dates are derived from unpublished letters.

36. Cella and Petrobelli, eds., *Verdi–Ricordi,* 51.

be able to transpose the entire Quartet block. He thus decided to transpose the passage during the period when he began to work with Pantaleoni. The most reasonable conclusion is that her voice was the principal cause.

Vocal range may well have been a factor. Desdemona's prolonged, solo, and *dolcissimo* high b^2 in the center of the Quartet—the point at which the Paris sketch begins—and throughout the Peroration is the highest note required for the role. It reappears in only one other passage: as a $c\flat^3$ in the Act III concertato, "le amare / Stille del mio dolor," 273/4/3, and its climactic repetition, 315/1/1. The descent from the high $c\flat^3$ is parallel to the situation at the midpoint of the Act II Quartet and doubtless forms part of the Desdemona *tinta*. On the other hand, Verdi might have been particularly impressed with the quality of Pantaleoni's low register: by lowering the quartet by a half-step, Verdi extended Desdemona's required range down to a low $b\flat$, the first note of "Dammi la dolce e lieta" (158/1/4). Whether or not he altered the tonality primarily to obtain this striking, deep pitch cannot be known for certain, but one may assume that Pantaleoni's low $b\flat$ had been sufficiently tested and approved before the decision to transpose was made.[37]

IV

It is evident that the likelihood that Verdi transposed a significant portion of *Otello* to maximize the qualities of a particular singer has implications for tonal analysis, both for an understanding of the opera as a whole and of this smaller portion of it. Of course, one could argue that the tonal shift indicates that specific keys do not mean much in Verdi—even in late Verdi—and without a doubt those lobbying for a close-knit tonal argument in *Otello* are put on the defensive. But the most reasonable position, I think, avoids extreme claims in either direction. What the composer has done with this transposition is not to nullify the significance of key but to subordinate it to another consideration; to agree for practical reasons to allow the Quartet to participate in the web of tonalities in a different manner, but not one that is random or without tonally expressive implications.

It seems clear that Verdi had conceived the original B major of the Quartet within the orbit of the preceding E-major Homage Chorus, Desdemona's entrance in Act II. More specifically, the Homage Chorus had proceeded in juxta-

37. Another factor in the transposition may have been the effect on Otello's (that is, Francesco Tamagno's) range. The "sketch" version of the Quartet required Otello to ascend twice to a high b^1 within an explicitly lyrical context. His high notes elsewhere in the opera tend to be more stridently urgent, and well suited to Tamagno's forceful voice. Otello sings a high c^2 once (his virtually shouted dismissal of Desdemona in Act III, "Quella vil cortigiana [che è la sposa d'Otello]," 225/1/1); a high b^1 twice, once as a grace note in his initial entrance in Act I ("[Dopo l'armi lo vinse] l'uragano," 22/2/3), and again, even more accented and *forte,* in one of his rages fairly early in Act II ("[Amore e gelosia vadan] dispersi insieme," 133/1/1, just before the first strains of the Homage Chorus).

posed sections whose keys largely arpeggiate the elements of the E-major triad: E (133/3/1), A modulating back to E (138/2/3, articulation of the lower fifth and return to the tonic), B (141/1/1, the articulation of V), G♯ minor (144/2/1, III), and back to E (148/2/3, I). The original keys of the ensuing rhymed Scena–set-piece complex stress similar elements, except that the arpeggiation now—significantly enough, considering the dark deeds to follow—is that of the E-minor triad. As was discussed earlier, subsection 1 of the rhymed Scena approaches its principal key, G major (III of E minor) through A minor (cf. the A major of 138/2/3) and also touches momentarily on B minor and E minor. Subsections 2 and 3 are more freely modulatory—their intention is to express surprise—but they ultimately prepare the B major of subsection 4 and the Quartet that immediately follows. B major, then, is to be considered in both the Chorus and the Quartet as a key articulating the upper fifth of the more structurally significant E.

As might be expected, this double arpeggiation of the E major/minor triad has its dramatic point. Throughout the first portion of *Otello,* before this Quartet, E major had been persistently associated with states of security such as victory, peace, and love.[38] Desdemona's request to restore peace by means of a "dolce e lieta / Parola del perdono," therefore, had been appropriately introduced in the expectant dominant of E, B major. Indeed, for her first four lines of the Quartet she fails to recognize any significant problem between her and Otello, and she sings in childlike, round-eyed anticipation of immediate forgiveness ("La tua fanciulla io sono / Umile e mansueta"). In any event, she instantly abandons both this poetic and this musical tone for her last six lines, after Otello has pulled the music out of her warm B major and into the suddenly chilly supertonic minor.

The key of B♭ major for the Quartet, on the other hand, lacks all these prior connotations of warmth. Quite the reverse: in terms of the discussion above, the fundamental E-minor triadic arpeggiation of the Scena and Quartet (E–G–

---

38. The E-major appearances (or significant gestures toward E major) before the Quartet are: the first announcement of victory, "È salvo! È salvo!" 18/1/3ff.; Otello's (more decisive) cadence of victory, "Dopo l'armi lo vinse l'uragano," 22/2/2ff.; the end of the "Vittoria! vittoria!" Chorus, 26/2/3ff. (along with "Si calma la bufera," 30/4/3ff.); the first shouts of "Fuoco di gioia!" (36/4/1ff.) and elsewhere in the chorus (e.g., 47/2/1, 49/1/2); fleetingly in Otello's statement about "this divine moment" in the Love Duet, "Temo che più non mi sarà concesso / Quest'attimo divino," 104/1/2ff.; the climactic moment of the "Bacio," 106/1/1ff.; a curious "sonority" (by no means a clear "tonicization") passed through briefly, and *aspramente,* in Iago's Credo, 114/4/1–2 (the E sonority seems to have no connotations of security here); and the main tonal center of the Homage Chorus, 133/3/1ff. Later in the opera the originally idyllic E major returns ironically, for instance, briefly—almost as a taunt—in Iago's narration of Cassio's dream, 188/2/3–4, sarcastically throughout the Act III Otello-Desdemona Duet (pp. 206–25), and, of course, with the poignant irony of loss at the end of Act IV. One might also notice that some fifteen measures before the Quartet proper in the original version, Desdemona had passed through E minor while offering Otello her handkerchief: "Se con questo / Morbido lino la mia man ti fascia." David Lawton, "On the 'Bacio' Theme in *Otello,*" *19th-Century Music* I (1977–1978), 211–20, argues (217) that early in the opera "the key of E expresses not only Otello's greatness but also, as an element of his greatness, his tragic destiny."

B) has been altered into a much more disturbing diminished triad (E–G–B♭). The deflection into B♭ major, which decisively shifts the tonal progress away from the gravitational pull of the more secure E major/minor, may now be considered a tonal and dramatic signal that something has gone wrong.[39] The most plausible explanation seems to be that B♭ major suggests a tonal spinoff of the F major at the opening of the act, that is to say, the F-major Iago-Cassio dialogue (followed by the F-minor Credo).[40] This presumed return to the sphere of influence of F is reinforced motivically, for, as mentioned earlier, Desdemona's Quartet melody begins by varying promises of pardon first made in that initial scene of Act II. Thus the choice of B♭ could well underscore Iago's prior plotting, of which this ensemble is the first direct consequence. But, whatever one's explanation of this transposition, the original, B-major connotations of brightness and expectant security are now lacking. A different tonal filter, or expressive filter, has been passed over the Quartet: not at all an ineffective or inappropriate one, to be sure, but certainly one that is in its context more expressively sober and cool.

Such late compositional transpositions as we find in this *Otello* Quartet—and elsewhere[41]—invite us to rethink what tonal choices and patterns might mean in Verdi. On the one hand, tonal processes are demonstrably an important concern: witness his organizing of individual sections around triadic axes; his sense of when to prepare a key elaborately and when to allow it to burst in unannounced; and, as Pierluigi Petrobelli has demonstrated, his manipulation of previously established sonorities to establish a particular *tinta* throughout a section or an entire work.[42] On the other hand, it is clear from these transpositions that tonal processes are not always his primary concern. Many of Verdi's tonali-

---

39. This is the only two-flat signature in the opera, and neither B♭ nor E♭ major has appeared for any significantly prolonged preceding music. (B♭ minor had been visited briefly here and there, but not in ways that illuminate this Quartet. And, of course, E♭ minor appears in the final version a few measures before the Quartet, where E minor had been before the transposition.)

40. It is perhaps worth mentioning that "Iago's" F major/minor at the beginning of Act II recalls (or prolongs?) the F major of the central core of the Act I Otello-Desdemona Love Duet, "Quando narravi," (97/ 1/1–103/2/1), a passage impossible to construe as malevolent. If the F major of Act II is intended to be related to that of Act I—and if one feels obliged to push the argument of tonal/dramatic associations—it may be that its point (with Iago) is to appropriate something idyllic and to stain it by using it for manipulative purposes; notice that Iago's later seizing of the handkerchief is an analogous dramatic (but not tonal) act.

41. Apart from the well-known key shifts in Verdi's revisions of, say, *Simon Boccanegra* and *Don Carlos,* two additional ones may be mentioned here. Verdi first entered the initial twenty-five measures of the last scene of *Aida* into the autograph score in F minor, not the present E minor: the *scena della tomba,* that is, originally began a half-step higher. (See the present author's "Compositional Emendations in Verdi's Autograph Scores: *Il trovatore, Un ballo in maschera,* and *Aida,*" forthcoming in *Studi verdiani* IV.) And, as I have pointed out elsewhere (*Giuseppe Verdi: Falstaff,* 43), Falstaff's Trill Monologue in Act III, Scene 1, originally ended in E♭ major, not the present E major: a change seemingly made for the possibility of producing a trill on the third flute.

42. See Pierluigi Petrobelli, "Osservazioni sul processo compositivo in Verdi," *Acta Musicologica* XLIII (1971), 129–32, and his further discussion in "Per un'esegesi della struttura drammatica del 'Trovatore,' " *Atti del 3° congresso internazionale di studi verdiani* (Parma, 1974), 387–400, translated by William Drabkin as "Towards an Explanation of the Dramatic Structure of *Il trovatore," Music Analysis* I (1982), 129–41.

ties seem to inhabit the vast middle ground between the two absolute poles of random keys to the left and unalterably fixed tonal logic to the right. It is precisely this delicate nuancing of the relative importances of keys that most challenges our powers of description, for in the tonal analysis of complex dramatic works one can easily claim too much.

With regard specifically to this *Otello* Act II Quartet, however, the key shift for Pantaleoni need not strike us as ill-founded or capricious, nor may we conclude that Verdi could have been persuaded to alter any of the other keys in *Otello.* (E major, in particular, plays a special role, and I would not like to learn that Verdi ever considered transposing the "Bacio" into E♭.) In its B-major version the opening measures of the Quartet had dual or multiple relationships with past music: tonally with the secure E-major Mandolin Chorus and the "Bacio"; motivically with the Iago-Cassio F-major dialogue at the beginning of Act II. These split associations are common in Verdi—they can occur, of course, whenever a motive is highlighted in another key—and they are some of the many strands that form the complex web of relationships holding a Verdi opera together. But in a dense network of multiple connotations, certain individual connotations may be altered without damage to the whole. With the transposition of the Quartet from B to B♭ major, Verdi realigned some of the split associations. These particular tonal and motivic associations now reached back, with differing intensities, to the same place, the earlier F-major Iago-Cassio dialogue—and the web of musical discourse remained sound.

Part 2

Motive and Harmony

Chapter 5

Verdi's Groundswells
Surveying an Operatic Convention

JOSEPH KERMAN AND THOMAS S. GREY

I

A musical tradition with such strong, sometimes nearly ineradicable, founda-
tions in conventional techniques and formulas as that of nineteenth-century
Italian opera seems to cry out for a comparative critical methodology. We are
thoroughly familiar nowadays with the basic elements of operatic musical convention from Rossini through middle-period Verdi: adagio and cabaletta; the
tempo d'attacco and *tempo di mezzo*; duet forms, similar and dissimilar; the largo
concertato; the stage *banda*; and so on. We have come to realize that an appreciation of the best works of Verdi and his predecessors depends heavily on acquir-
ing a feeling for these conventions with which they worked, for standard text
forms and aria types, as well as the voice types and singing styles of their interpreters (as far as these can be ascertained).

While our appreciation of Verdi's musical and dramatic achievements has
been greatly enriched over recent years through investigations into the context
of *primo ottocento* operatic repertory and traditions, surprisingly little work has
been done with regard to Verdi's own manipulation of specific conventions in
the course of his career.[1] It is well known that he defended (at least in principle)

---

1. Two major comparative studies in this area are concerned with the role of text structures in determining melodic and formal elements: Friedrich Lippmann, "Der italienische Vers und der musikalische Rhyth-
mus: Zum Verhältnis von Vers und Musik in der italienischen Oper des 19. Jahrhunderts, mit einem Rück-
blick auf die 2. Hälfte des 18. Jahrhunderts," *Analecta Musicologica* XII (1973), 253–369; ibid. XIV (1974),
324–410; ibid. XV (1975), 298–333; and Robert Moreen's dissertation, "Integration of Text Forms and
Musical Forms in Verdi's Early Operas," Princeton University, 1975. Lippmann's lengthy article is a com-
pendium of rhythmic treatment of Italian verse meters by composers from J. A. Hasse through Verdi. Within
a more limited repertory, Moreen examines the relationship of traditional text forms to full aria and duet
structures. An example of comparative methodology by one of the present authors is Joseph Kerman's "Ver-

one of Italian opera's most notorious conventions, the cabaletta, as late as the time of *Aida*.[2] Indeed, much of Verdi's greatness can be seen to lie in the balance he established between conservatism and innovation, a respect for traditional idioms coupled with a vigorous dramatic and musical imagination. A natural and effective critical avenue would seem to be the investigation of other such musico-dramatic types that can be traced throughout his operas, even if they are not all as easily codified as the cabaletta. Julian Budden's epochal study of Verdi's operatic oeuvre provides many insights along these lines. It also provides much material for further detailed typologies of this sort, and in the first volume Budden suggest one that we will examine here, which he terms a *groundswell*.

This "groundswell" effect is in part a stereotyped phrase-pattern and concomitant harmonic formula, which typically functions as an emphatic cadential period to the largo concertato section of a large-scale ensemble finale. It tends to form, indeed, the most impressive and memorable element of the finale. Budden coins the term in his discussion of aria and ensemble forms in *primo ottocento* opera, but he refrains (perhaps wisely) from identifying the convention in precise terms.[3] He traces the origin of the largo concertato in general to Rossini and late-eighteenth-century comic opera, namely to the slow (often a cappella or quasi-a cappella) middle movement of a sectional finale expressing the characters' common astonishment at some dramatic reversal or unforeseen incident (cf. *Il barbiere di Siviglia,* Act I Finale, Adagio, which Rossini marks "quadro di stupore"). The specific groundswell effect found in serious opera of the next generation can in fact be more distinctly circumscribed than Budden lets on. To form an idea of the salient musical and dramatic features of this convention, let us turn first to classic examples from two of the most familiar pre-Verdian Italian operas.

The concluding Finale of Bellini's *Norma* offers one of the earliest and finest examples of the device where it functions as part of the opera's climactic final ensemble. As a musical formula, it can be understood to be derived from one of the most basic phrase patterns of bel canto melody, an a-a'-b-c pattern, in which c signifies little more than a cadential rounding-off.[4] The groundswell itself con-

di's Use of Recurring Themes," in Harold S. Powers, ed., *Studies in Music History: Essays for Oliver Strunk* (Princeton, 1968), 495–510.

2. Philip Gossett has written about the use of the cabaletta in *Aida* in the context of the opera's genesis (Verdi's correspondence with Antonio Ghislanzoni) and of the ever-present tradition of the Rossinian four-part aria and duet form, in "Verdi, Ghislanzoni, and *Aida*: The Uses of Convention," *Critical Inquiry* I, no. 2 (1974), 291–334. A major point of Gossett's article is the ambivalence Verdi continued to display toward Rossinian conventions at this late date; beside the oft-quoted exhortations to his librettists for new, freer verse forms, Verdi's correspondence reveals a contrasting tendency to preserve the older forms when he found them appropriate or when nothing better could be provided.

3. Julian Budden, *The Operas of Verdi,* 3 vols. (London, 1973, 1978, 1981), I, 19. Budden's own application of the term *groundswell* proves to be very sparing; of the examples discussed in this paper, only one rather atypical case, the Act IV Quartet from *Don Carlos,* elicits the term from him again (III, 129).

4. See also the discussion of typical Verdian melodic forms in Joseph Kerman, "Lyric Form and Flexibility in *Simon Boccanegra,*" *Studi verdiani* I (Parma, 1982), 49–51.

stitutes either a final or penultimate cadential period within the variable series of sections that make up an ensemble finale. In this case it is the major-mode conclusion of a minor/major binary structure, beginning as Norma's plea to Oroveso for the sake of her children (Ex. 5.1). This example reveals the following more specific traits of the device: (1) a regular alternation of tonic and dominant harmonies (normally *a-a'*—in this case Bellini includes an extra, introductory statement without soloists); (2) a contrasting, tension-building phrase (*b*) involving sequential harmonic progressions with rising treble and bass lines; (3) a grandiose cadential descent, here capped by crashing cymbals on the downbeat; and (4) the repetition of the whole series for an added sense of weight and expansiveness.

Bellini makes perhaps unsurpassed dramatic use of the device. Instead of providing mere musical ballast, as it later came to do all too often, this groundswell accompanies Oroveso's process of relenting, already signaled subliminally by the shift to E major. The exchange between Norma and Oroveso is carefully kept audible above the discreet choral commentary:

NORMA:	Padre, tu piangi!
OROV.:	Opresso è il core.
NORMA:	Piangi, e perdona!
OROV.:	Ha vinto amore!
NORMA:	Ah, tu perdoni—quel pianto il dice.
POLL., NORMA:	Io più non chiedo, io son felice; Contento /a il rogo ascenderò.
[CHORUS:	Piange! Prega! Che mai speri? Quì respinta è la preghiera (etc.)]

The seesawing V–I harmonies depict Norma's urgent entreaties, while only at the climax of the *b*-phrase does she fully realize that she has prevailed ("Ah, più non chiedo"). Bellini has also reserved a few clinching lines of new text for the second cursus, so as to further justify the musical repetition: Oroveso's promise to Norma that her children will be spared ("Ah, cessa infelice! Io tel prometto / Ah, sì").

The dramatic context and function of this example serve to define it as one of two basic groundswell subtypes, which we could call the *finale ultimo*. It serves to draw out the climactic moment of the opera, gathering together soloists and chorus in an extended moment of lyrical expansion and giving weight to the final tonic key through its slow-paced V–I reiterations and emphatic cadential phrase. As in this case, however, the final phrase is typically cut off by a harsh

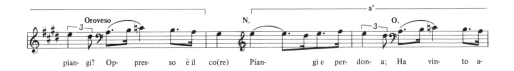

EXAMPLE 5.1. The groundswell of the Act II Finale, *Norma.*

orchestral *tutti,* initiating a sudden return to the minor mode and a swift, san-
guinary denouement in a fast tempo.

The second broad contextual subtype, the groundswell in a mid-opera finale,
is exemplified by Donizetti's celebrated sextet in Act II of *Lucia di Lammermoor.*
The sextet forms the middle section of a lengthy sectional Finale, a frozen-

EXAMPLE 5.2. The groundswell of the sextet in Act II, *Lucia di Lammermoor*.

action tableau (*larghetto*) initiated by Edgar's unseemly interruption of Lucy's betrothal ceremony. As in *Norma,* the groundswell forms the concluding period of a slow-tempo binary structure, beginning at the point where the chorus joins the solo ensemble. This position of the groundswell, as the second period of a two-part adagio movement, remains one of its most consistent features. The standard phrase-pattern is present (*a-a'-b-c,* repeated once), with the usual addition of a brief cadenza/coda (Ex. 5.2). Following a standard practice for such concerted numbers, Donizetti introduces all of the text in the initial solo period preceding the groundswell; the chorus merely harmonizes to second-hand verses. Even so, he does not take Bellini's pains to render much, if any, of it intelligible. Donizetti's ensemble is the outcome of the classic mid-opera peripeteia mentioned earlier, inherited from the comic finales of Mozart and Rossini. The assembled cast is struck dumb, and the sentiments of the various factions are interpreted easily enough by the audience even without knowing just what is said.

What counts here is the opportunity for a moment of full-bodied lyric effusion. And it is for this that the groundswell is principally designed, normally offering the soprano the opportunity to top off the proceedings with a measure's worth of high B♭ or the like over the cadential $^6_4$ chord. In the present case, the peculiarly operatic stasis is rationalized well enough in the text, as the two mortal enemies, Edgar and Henry, exchange rhetorical questions about the invisible force that "stays the fury of their vengeance." The broad harmonic rhythm of the groundswell, with its slow tonic-dominant reiterations, emphasizes the static character of the situation, while the brief "swelling" modulations of the *b*-phrase suggest something of the characters' pent-up tensions.

Two further characteristic features of the mid-opera type are exemplified in Donizetti's sextet: (1) the striking tonal contrast with its flanking sections (D♭, surrounded by large units in G and D); and (2) a subsequent extended stretta in fast cut-time—another trait inherited from the comic-opera prototype. The D♭ of Donizetti's ensemble, incidentally, emerges as a favorite key for Verdi's groundswells, along with neighboring flat keys. Among the earlier Verdi operas, the formula occurs most frequently in the *finale ultimo* context; examples include the endings of *Giovanna d'Arco, Il corsaro, I due Foscari,* and *I masnadieri.* But one of its more successful applications, one possibly inspired by *Norma,* is actually a kind of cross between the two types: the Act I Finale of *Macbeth.*

II

As a purely formal type, the groundswell can of course be applied to any number of operatic circumstances, and we eventually find Verdi using it in smaller ensembles, without chorus (as in *Rigoletto, Les Vêpres siciliennes, La forza del destino*). The full-scale device, however—as part of an ensemble finale—seems almost always to be reserved for a single occasion within an opera. In *Macbeth* (1847), we find it in the adagio concertato of the first Finale. The adagio is precipitated by an appropriately horrific peripeteia, the discovery of Duncan's murder (Piave has indicated a "stupore universale"). The groundswell occupies the last of three stanzas. In the first stanza a massed outburst for full forces invokes the flames of hell to consume the murderer ("Schiudi, inferno, la bocca"). The second stanza is an extended a cappella prayer for divine assistance. As in *Norma,* then, the groundswell introduces new words (third stanza: "L'ira tua formidabile e pronta"). Some intelligibility is vouchsafed in this case by presentation of the initial text as a single melodic line, either in octaves or sixths.

The groundswell follows the standard formula, although the V–I alternations last a full eight measures (Ex. 5.3). Again there are rising treble and bass lines in the contrasting phrase and climactic cymbal crashes at the cadence. The broad, swinging dotted rhythms and minor-sixth inflections in the accompaniment both recall the passage from *Norma,* and the cadential phrases of the two examples are essentially identical.

What further suggests the influence of *Norma* is the fact that Verdi has applied to this dramatic context (the first-act Finale crisis) musical elements of the *finale ultimo* type. There is an overall minor/major contrast (B♭ minor to relative major, D♭), but not the striking tonal contrast traditionally found in this position. Thus instead of a long concluding stretta in a contrasting key, Verdi's allegro is cut down to perfunctory proportions, remaining in the key of the groundswell. The focus of this vestigial stretta is on the drawn-out solo exclamations, "Gran Dio!" These underline the hypocrisy of the Macbeth couple, who have of necessity joined in the prayer. At this point, they are certainly not praying but expressing apprehension. The prayer itself is given an ironic edge by the apprehension Macbeth has just expressed in the preceding duet: "Perché, perché ripetere / Quell'*Amen* non potei?"

The setup of this example is perhaps less powerful than in *Norma,* though Verdi certainly does his best to enhance it. Like Bellini, he gives directions for a series of gradual dynamic swells, beginning hushed but *grandioso.* The broad rhythmic sweep is matched to the momentum-gathering effect of the V–I seesaws. Verdi also introduces a new and henceforth characteristic touch in relating the groundswell to the preceding material thematically. As Julian Budden has pointed out, the motivic connection derives originally from Macbeth's striking, unaccompanied pronouncement, "tutto è finito," as he reappears after Duncan's murder (Ex. 5.4).[5]

---

5. Budden, *The Operas of Verdi* I, 292. The motive also introduces the Prelude to Act II.

[soloists and chorus, *unisono:* "L'ira tua formidabile" etc.]

EXAMPLE 5.3. The groundswell of the Act I Finale, *Macbeth*.

EXAMPLE 5.4. The thematic derivation of the Act I Finale groundswell, *Macbeth*.

III

More than a formal element in a musical design, the groundswell has the dramatic function of focusing on the Macbeths' guilt. But is the effect out of proportion with the dramatic impetus? Is it perhaps an example of the "besetting sin of Verdi's early style—emphasis without depth";[6] that is, does it strike us as truly grandiose or simply as bombastic? Verdi seems to have wrestled with this device in a number of the middle-period operas and even beyond. To put the problem one way: from the standpoint of a composer of Verdi's radical dramatic instincts, what situations were strong enough to earn one of these groundswells? To put it another way: for a composer of Verdi's conservative musical tastes, how could dramatic pretexts be concocted for the application of this device? An example from a slightly earlier opera is interesting from this point of view, the concluding Finale of *I masnadieri* (1847), Andrea Maffei's adaptation of Schiller's *Die Räuber*.

The musical formula should by now be familiar: the double statement of a melody over a tonic-dominant alternation (in this case, the opening tonic bar is omitted); a rising melodic line in the *b*-phrase—though less forceful here than in *Macbeth*; a cadence; and the subsequent repetition of the series, with partially new text. The climax on the mildly remote chord of ♭VI is, like the ♭III in *Macbeth*, a favorite goal of these middle phrases (Ex. 5.5).

The fresh element here is the dramatic intervention of the chorus. The repentant and remorseful Carlo wants to abdicate his position as leader of the outlaw pack. The Finale begins to evolve as a chain of lyric periods but is harshly interrupted by the chorus of *masnadieri*, reminding Carlo of their communal oath. This oath, from the Finale of the previous act, is also evoked musically by the descending minor triad in dotted rhythm, "Spergiuro, ascoltaci! più non rammenti / Gl'irrevocabili tuoi giuramenti?" It is this intervention that sets off the groundswell, a temporary, last-minute escape from the tragic realities of the moment. (This is, of course, a characteristic dramatic function of the device in the *finale ultimo,* frequently accompanying one of those protracted operatic death scenes.) Not only do the chorus precipitate the groundswell here, they soon insist on participating in it. By contrast, Carlo's father, Massimiliano, is present only to fill out the texture of the solo ensemble (in Schiller's play he has already expired). Verdi cleverly contrives the entrance of the chorus by having it fill in that "missing" first bar of tonic harmony in the second cursus, and their dotted rhythms continue to suggest the fatal oath (cf. Ex. 5.5).

This use of the chorus certainly represents an attempt to make the essentially lyrical formula more dynamic. Verdi even saves the *fortissimo* climax for the cadence of the second cursus, where he also adjusts the vocal lines, bringing

---

6. Ibid., 337.

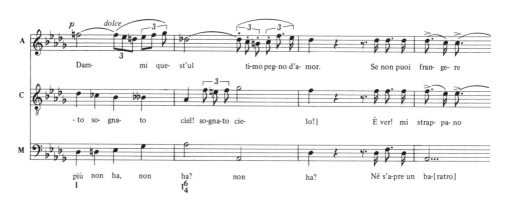

EXAMPLE 5.5.   The groundswell from the Act IV Finale, *I masnadieri*.

the soprano and tenor up to a high Bb. And while Amalia has sung her entire stanza during the first statement of the music, as expected, Carlo's last two lines are saved for the repeat, his final *tronco* syllable ("mi trae con *se*") arriving only with the sudden, hammered minor chord that initiates the brief denouement. Granted, it seems doubtful that anyone will readily perceive these new lines within the busy texture of the ensemble.

We have suggested that the first choral entry ("Spergiuro, ascoltaci!") precipitated the groundswell. A further musico-dramatic twist is suggested by the short lyrical trio that precedes this. For this eight-bar period (Ab) is itself a single statement of the formula. It is in this first quasi-groundswell that the two lovers express their hopes for eternal bliss:

> CARLO: M'ama quest'angelo,
> M'ama ed oblia
> Amalia!
>
> AMALIA: Mio Carlo!
>
> BOTH: Per sempre mia;
> Cadranno [morrano] i secoli,
> Cadranno i mondi,
> Ah! in noi, coll'anima
> L'amor vivrà.

By the time the two launch into their second, complete groundswell, they realize that their time is indeed up.

IV

A comparative typological survey must guard against the tendency to chart a steady graph of improvement in the application of the type or technique in question, forcibly interpreting the artistic evidence to this end. Nonetheless, it seems fair to say that Verdi's use of the groundswell in both *I masnadieri* and *Macbeth* compares favorably with instances in some of the earlier operas. The Act I Finale of *I Lombardi* (1843) contains a situation quite similar to that of *Macbeth,* the sudden revelation of Pagano's parricide ("Mostro d'averno orribile, / Nè a te si schiude il suol?"). "Orrore universale" is expressed, as in the later opera, by loud, double-dotted, minor-mode choral outbursts. But the ensuing groundswell variant (*a-a'-b-b'*) involves a shamelessly jaunty F-major tune, resulting from Verdi's too-ready capitulation to the traditional injunction against an *abuso dei minori*; he merely changes the mode and tempo of the original melodic material.[7] *I due Foscari* (1844) and *Giovanna d'Arco* (1845) each offer examples of the groundswell as climax of a *finale ultimo* complex, like that of

---

7. Cf. ibid., 121.

Masnadieri. The contrasting phrase (*b*) in both cases is harmonically milder than usual, seemingly underemphasized. They rely mainly on the soprano's high note for a climactic effect at the cadence. In *Giovanna d'Arco* there is only a single cursus of the formula, following an incomplete false start somewhat akin to the *Masnadieri* finale. Neither here nor in *I due Foscari*, however, does the formula impress one as much more than a half-conscious response to the situation, a routine tragic demise. Verdi and his librettists have failed to concoct an adequate pretext, or at least one that could inspire the composer to integrate the device in a fully satisfying manner.

If Verdi himself sensed that he ought to avoid "emphasis without depth," this may be manifested in his application of the groundswell in *Rigoletto,* where it turns up in the new, more intimate context of the famous third-act Quartet. This new context, outside of the usual finale-complex and lacking the participation of the chorus, seems appropriate to what Abramo Basevi identified as Verdi's second, "personal" or intimate stylistic period.[8] The groundswell still serves its accustomed function as the culminating cadential period of a multisectional ensemble (the final sixteen bars of the number, plus an additional nine bars of coda). But the impression here is more organic, not that of a reflex reaction to a stock situation.

Indeed, there is no universal stupor in this case: the dramatic *colpo* is experienced by Gilda alone, and her isolation is effectively realized, of course, in the famous divided stage setting. In the opening E-major allegro, Rigoletto has shown his daughter evidence of the Duke's infidelity; but unlike the immediate, rather artificial outrage that characterizes many groundswells involving full chorus, Gilda's reaction is depicted in a gradual, naturalistic manner. Only in the course of the concerted mid-section of the andante ("Bella figlia dell'amore") does Gilda's line start to assume prominence in the musical texture. This contrasting mid-section, beginning with Maddalena's laughing figure, "Ah! ah! Rido ben di core," is in itself a compact groundswell period, recalling the false-start technique seen in *I masnadieri*. In the present number, the second statement of the false groundswell is not simply cut off, but skillfully elided with and foreshortened by the return of the Duke's melody. The moment at which Gilda finally asserts her melodic prominence coincides with the *b*-phrase of this quasi-groundswell, where the sense of her text ("Infelice cor tradito, Per angoscia non *scoppiar*") effectively matches the typical harmonic swell toward ♭III and V (F♭ major and A♭ minor) (Ex. 5.6). After this, Gilda's line continues to float above the ensemble until her sighing appoggiaturas become the main melodic substance of the groundswell proper. As in the *Macbeth* example, there seems to be

8. Andrew Porter, "Verdi," in *The New Grove Masters of Italian Opera* (New York, 1983), 207.

EXAMPLE 5.6. The *b*-phrase of the quasi-groundswell, Act III Quartet, *Rigoletto*.

a motivic connection implied here with Gilda's earlier phrase, "Ah, così parlar d'amore!" which is similarly shot through with these pathetic appoggiaturas.

The subsequent, full groundswell serves as a stabilizing, summarizing element. While it contains the usual upward rising lines, driving toward the cadence, the harmonic swell is deemphasized in comparison to the preceding partial groundswell. Here it is limited to somewhat tame progressions through the dominant and relative minor. Even so, Verdi carefully avoids letting it become mere cadential ballast. While the three upper parts are repeating earlier verses, Rigoletto's final stanza has been reserved until now:

> Taci, e mia sarà la cura
> La vendetta ad affrettar.
> Sì, pronta fia, sarà fatale,
> Io saprollo fulminar.

His vengeful fury, like his desperation in the duet with Gilda at the end of the opera, is depicted through the inexorable sequential rise of his line. And unlike Carlo's new lines in the *Masnadieri* Finale, these are made at least partially intelligible when Rigoletto breaks out of the prevailing texture at the cadence with a cascade of accentuated sixteenth-notes ("Io saprollo fulminar"). Within the general lyrical expansion of the period, Verdi thus manages to underline the matter of essential dramatic force, Rigoletto's projected vengeance upon the Duke.

V

By the time of his middle period, Verdi was certainly becoming wary about using the groundswell formula in its more traditional guises. Almost its last conventional appearances occur in *Trovatore* and *Traviata,* and not without some modifications. The big ensemble of the Act II Finale in *Il trovatore* ("E deggio e posso crederlo?") recalls the *Rigoletto* Quartet musically (Gilda's breathless appoggiaturas) but, all in all, it is unremarkable in both musical and dramatic terms. The tempo is slightly faster than usual, as it had been in *Rigoletto,* and here Verdi is careful to maintain a subdued dynamic level up until the concluding allegro. (He was to experiment further with this subdued, up-tempo version in *Un ballo in maschera.*) The groundswell is precipitated in typical fashion by the startling nick-of-time appearance of Manrico at Leonora's convent, while its slightly unusual tempo and character are explained by her reaction, obviously not horrified but elated. It may well have been the outward similarity of the dramatic situation to that of the *Lucia* sextet that prompted Verdi's use of the device.

The situation in the second-act Finale of *La traviata* is one that was to lead Verdi back to the groundswell idea as late as *Otello,* namely, the swooning and gradual revival of the unjustly accused heroine. Budden calls this largo concertato "in some respects an old-fashioned piece, appropriate to the figure who dominates it," namely, Germont.[9] No doubt the groundswell formula is one of the respects Budden has in mind, although he does not identify it as such. Its position as the concluding period of the ensemble is standard. One small refinement in musical terms is the modulation (at [x] in Ex. 5.7) between the *a'-* and the *b*-phrase.

As in earlier examples, there is evidence of a concern for musical connections across the number. Here the tendency toward C minor (B♮ to C progressions) links up to material on either side of the groundswell passage: (1) to the C-minor chorus, "Oh, infamia orribile tu commettesti!"; (2) to the precadential climax (C minor, first inversion) in the immediately preceding period (Schirmer vocal score 174); and (3) to the expansive coda that follows (vocal score 187). Nothing new happens in the drama after Violetta revives, early in the ensemble (one waits in vain for the Baron to take action against Alfredo), so Verdi dispenses with any fast-tempo conclusion. Instead, he has transferred a kind of

---

9. Budden, *The Operas of Verdi* II, 152. It could certainly be argued, however, that Germont does *not* dominate the scene past his solo—and that neither does the Baron, who should. As Budden comments elsewhere, had Massenet or Puccini set *La Dame aux camélias,* "there would be no entry of Germont, and no concertato of sad sweet melody. Instead, Baron Duphol would have struck Armand [Alfredo] across the face with his glove and the curtain would have descended to Dumas's ringing phrase: 'Monsieur, vous êtes un lâche!' " (*The Operas of Verdi* III, 306). See also Joseph Kerman, "Opera, Novel, Drama: The Case of *La traviata,*" in *Literature and the Other Arts* (= *Yearbook of Comparative and General Literature* XXVII [1978]), 50 and n.6.

EXAMPLE 5.7. The groundswell of the Act II Finale, *La traviata*.

vestigial stretta back to a dramatically more apposite spot, the actual *colpo,* the point at which Alfredo vents his mistaken contempt of Violetta by throwing a purse of money at her feet (chorus et al.: "Oh, infamia orribile," C minor, *velocissimo*). This is the moment of outrage and indignation, while subsequent verses concentrate on emotions of sympathy or remorse.

Honing down the customary stretta or omitting it altogether has become a common procedure for Verdi since *Macbeth*. He is still willing to take advantage of the conventional harmonic and metric proportions of the groundswell to achieve a desired effect but is by now determined to avoid the kind of musical-dramaturgical cliché on a larger scale that the formula had often previously incurred.

VI

Attempts to streamline or otherwise modify a conventional formula are likely to run up against a problem at some point: when does a convention cease to be conventional? How far can it be modified and still produce the desired effect? Verdi seems to have posed the question to himself in revising the closing scene of *Simon Boccanegra*. In the first version, Verdi had concluded the opera with a concerted groundswell of only a single cursus, followed by a melancholy, almost silent denouement rather than the violent, frenetic type we have seen in *Norma* and *I masnadieri* (or the groundswell-Finale of *Il corsaro,* where the hero afterward leaps off a cliff into the sea, in true melodramatic fashion). The inversion of the cliché in *Boccanegra* must have appealed to Verdi. But in revising the score in 1881, Verdi reinstated the missing repeat, in addition to touching up some harmonic and melodic points.[10] Even in its more sophisticated later guise (with regard to texture and instrumentation, for instance), the rudimentary dynamic of the formula seems to depend on this basic architectural symmetry.

It is true that, as in some earlier cases, the groundswell performs no real dramatic function here beyond joining the characters in a communal expression of grief which has already been voiced individually or at least in smaller groups. But in turning to this formula, Verdi always had to draw a line between musical weight and dramatic redundancy. The 1857 *Boccanegra* made unusually few concessions to convention or popular taste, so it is not surprising to find that Verdi opted for trimming the cadential ballast of the groundswell.[11] The mellowed composer of 1881, on the other hand, reconsidered in favor of lyric grandeur. The basic function of the device, after all, is to provide a kind of catharsis for preceding dramatic tensions, in addition to a strong sense of tonal arrival. And in the case of the *Boccanegra* Finale, the repetition seems more than usually merited in view of the admirable concision and continuity of the scene it concludes. (It is also possible that the original motivation to delete the repetition was merely to curtail somewhat the Doge's protracted death-pains, from a poison he had imbibed in the previous act.)

Several improved musical details of the revised passage also make the repetition welcome. For example, the bass line is given a stronger sense of direction in the *b*-phrase, and the blandly traditional II–V7–I cadence is enriched by a secondary dominant (V$^4_3$/III) (Ex. 5.8). The final cadence of the period is deceptive (diminished seventh), as is typical of the *finale ultimo* groundswell, though this time the chord is given in hushed tones by the low brass. And in maintaining the slow tempo to the end, fading to a somber *ppp* conclusion, Verdi otherwise defies the tradition.

VII

After *Simon Boccanegra* Verdi did not employ the *finale ultimo* groundswell again (the revised finale of *La forza del destino* represents only a qualified exception). From the 1850s on, in fact, it seems that he generally did not allow himself to fall back on the convention without modifying it in some way. Even in his fairly conservative offering to the Paris stage, *Les Vêpres siciliennes,* the groundswell occurs not in any of the full-blown concerted Finales, but in the fourth-act Quartet, "Adieu, mon pays." The dramatic motivation of the number and the position of the formula within it are conventional enough, how-

10. The music for both the 1857 and 1881 versions is given in full by Budden, *The Operas of Verdi* II, 330–33.

11. Cf. Kerman, "Lyric Form and Flexibility in *Simon Boccanegra,*" 60.

ever, as is the following turbulent stretta—cut-time, allegro vivace—in the sharply contrasting key of E (the Quartet is in F).

Two instances from *Un ballo in maschera* are, by comparison, so musically transformed as nearly to escape recognition. The first occurs within the final Quartet with chorus in Act II. Renato discovers the identity of the veiled woman he is to accompany ("Che! . . . Amelia! Sua moglie!")—another traditional motivation for the device, but the device itself is incorporated into a larger symmetrical scheme, surrounded by the mocking refrain of Sam, Tom, and their band of conspirators. Verdi achieves an unusually effective continuity by running this choral mockery and its orchestral grace-notes underneath the groundswell, placing this scherzo-like material in musical and dramatic counterpoint with the dilemma of Renato and Amelia (Ex. 5.9*a*). The tempo (*quasi allegretto*), the light texture and dynamics, and the exceptionally brief *a*-phrases (two measures) all combine to mask the formula.[12]

The second instance, the cadential period of the Act III Quintet, "Di che fulgor, che musiche," moves at a genuinely fast clip (Ex. 5.9*b*). Was Verdi perhaps attempting to adapt the device to the *tinta* of the opera, with its predominance of light textures and quick, scherzo-like tempos? Both examples include an accelerating chromatic descent, a feature that becomes characteristic of the vocal parts in the later groundswells. It seems that Verdi was by now trying to slip the device into his operas almost without its being noticed. Indeed, when the formula is both musically modified and divorced from its conventional contexts, as in the second example here, it may seem doubtful whether we can identify a convention at all. Nonetheless, Verdi continues to apply one or both of these methods of modification—musical or contextual—whenever he turns to the groundswell idea in the later operas.

VIII

In both *Don Carlos* and *La forza del destino* Verdi uses the groundswell in modified dramatic contexts, intimate rather than grandiose, and without choral participation, as we have seen it already in *Rigoletto* and *Vêpres*. The tenor-baritone Duettino in Act III of *Forza* ("Solenne in quest'ora") is perhaps the

---

12. Budden scans this Quartet-Finale as a rondo, in which the scherzando B♭ tune ("Ve' se di notte qui colla sposa") functions as the main theme, while the material belonging to Renato and Amelia ("Così mi paga, se l'ho salvato," G minor, and the groundswell passage itself) constitute episodes (*The Operas of Verdi* II, 407). This does draw attention to the new, more consciously architectural treatment of the device within a larger scheme, which was to be further amplified in *Otello*. Yet it is difficult to see the function of the groundswell here as really episodic. For one thing, it is in the tonic key (B♭) and establishes the principal structural return to this. Furthermore, the first (and only) return of the so-called rondo main theme, following the groundswell, has more the function of a coda, in both a musical and a dramatic sense ("Andiam. Ve' la tragedia mutò in commedia. . . ").

EXAMPLE 5.8. *B*-phrases from the original (1857) and revised (1881) groundswells
of the Act III Finale, *Simon Boccanegra.*

smallest scale on which it can be found. It may thus raise a taxonomical question: at what point is the presence of the musical formula merely accidental? To
what degree does the status as a convention rely equally on both dramatic and
musical physiognomy? A single cursus of the phrase-pattern in a solo entrance
aria, for instance, does not seem to qualify. From this point of view, the concluding half of the Duettino might possibly be interpreted as a sort of parody-
groundswell. It contains the full musical formula, with repeat and coda, and
constitutes the second period of a minor/major romanza-type movement; it

EXAMPLE 5.9. Concluding portions of two groundswells, *Un ballo in maschera*.

thus has a fairly typical musical context. Don Alvaro appears to be *in extremis* from wounds inflicted in battle ("Or muoio tranquillo"), although the force of destiny is of course not yet finished with the hapless Don. His putative hour of death has evoked the musical phraseology of the *finale ultimo,* yet its unusually modest scale (the orchestra never rises above *piano*) and restrained vocal and orchestral textures lead us to suspect that this is not really the end.

Another groundswell seems to materialize in a more traditional context, the last-act Finale of the opera (1869 version), beginning with Leonara's A♭

melody "Lieta poss'io precederti." Once again, it forms the second period of a lyrical, minor/major binary structure. It is still a relatively intimate ensemble, with only three soloists and no chorus, and again is restrained in terms of orchestral texture and dynamics. And as if further to compensate for the traditional context, the musical structure has been modified, its phrases shrunken to the smallest possible proportions: 4 + 4 measures altogether, with Alvaro's contrasting phrase appended ("Tu mi condanni a vivere") (Ex. 5.10). The repetition gets only as far as the *b*-phrase, which had provided only the slightest tonal contrast in the first place, and then gives way to freer cadential material. Leonora's end is not the grandiose death and transfiguration of such earlier heroines as Giovanna d'Arco; the tone here remains one of remorse and resignation.[13] The intimate scale of the musical phrases and the ethereal, high string sounds look forward to the end of *Aida*. The familiarity of the musico-dramatic context—the central period of a *finale ultimo* ensemble, concerned with the expiring heroine—permits this large degree of modification without entirely vitiating the identity of the groundswell. (At the same time, we must not assume that such a passage was consciously conceived by Verdi as a modification of a fixed device; the musical kinship to "O terra, addio," which is no longer a groundswell, is perhaps more significant here than that to the full-scale groundswells of *Giovanna d'Arco* or *La traviata*.)

Like the *Forza* Duettino, the Quartet in Act IV of *Don Carlos* recalls a conventional dramatic situation outside the usual concerted-finale context. (And like *Simon Boccanegra*, it is another groundswell passage for which we have Verdi's second thoughts from his latest period, the 1884 revision.) The situation here is very similar, of course, to the Act II Finale of *La traviata*. The heroine, Elisabeth, has just been subjected to the violent reproaches of a jealous husband/consort; she swoons, awakes, and delivers a pathetic speech which incites the others present to join in an ensemble, each having sung a stanza more or less alone in the interim. In this case, Verdi has modified both dramatic context and musical scheme. In the 1867 version, the usual tension-building phrase (*b*) is replaced by a kind of lyrical parenthesis in G♭ (linking up with several quasi-modulations to this key area earlier in the ensemble) (Ex. 5.11). This static contrasting phrase somewhat alters the essential dynamic of the device,

---

13. This trio does not exist, of course, in the first version (1862), where the opera ends with Alvaro's somewhat preposterous suicide leap, to a chorus of monks singing "Miserere," a restless series of modulations, and chromatic rumblings in the bass. Verdi's revised Finale replaced one that was dramatically frenetic and musically disjointed with one colored, it has been suggested, by "Manzonian" spiritual resignation (and with the key changed from E to A♭). The more classically balanced form of the minor/major romanza is thus appropriate to the tone of the new ending.

The terse economy of the groundswell here perhaps reflects Verdi's initial reservations about a lyrical trio-finale: "De Lauzières wanted to do a trio like the one in *Ernani*," he writes to Léon Escudier in 1864, "but in *Ernani* the action continues during the entire trio, whereas here it finishes just as the trio begins; therefore it's pointless to write one" (letter of 29 July 1864, *Rivista musicale italiana* XXXV [1928], 180; trans. Budden, *The Operas of Verdi* II, 436).

EXAMPLE 5.10. The groundswell of the Act IV Finale of
La forza del destino (1869 version).

EXAMPLE 5.11. The groundswell of the Act IV Quartet, *Don Carlos* (1867 version).

and it is perhaps the lack of the usual harmonic activity here that led Verdi to omit the customary repetition. Like the tonal connections to the first part of the ensemble (G♭), the sixteenth-note activity in the lower parts recalls earlier material: the accompaniment figure that opens the Quartet, and the nervous triplet sixteenths of Rodrigue's aside, "Il faut agir, et voici l'heure."

In the final revision, the Milan *Don Carlo,* this Quartet was considerably tightened up and rewritten. There is no G♭ episode in the groundswell, since the earlier modulations to this key have also been excised. As a pitch, however, the G♭ (minor-sixth degree) remains significant; Verdi now emphasizes the modal ambiguities within the overall number, which begins to take on aspects of the minor/major binary romanza form so often associated with the groundswell. The contrasting phrase (*b*) has been reduced to little more than a prolongation of the tonic $^6_4$, but it is interesting that Verdi has inserted a new secondary dominant to enliven the cadence at the same point that he did in the revised *Boccanegra* example (there a V$^4_3$/III, here V$^4_3$/VI, at the [x] in Example 5.12).

Unlike the *Boccanegra* revision, the groundswell here retains its low profile; though shortened, the formula is still not repeated. It is well known that Verdi generally cooled off the political side of Rodrigo's character in the revision, and Rodrigo is accordingly deemphasized in the Quartet, while greater attention focuses on Elisabeth. Similarly, and interestingly, the motivic connections have been transferred from his part to hers. Rodrigo's anxious sixteenth-notes are gone, but an even clearer relation is established between Elisabeth's line in the *b*-phrase and her first words in the ensemble, "Che avvenne? O ciel!" (Ex. 5.13).

Perhaps even more significant than the musical and contextual modifications presented by the *Don Carlos* Quartet is the fact that Verdi refrained from using it in a more prominent and typical spot, the Grand Finale of Act III. Instead, when Carlo rashly threatens the king at the climax of this Finale, the expected formula is replaced by a hushed six-bar reminiscence of the Carlo-Rodrigo Friendship Duet. By defending the King at the critical moment, Rodrigo has in a sense defused the groundswell situation, and the stately procession is quickly resumed.

IX

The third-act Finale of *Otello* offered Verdi an irresistible opportunity to turn once again, and for the last time, to this now nearly obsolete musico-dramaturgical convention. Here again is the wronged heroine, now within the traditional groundswell context of a full-scale concerted Finale. While the dramatic situation may recall both the *Traviata* and *Don Carlos* examples, the musical conception is at once grander and more original. While the ensemble may at first give the impression of a slightly old-fashioned, large set-piece, its construc-

EXAMPLE 5.12. The groundswell of the Act IV Quartet, *Don Carlo* (1884 version).

EXAMPLE 5.13. Motivic connections in Act IV Quartet, *Don Carlo*.

tion is actually far less conventional than we might assume. Verdi modifies the local harmonic pattern of the groundswell and integrates it into a larger, more complex formal scheme, so that one is almost forced to rely on the situation and the metrical arrangement of the melody to identify a groundswell at all.

The largo concertato is precipitated, of course, by Otello's rabid outburst, "A terra, e piangi!" followed by a grinding series of modulations in the low brass; a familiar tableau of stupefaction and horror provides the background for Desdemona's sweetly intoned lament. The groundswell occupies the concluding period of a (very condensed) tripartite structure, rather than a binary one. The first period consists of Desdemona's broken exclamations ("A terra! sì . . . nel livido / Fango"), which modulate to a sweeping melody in the dominant, "E un dì sul mio sorriso."[14] The phrase-structure of this second, brief period already suggests a groundswell, an *a-a'* pair followed by chromatically descending diminished-sevenths (*b*). But a more complete groundswell formula follows, picking up this chromatic descent in both its *a* and *b* members (Ex. 5.14, at the [x]). The tonal scheme is unusual. The initial phrases this time occur in a foreign key area (F), while the *b*-phrase begins on a tonic $^6_4$ chord, functioning momentarily as ♭III of F. The overall tonal progression of Desdemona's solo section is thus A♭–E♭–F–A♭, so that the harmonic swell is extended over the entire group instead of just its middle phrase. Verdi was undoubtedly not willing to risk the banality of the groundswell in its primitive guise, and this added dimension of harmonic interest prevents the listener from tuning out Desdemona's plight as just a well-worn cliché.

Equally unusual is the manner in which the groundswell fits into the overall structure of this huge ensemble. The initial exposition has involved only one voice. The repeat, with the full complement of soloists and chorus, is postponed until the very end of the largo, creating a large-scale symmetry but also imbuing the repeated material with greater structural weight. In between these two thematic pillars Verdi constructs a gradual textural and dynamic crescendo, starting from an unaccompanied vocal quartet. Chart 5.1, in which Desdemona's tripartite material is designated as *A1–3*, outlines the form of the whole movement.

Verdi and Boito pondered at length about this Act III ensemble. The composer was not willing to forego the impressive musical and scenic weight that a largo concertato, that "last bastion of artificiality," could provide.[15] Yet neither Verdi nor Boito could be satisfied with an extended frozen-action effect. In the end, they managed to embed a thread of action in the number in the form of Iago's sotto-voce machinations—sotto voce in terms of dramatic presentation, at least; it would require a minor miracle of vocal projection fully to articulate these lines above the commotion. But perhaps the real dramatic action is constituted by Otello's silently kindling fury—depicted through the inexorable rise in musical temperature across this ensemble—which finally explodes to interrupt the great unison cadence (m. 97, "Fuggite!"). Verdi has capitalized on the traditional orchestral hammer-stroke that signals the fast-tempo denouement by putting it in Otello's hands, so to speak.

This moment normally involves an abrupt change of mode, but here the chorus has already swung into A♭ minor, which Verdi now harshly juxtaposes with an E^7 chord. He also skillfully manipulates our perception of the groundswell within the return of the *A* material. By replacing the brief chromatic sequences

14. The similarity to earlier situations, which extends to such features as the high, light-textured string writing, is noted by Budden, who relates the passage to "the tradition of lyrical transfiguration into which wronged Verdian heroines often escape" (*The Operas of Verdi* III, 385).

15. Budden, *The Operas of Verdi* III, 306. Budden offers a detailed account of the genesis of the libretto for the Act III Finale (306–14).

EXAMPLE 5.14. The groundswell of the Act III Finale, *Otello*.

that had originally provided the contrast in *A2* ("Ed or . . . l'angoscia in viso") with a dense six-measure contrasting section, drawn from the end of *C'*, he may lead us to think of *A2* and *A3* combined as a single large groundswell idea. In this way, Desdemona's "E un dì sul mio sorriso" becomes the initial tonic-dominant phrase-pair (as it had first suggested itself), the new contrasting section (mm. 83–88) functions as the tension-building *b*-phrase, and the F-major *A3* phrase (now starting in a $\frac{6}{4}$ position, *ff*) becomes an extended cadential phrase, together with the proper Ab cadence from measure 93 on:

Groundswell phrase	*Measures/key*
a, a'	79–80, 81–82
	Eb
b	83–88 (*animando*)
	C min., D min., E min., G min.
c	89–96 (*ritenuto*)
	F–Ab major/minor

CHART 5.1. *Otello*, Act III, largo, A♭.

section:	A1	A2	A3 (groundswell)	B (Quartet)	A2'
key:	A♭	E♭	F–A♭	A♭	E♭
mm.:	1–9	10–17	18–25	26–33	34–37

section:	C	B' (w/choral *pertichini*)	+ extension	C'
key:	e♭*	B♭*	D♭*	c*
mm.:	38–48	49–52	53–60	61–71

section:	A1'	A2' (+ material from C')	A3' (groundswell)
key:	A♭	E♭–c	F–A♭–a♭
mm.:	72–78	79–88 (cf. 67–70)	89–96

* Modulatory or unstable passages.

By using the groundswell within a thoroughly conventional context, the large-scale largo concertato, Verdi is able to enrich it harmonically and endow it with greater formal significance and complexity without the risk of completely obscuring its identity. The effect is an appearance of conventionality that belies, on closer inspection, a truly original and powerful musical design.[16] It is a grandiose and traditionally operatic effect, perhaps not "Shakespeare," but certainly Verdi.[17]

We may still wonder whether such a convention can fit comfortably in an opera that has generally outgrown such techniques. Is it properly at home only in the "naive" style of Bellini or early Verdi? By the time of *Otello*, it cannot be denied that Verdi has become a somewhat more "sentimental" composer (*pace*

16. Cf. Joseph Kerman, *Opera as Drama* (New York, 1956), 152–53.

17. Some mention must be made of the revisions this concertato underwent for the 1894 Paris production. The piece as a whole was scaled down, in length and general volume, largely with an eye to making Iago's crucial participation more evident—the "dramatic truth" of the ensemble depends entirely on this, Verdi stated. It has also been suggested that Verdi wished to compensate for the added length of the ballet in this act (Carlo Gatti, Spike Hughes) and that he feared the Parisian cast lacked the skill to control the complicated textures of the original ensemble (Francis Toye; see Budden, *The Operas of Verdi* III, 406–12). In any case, it should be noted that Verdi never gave the Paris revisions a "definitive" status.

The expanded groundswell effect we have described is consequently scaled down, but not eradicated. The most significant modification is the elimination of the F-major parenthesis ("Quel sol sereno e vivido") from the opening group, which certainly skews the grand symmetry of Verdi's original structure. But the "new" appearance of this music at the climax of the revised ensemble (original m. 89) still serves as a substitute cadential $^6_4$ of the large-scale reprise, adding extra weight to the (delayed) repetition of the groundswell.

Sir Isaiah Berlin). Yet the *Otello* Finale can exert a great impact, and one not out of keeping with the style of the opera as a whole. After having long approached the device with an almost apologetic attitude, often reducing it to the smallest possible proportions (as in the revised Finale to *La forza del destino*), Verdi has returned it here to full-blown, grandiose proportions. As with the cabaletta in *Aida,* Verdi returned to a conventional technique where the dramatic situation justified it—and where it simply seems to work. But in this case, he has taken the convention apart and reconstructed it along broader lines to fashion what is arguably the most impressive of his large-scale ensembles.[18]

18. Effective parodies of the groundswell may be found in Sullivan's *Trial by Jury* (1875: "A nice dilemma"—one of the opera's most popular numbers) and *The Sorcerer* (1877: "O marvellous illusion," Act I Finale).

Chapter 6

Isolde's Narrative
From Hauptmotiv *to Tonal Model*

MATTHEW BROWN

Few composers have written more extensively or more self-consciously about the nature of unity in art than Richard Wagner. Spurred on by a belief that traditional number operas represent an "arbitrary conglomerate of separate, smaller forms," he conceived of a new dramatic form: a continuous organic whole uniting word, feeling, and tone, whose individual sections shape one another in a mutually dependent way.[1] In Wagner's words, "This drama, both in content and in form, consists of a chain of . . . organic members conditioning, supplementing, and supporting one another, exactly like the organic members of the human body."[2] How, then, did Wagner achieve this goal? How did he solve the compositional problem of constructing episodes that are internally unified yet still promote the continuity and coherence of the whole?

We will address these questions by examining the structure of one episode, Isolde's Narrative from *Tristan und Isolde,* Act I, Scene 3. As a test case, the Narrative has certain obvious strengths. Dramatically, it is clearly one of the most important sections at the beginning of the opera and is both self-contained and quite distinct from the surrounding action (Kurwenal's Song, Scene 2, Brangäne's Consolation, Scene 3). The immediate purpose of the Narrative is to describe the events that preceded the opening of the curtain and

I would like to thank David Lewin, James Webster, Arnold Whittall, and Jennifer Williams Brown for comments on earlier versions of this paper.

1. "Ein willkürliches Konglomerat einzelner kleinerer Gesamtstücksformen": Richard Wagner, "Eine Mittheilung an meine Freunde," *Gesammelte Schriften und Dichtungen* IV (Leipzig 1871–1873, 1883), 391 (henceforth *GS*); translated by William Ashton Ellis as *Richard Wagner's Prose Writings* (London, 1892), I, 367 (henceforth *PW*).

2. "Das den Inhalt und der Form nach aus einer Kette solcher organischer Glieder besteht, die sich gegenseitig so bedingen, ergänzen und tragen müssen, wie die organischen Glieder des menschlichen Leibes": Richard Wagner, *Oper und Drama,* in *GS* IV, 245.

thereby explain Isolde's bitter rage in the first three scenes. On a deeper level, the section establishes the fundamental conflict between loyalty and love that motivates the entire drama. The significance of the Narrative to the overall structure of the opera can be gauged by Wagner's use of the material later in the opera: the music and text recur at a crucial moment toward the end of Act I and again in Tristan's Act III delirium.

Musically, the complex two-part structure of the Narrative offers a good opportunity to study the ways Wagner balances the needs for large- and for small-scale coherence. Moreover, this episode provides an ideal basis for discussing many of the general problems faced by Wagner analysts, both surveying familiar approaches and testing new ones.

Obviously, before any detailed analysis of the Narrative can be done one must digest a tremendous volume of textual and musical material and examine how the two elements interact. To a large extent these problems were solved at the turn of the century in the surveys of writers such as Heinrich Porges and Karl Grunsky.[3] Once the essential geography had been charted, Alfred Lorenz and Robert Bailey then tackled the more perplexing task of identifying patterns in the large-scale tonal and motivic design.[4] As we shall see, although both writers accept that the Narrative is built from large tonal units that correspond to the two-part structure of the text, they disagree on what those sections are. Whereas Lorenz divides the episode into two periods, the first a *Bogen* form in E minor, the second—including the Curse—a *Bar* form in C major, Bailey suggests that the two parts combine to make a single cycle in E with the Curse as a new section.

Important issues that have not yet been raised, however, force us to reconsider the validity of the readings by Lorenz and Bailey. First, in separating themes from their harmonic and contrapuntal contexts, both writers underestimate the extent to which the formal function of a motive depends on its tonal and voice-leading properties. While they recognize that Part 1 is based on the "Sick Tristan" theme and Part 2 on the "Zorn" theme, neither examines the structure of these themes to see how their voice-leading properties dictate the ways they are manipulated to produce larger tonal spans. Lorenz and Bailey are by no means the only commentators to sidestep this issue: Wagner himself

---

3. For discussions of the function and importance of Isolde's Narrative see Heinrich Porges, "Tristan und Isolde," *Bayreuther Blätter* XXV (1902), 196–98; Karl Grunsky, "Das Vorspiel und der erste Akt von 'Tristan und Isolde,' " *Wagner-Jahrbuch* II (1907), 254–62; Ernest Newman, *The Wagner Operas* (New York, 1949), 223–36; Joseph Kerman, *Opera as Drama* (New York, 1956), 210–11; Jack Stein, *Richard Wagner and the Synthesis of the Arts* (Detroit, 1960); H. F. Garten, *Wagner the Dramatist* (London, 1977), 107–8; Carl Dahlhaus, *Richard Wagner's Music Dramas,* trans. Mary Whittall (Cambridge, England, 1979), 51–52.

4. Alfred Lorenz, *Das Geheimnis der Form bei Richard Wagner* III (Berlin, 1926), 38–45; Robert Bailey, "The Genesis of *Tristan und Isolde*," diss. Princeton University, 1969, 151–52, 191–206. In a brief but fascinating article, Joseph Schalk proposes that the Narrative forms a single period in E major/minor: "Das Gesetz der Tonalität," *Bayreuther Blätter* XI (1888–1889), 194–96.

complained that his friend Hans von Wolzogen "viewed the characteristics of what he calls my 'Leitmotive' rather in the light of their dramatic significance than in that of their bearing on musical construction."[5]

Second, by identifying keys purely on the basis of local cadences rather than by large-scale prolongations, Lorenz and Bailey oversimplify the analysis of the Narrative in terms of closed tonal units. No one would deny that the coherence of the Narrative depends on tonal as well as motivic recall; however, as Carl Dahlhaus and Anthony Newcomb stress, the recurrence of particular cadence points, especially over extended periods of time, does not itself guarantee the overall harmonic unity of an episode.[6] According to Newcomb: "With Wagner one can no longer simply assume the shaping and connecting power of functional tonality alone over sizeable stretches of time. It must be demonstrated in the music itself . . . [tonality] must be built up carefully through the small scale to the middle to the large."[7]

Finally, in stressing the tonal coherence of the episode, Lorenz and Bailey circumvent the difficult problems posed by Wagner's persistently chromatic style. Lorenz tries to apply Riemann's theory of functions, a theory that is quite unable to deal with the extreme chromaticism of the Narrative's second part. Bailey, though presupposing a fully chromatic tonal theory, offers no mechanism for determining hierarchies among secondary key areas, a fact that undermines his popular notion of double tonality.[8]

5. "Ich habe nur des einen meiner jüngeren Freunden zu gedenken, der das Charakteristische der von ihm sogenannten 'Leitmotive' mehr ihrer dramatischen Bedeutsamkeit und Wirksamkeit nach, als ihre Berwerthung für den musikalischen Satzbau in das Auge fassend, ausführlicher in Betrachtung nahm": Richard Wagner, "Über die Anwendung der Musik auf das Drama," *GS* X, 241–42; trans. *PW* VI, 367.

6. Carl Dahlhaus, *Between Romanticism and Modernism,* trans. Mary Whittall (Berkeley and Los Angeles, 1980), 40–78; Anthony Newcomb, "The Birth of Music out of the Spirit of Drama," *19th-Century Music* V (1981–1982), 38–66. For another appraisal of Lorenz, see David R. Murray, "Major Approaches to Wagner's Musical Style: A Critique," *Music Review* XXXIX (1978), 211–22.

7. Newcomb, "The Birth of Music," 51. Dahlhaus goes further than Newcomb and suggests that in Wagner's music tonal forces do not generally operate on the large scale: "As they change in quick and often 'rhapsodic' succession, the keys, or fragmentary allusions to keys, do not always relate to a constant center, around which they are to be imagined as simultaneously grouped; they should rather be seen as joined together like the links in a chain, without there necessarily being any other connection between the first and third links than the second": *Between Romanticism and Modernism,* 66. For criticisms of this view, see Newcomb, "The Birth of Music," 48–50; Murray, "Major Approaches," 218–20; and Christopher Wintle, "Issues in Dahlhaus," *Music Analysis* I (1982), 344–50.

8. Bailey, for example, proposes that in late-nineteenth-century music, composers worked with twelve keys of interchangeable mode rather than with twenty-four major and minor keys (see "The Genesis of *Tristan,*" 149). Schoenberg in his theory of regions had, of course, attempted to demonstrate that all twelve chromatic keys might be derived from the home key (see Arnold Schoenberg, *The Structural Functions of Harmony* [New York, 1969], 19; also Heinrich Schenker, *Harmonielehre: Neue musikalische Theorien und Phantasien I* [Stuttgart, 1906]). According to Bailey's notion of double tonality, many late-nineteenth-century works center, not on a single key, but on a pair of tonics often a minor third apart, the locus classicus for such procedures being the *Einleitung* to Act I of *Tristan,* which is in the double tonic A/C. Whether these two tonics operate at the same level throughout the piece is debatable; most "double tonics" could also be explained as third mixtures within some principal key (see "The Genesis of *Tristan,*" 239), and Bailey's *Prelude and Transfiguration from "Tristan und Isolde"* (New York, 1985), 113–46.

Of the various tools available for handling these issues, one of the most useful is Schenkerian theory. On the first issue, Schenker's methods are particularly well suited to showing how thematic successions interact with their harmonic environment. On the second, his notion of *Schichten* provides a flexible means of identifying the hierarchic significance of particular inflections of modulations. And on the final issue, Schenker's theory of harmonic relations—contrary to the recent claims of Gregory Proctor and Patrick McCreless—is intrinsically fully chromatic and hence far more applicable to highly chromatic passages than rival theories such as those of Riemann.[9] My aim, then, is to reconsider the structure of the Narrative from a Schenkerian perspective and to take another look at the issues of tonal/motivic interaction, large-scale tonal planning, and chromaticism. In particular, I hope to show that each *Hauptmotiv* or form of a *Hauptmotiv* serves a specific formal function and that each articulates distinct voice-leading spans and motivic complexes.

Although a Schenkerian analysis can demonstrate the complex tonal and motivic connections that lie beneath the surface of Wagner's music, it is a moot point whether these operas display the sort of deep-level coherence that Schenker ascribed to organic masterworks.[10] In dealing with the Narrative, at least, I tend to support Schenker's claim that the structure breaks down at deeper levels of the middleground. Yet, unlike Schenker, I do not regard this feature as an inherent flaw in the music. Rather, I believe that tonal modeling provided Wagner with one ingenious way of creating self-sufficient episodes that can be transplanted and transformed at subsequent points in the opera—in short, with a way of achieving the type of organic unity he sought.

9. According to Gregory Proctor, "Schenker was forced to narrow his system to the inclusion of Mozart and the exclusion of Wagner": "Technical Bases of Nineteenth-Century Chromatic Tonality," diss. Princeton University, 1978, 7. Proctor proposes that there are two main types of tonal practice: "classical diatonic tonality," and a tonal practice based on "one chromatic scale from which all diatonic scales are derived as subsets" (iii–v). Patrick McCreless endorses Proctor's view in his recent article "Ernst Kurth and the Analysis of Chromatic Music of the Late Nineteenth Century," *Music Theory Spectrum* V (1983), 60–62. While Proctor and McCreless are justified in distinguishing stylistically between diatonic tonality and chromatic tonality, Schenker himself appears to have made no such distinction. In *Harmonielehre*—admittedly an early work—he conceived tonality as a single, fully chromatic system (*Harmonielehre*, see the tables on p. 395—the second table, which contains a typographical error in the original, is cut from the English translation). Nevertheless, in the Introduction to *Der freie Satz* Schenker reiterated his view that tonality is fully chromatic, in a sentence reminiscent of the *Harmonielehre*: "Eine wirklich gegründete Tonalität leitet auch das grösste Mass von Chromen sicher in den Grundklang zurück": *Der freie Satz* (Vienna, 1935), 5. See my article, "The Diatonic and the Chromatic in Schenker's Theory of Harmonic Relations," *Journal of Music Theory* XXX, no. 1 (1986), 1–31.

10. It is important to stress that Schenker criticized Wagner not for writing music that goes beyond the realm of tonality but because he failed to coordinate the dissonances and chromaticism at the middle ground—see, for example, *Harmonielehre*, para. 89; *Das Meisterwerk in der Musik* II (Munich, 1926), 29–30, 54. For a listing of Schenker's analyses of extracts from Wagner, see Larry Laskowski, *Heinrich Schenker: An Annotated Index to His Analyses of Musical Works* (New York, 1978), 154–57. Newcomb exaggerates the absence of graphs by other Schenkerians. Besides William Mitchell's well-known graph of the Prelude to *Tristan,* see Adele Katz, *Challenge to Musical Tradition* (New York, 1945), 194–247; Felix Salzer and Carl Schachter, *Counterpoint in Composition* (New York, 1969), 448–57; Robert P. Morgan, "Dissonant Prolon-

*   *   *

Before considering the Narrative as a whole, let us first examine each of its two parts separately. It is perhaps easiest to begin by discussing the text, since the poem provided Wagner with the essential skeleton for his music. Chart 6.1 gives the entire text of Part 1, indicating the major sections and their location in the score.

Part 1 has five main sections, each one built from complete sentences of six or twelve lines and each revealing a distinctive pattern of line length, rhyme, and word sound. Set sometime in the past, the first two sections describe how Tristan was wounded in mortal combat with Morold and came to Ireland to seek Isolde's celebrated powers of healing. Though he was disguised as "Tantris," she soon recognized him and intended to stab him in revenge for the death of Morold. To reinforce the basic rhetorical form of the Narrative, Isolde describes these events in a regular and detached manner—the lines are almost naively metrical and the verbs are all in the third person (she even refers to herself in the third person). In Section 3, Isolde becomes more violent (the verbs are now in the first person) as she recalls the rage that made her seize the sword to kill Tristan. This outburst quickly subsides in Section 4 when she remembers the peculiar glance Tristan gave her that moved her to drop the blade. As if to set this section apart from the surrounding material, Wagner abandons the prevailing metrical and rhyme schemes and splits the section into three sentences: the first leads up to the glance, the second describes the dropping of the sword, and the last tells of Tristan's recovery. We are jolted back to the present at the start of Section 5 with Brangäne's interjection and Isolde's sarcastic quotation of Kurwenal's Song from Scene 2.[11]

Perhaps the most striking feature of Wagner's music for Part 1 is its almost total saturation with the "Sick Tristan" theme, a figure that appears here for the first time in the opera. "Sick Tristan" recurs some nineteen times within a hundred bars; in the few places where the motive is not stated explicitly, its presence can still be felt through a variety of related or derived gestures. Most writers accept that the statements of the theme appear in two main forms that Lorenz

---

gation: Theoretical and Compositional Precedents," *Journal of Music Theory* XX (1976), 62–72; Robert Gauldin, "Wagner's Parody Technique: 'Träume' and the *Tristan* Love Duet," *Music Theory Spectrum* I (1979), 35–42.

11. Significantly, Brangäne's interjection is missing from Wagner's prose draft. Indeed, she interrupts Isolde much earlier in the narrative, claiming to have recognized Tristan. This is, of course, the opposite of what Brangäne says in the finished poem (see *GS* XI, 329). For a brief survey of the differences between the finished poem and the story as transmitted by Gottfried von Strassburg, see Garten, *Wagner the Dramatist,* 107–8.

		MOTIVE
	IS.:	
Section 1	Von einem Kahn,	S1
(31/2/2)	der klein und arm	
	an Irlands Küsten schwamm,	
	darinnen krank	S1
	ein siecher Mann	
	elend im Sterben lag.	
	Isoldes Kunst	"Sehnsucht"
	ward ihm bekannt,	
	mit Heilsalben	
	und Balsamsaft	
	der Wunde, die ihn plagte,	S1
	getreulich pflag sie da.	
Section 2	Der „Tantris"	"Tantris"
(32/1/4)	mit sorgender List sich nannte,	
	als „Tristan"	
	Isold' ihn bald erkannte,	Kurwenal
	da in des Müß'gen Schwerte	
	eine Scharte sie gewahrte,	
	darin genau	
	sich fügt' ein Splitter,	
	den einst im Haupt	
	des Iren-Ritter,	
	zum Hohn ihr heimgesandt,	
	mit kund'ger Hand sie fand.	
Section 3	Da schrie's mir auf	S2
(33/2/1)	aus tiefstem Grund!	
	Mit dem hellen Schwert	S2
	ich vor ihm stund,	
	an ihm, dem Überfrechen,	M1
	Herrn Morolds Tod zu rächen.	S2

CHART 6.1. Text divisions in Part 1.

continued

CHART 6.1. *continued.*

Section 4	Von seinem Lager	M1
(34/1/3)	blickt' er her —	M2
	nicht auf das Schwert,	M1
	nicht auf die Hand —	M2
	er sah mir in die Augen.	"Sehnsucht"
	Seines Elendes	Glance
	jammerte mich! —	
	Das Schwert — ich ließ es fallen!	
	Die Morold schlug, die Wunde,	M1
	sie heilt' ich, daß er gesunde	M1 variant
	und heim nach Hause kehre —	S2
	mit dem Blick mich nicht mehr beschwere!	
Section 5	**BR.:**	
(35/3/4)	O Wunder! Wo hatt' ich die Augen?	S2
	Der Gast, den einst	M3
	ich pflegen half?	M3
	IS.:	
	Sein Lob hörtest due eben:	Kurwenal
	„Hei! Unser Held Tristan" —	
	der war jener traur'ge Mann.	S1

rather quaintly dubbed "Stormy" and "Mild."[12] Example 6.1 gives both forms reduced to their basic outlines.

It is clear from Example 6.1 that both versions begin with the characteristic $^6_3$ sonority followed by chromatic contrary motion in the outer parts. Rhythmically, the top part moves in a distinctive ♩. ♪ ♩. ♪ pattern, with the accompaniment in triplets and the bass in even half-notes (or ♪ 𝄾). The two forms deviate, however, on the seventh beat: whereas "Stormy" continues the chromatic lines to converge on a major triad (which completes the first phrase of an antecedent-consequent pair), "Mild" ends here with a half-cadence. Since the half-cadence

12. Lorenz, *Das Geheimnis der Form* III, 41. Some twenty years earlier Karl Grunsky identified four forms—forms I–III correspond to transpositions of "Stormy" to E, C, and G, while form IV corresponds to "Mild": "Das Vorspiel," 254–56. For other brief discussions of the harmonic structure of the "Sick Tristan" motive, see Georg Capellan, "Harmonik und Melodik bei Richard Wagner," *Bayreuther Blätter* XXV (1902), 13; Emil Ergo, *Über Richard Wagners Harmonik und Melodik* (Leipzig, 1914), 144; Ernst Kurth, *Romantische Harmonik und ihre Krise in Wagners "Tristan"* (Berlin, 1919), 224–25, 553–54; and Horst Scharschuch, *Gesamtanalyse der Harmonik von Richard Wagners Musikdrama "Tristan und Isolde"* (Regensberg, 1963), 10.

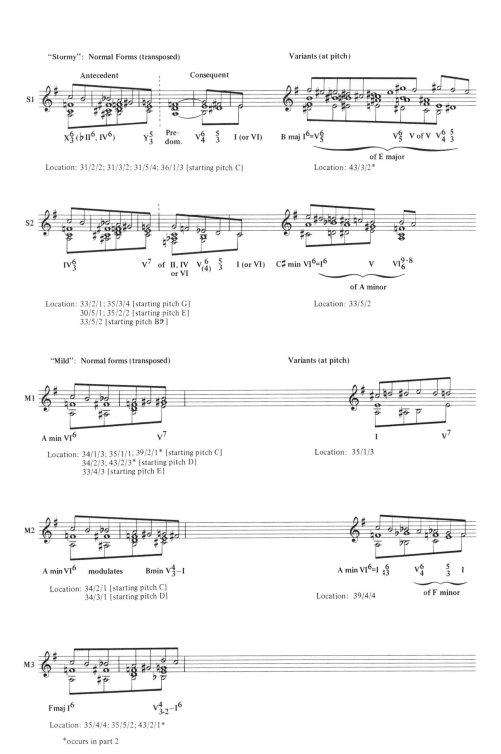

EXAMPLE 6.1. "Sick Tristan" theme.

can occur on various degrees relative to starting pitch, the "Mild" form can modulate, sequence, or repeat itself in the same key.

The second phrase of "Stormy" is basically a cadence pattern, V^6_4–$^7_{5\atop3}$–I (VI). The time span between the end of phrase 1 and the $^6_4$ of phrase 2 can be filled in several ways, thereby producing a modulation to almost any key. In S1, we find a simple pre-dominant at this point (V of V, IV or ♯IV). In S2, the scheme is more elaborate: the major triad closing phrase 1 is reinterpreted as a dominant seventh that resolves at the beginning of phrase 2. The latter sonority can serve as II, IV, or VI of the new key and may also be followed by other pre-dominants before reaching the cadential $^6_4$.

The syntactic differences between "Stormy" and "Mild" also have metrical implications. Whereas the former makes a four-bar phrase starting on the third beat of a 4/4 bar, the latter initiates a two-measure unit beginning on the downbeat. Since the final triad of "Mild" occurs halfway through the second bar, the resolution and next phrase can start on the following downbeat.

Two aspects of "Sick Tristan" make it an ideal building block for large-scale structures. First, the shifting chromatic character of the antecedent phrase and the flexibility of the cadence allow Wagner to mold the theme into various tonal contexts. For example, the initial $^6_3$ may be appear locally as I^6, ♭II^6, IV^6, or VI^6. Sometimes, however, the larger function of these sonorities may be quite different; for example, since the statements beginning with VI^6 often complete emphatic perfect cadences, the VI^6 may serve as a substitute tonic, with the root in the bass and the third in the soprano.

Second, since the rhythmic and melodic profile of "Sick Tristan" resembles that of other motives, Wagner is able to merge one theme unobtrusively into another. Even at the earliest stages of composition, Wagner decided to highlight the resemblance between the "Mild" form and the "Sehnsucht" motive near the start of Part 1—as Bailey notes, he sketched the two together in Mathilde Wesendonck's copy of the poem.[13] More significant, in the composition draft for Section 4 Wagner originally included a statement of "Mild" in 34/3/3, but in later stages he replaced this theme with a statement of the "Sehnsucht" motive that seems to grow out of the "Mild" theme's inner parts.[14] "Sick Tristan" is also related to the "Glance" motive, which is later woven into the Narrative, and more remotely to new gestures such as the A-major tune from the end of Part 2 (41/3/3). Striking as they may be, these family relationships among motives do not undermine the independence of each gesture. On the contrary, throughout the opera Wagner is extremely careful to preserve the particular dramatic and musical associations of each theme.

13. In the ensuing discussion, (00/0/0) refers to page number, system number, and measure number within the system in the widely available vocal score arranged by Karl Klindworth and published in the United States by G. Schirmer. Bailey quotes the sketches in his Example 10: "The Genesis of *Tristan*," 57.

14. See Bailey's transcription in example 14, "The Genesis of *Tristan*," 195.

While it is certainly interesting to identify and compare the two forms of the *Hauptmotiv,* such observations would have little significance if Wagner did not exploit the differences on some larger level. Indeed, as we shall see, each form is used to articulate distinct middleground spans that reinforce the structure and moods of the five sections of the poem. Thus, after its initial appearance in a brief introduction (30/5/1), the "Stormy" form becomes the prime agent for tonal and motivic development in Sections 1/2, 3, and 5. The "Mild" form, similarly prefigured at the end of Section 3 (33/4/3), is primarily reserved for Section 4, a unit that is exceptional in other respects as well.

As is shown in the voice-leading graph (Ex. 6.2), Sections 1 and 2 together form a unit in E minor that is supported by a large-scale arpeggiation of the tonic triad (indicated by lower beamed notes), with chromatic passing notes between the G and the B. E minor is, in fact, prepared in the introduction: having reached C♯ in 30/4/3–30/5/1, the first statement of "Sick Tristan" takes us to B major (31/1/2–3). This sonority is immediately reinterpreted as the dominant of E in the descending scale B–A–G–F♯–(E) of 31/1/1–2. Although the decisive tonic chord is withheld until 31/4/2, the first eight measures of the Narrative clearly implicate E minor.

Section 1 (31/2/2–32/1/4) contains four rather square phrases that seem to mirror the matter-of-fact tone Isolde has adopted to begin her story. The vocal phrases neatly match those of the orchestra, a correspondence that gradually breaks down as the Narrative progresses (and as Isolde's self-control crumbles). After two statements of S1 in E minor—the first ending deceptively, the second reaching full closure—Section 1 continues with the "Sehnsucht" motive and concludes with "Sick Tristan," this time cadencing in the relative major, G. Section 2 (32/1/4–33/2/1) then balances the previous motion from E to G with a long linear progression in parallel sixths, from the A♭ and A of the Tantris/Tristan passage (32/2/1), via A♯ (V⁶₅ of V) to C (augmented sixth), and back to the dominant of E for the final word "fand." This dominant immediately resolves at the beginning of Section 3, with the orchestral statement of S2 starting on G in the upper voice (33/2/1).

The bass pattern underlying Sections 1 and 2 is clearly framed by statements of S1 starting on C in the upper line and S2 on G. Significantly, Wagner uses the same two thematic gestures, in reverse order, to articulate the identical bass pattern in Section 5 (35/3/4–36/3/1; Ex. 6.2). The opening statement of S2, which marks Brangäne's interjection, begins in the tonic E but modulates to G at the end of its consequent phrase. This local tonic is then prolonged by two statements of the "Mild" theme and by Isolde's quotation of Kurwenal's Song, "Hei! unser Held Tristan!" from Scene 2. E minor is eventually restored, not by the involved chromatic sixths heard in Section 2, but by a final statement of S1 whose bass rises chromatically from A via A♯, B, C, and C♯ to the dominant B and a cadence on E at 36/3/1. In short, Section 5 offers a recomposition of the underlying progression of Sections 1 and 2.

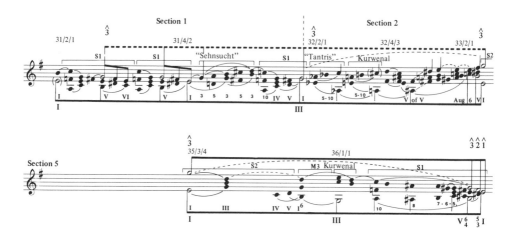

EXAMPLE 6.2. Voice-leading models in Sections 1, 2, and 5.

Just as Wagner is consistent in his larger treatment of "Stormy," so is he in the handling of the "Mild" theme in Section 4 (34/1/3–35/3/4; Ex. 6.3). Again we see clear signs of tonal modeling, but this time the model, like the theme itself, is much simpler. As was mentioned earlier, Section 4 has three sentences. Wagner captures this three-part form musically in an extremely subtle manner: he sets the first and third sentences to the same tonal model and fashions the central sentence, the mesmerizing "Glance," as an interpolation.

The structure of this new model is simple enough: after tonicizing A, it prolongs this *Stufe* through the mixed third C♯ before moving up to V⁷ of E. In the first sentence (34/1/3–34/4/2), the bass A ascends to C♯ through sequential statements of the "Mild" theme; the upper line, C♯–D–E, follows the bass in parallel tenths. Next, the final portion of the "Sehnsucht" motive, with its striking deceptive cadence, brings us to the dominant of E and thence to C. The third sentence (35/1/1–35/4/2) follows the same general plan: after returning locally to A minor for the "Mild" theme, Wagner slides up to C♯ (I⁶) through a major-mode version of the same motive. Section 4 ends with a clear cadential $^6_4$ in E minor, with the "Glance" motive skillfully woven into the inner parts (35/3/1–2).

Wedged between the two statements of the model, Wagner's setting of the middle sentence is nothing short of inspired. The deceptive cadence at 34/4/2 breaks the forward motion of the music, creating a sense of timelessness barely inferable from the surface of the text, yet crucial to our understanding of Isolde's nascent love for Tristan. Wagner sets up this discontinuity beautifully in the poem by delaying the object "die Augen" until the end of the sentence: "Nicht auf das Schwert, / Nicht auf die Hand, / Er sah mir in die Augen." The second sentence then consists of a complete statement of the "Glance" theme, welling up from the submediant chord in the same way it did in the Einleitung, and cadencing in A minor (34/5/4). The "Glance" theme appeared several times in Scenes 1 and 2—most memorably at the moment where Tristan avoids looking Isolde "in die Augen" (16/3/4, also 18/3/3)—but always fragmented, with its harmony poignantly twisted. In this second sentence, Wagner brings the "Glance" motive into the open for the first time, affording us a brief glimpse of Isolde's true feelings.

Given, then, that the two forms of "Sick Tristan" articulate different voice-leading spans, how does Wagner fit them together? Whereas Sections 4 and 5 are abruptly juxtaposed—this is entirely appropriate, since Brangäne interrupts Isolde at their interstice—Sections 2 and 4 are joined by a transition, namely, Section 3, 33/2/1–34/1/2 (Ex. 6.4). Thematically, this transition is achieved simply by three sequential statements of S2, the first on starting on G in the upper voice, the second on B♭, and the third on E (Wagner reinforces the latter with an additional statement of the "Mild" theme). Tonally, however, the modulation from E minor to A minor is rather complex. Wagner moves toward G at the end of the first S2, and then via E♭ (VI of G minor becomes II of D♭) to D♭ at the end of the second statement. The D♭ subsequently becomes the third degree of an A-major triad in the final statement of S2, which cadences in A minor to begin Section 4. The contrapuntal framework guiding this transition, a succession of parallel tenths, is shown as the stemmed notes in Example 6.4.

We have seen, then, that Wagner uses the "Stormy" form of "Sick Tristan" to articulate the tonal patterns of Sections 1/2 and 5 and the "Mild" form for Section 4. By isolating the "Mild" form, Wagner treats Section 4 as an episode inserted into the basic framework of Part 1: in fact, since Sections 3 and 5 begin with essentially the same material, Section 4 could even have been omitted without any obvious loss of musical sense. The fact that Section 3 ends with an incomplete statement of S2 (missing the last three chords) heightens the sense of interruption in Section 4.

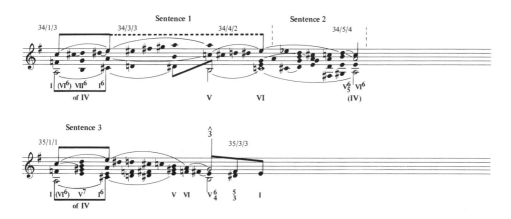

EXAMPLE 6.3. Voice-leading models in Section 4.

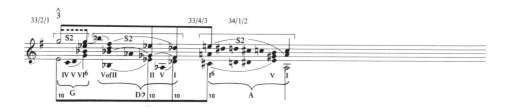

EXAMPLE 6.4. Section 3.

This interpretation of Section 4 as an episode is, however, almost the antithesis of the view presented explicitly by Lorenz and Newcomb and implicitly by Bailey.[15] According to these writers, Part 1 consists of a large *Bogen* form, the first member of which corresponds to Section 1, the middle section to Sections 2 and 3, the reprise to Section 4, and the coda to Section 5. This reading is, however, implausible for several reasons: first, as was shown earlier, the text and music of Section 2 are more closely connected to Section 1 than to Section 3; second, since Section 4 is based on the "Mild" form and begins in A minor, it is an unlikely reprise for a period dominated by the "Stormy" one and in E minor; third, since the function of Section 5 is to restore the *Hauptmotiv* in the tonic, it serves not as a coda but as a reprise. One might also point out that Bailey's "modulations" to G and C in Section 5 are not genuine changes of key, since neither controls any secondary spans: they are merely local tonicizations of *Stufen* within the key of E minor. Certainly there is no reason to accept either G or C as "double" tonics to E in Bailey's sense.[16]

*   *   *

Part 2 is somewhat more loosely organized than its predecessor. Its sectional divisions are less clearly drawn, its thematic structure is less concentrated, and its tonal plan is less fluid, at times even equivocal. Yet on close inspection a double cycle emerges, subtly articulated by motivic recall and parallel middleground designs.

Part 1 describes Tristan's first journey to Ireland; Part 2 tells of his second, when he returned to claim Isolde as the bride of Marke and thereby secure a truce between the two feuding nations. Isolde is furious: she feels she has been forced to bear not only the humiliation of the entire Irish people, but also Tristan's betrayal of her confidence.

The cyclic arrangement of Part 2 was first identified by Lorenz, and although his scheme needs certain refinements it is nonetheless basically plausible.[17]

15. Lorenz, *Das Geheimnis der Form* III, 41; Newcomb, "The Birth of Music," 45.

16. Bailey, "The Genesis of *Tristan*," 191.

17. Lorenz divided each cycle into four sections: his Sections 1, 3, and 4 correspond to my Sections 1, 2, and 3. As Lorenz pointed out, his second section, the Tantris/Tristan passage in Cycle 1, is missing in Cy-

Chart 6.2 shows that each cycle has three main sections, each built from poetic units whose structure and proportions are similar to, though slightly less regular than, those of Part 1. Both cycles begin with oaths—in Section 6 (Cycle 1) Isolde bitterly recalls Tristan's oath of loyalty, while in Section 9 (Cycle 2) Brangäne reminds her mistress of the oath of friendship taken by the two countries. In the central portion of each cycle (Sections 7 and 10), Isolde describes with increasing sarcasm the sacrifices she has been forced to make since Tristan's return. Sections 8 and 11 briefly ease the tension, as Isolde remembers the strange tenderness she had felt for her patient, especially as she let the sword fall to the ground. But her resentment for Tristan again wells up: the first time she bursts out "O blinde Augen!"; the second time she sings a vicious parody of the speech she imagines Tristan used to convince Marke to send him to woo her.

As was mentioned earlier, the *Hauptmotiv* for Part 2 is the "Zorn" motive (Ex. 6.5).[18] "Zorn" claims this distinction by appearing more often than any theme; yet, compared to "Sick Tristan," the motive plays only a small role in the generation of middle-ground spans. This discrepancy in formal function stems from differences in the internal design of each theme: whereas "Sick Tristan" forms distinct chord progressions, "Zorn" is basically inert and merely elaborates a single diminished-seventh sonority. The function of "Zorn" is, therefore, to punctuate harmonic spans; in almost all cases it is preceded by a V^7 chord and hence it usually appears within some sort of deceptive cadence. Wagner exploits this capacity to break harmonic flow by reserving "Zorn" for textual divisions such as sentence endings.

Various other themes surface in Part 2 to reinforce the cyclic organization of the text (Ex. 6.6). For example, Wagner connects the first two sections of the cycles with direct motivic repetitions: Sections 6 and 9 both begin with the same orchestral theme and vocal melody (Ex. 6.6, motive O) while Sections 7 and 10 start with the "Zorn" theme plus a new vocal gesture (Ex. 6.6, motive P); Section 8 presents two statements of "Mild" and is answered by a double statement of the distantly related A-major theme (Ex. 6.6, motive Q) in Section 11. (This theme will return at the end of Act II when Marke remembers how Tristan brought him his "wondrous bride.") Sections 8 and 11 are further linked by presenting fully formed melodic phrases in more or less stable keys—a sharp contrast to the motivic snatches that characterize other sections of Part 2. The remainder of Part 2, Section 12, likewise restates themes heard earlier in the Narrative, but not in Part 2. By bringing back "Sick Tristan" in its "Mild"

cle 2. See the chart in *Das Geheimnis der Form* III, 43. The cyclic element of Part 2 is missing in the prose draft. Although Wagner originally conceived an interruption by Brangäne, no mention is made of any vow; she merely claims that she had no idea Isolde found betrothal to Marke so repugnant. At a later stage Wagner added the Curse and the two reminiscences to Part I: the Tantris/Tristan passage of Section 2 in Section 7, and the dropping of the sword of Section 4 in Section 8.

18. Kurth discusses this motive at length; see *Romantische Harmonik,* 471–74.

CHART 6.2. Text divisions in Part 2.

CYCLE 1	MOTIVE	CYCLE 2	MOTIVE
Section 6 (36/3/1) **IS.:**		**Section 9** (39/5/3) **BR.:**	O
Er schwur mit tausend Eiden	"Zorn"	Da Friede, Sühn' und Freundschaft	
mir ew' gen Dank und Treue!		von allen ward beschworen,	
Nun hör, wie ein Held	"Zorn"		
Eide hält!			
Den als Tantris	"Tantris"		
unerkannt ich entlassen,			
als Tristan	"Zorn"		
kehrt' er kühn zurück;			
auf stolzem Schiff,		wir freuten uns all' des Tags;	
von hohem Bord,		wie ahnte mir da,	
Irlands Erbin		daß dir es Kummer schüf'?:	"Zorn"
begehrt' er zur Eh'			
für Kornwalls müden König,	"Zorn"		
für Marke, seinen Ohm.			
	P		P
Section 7 (38/2/2):		**Section 10** (40/4/2) **IS.:**	
Da Morold lebte,	"Zorn"	O blinde Augen!	"Zorn"
wer hätt' es gewagt		Blöde Herzen!	
uns je solche Schmach zu bieten?		Zahmer Mut,	
Für der zinspflicht'gen		verzagtes Schweigen!	
Kornen Füsten	"Zorn"	Wie anders prahlte Tristan aus,	"Zorn"
um Irlands Krone zu werben!		was ich verschlossen hielt!	
Ach, wehe mir!			

Section 8 (39/1/4)	Ich ja war's,	
	die heimlich selbst	
	die Schmach sich schuf!	"Mild"
	Das rächende Schwert,	"Glance"
	statt es zu schwingen,	
	machtlos ließ ich's fallen!	"Mild"
	Nun dien' ich dem Vasallen!	

Section 11 (41/3/3)	Die schweigend ihm das Leben gab,	Q
	vor Feindes Rache	
	ihn schweigend barg;	
	was stumm ihr Schutz	
	zum Heil ihm schuf —	
	mit ihr gab er es preis!	"Zorn"

Section 12 (42/1/3)	Wie siegprangend heil und hehr,	W
	laut und hell	
	wies er auf mich:	
	„Das wär' ein Schatz,	R
	mein Herr und Ohm:	
	wie dünkt Euch die zur Eh'?	
	Die schmucke Irin	Q
	hol' ich her;	
	mit Steg' und Wegen wohlbekannt,	M
	ein Wink, ich flieg' nach Irenland:	M
	Isolde, die ist Euer! —	
	Mir lacht das Abenteuer!"	S

Curse (43/5/2)	Fluch dir, Verruchter!	
	Fluch deinem Haupt!	
	Rache! Tod!	"Zorn"
	Tod uns beiden!	

EXAMPLE 6.5. "Zorn" motive.

form (M3), the theme from Kurwenal's Song, and a variant of the "Stormy" motive, Wagner clearly intends us to hear the concluding section of Part 2 as analogous to the reprise of Part 1 (Section 5) and thus to conceive of the Narrative as unified.[19]

Though vital to our perception of the double cycle in Part 2, these motivic parallels are only surface manifestations of a much deeper voice-leading correspondence. This common framework is all the more remarkable because it remains at pitch even though the two cycles move between different key areas: Cycle 1 modulates from V^9 of C to F minor, and Cycle 2 moves from V^9 of D♭ to E major.

The basic pattern is set up in Sections 6 and 9. Although these sections open in different keys, both subsequently twist around to the dominant of E♭ (Ex. 6.7).

19. Bailey discusses this motivic connection in "The Genesis of *Tristan*," 200, 203.

EXAMPLE 6.6. Cyclic themes in Part 2.

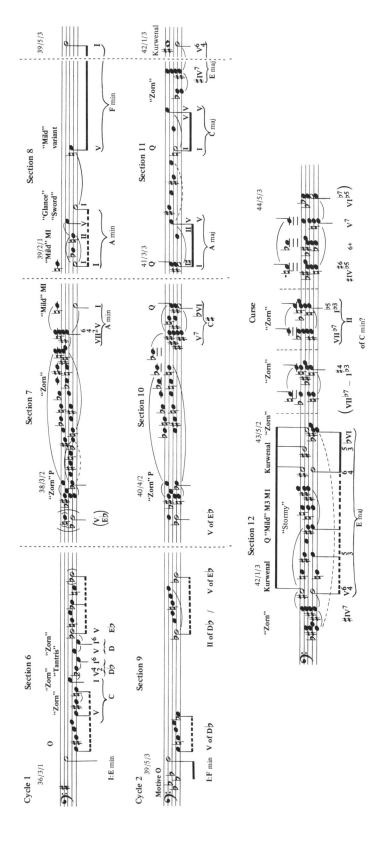

EXAMPLE 6.7. Tonal models in Part 2.

In Section 6 (36/3/1–38/2/2), Wagner immediately moves away from the tonic E minor at the end of Part 1, to the dominant of C (V of VI) for the new theme, motive O. Having cadenced onto C at 37/2/1, Section 6 proceeds with an extended segment based on the Tantris/Tristan material from Part I, intermingled with the "Zorn" motive. Wagner then approaches the dominant $^6_4$ of E♭ by a chain of ascending parallel sixths. Section 9 (39/5/3–40/4/2) follows a similar though more compressed plan, shifting from the tonic F minor at the end of Cycle 1 to the dominant D♭ (V of VI) with the repetition of motive O. The latter dominant resolves deceptively to B♭ (VI), which is then reinterpreted as the dominant of E♭. In both sections, closure in E♭ is thwarted by the intrusion of "Zorn" on A.

In Sections 7 and 10 (38/2/2–39/2/1; 40/4/2–41/3/3), the similarities between the two cycles become even closer. Having announced the commencement of each section with "Zorn" on A, both sections move up to B♭/G for a new vocal motive, P. The two sections then articulate a long chromatic ascent in sixths that extends from B♭ and G up to a diminished seventh on E (38/5/3/; 41/1/3), marked in Cycle 1 by yet another statement of "Zorn." Eventually we reach a chord on F. In Section 7 the chord is a diminished seventh (VII^7 of A) that tonicizes the dominant of A minor, passing through the Tristan chord at pitch on the way (39/1/3). In Section 10 the F chord is followed by V^7 of C♯/ D♭, which resolves onto ♭VI (I of A major) at the beginning of the next section.

Wagner conveys the reflective mood of the next sections (8 and 11) by temporarily suspending the momentum of Sections 7 and 11 and by restoring tonal stability. Section 8 (39/2/1–39/5/3) is firmly rooted in A minor and only relinquishes A two bars before the end with a cadential $^6_4$ in F minor (end of Cycle 1). Section 11 (41/3/3–42/1/3) begins in A major with motive Q. Wagner then moves to C for a repetition of Q, but before this new tonic can be established conclusively he interrupts the cadence with "Zorn." He then adds a short transition to E major for the start of Section 12.

Section 8 is interesting for another reason. Just as the poem here refers back to the incidents described in Section 4—the "Glance" and the dropping of the sword—so the music recalls the entire motivic complex in the same key, a sort of reminiscence within a reminiscence. Both sections begin with "Sick Tristan" in "Mild" form (M1) in A minor, then proceed to statements of "Glance" (with the cadential figure associated with the sword) and the "Mild" variant again in A. The similarity breaks down only near the end: whereas Section 4 cadences in E minor, Section 8 goes to F minor for the start of Cycle 2.

There can be little doubt that the overall impression of Section 12 (42/1/3– 43/5/2) is that of closure, an effect Wagner produces both by evoking the motives of Section 5 and by restoring the original tonic of E minor. From a harmonic perspective, the entire section can be seen as an expanded perfect cadence: the V$^6_4$ on B four bars from the very end clearly refers back to the opening chord of the section and is even marked by the recurrence of the same motive from Kurwenal's Song. The intervening music prolongs B as a tonic with the new theme R (42/4/3—this melody will reappear in Act I, Scene 5). A brief pause on I^6 of G (VI^6) at the end of R (43/1/1) sets up "Sick Tristan" (form M3); the latter soon yields once more to the $\frac{6}{3}$ on B (43/3/2) and then $\frac{6}{4}$ in the "Stormy" variant of "Sick Tristan" that brings the Narrative to a close. Although the resolution to the tonic in the full cadence dissolves into a diminished-seventh chord, signaling the start of Isolde's Curse, the Narrative proper ends at this point. Seen in this context, the Curse functions as a transition to E♭, the key of Brangäne's Consolation. Although its profusion of diminished sevenths make it tonally ambiguous, the Curse clearly inflects C minor in the strong augmented 6th–V–(I) cadence with which it ends (44/5/3; see Ex. 6.7). The distinctive pattern of diminished sevenths here serves to adumbrate the crucial Curse sections in Tristan's delirium in Act III.

We have seen, then, that Part 2 is constructed from a chain of discrete units arranged cyclically. The question now is whether this succession is controlled by a single tonic, as was suggested by Lorenz and Bailey. Certainly it is difficult to accept Lorenz's claim that Part 2 is a self-contained period in C major. On the one hand, C *minor* (not C major) is established, though only in passing, at the beginning of Cycle 1 (37/2/1) with the "Zorn" theme and, at the end of the Curse (44/5/3), again with the "Zorn" theme; in neither case does it generate any decisive secondary spans. On the other hand, the sense of closure at the end of Section 12 is so strong that any attempt to hear E as parallel dominant to the real tonic C (Lorenz's Riemannian explanation) seems farfetched. It is perhaps worth noting briefly that the only secondary keys mentioned by Lorenz throughout Part 2 are F minor at the end of Cycle 1 and D♭ at the start of Cycle 2.[20]

Given the strong connections between Sections 5 and 12, Bailey's hypothesis that the whole Narrative is in E major/minor seems sensible; however, even here the evidence is far from conclusive. The problem is not that the sequence of secondary keys (C major/minor, A minor, F minor, A major, and so on) cannot be explained in Schenkerian terms as *Stufen* within E—as was mentioned earlier, Schenker clearly accepted the possibility of local tonics in all chromatic keys—but, rather, that the voice-leading and motivic content of the double cycles has no direct relationship with that of Part 1. It is important to remember that in Part 1 the tonic was defined by the "Stormy" form of "Sick Tristan." Excluding Section 12, the most significant cross-reference between Parts 1 and 2 is Section 8; yet, as was outlined earlier, this material is in the key of A rather than E and recalls Section 4, which is an interpolation within the main prolongations of E in Part 1. Indeed, if we did not have Section 12, there would be no reason at all to suppose that Part 2 would end in E. In this sense, the double

20. See Lorenz, *Das Geheimnis der Form* III, 42; Bailey, "The Genesis of *Tristan*," 191.

cycle in Sections 6–11 seems sufficiently removed from E minor to subvert any deep middleground connection between Sections 5 and 12. Thus, whereas Part 1 is continuously in E minor, Part 2 is in E only in some more remote, discontinuous sense. By weakening the tonal framework of Part 2, Wagner is able to preserve the overall continuity of Scene 3. What we see, in effect, is that while an extensive use of tonal models may provide coherence on one level, on another it may prevent unity. It was doubtless observations such as these that led to Schenker's comments on Wagner's music.

∗   ∗   ∗

It would be premature to offer any broad generalizations about Wagner's compositional practice on the evidence of a single extract, but one point is, I hope, clear. Thanks to the work of Lorenz, Bailey, and others the tonal and motivic geography of *Tristan* has been charted; the next task for analysts is to establish precisely what role a given motive plays in articulating specific tonal spans, and also to show not just whether a span *is* tonal but *how* it is tonal. While it is too early to claim that tonal modeling might pervade the entire fabric of an opera, the extremely self-referential nature of Wagner's compositions suggests that Isolde's Narrative is by no means an isolated case. If, as Arnold Whittall has recently suggested, the second century of Wagner analysis should focus on details of the music, I hope this essay is a step in the right direction.[21]

21. Arnold Whittall, "Wagner's Great Transition? From *Lohengrin* to *Das Rheingold*," *Music Analysis* II, no. 3 (1983), 269.

Chapter 7

Ritornello Ritornato

A Variety of Wagnerian Refrain Form

ANTHONY NEWCOMB

In *The New Grove Wagner,* Carl Dahlhaus argues that the technique of leitmotive offers an adequate basis for a theory of large form and of local detail in Wagner's music. "What is missing, for the most part, are forms of intermediate size; Alfred Lorenz's efforts to establish their existence were a failure."[1] Can we, in fact, define the intermediate forms about which he speaks, forms from 150 to 600 measures, from five to thirty minutes in length? As a premise for the discussion, we must recall that forms—large, small, and intermediate alike—are intrinsically separate from the leitmotivic web, and that the distinction has long been recognized in Wagnerian analysis.[2] Form and leitmotivic web may of course interact and may even be in total agreement at times, but they are by no means the same.

Form may be viewed as a set of conventions establishing standard successions of functional events. In a sense such a standard succession is analogous to the standard plots structuralists find in folktales, detective stories, even complicated novels, save that in music each of these events is defined not by such descriptions as "chieftain marries princess" or "ruler builds castle," but by a partic-

---

1. Carl Dahlhaus, *The New Grove Wagner* (New York, 1984), 79. This sentence as not in the article on Wagner written by Dahlhaus for *The New Grove* XX, 117–18. Dahlhaus posed the same challenge a bit more carefully in his pioneering article of 1969, "Formprinzipien in Wagners *Ring des Nibelungen*," in Heinz Becker, ed., *Beiträge zur Geschichte der Oper* (Regensburg, 1969), 95–129, 105: "Der Motivzusammenhang, der das ganze Drama umfasst, ist also, ohne selbst Form zu sein, eine der Voraussetzungen für die Formen der einzelnen Teile; sie isoliert zu analysieren, wie es Lorenz versucht, ist inadäquat. Und umgekehrt müssen in den einzelnen Teilen überschaubare symphonische Formen ausgeprägt sein, wenn nicht das Motivgewebe, in dem alles mit allem verknüpft ist, als wirrer Knäuel wirken soll. Das Formproblem in Wagners *Ring* ist das Problem der Vermittlung—der mittleren Stufen—zwischen dem einzelnen Motiv und dem ganzen Drama."

2. For the history of this subject in Wagnerian criticism, see the Introduction to the present volume.

ular combination of such characteristic elements as tempo, tonality and tonal stability, instrumentation, texture, and melodic style, all of which together suggest its *function* as defined by its relation to other events in a succession of events. Examples of musical functions in this sense might be introduction, closing section, retransition, as well as *tempo di mezzo* and cabaletta. A conventional ordering of such musical functions into an intelligible plot or unit of discourse is what I understand by *musical form* in the general sense. Such a definition of form in the general sense is quite different from a schematic definition such as A–B–A or A–B–A′–B′–A″, since it is particularly concerned with such matters as the typical melodic style of the A section, the typical nature of the contrast between B and A, how the transition is accomplished from one to the other, and so on. Form in the individual piece is the result of the interplay between some such conventional succession(s) and the actual succession of musical functions or events. As we listen to the individual piece, especially to those in which the formal type is part of the problem posed, rather than being among the premises for the piece, we are engaged in identifying the function of the musical event that we are hearing, and in placing this event in some larger, more or less conventional succession of functional events that is a form.

The technique of leitmotive does not determine any succession of events in this sense;[3] the *Bar* form, on the other hand, does. So does the *Reprisenbar,* the *Bogen,* the strophic variation, even the sonata. Wagner appeals to all of the above forms, or conventional orderings of musical events, in giving intelligibility and shape to the musical side of his musico-dramatic structures. I should like here to propose that he uses a further set of musical-formal conventions as background to his musical shapes: those of the eighteenth-century ritornello procedure. This set of conventions, though highly developed and though much closer than concepts like *Bar* form to the surface of the musical culture of which Wagner was part, has not, as far as I have seen, been reckoned as a component in his formal vocabulary.[4]

The conventions of ritornello procedure, as used by Wagner, operate on two formal levels: first on the level of the thematic unit, and second on the level of the larger formal unit, which proceeds as an alternation of episode and (usually incomplete or varied) ritornello material.

On the first level, some of Wagner's thematic units analogous to ritornellos play with the conventions of thematic structure put forth exhaustively by Wilhelm Fischer in a famous article on the development of style in the eighteenth century, printed nearly seventy years ago in Guido Adler's *Studien zur*

---

3. In fact there is often a tension between the demands made by leitmotivic commentary on the dramatic situation and those made by the melodic articulation of form; I explore this dilemma in more detail in "The Birth of Music out of the Spirit of Drama," *19th-Century Music* V (1981–1982), 47–48, with relevant citations.

4. Carl Dahlhaus ("Formprinzipien," 123–27) comes as close as any commentator to the concept of the ritornello procedure in opera. See footnote 15 below.

Musikwissenschaft.[5] Fischer identified two basic thematic types in early-eighteenth-century music. One he called the *Liedtypus,* or song-type; the other he called the *Fortspinnungstypus,* associating the latter particularly with larger forms in the earlier eighteenth century.[6] In such a theme, he identified the following succession of events in functional terms: first, a clearly formed, arresting opening section (labeled A in Examples 7.1 and 7.3 below), the strongest thematic idea of the ritornello; then a sequential continuation, melodically less differentiated and less closed in shape, harmonically less stable and perhaps modulating, of indefinite length, though usually longer than the initial section (B1 and B2 in Examples 7.1 and 7.3); finally, a cadential section (which Fischer for some reason misleadingly called the *Epilog*), a section that often has distinctive motivic content and that firms up harmonically around a cadence, proclaiming the end of the unit (X in Examples 7.1 and 7.3).[7] We might speculate that the attraction for Wagner of this thematic type—especially as opposed to the other type identified by Fischer, which is basically the antecedent-consequent phrase—can be seen in its aperiodicity, its lack of complementary, architectonic repetitions and symmetries, its encouragement of sequential growth, especially in the central section, and its establishment of a logic for a thematic sentence that is based on a succession of functions, without emphasizing tonal closure or cadential complementarities between balanced sections.

On the level of the larger formal unit, Wagner often invokes the conventional alternation between ritornello material on the one hand (usually just one or two of the functionally distinct sections of the ritornello) and non-ritornello, or episodic, material on the other, in the manner of many an early-eighteenth-century concerto movement, aria, trio sonata movement, or fugue. The episodic section in Wagner is often characterized in ways similar to those in eighteenth-century movements: by a lighter texture and emotional tone, especially as effected by lightened instrumentation and harmonic or motivic density.

We shall look here at a pair of scenes that use the conventions of ritornello movements in a relatively clear way. To say this is not to assert that these scenes are in ritornello form. As I have argued elsewhere, it is a mistake to assert that most Wagnerian units are in any single form.[8] Rather, each appeals to various formal conventions as it proceeds, plays with them, intermixes them, and asks

5. Wilhelm Fischer, "Zur Entwicklungsgeschichte des Wiener klassischen Stils," *Studien der Musikwissenschaft* III (1915), 24–84. Wagner's thematic units discussed in the present essay are distinct from leitmotives; they are, for one, much too long. Leitmotives are often extracted from them or embedded in them, however, especially in the opening section (A).

6. Fischer's ideas about the role of this thematic type in the development of the Viennese style are not at issue here.

7. The ritornellos to the first movements of Vivaldi's Concerto for two violins in A minor, Op. 3, No. 8, and to J. S. Bach's Brandenburg Concerto No. 5 offer familiar examples of the thematic type. The Vivaldi has, somewhat unusually, two distinct cadential sections.

8. Anthony Newcomb, "Those Images That Yet Fresh Images Beget," *Journal of Musicology* II (1983), 227–45.

us to interpret and reinterpret the succession of musical events that we hear as particular functions within those conventional successions. In the units that I shall look at here, the conventions of the ritornello form are among the most prominent. This is also not to assert that all of Wagner's many refrain forms use this same set of conventions. The particular kind of refrain form I shall study here is only one of the many varieties that Wagner uses in his operas.[9]

The instances of the use of the ritornello conventions to be considered here are from the late 1850s and seem to be Wagner's first experiments with the device. The question of what models he may have known and been thinking of at the time is an intriguing one. Although it cannot be the primary concern of this essay, we shall return to it briefly in closing.

I

Tristan, Act II, Scene 1, is one of the clearest instances of a larger unit involving the conventional successions of the ritornello form. Its ritornello (Ex. 7.1) is introduced as the prelude to the act, immediately following two introductory gestures that return later. The distinctive characteristics of this ritornello are its climactic cadential section, toward which the entire ritornello moves strongly, and its repetition of the opening and sequential sections as a sequence in themselves, leading up to the arrival of the emphatic cadential section. Particularly important is the stylistic and functional differentiation of the sections within this sizable thematic unit: the opening section (Rit. A in Ex. 7.1) is harmonically relatively stable (especially in the context in which it occurs the first time), melodically relatively clearly formed, establishing the principal thematic-motivic material of the unit, and metrically solid, continuing the four-measure periodicity of the beginning of the prelude.[10] The ensuing sequential sections (Rit. B1 and B2 in Example 7.1) are harmonically most unstable, melodically motivic and fragmented, and increasingly syncopated and irregular in length; their function is neither to begin nor end, but to stretch powerfully toward resolution of some kind; the final, cadential section (Rit. X in Example 7.1—so named to stress its particular function and the indeterminate number of sections that may precede it) returns to metrical regularity and to the more clearly struc-

9. For example, Reinhold Brinkmann (" 'Drei der Fragen stell' ich mir frei': Zur Wanderer-Szene im 1. Akt von Wagners 'Siegfried,' " *Jahrbuch der Staatlichen Instituts für Musikforschung* V [Berlin, 1972], 141–52) gives an exhaustive analysis of the refrain elements (not ritornello procedure) in the first question set of the Wanderer-Mime scene.

10. The first occurrence of Rit. A in the piece, labeled "proto-form" in Example 7.1, is particularly stable, appearing as it does over a functionally unmistakable V pedal. The immediately ensuing form, labeled Rit. A in Example 7.1, is the most common one in the scene as a whole and uses less stable harmonies, though still over a strong $\hat{3}$–$\hat{4}$–$\hat{5}$ bass line. (The "proto-form" also shows Wagner's typical care in soldering the joints between thematic sections, in that it introduces the melodic material of the new ritornello as a countervoice to the previously exposed introductory theme of the prelude.)

EXAMPLE 7.1. *Tristan*, Act II, Scene 1, ritornello pattern.

EXAMPLE 7.1. *continued.*

tured melodic material of the opening section, and settles into a strong cadential arrival on the dominant chord.

The resolution of the final dominant is, of course, interrupted, here by the material that will be the basis of episodic contrast in the larger unit: the onstage horn calls. One of the elements defining the contrast between ritornello and episode here is typical—the drastic thinning of texture (the pit orchestra drops out) and the introduction of solo instruments. As Reinhold Brinkmann has pointed out, another is a striking contrast in tone, brought about principally by a contrast in the way of handling time and pulse—the ritornello giving the impression of many fast pulses and highly articulated time, the episode one of much slowed or suspended pulses and of vague articulations.[11]

The major musical elements of the scene are now before us. Its formal conventions are suggested; its musical materials are exposed. The unit proceeds by an alternation and intermingling of the forward-hurtling, highly goal-directed ritornello and the static, hovering episode. The thrust of the entire scene will be to obliterate the characteristic and contrasting tone of the episode through the ritornello's musical insistence. Put in those terms, the logic of the scene seems clear enough. But there are subtleties: canny manipulations of the *functions* served by the three typical ritornello sections—opening, continuation, and cadence—in the many varied and incomplete interior recurrences of that ritornello. Such manipulations are also one of the most powerful sources of formal interest in eighteenth-century ritornello movements.

11. Reinhold Brinkmann, "Mythos-Geschichte-Natur," in Stefan Kunze, ed., *Richard Wagner—Von der Oper zum Musikdrama* (Bern, 1978), 61–77, 63.

CHART 7.1. *Tristan,* Act II, Scene 1, ritornello structure.

Introduction	
Ritornello (mm. 33–74)	A B$_1$ B$_2$ (A B$_1$ B$_2$ repeated up major 2nd) X
episode 1 (mm. 75–96)	horns
Ritornello (mm. 97–111)	A B$_1$ B$_2$ (compressed)
episode 2 (mm. 112–38)	("des Laubes säuselnd Getön") horns, solo clarinet
Ritornello (mm. 139–46)	A B$_1$ B$_2$ (compressed)
episode 3 (mm. 147–77)	("des Quelles sanft rieselnde Welle") horns, ww. tremolo, string tremolo
Ritornello (mm. 178–99)	A A A A B$_1$ B$_2$ lead to a cadence, but *no* X
episode 4 (mm. 200–251)	Brangäne's warning—transition and 2 strophes in quasi-recitative style
Ritornello (mm. 252–342)	Sizable development of Rit. A alternating with motives from episodes 2 and 3 (mm. 252–89) leads finally to B$_1$ B$_2$ X (mm. 290–313) and extended cadential development of X (mm. 314–42)
episode 5 (mm. 343–418)	Frau Minne
Ritornello (mm. 419–97)	Sizable development of Rit. A transformed (mm. 419–64) leads to B$_2$ X (mm. 465–97) and a motivically dense, harmonically emphatic, confirmatory cadence

Chart 7.1 gives the sectional disposition of the ritornello recurrences and a digest of the contents of the episodes. The first recurrence gives a much compressed, bleached-out version of just the opening and sequential sections (Rit. A and Rit. B1 and B2). As in most ritornello pieces, a second episodic interruption quickly appears, modulates, and is developed a bit further than the first. Here the soloistic textural motive of the episodes in general is borne by a lovely clarinet solo, subtly related by free inversion to the opening motive of the ritornello.[12] The strong expectation of a return to the ritornello aroused by the formal convention helps Wagner to get away once more with a much understated recurrence of the ritornello, sweeping quickly through abbreviated and unemphatic thematic sentence, which again proceeds up to but does not include the cadential section. The third episode is one of the most ravishing of the group, developing the delicate instrumentation and the suspended pulsation of the episodic material in a longer and more distant excursion, from which Rit. A must insist a bit more in order to return. After this return the thematic sentence continues to a quick deceptive cadence, but it still lacks the proper, emphatic cadential section. A new thinning of texture and slowing of rhythmic momentum lead to the fourth episode. As in many eighteenth-century ritornello move-

---

12. Such motivic relations between episode and ritornello are frequent in the ritornello movements of J. S. Bach.

ments, this later episode is also larger and leads in turn to a more complicated intercutting of episodic material with ritornello material as an extended transition back to the ritornello sentence, or—perhaps better put—as an extended effort to complete the ritornello sentence. In Wagner's version the head motive of Rit. A serves to push back toward the ritornello, but it is resisted, so to speak, by materials from all the previous episodes. Rit. B1 and B2 finally follow Rit. A (mm. 290–99) and lead, for the first time since the initial statement of the ritornello, to the proper cadential section (following m. 300). This is then considerably expanded and leads to a linearly and metrically vigorous, if harmonically deceptive, cadence (m. 342).

Thus my sketch of the musical formal conventions behind this unit and of the particular, not highly idiosyncratic way in which Wagner adapted them to at least its first part. As is usual with Wagner, this set of formal conventions is used not to satisfy any traditional generic requirements, but because of the closeness with which its musical events could parallel the dramatic events.[13] Of course, all great composers of opera must find musical analogies for drama. But the interplay of musical-formal conventions with dramatic logic is in this instance particularly artful.

The forward-hurtling, strongly goal-directed ritornello sentence makes a fine musical symbol for Isolde's obsession with achieving her goal, and it is associated with Isolde from her first entrance. The conventional musical shaping of the larger formal unit by the struggle of the ritornello sentence to complete itself offers a musical-formal parallel to the dramatic direction of the scene. The conventional clarity, activity, and eventual dominance of the ritornello material in the form are effective symbols for Isolde's dominant will. The conventional soloistic episodic contrast can be fulfilled instrumentally by the (gradually disappearing) horns of Marke's hunting party; this dramatic element is given human voice, again from the beginning of the scene, by Brangäne. As the horns fade from hearing altogether, Brangäne's voice becomes more vehement, but it finds nothing thematically strong enough to combat the push of Isolde's forward-tumbling ritornello, which grows in vigor, definition, and completeness from its first occurrence within the scene (the first, that is, after its complete exposition in the prelude) to its final triumph. At each recurrence of the ritornello material Brangäne plunges in to stop the logic supplied by the conven-

13. The availability of musical formal conventions that might parallel a dramatic evolution, and hence enable the music to follow the evolution while still remaining musically coherent and intelligible, was the principal concern of Wagner's essay *Über Franz Liszts symphonische Dichtungen* of early 1857. The availability of such a form was a primary criterion in judging whether a program was appropriate for music (see especially *Sämtliche Schriften* V, 189–95). I read this passage as a reflection of Wagner's experience as a composer of dramatic music over the past dozen years. He had come to realize that not all dramatic evolutions could be effectively followed musically, because their shapes could not be adapted to any combination of musical-formal conventions. Consciously, unconsciously, or subconsciously Wagner came to design more and more of his dramatic evolutions so that they could fit some set of conventions more or less naturally—so that they could be accommodated to the needs of musical growth.

tional design of the ritornello sentence. Each time, Isolde takes Brangäne's episodic diversions and turns them back into her ritornello material.

Nowhere is the expressive potency of this symbolism of dramatic design through musical design more beautifully and economically exemplified than in episode 3. Brangäne asserts that she still hears the horns, stopping the drive of Isolde's ritornello and calling up an episode (m. 147). Interrupted, Isolde listens for Brangäne's *Hörner Schall*. But, as Wagner's handling of the conventional instrumental contrast tells us, Isolde truly does not hear it—as Brangäne says, "Dich täuscht des Wunsches Ungestüm, / zu vernehmen was du wähnst." Isolde listens, and we hear her ears transform the horns of the episode first into solo woodwind tremolos (m. 159), then into string tremolos (m. 161)—just the rustling of nearby water, she says. Over the string tremolos floats the opening phrase of her ritornello (m. 178), and her powerfully insistent desire resumes its push toward fulfillment.

The abbreviated cadence of m. 200 is, of course, not the end of this formal unit. There follow the larger episode of which I have already spoken (Brangäne's warning about Melot) and Isolde's sizable counter-argument to that warning, which leads to her first completion of the ritornello sentence. Brangäne leaps into this sentence right at the point of cadence (m. 342), hurling desperate cries of self-accusation. The following transition, dense with leitmotives, leads to the last and largest episode, the delicately orchestrated Frau Minne section (mm. 380–418)—appropriately given to Isolde herself, for Brangäne's resistance has faded. From the self-induced swoon of this episode, Isolde leads back to a new, extremely clearly formed if slightly vulgar transformation of Rit. A (see Ex. 7.2, in which elements common to the two are circled). This transformed opening section works its way across a sizable development to a supremely emphatic statement of Rit. B (mm. 465–71) and Rit. X (477ff.), the whole culminating in a weighty cadential combination of Rit. A and the "Todgeweihtes Haupt" motive, recently invoked by Isolde at the end of her final episode, as the torch is extinguished to close off the larger unit.

The transformation of a section of the ritornello at some point in the structure, such as happens here with the opening section in the final recurrence, is a characteristic aspect of Wagner's handling of the ritornello form. Such transformations generally have a dramatic purpose. It may be, as here, a transformation to a new form of the previous ritornello section, now altered to express with a musical metaphor a psychological change in the situation: the increasing strength and directness of Isolde's willful drive toward her goal. It may be a transformation to a form of a motive that had existed before the ritornello. The latter device reveals a previously concealed dramatic relationship between the separate psychological fields associated with the preexistent motive and ritornello section. We shall encounter an example of this second type below. First, however, a more general consideration.

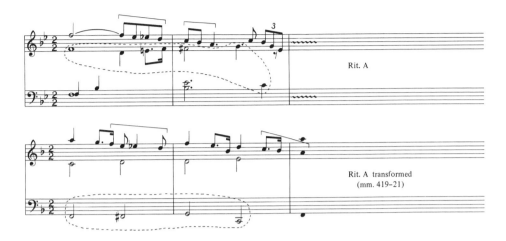

EXAMPLE 7.2. *Tristan,* Act II, Scene 1, mm. 29–31.

I have claimed that the principal set of formal conventions governing this formal unit is that of a refrain structure, and that the specific kind of refrain structure at work is much like the early-eighteenth-century ritornello movement. The other, closely related set of musical-formal conventions that one might propose is clearly the rondo. The ritornello is preferable partly because of the nature of the episodic sections, that is, their lightness of scoring and their lack of strong thematic profile in comparison to the ritornello. But it is preferable mainly because of the structure of the principal theme, and the manipulation of this structure in the internal recurrences. Rondo themes are conventionally some variation on Fischer's *Liedtypus,* while ritornello themes are conventionally some variation on his *Fortspinnungstypus.* Since the idea of a principal thematic sentence made up roughly according to Fischer's *Fortspinnungstypus*—that is, made up of a conventional succession of functionally and stylistically distinct sections, whose order and completeness are manipulated in recurrences—is an important one to my thesis, I should now like to examine one further instance.

II

In *Siegfried,* Act I, the sections of the Wanderer-Mime scene that surround the two question sets—the sections before, between, and after—have a similarly structured principal theme.[14] These sections can be heard as shaped by the in-

14. In the ensuing discussion (00/0/0) refers to page number, system number, and measure number within the system in the widely available vocal score arranged by Karl Klindworth and published in the

complete recurrences of what one might call the thematic sentence, with some of its sections either omitted or substantially varied upon repetition, and in alternation with less weighty episodic passages. The thematic sentence itself (Ex. 7.3) begins with a striking opening section four measures long (mm. 1289–92, 50/3/1–4), given the strong and arresting quality customary for an opening section especially by its lapidary rhythmic solidity (highlighted by contrast with what precedes it) and by its metrical foursquareness. It also has something of the usual harmonic stability of an opening section, in that it can be heard from the second chord as a series of $IV^6–N^6–V–I$ cadences. But it is always stated as a real sequence, with no clear tonal orientation. This opening section is followed by a sequential series, here characteristically ascending (mm. 1293–98, 50/3/5–51/1/4), and a two-measure cadential section with a characteristically descending melodic gesture. The last two are similar in rhythm and instrumentation, but differ in melodic direction and harmonic function.[15]

One of the fascinations the ritornello form offers is to follow across the larger formal unit the fate of the particular music that fills the three functions in the thematic sentence. The point here concerns particularly the smaller of the two formal levels mentioned at the outset of this essay—that is, the structure of the thematic sentence itself, in its various recurrences. The balance between the sec-

---

United States by G. Schirmer; measure numbers alone are counted from the beginning of the act. To convert these measure numbers to measure numbers for scene 2 alone, subtract 1,288.

15. Dahlhaus ("Formprinzipien," 124–25) makes the point that in some formally free operatic scenes (his primary example is from Mozart: the Act II Finale of *Figaro*) specific motives function as beginning, continuing, and closing motives, and that their functional character is so clear that their grouping can be unschematic without being amorphous. He adduces the Wanderer's thematic unit as an example of such functional motives in Wagner. He does not, however, see measures 1316–17 as a development of the original sequential section but calls their content an independent motive; furthermore, he does not identify the cadential section.

The sequential central section of the thematic unit here (Rit. B) seems so close to the important section beginning at measure 38 of Liszt's *Orpheus* as explicitly to allude to and emulate that section: the two sections have in common key, instrumentation (horns over strings), harmonic vocabulary, rhythmic motive and general level of rhythmic activity, motion in parallel tenths between alto and bass, and overall sequential rise. Wagner's interruption of work on *Siegfried*, Act I, Scene 1, because of an extended visit by Liszt in October through November of 1856 has long been known, as has Liszt's performances of *Orpheus* and *Les Préludes* in St. Gallen in a concert on 23 November 1856, at which Wagner also directed Beethoven's Third Symphony. See Peter Raabe, *Franz Liszt* (2d ed. Tutzing, 1968), I, 176–77; and Robert Bailey, "The Method of Composition," in Peter Burbridge and Richard Sutton, ed. *The Wagner Companion* (Cambridge, England, 1979), 304. Given this background, and Wagner's careful control over thematic resemblance, it seems likely that the allusion was intended. The juxtaposition implied by the allusion dramatizes how much more extensively and essentially Wagner is able to develop the shared basic idea (Liszt, mm. 38–39; Wagner, mm. 1293–94), both in the measures immediately following, and in later recurrences within the scene (e.g., mm. 1309–13, 51/4; or mm. 1316–21, 52/1). Might we be justified in hearing this reworking of a Lisztian motive as a musical parallel to the puzzling passage in the essay *Über Franz Liszts symphonische Dichtungen* (like *Siegfried*, Act I, Scene 2, written shortly after Liszt's visit to Wagner in Zurich), in which Wagner pays a backhanded compliment to the quality of Liszt's thematic invention by saying that Liszt's themes are so definite and full of meaning at their initial presentation "dass ich oft nach der ersten sechzehn [!] Takten erstaunt ausrufen musste: 'genug, ich habe alles' " (Richard Wagner, *Sämtliche Schriften* V, 195–96). Do the passage from the essay and the passage from *Siegfried* both criticize Liszt indirectly for not developing the full potential in his motives?

EXAMPLE 7.3. *Siegfried,* Act I, Scene 2, ritornello (mm. 1289–1300).

tions may alter; some may be radically transformed; others may disappear entirely.[16] The essential matter is that the arresting, opening function and the cadential function be represented in the final recurrence of the sentence.

The evolution of the present ritornello from *Siegfried,* Act I, is almost diametrically opposed to that of the ritornello from *Tristan,* Act II, partly as a result of its particular makeup. In *Siegfried* the cadential gesture is fairly unemphatic and not highly characteristic, while the opening section is emphatic and full of distinctive character—which is to say that while Isolde's ritornello is heavily end-accented and yearns for its emphatic conclusion, the Wanderer's is heavily beginning-accented and tends to finish inconclusively (or, by a neat reversal of gender, that Isolde's is a masculine phrase and the Wanderer's a feminine one). In repeating the Wanderer's ritornello across the center of the scene, Wagner, surprisingly, suppresses its opening section, only to have it reappear triumphantly in a kind of dramatic reversal, to articulate the close of the entire musico-dramatic unit, which is the scene. (There are obvious dramatic parallels to this musical-formal procedure.) And the seemingly meek cadential section of the ritornello, which had long since slipped from sight, reappears at the end of the scene (as it should by convention), now transformed to reveal a powerful significance. The central sequential section, which was associated with the Wanderer's stately progress toward the hearth, had dominated the beginning of the scene. It disappears in the end, its dramatic function used up, its musical one

16. The same is true of early-eighteenth-century ritornello movements, of course. In the first movement of the Vivaldi Concerto referred to in footnote 7, for example, one of the two cadential sections is used up, so to speak, by functioning emphatically as preparation for the principal return of the opening section of the ritornello in the tonic toward the end of the movement, and it disappears from the final thematic sentence.

dispensable. The concision of a final ritornello made up of just the opening and closing gestures, plus the dramatic reversal attendant on their reappearance, give Wagner an economical but weighty way of closing the scene and the form.

This point may be expanded by considering more closely Wagner's deployment of this thematic sentence in the initial, central, and closing parts of the scene, and in particular his variations of the relative weight of the three functional sections of the theme according to the structural needs of the moment (see Chart 7.2). After Mime's short first episode (mm. 1301–4, 51/2/1–3/1), the Wanderer ritornello returns, now with the central section, initially a tonal sequence, destabilized into a real sequence. Mime then interrupts the ritornello before the cadential section, interjecting his sharply contrasting episodic textures and agitated rhythms. The suppression of the opening section of the ritornello across the ensuing part of the scene begins here with its surprising return as part of Mime's interruption, in rhythmic diminution and in the light textures of Mime's episode (m. 1315, 52/1/2). The model of the thematic sentence then proceeds correctly to the central section, which appears now with normal instrumentation, rhythm, and motives, but in a variant that will be important to the center of the scene (mm. 1316–19, 52/1/3–2/1).[17] This central section leads, again without the cadential section, to a second episodic development—and a further step in the erosion or suppression of the opening section.[18] The Wanderer answers this by returning to the thematic sentence, now completely deprived of the opening section, but with a vigorous, upward-sequencing version of the central section rising in three stately members to a downward-sequencing triple statement of the cadential section, marking the first big articulation in the formal unit as a whole. This ritornello recurrence (which marks the Wanderer's first offer of information to Mime) is emphatic, but still lacks the opening section. There follows another episode by Mime (mm. 1343–49, 53/2/6–54/1/3), the largest so far, incorporating an even more surprising disguise of the opening section of the ritornello in Mime's instrumental textures and rhythms (mm. 1347–49, 54/1/1–3) and to a sizable episodic development of elements of the opening and central sections by the Wanderer. This finally leads, as it had in the previous episode, to a threefold upward statement of the central ritornello section (mm. 1357–63, 54/2/6 = mm.

17. That this is a variant of the initial sequential section, with slightly more expansive harmonic and melodic gestures, is suggested from the outset by the close similarities in instrumentation, harmony, texture (parallel tenths between alto and bass), and principal rhythmic-melodic motive (compare the alto in measure 1294 with the soprano in measure 1317). It is confirmed by Wagner in the version of measures 1350ff. (54/1/4ff.) that brings together elements of the two versions.

18. Measures 1322–23 repeat the second and third chords of the opening section, but cannot find the other chords to go with them; this overlaps with the Wanderer's singing, in measures 1323–24, the top voice of the opening section, but without the proper harmonies. The orchestral top voice of measures 1326–27 then echoes the top voice of 1322–23, but now without the correct harmony—that is, without the chords that in 1322–23 had made the connection to the opening section. The process is one of progressive dissolution of the opening ritornello section.

CHART 7.2. *Siegfried,* Act I, Scene 2, ritornello structure.	
Ritornello 1 (mm. 1289–1300)	A B (3x, tonal sequence) X (cadential segment)
episode (mm. 1301–4)	Mime; clear textural contrast
Ritornello 2 (mm. 1305–12)	A B (3x, real sequence)
episode (mm. 1313–15)	Mime; clear textural contrast; ⟶ Rit. A disguised
Ritornello 3 (mm. 1316–19)	B (2x, varied)
episode (mm. 1320–29)	Wanderer and Mime; Rit. A varied and dissolved
Ritornello 4 (mm. 1330–42)	B (3x, real sequence) X (3x, real sequence)
episode (mm. 1343–56)	Mime; textural contrast; ⟶Rit. A disguised
Ritornello 5 (mm. 1357–63)	B (3x, real sequence) X (Dissolved)
episode (mm. 1364 ff.) ⟶	Mime; textural contrast
Question Set 1	
Ritornello 6 (mm. 1598–1608)	B (3x, real sequence) A (varied)
episode (mm. 1609–16)	Wanderer; no textural contrast
Ritornello 7 (mm. 1617–25)	B (3x, varied)
episode (mm. 1626 ff.) ⟶	
Question Set 2	
Ritornello 8 (mm. 1855–67)	A X (transformed)

1330–36, 52/3/5–53/1/4). According to both the previous occurrence (mm. 1330–36) and the formal convention of the ritornello sentence, we should now hear the cadential section. In one of the nicest effects of the unit, this section does in fact begin, but is suddenly interrupted and deflected as Mime, increasingly agitated, leaps in with what will be the musical material of the first question set (see Ex. 7.4*a* and *b* for a comparison of mm. 1364–65, 54/3/6–7, the deflected cadential section, and the proper cadential section of the ritornello, transposed to the appropriate pitch).[19] At this point, then, the ritornello, has been eroded until only its central section remains.

The ensuing question set functions as an episode on another level—like Brangäne's warning in the scene from *Tristan* just discussed, it acts as a musical unit with independent structure, but framed by the larger ritornello structure of the entire unit.

When the ritornello comes back between the two question sets, its opening section is again drastically changed, either texturally (mm. 1598–1600, 64/3/1–3) or harmonically (mm. 1607–8, 65/1/4–5), its cadential section is absent, and its central section (mm. 1601–6, 64/3/4–65/1/3) becomes successively less stable (cf. mm. 1601–6 with mm. 1617–25, 65/2/7–4/2).

19. Since this cadential section is a (prolonged) N–V–I cadence, it bears a close harmonic relationship to the initial section of the ritornello. Both are echoed harmonically in the large N^6–V–(I) cadences that articulate major divisions in the question sets (e.g., mm. 1392–94, 56/1/1–3; mm. 1593–94, 64/2/2–3; mm. 1634–35, 66/1/4–5; mm. 1869–70, 76/2/2–3). Only in the final cadence of the unit is the $♭\hat{2}$ decisively replaced by the $♮\hat{2}$ (mm. 1881–82, on the way to the cadence at m. 1885).

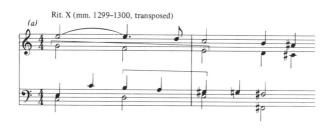

EXAMPLE 7.4. *Siegfried,* Act I, Scene 2, transformation of the
cadential section of the ritornello.

An ingenious and dramatically telling transformation of ritornello material (and a subtle play on the function of the various ritornello sections) comes with the surprising reappearance, at the end of the second set of questions, of Mime's cry of despair, which had directly preceded the beginning of the entire scene. This reappearance creates what can be heard as a double allusion: first and most obviously, to the first occurrence of this music just before the beginning of the scene; and second, ironically now, to the Wanderer's threefold statement of the cadential section near the end of the initial part of the scene (cf. mm. 1337–42, 53/1/6–2/5 with mm. 1843–54, 75/2/7–9). Thorough acquaintance with the cadential section of the ritornello across the body of the scene now leads us to hear Mime's outcry, when it recurs at the end of the second set of questions, in a new light, as a transformed version of that cadential section. Similar in melodic contour and rhythm, Mime's outcry and the Wanderer's cadential section differ principally in that Mime's outcry sequences upward in ever shriller desperation rather than calmly downward as the Wanderer's cadential section had done, and, more strikingly still, in that Mime's unit is crunchingly dissonant—a real cry of despair akin to Wotan's Blessing of Alberich's unborn son in Act II, Scene 2 of *Die Walküre*. (See Example 7.4*c–d,* where the cadential section of the ritornello, again at the appropriate pitch [*c*], is juxtaposed with Mime's phrase as it appears at the beginning of the scene and the end of the question set [*d*].)[20]

Thus the goal of the Wanderer's ritornello, that is, its cadential section, and the end point of the second set of questions both lead Mime back to the question that was tormenting him before the Wanderer's entrance, the question whose answer he is now fully prepared to receive. Wagner now completes both the dramatic scene and the musical structure quickly and economically by answering Mime's question and by bringing back the ritornello, pared down to just its weighty initial section (which appears in correct form for the first time since the beginning of the scene) and its emphatically transformed cadential section.

This discussion of the Wanderer-Mime scene has concentrated on a single musical process and a single set of thematic materials. It has necessarily skipped over musical factors of great importance in creating the overall shape of the scene, thus excluding the interrelations between the thematic material of the flanking sections and of the question sets they surround—and also excluding tonality. Both exclusions were made to concentrate the focus of the presentation, but the exclusion of tonality had an additional, more polemical point.

Both scenes discussed here are also structured tonally—that from *Tristan* a good deal more clearly than that from *Siegfried*. In omitting mention of tonality I meant to stress that the ritornello form offers a structure that can be under-

---

20. Both motives are derived from the "Weibes Wonne" motive first heard in its characteristic form at measures 1338–40 of *Das Rheingold,* a point Wagner makes by transforming the cadential section in its final occurrences in the scene to a version still closer to the motive from *Das Rheingold* (see the final version in Example 7.4*e*).

stood in much of its subtlety and complexity on the basis of thematic manipula-tions alone, without reference to large-scale tonal motion. Ritornello forms gain a sense of large-scale direction from varying degrees of completion of a recurring thematic sentence and from local harmonic modifications of the three functional sections of that thematic sentence, rather than (or as well as) from large-scale tonal motion. One does not have to depend on apprehension of large-scale tonal movement in order to place the structuring thematic recurrences in some sort of hierarchy. This is a particular advantage for a scene like the one from *Siegfried,* whose principal material is highly unsettled tonally, whose more than six hundred measures must incorporate a tremendous variety of referential tonal incident, and whose tonal structure is thus not easy to follow without close study and multiple hearings. The thematic logic provided by the conventions of the ritornello form gives the listener an alternative way of structuring his experience while he is working his way gradually to a fuller understanding of the tonal rein-forcement.

III

A formal interpretation such as the one advanced above inevitably raises cer-tain questions—first, whether this structural technique may have been bor-rowed, consciously or subconsciously; second, about the likelihood that Wagner's mind might have turned to music of the early eighteenth century at this point in his career; third, about the specific music to which he might have turned in such a case. I cannot claim to answer these questions here. Their an-swer seems to lie in the attitude of Wagner and those in his circle to J. S. Bach. (Although he owned many Handel scores, Wagner had scarcely a good word for the other composer of the early eighteenth century prominent in the concert halls of the early nineteenth, perhaps because Handel represented for him the generally conservative forces of the *Singacademien* and the large music festivals, both English and German.) Bach reception in the nineteenth century has been only spottily investigated so far. By way of a true *Epilog,* I offer one interpreta-tion of the current knowledge.

Wagner's published writings and letters, like his music, show no particular concern with the music of Bach (or with any other early-eighteenth-century music) in the 1840s and early 1850s.[21] By the early 1860s, that attitude had

---

21. An exception here might be made for the motets, and especially *Singet dem Herrn,* which Wagner performed in Dresden in 1848 and to which he repeatedly referred with respect. Familiarity with this piece probably came from Wagner's early training: the performance of Bach's motets was a tradition in Dresden kept alive by Wagner's teacher Theodor Weinlig.

Beyond this, Wagner clearly had in his library in Dresden the scores of both Bach Passions, presumably in the Berlin editions of the early 1830s published by Trautwein (*Johannespassion*) and Schlesinger (*Matthäus-passion*). While in exile he repeatedly wrote to Fischer in Dresden asking him to send his [Wagner's] scores of

changed.[22] The change is emphatically and publicly recorded, so to speak, in the diary entry of 23 September 1865, meant for King Ludwig and later (1878) published in *Was ist deutsch*?[23]—a panegyric to Bach as the great ancestor of the German musical spirit. Private signs turn up earlier, right around the time of *Siegfried,* Act I, and *Tristan.* In a report first transmitted only over fifteen years after the fact and coming down to us in various versions, Robert Franz says that when he visited Wagner in Zurich in the summer of 1857, Wagner led him to his studio and showed him either "*Alles, was ich an Musikalien besitze,*" or "*Was jetzt mein Studium bildet,*" depending on which version you read. The music case, reported Franz, contained nothing but Sebastian Bach, Beethoven, and Franz's Lieder. Though (as Franz himself recognized) the Franz Lieder were clearly included in order to flatter the visitor, and though the remainder clearly did not comprise Wagner's entire music library, this remainder may indicate, as Wagner claimed, what he was particularly concerned with at the time.[24] In a well-known letter to Mathilde Wesendonck of 9 July 1859, Wagner wrote, "How it delighted me that I introduced Sebastian Bach to you the other day! Never had he given me such pleasure, and never had I felt so close to him."[25] In a passage from "*Zukunftsmusik*" (mid-1860), while talking of an ideal kind of phrase construction that is aperiodic and polyphonic, Wagner recommends Bach as a model.[26]

---

the Bach Passions (see letters of 2 March 1855 and 7 November 1856—the latter during Liszt's visit and just before resumption of work on *Siegfried,* Act I).

In *Mein Leben,* Wagner reported a couple of other incidents from the late 1840s: that a triple concerto by Bach as played in a concert by Hiller in early 1847 moved him to "true astonishment," and that during an evening's visit of July 1848 in Breslau to [Johann Theodor] Mosewius, an old family friend and the director of Breslau's *Singacademie,* he had been primarily interested by Mosewius's rich collection of copies of Bach cantatas. Both these recollections were written in the late 1860s, however, and may be colored by Wagner's attitude toward Bach at that time. In his letter to Minna of 11 July 1848 (Richard Wagner, *Sämtliche Briefe* II, ed. Gertrud Strobel and Werner Wolf [Leipzig, 1970], 608), Wagner reported the Breslau visit to Minna ("Abends um 8 Uhr kam ich erst in Breslau an: nachdem ich mir schnell noch die Stadt etwas angesehen besuchte ich *Mosewius* der eine unmässige Freude hatte mich zu sehen; bis 1 Uhr in der Nacht haben wir zusammengesessen"), but said nothing about any impression the cantatas may have made.

22. Martin Geck, "Richard Wagner und die ältere Musik," in Walter Wiora, ed., *Die Ausbreitung des Historismus über die Musik* (Regensburg, 1969), 128. Martin Gregor-Dellin, *Richard Wagner* (Munich, 1980), 493: "Der Choral [at the beginning of *Die Meistersinger,* Act I] legt auch von Wagners Bach-Studium Zeugnis ab, dessen Intensität gerade in den *Tristan* und *Meistersinger* Jahren nicht unterschätzt werden darf."

23. See Otto Strobel, ed., *König Ludwig II. und Richard Wagner: Briefwechsel* (Karlsruhe, 1936), V, 23–24. The entry of 10 September 1865 comparing Wagner's and Cosima's life together to a Bach double fugue appears in I, lxiii. The passage is available in translation in Joachim Bergfeld, ed., *The Dairy of Richard Wagner, 1865–1882: The Brown Book,* trans. George Bird (Cambridge, England, 1980), 72.

24. Carl Friedrich Glasenapp, *Das Leben Richard Wagners* III (Leipzig, 1905), 154–55. Glasenapp notes that this anecdote was transmitted in differing versions, the earliest of which he dates 1873. William Ashton Ellis, *Life of Richard Wagner* VI (London, 1908), 285, gives as his source a letter by Franz of 1882. Since all sources for this anecdote come well after the time when Bach was firmly established in the pantheon of Wagner and his circle, the anecdote may not be reliable, even to the extent of telling us what was included in Wagner's limited current *Studium.*

25. *Richard Wagner an Mathilde Wesendonck* (Berlin, 1904), 160.

26. Richard Wagner, *Sämtliche Schriften* VII, 108.

If this sketchy evidence suggests that Wagner was turning increasingly to Bach's music in the 1850s, what may have caused this turn? Wagner does not refer particularly to the Bach Gesellschaft edition (begun in 1850) or to those around it, most of whom were of the opposite *Partei*.[27] His increasing interest in Bach may have been due to a combination of his interest in Schopenhauer and his own conservative turn in the mid-1850s on the one hand and of the nineteenth-century association of Bach with absolute music and with the *Altdeutsch* on the other.[28] It is also likely that his close friends and colleagues of these years, Franz Liszt and Hans von Bülow, played a part.

Liszt, whose long visit to Wagner in October and November 1856 has already been mentioned, was one of only twenty-four signatories of the announcement and call for subscribers to the Bach Gesellschaft in July 1850, and the only one from Wagner's circle. In 1852, he published his piano transcriptions of six Bach Preludes and Fugues for organ, which contain several large ritornello movements.[29] In early 1856 he had just finished his own Fantasia and Fugue on B–A–C–H.[30]

Von Bülow joined Liszt in performances of a Bach Concerto for three pianos, doubtless the D minor, in concerts of the early 1850s; he also played the D-minor solo Concerto in these same years.[31] In a review from October 1855, von Bülow sang the praises of the two Bach Passions, especially as against Handel's *Messiah,* so often done by the *Singacademien*.[32] Von Bülow's letters record that he played the Italian Concerto in Berlin in December 1858, shortly after a month-long visit to Wagner in Zurich in July and August 1858. His arrangement of the piece was published by Bote and Bock the following year.[33] All of these pieces, of course, contain large ritornello structures.

This evidence, though sketchy, is enough to show that two of Wagner's closest friends and colleagues of the middle and late 1850s were, during those same years, thinking about, transcribing, editing, and performing large instrumental

27. See Hermann Kretzschmar, "Die Bach-Gesellschaft: Bericht über ihre Thätigkeit," in J. S. Bach, *Werke,* ed. Bach Gesellschaft, XLVI (1899), xxiv–xl.

28. See Carl Dahlhaus, "Zur Entstehung der romantischen Bach-Deutung," *Bach Jahrbuch* LXIV (1978), 192–210, esp. 193–96.

29. Item No. 119 in Peter Raabe's catalogue of Liszt's works: see footnote 15. One of the Preludes transcribed, that in B minor (BWV 544), is among the grandest of Bach's keyboard movements in ritornello form. Raabe (*Franz Liszt* II, 63–67) cites evidence of Liszt's particular concern with Bach's music during the Weimar period.

30. Raabe, *Franz Liszt* II, 293–94, Catalogue No. 381.

31. The D minor Triple Concerto, which Mendelssohn, together with Hiller and Liszt, had played publicly as early as 1840, had been published in an edition by F. Griepenkerl in 1845 (Leipzig: Peters). Though the C-major Concerto followed from the same publisher in 1850, the D-minor remained much the better known in the mid-nineteenth century. In a remark of 1878 (cited in Kretzschmar, "Die Bach-Gesellschaft," xxx), Hiller did not seem to know that there was a concerto for three keyboard instruments in C major.

32. Hans von Bülow, *Briefe und Schriften* (Leipzig, 1896), III, 125–26.

33. Hans von Bülow, *Briefe* IV, 206, 286, 289.

ritornello pieces by Bach. It is, of course, not positive evidence that they played the pieces for him or led him to think anew about their musical structures. Perhaps when combined with the structures in Wagner's own music of the same period, however, it may add to the circumstantial evidence pointing to a new attitude toward, and emulation of, the music of Bach by Wagner in the later 1850s.

Chapter 8

Motives and Recurring Themes in *Aida*

ROGER PARKER

The obvious reason for discussing *Aida* in a volume devoted to Verdi and Wagner is that, particularly in its treatment of "motive" and "recurring theme," it is the most nearly Wagnerian of Verdi's operas. Or perhaps one should immediately say "least remotely Wagnerian." Much of the opera sounds anything but motivically developmental, and its handful of recurring themes forms a sorry list beside those impressive tables that offer to guide us through the scores of late Wagner operas. But this simplicity, this only very partial commitment to ensuring musical and dramatic continuity by motivic means, may prove useful. Various types of activity may be isolated with greater security; the risk is lessened of diversions into that Klingsor's garden called Semantic Labeling (a byway which, in uncharitable moments, one may feel enthralled and ensnared virtually an entire century of questing Wagnerians). Furthermore, just because the recurring themes in *Aida* are easily identifiable, it does not necessarily follow that their deployment within the score is rudimentary or merely mechanical. In fact it will be my main contention that the subtlety Verdi employs in this area has largely gone unrecognized, and may even offer us valuable clues to his broader aims as a musical dramatist.

But first I should like to discuss briefly the workings of a further kind of motivic activity, that involving units smaller than the recurring themes mentioned above. Again, the comparison with Wagner is instructive. It is often impossible in Wagner's mature music dramas to draw a clear line between fully fledged leitmotives and what Ernst Kurth called "developmental motives." Carl Dahlhaus puts the matter with characteristic elegance when he compares the motives in *Tristan* to "threads in a woven fabric that come together, surface, disappear and divide, rather than [to] building blocks that are placed beside and above each other."[1] No such problem of classification exists in *Aida*. The recurring themes are all clearly identifiable melodic units, which are repeated with only surface harmonic variation; they are "building blocks" in the Dahlhaus sense, although (as I hope to demonstrate later) the flexibility and subtlety with which they adapt to changed contexts may cause us to question the aptness of that particular metaphor. There is no danger of confusing them with "developmental motives"—a fact that allows us to approach the latter with the minimum of semantic baggage. Perhaps—Wagner as ever stalking the wings—it is this lack of immediately translatable, reassuring "meaning" that has led to the seeming neglect of small-scale motivic working in Verdi analysis, though one need hardly stress that the lack of a semantic label does not necessarily mean any lack of dramatic relevance and articulation.

For a specific example, we might turn to what is probably the opera's most intense area of motivic activity: its Prelude and opening scene. There are several reasons for the relative density of this section. One is historical: the scene is, broadly speaking and with necessary adjustments, an old-fashioned *introduzione,* and as such is a section in which various disparate elements are welded together, in part through motivic means.[2] A second reason concerns the particular nature of this opera. *Aida* is unique in Verdi's work in the extent to which it engages local atmosphere. As do nearly all of Puccini's mature operas, it seems constantly to allude to its ambience. This means that the *tinta* (or identifying color) of the work is of great importance, and that we need a tightly unified opening scene in which to set forward some elements of this *tinta* with special clarity.

The Prelude to the opera is, of course, overtly developmental, its two main themes undergoing a continual series of intervallic transformations. The themes (Ex. 8.1*a* and *b*) are later to be associated with two of the opera's central opposing forces—the first with Aida and her love for Radames, the second with the Egyptian priests—and so it is hardly surprising that they are contrasting in register, rhythm, and degree of chromaticism. However, Example 8.1 shows that they are also musically complementary, and derive from one another. Verdi makes part of this relationship explicit when he combines the themes contrapuntally at an early stage of the Prelude (Ex. 8.1*c*).

What is perhaps less obvious is the extent to which this motivic development spills into the first scene. Example 8.1*d* isolates a small idea from measure 8 of the Prelude, a point that signals the end of the first period and a move to F♯ major. Example 8.1*e* identifies an important moment from near the end of the

1. Carl Dahlhaus, *Richard Wagner's Music Dramas*, trans. Mary Whittall (Cambridge, England, 1979), 63.

2. For an account of the Rossinian *introduzione*, see Philip Gossett, "Gioachino Rossini and the Conventions of Composition," *Acta Musicologica* XLII (1970), 48–58.

EXAMPLE 8.1. Motivic transformations in the Prelude and opening scene of *Aida*.

Prelude, in which this same idea (as its preceding measures show, one that has been particularly protean in its intervallic transformations) again appears. And these two moments together offer a clue to an important level of structural balance in the overall tonality of the Prelude: eight measures into the piece, we abandon D major, achieve an F♯ pedal, and begin an enormous tonal digression; eight measures from the end, the digression ends, an F♯ pedal is quitted, and the "home" key of D major is, for the first time, unequivocally established. The tonal context gives the motive at Example 8.1*e* considerable significance and weight—so much so that, when the first scene begins, and those same four pitches are immediately repeated and contrapuntally developed (Ex. 8.1*f*), the sense is of a gentle continuation of musical activity rather than of any new musical event.

Such an unemphatic opening is of course dramatically appropriate. Ramfis and Radames are in mid-conversation as the curtain rises. But, more important, it is as if the "inner drama" of the orchestral Prelude, with its play of opposing motives, carries on underneath the external action.[3] To strengthen this impression, and immediately to associate the "Priests" theme (Ex. 8.1*b*) with Ramfis, his first vocal statement is underpinned by a clear, accented version of that theme. However, motives becoming ever more entwined as they develop, the descending scale is now formed from "Aida-like" appoggiaturas (Ex. 8.1*g*).

Perhaps the point has been sufficiently stressed. It will, however, be instructive to mention a few places in this first scene where motivic transformations are used to particular effect. Certainly the densest and most telling episode comes during Amneris's jealous interrogation of Radames. With highly pointed meaning, she asks him:

> Nè un altro sogno mai
> Più gentil, più soave,
> Al core ti parlò? Non hai tu in Menfi
> Desiderii, speranze?

> Has another dream
> Gentler, sweeter,
> Never spoken to your heart? Don't you have in Memphis
> Desires, hopes?

It is not, of course, difficult for the audience to divine exactly what this "altro sogno" is. Unless they have just slept through "Celeste Aida," they can be in no doubt as to the object of Radames's *amour fou*. The music that illustrates Amneris's warring emotions and as yet inchoate suspicions also teeters on the edge

---

3. A sketch of this opening conversation is published in Carlo Gatti's *Verdi nelle immagini* (Milan, 1941), 187. In that earlier version, the sense of an essentially orchestral argument is even stronger: the voices—as so frequently in Verdi's early sketches—do little more than recite on fixed pitches.

EXAMPLE 8.2. Motivic transformations of the Aida theme in *Aida,* Act I, Scene 1.

of discovery. As is shown in Example 8.2*a*, "Nè un altro sogno mai" is a fragmentary, unrealized conflation of the Aida theme; and, for good measure, the entire phrase describes another heavily chromatic, appoggiatura-laden version of the "Priests" theme. The ensuing allegro between Radames and Amneris, "Quale inchiesta!" is then based on a further version of "Nè un altro sogno mai" (Ex. 8.2*c*). It is thus a moment of extraordinary musical and dramatic clarification when this duet is itself interrupted by a definitive version of the Aida theme, as the heroine appears on stage for the first time. We shall return to this passage in another context shortly.[4]

Other moments of motivic clarification are perhaps more obvious, though not always easier to interpret dramatically (at least in any narrow sense of the word). In the context of the following scene it is hardly surprising that a message from the gods is announced by means of a kind of *Ur*-version of the "Priests" theme, one in which all decoration is eschewed and in which the original gesture toward counterpoint is fused into a monolithic, static single voice (Ex. 8.3*a*). And it is similarly fitting that Ramfis's verse in the final chorus ("Su! del Nilo") subtly combines an outline of the "Priests" theme with elements of the contrapuntally developed subject that underpinned his earlier conversation with Radames (Ex. 8.3*b*). More problematic is the identity between the bass parts charted in Example 8.4. It is of course appropriate that the solemn brass fanfare that heralds the King's first entrance (Ex. 8.4*a*) should have an identical bass progression to the final chorus, which the King himself leads off (Ex. 8.4*b*); but when the same figure underpins the first bars of Aida's closing peroration, "Numi pietà" (Ex. 8.4*c*), we are given pause. We could explain this in

4. This is perhaps the place to draw attention to the Overture Verdi wrote for *Aida* at the time of its Milan premiere in 1872. In its early stages, the Overture is identical with the Prelude, but later on Ex. 8.2*c* and "Numi pietà" are given an extended airing, with contrapuntal working in plenty. Though this is certainly further evidence that Verdi was actively pursuing the "symphonic" possibilities of motivic combination and juxtaposition, one hesitates to make much of it, for the simple reason that the end product is one of the composer's most startlingly vulgar creations.

EXAMPLE 8.3. Motivic transformations of the "Priests" theme in *Aida*, Act I, Scene 1.

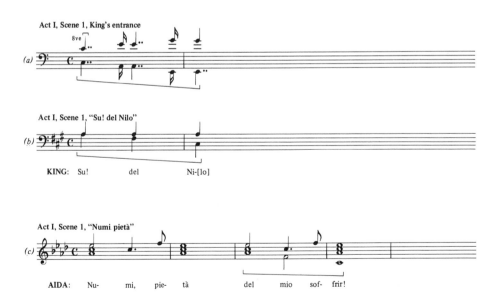

EXAMPLE 8.4. Repeated bass progressions in *Aida*, Act I, Scene 1.

semantic terms only by relying to a dangerous degree on hindsight: Klingsor's garden stretches welcomingly before us. The bass is, after all, a clearly audible version of an important figure from the Prelude (Ex. 8.1*d–f*), and "Numi pietà" is no more than the final, lyrical stage of the complex transformational journey of this figure through the opening scenes of the opera. No simple equation of music and meaning is needed to feel the aptness and persuasiveness of its repetition.

As everyone knows, in good music a search for "motivic coherence" will almost always be rewarded in overabundance. Then comes the frightening moment when one realizes that the more levels of coherence the music displays, the less coherent one's own exegesis is likely to become. In operatic analysis, perhaps more so than in "purer" musical forms, it is certainly valuable to nurse such ambiguities. Nevertheless, and critical incoherence notwithstanding, motivic cross-reference and development do play an active part in Verdian music drama and certainly deserve more attention than they receive.[5]

* * *

In comparison with the motivic complexity and richness of this opening scene, Verdi's use of recurring themes in *Aida* may seem rather unimaginative. Unlike those much-discussed "curses" and "kisses" from other famous works, repetitions do not coincide with obvious dramatic climaxes, and frequently involve the old "visiting card" function that Verdi had experimented with so doggedly in *I due Foscari* some thirty years earlier. Joseph Kerman, in an interesting general consideration of thematic recurrence in Verdi, goes so far as to call this aspect of *Aida* "in general . . . stiff and uninteresting," making an exception only for an appearance of the "Priests" theme during Act III.[6] If this is indeed the case, it would be a curious anomaly in a work so calculated in musical design and structure as *Aida*. While the Verdi of the 1840s may occasionally have employed such a device in an external, experimental manner, by 1870 he would surely use it only if it fitted into the larger pattern of the work.

As a test case, we might concentrate on the principal recurring theme of the opera, that connected with Aida. A summary chart of its appearances, given in Example 8.5, already calls into question the justness of terming it merely a "visiting card." After the Prelude, it appears twice in each of the first two acts, and once more near the beginning of Act III; repetitions neatly alternate between orchestral announcements of Aida's entrance on stage and vocal statements by

5. Readers may like to consult two earlier essays that discuss the issue: Frits Noske's "*Otello*: Drama through Structure," in his *The Signifier and the Signified: Studies in the Operas of Mozart and Verdi* (The Hague, 1977), 133–70; and my own "Levels of Motivic Definition in Verdi's *Ernani*," *19th-Century Music* VI (1982–1983), 141–50. But see the comments on Noske's idea of a "musico-dramatic sign" in the editors' Introduction to the present volume, 12–13.

6. Joseph Kerman, "Verdi's Use of Recurring Themes," in Harold S. Powers, ed., *Studies in Music History: Essays for Oliver Strunk* (Princeton, 1968), 503.

EXAMPLE 8.5. Appearances of the Aida theme.

Aida herself. The texts accompanying the vocal statements immediately make it clear that the theme represents Aida by reference to just one aspect of her character: her timorous, uncertain love for Radames. The absence of the theme in the body of Act III and in Act IV thus immediately assumes some dramatic significance. The Aida of Act III is for the most part involved with Amonasro. In Act IV, for the first and only time, she takes matters into her own hands, ceases to be torn between love and duty, and makes a final commitment to Radames. The tentative eroticism of her identifying theme would be quite out of place in their deathbed reunion.

The first appearance of the theme after the Prelude alerts us to its potential for dramatic and musical impact. In view of the stage action, the possibilities for music drama might seem unpromising: Amneris's "Nè un altro sogno mai" (already discussed) causes Radames some confusion, and her suspicions are intensified as she notices the change that comes over him when Aida is seen in the distance. The fact that Aida is accompanied by "her" theme would seem naively redundant—a "visiting card" in an embossed envelope. However, the manner in which the theme is linked to its musical context is by no means routine. We have already mentioned something of the motivic preparation that precedes it; the tonal context is, if anything, even more revealing. Example 8.6*a* gives the music of the episode, together with a summary graph of the context (Ex. 8.6*b*), showing how the theme acts as an interruption within a closed tonal form in E minor, the allegro "Quale inchiesta!" The theme gestures persistently toward, but never quite reaches, G major. As we can see, the repeated dissonances of the E-minor music, in particular C–B and F♯–E, are taken up in the Aida theme and, despite an increase in local chromaticism, are gently resolved in the new context. Even secondary dissonances around the tonic and dominant of E minor, D♯ and A♯, become absorbed enharmonically into the Aida theme as E♭ and B♭. The appearance of Aida and "her" theme act, in other words, as a moment of tonal release, but not a permanent one; the tensions are resolved only locally and, when E minor returns, its characteristic dissonances reappear unchanged.

This accords precisely with the dramatic situation. Aida's appearance occasions Radames's longing glances and (albeit involuntarily) releases him from Amneris's probing questions; but, on the larger level, there is no true resolution, merely an intensification of Amneris's suspicions. It is telling that Radames's one comment during the interruption, "Dessa!" ("It is her!"), is "consonant" with the orchestral Aida theme, coinciding in pitch and rhythmic placement with the final note of its first statement. On the other hand, Amneris's vocal line weaves deviously underneath the theme, meeting it only at the moment of greatest dissonance, on the key word *sguardo* ("look").

Incidentally, the vocal focus on scale degree 6̂ of E minor is certainly not fortuitous, and has wider implications for the scene. The note C, as shown on the graph, is plainly the suspended link between the allegro sections and the Aida theme, and on a larger level the neighbor-motion B–C–B seems to carry an exceptional weight of verbal significance. As we see from Example 8.7, isolation of the motive results in a succinct verbal summary of the action, from tentative probing to vicious condemnation: "*Radames*: 'l'arcano amore . . .' *Amneris*: 'Oh guai! . . . se un altro amore . . .' *Radames*: 'Mi lesse nel pensier! . . .' *Amneris*: 'Aida! . . . o rea schiava! . . . Ah! Trema rea schiava, trema.' "

The second appearance of the Aida theme, at the center of the famous soliloquy "Ritorna vincitor," is at once more extreme, more personal, and more complex. Aida's exposure to the militaristic exhibition of "Su! del Nilo" swings her violently in favor of family and homeland, but condemnation of the Egyptians is suddenly cut short by recollection of her love for Radames, a recollection that takes the form of a vocal statement of her theme. The theme in turn gives way to further anguished confusion, in "I sacri nomi del padre, d'amante," and eventu-

EXAMPLE 8.6. Aida theme, Act I, Scene 1: first appearance after Prelude.

EXAMPLE 8.6. *continued*.

ally leads to the pathetic capitulation of "Numi pietà." We are, then, in a more kinetic situation: the theme illustrates one link in a chain of emotional events. It is thus to be expected that here we have a tonal motion that develops *through* the theme rather than being interrupted by it (see Ex. 8.8*a*).

Most immediately striking, however, is the fact that even though the theme appears a tone lower than earlier it is nevertheless preceded again by a passage in E minor, "L'insana parola." And the identity of the two E-minor sections is not merely a matter of pitch but is strengthened by thematic recall (Ex. 8.8*b*) and by rough equivalence of tempo and "affect." However, before the Aida theme appears, E minor is brutally invaded by a diminished chord, the two tritones of which are set in stark vocal opposition by Aida (Ex. 8.8*c*). The vivid association of each tritone with her warring passions is evident.[7] Her theme then proceeds to resolve the latter of these tritones (B♭–E) in a manner similar to that we saw in Example 8.6, thoughts of love temporarily releasing tonal tension, absorbing chromaticism. But the force of the first tritone (G–D♭[C♯]) remains, the strength of its articulation too great to find enharmonic release in the Aida theme's rising chromatic line. D♭ reappears as a dominant ninth in the final cadence of the theme and is taken up by Aida in her move away from F major. And, as her vocal D♭ returns, she recalls her wish to destroy Radames: "Imprecherò la morte a Radames." Again, as in the first instance, the Aida theme is a small tonal island of refuge, affording brief respite from the gathering tide of conflicting emotion. In this sense, its deeper implication with surrounding musical events on this second appearance is a strong indication of the direction the drama is taking.

Our sense that the Aida theme becomes more thoroughly involved with its surroundings is certainly intensified by events in Act II. Its two appearances there are intimately bound into a closed structure (the Amneris-Aida Duet) that engages traditional formal expectations—so much so that they are not fully comprehensible without a preliminary glance at the larger form. As we see from

7. G–D♭(C♯)—"Struggete le squadri / Dei nostri oppressor!" ("death to the enemies of our homeland!"); B♭–E—"Sventurata! che dissi?" ("But what am I saying?" [this will mean the death of Radames]).

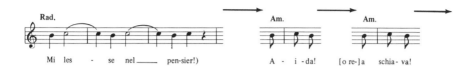

EXAMPLE 8.7. Verbal implications of the neighbor motive B–C–B.

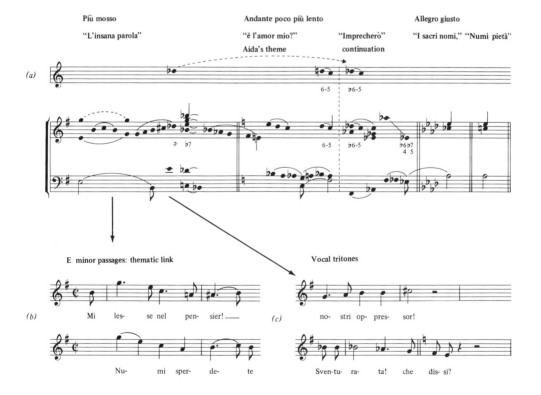

EXAMPLE 8.8. *Aida*, Act I, Scene 1, Aida's "Ritorna vincitor!"

Chart 8.1, the Duet follows only partially traditions of nineteenth-century duet structure. Instead of a four-part form (plus Scena), with a patterned alternation of "kinetic" and "static" movements, we have one large "kinetic" movement (the *tempo d'attacco*) followed by two "static" ones (the adagio and cabaletta). The confrontation is preceded by an orchestral statement of the Aida theme, as Amneris watches the heroine approach. In the opening Scena (in free verse, *versi sciolti*), Amneris tries to ingratiate herself with Aida. The *tempo d'attacco* begins, as it so often does in nineteenth-century Italian opera, with a patterned statement of opposing attitudes: Aida's tormented, hidden love for Radames (again articulated through her theme); and Amneris's tormented, hidden jealousy. The verse becomes fixed, into *doppio quinario*. From there the action develops with increasing momentum and verbal freedom as Amneris breaks down Aida's defenses, first by the false announcement of Radames's death, and then by its contradiction.[8]

The adagio then restores verbal and musical order with the static definition of a new level of opposition. Aida has capitulated, and pathetically admits her love; Amneris gives unrestrained vent to her hatred. The cabaletta follows immediately, to restate these positions against the distant background of a choral reprise of Act I's "Su! del Nilo." Amneris strides off. Aida remains for a final, imploring reprise of "Numi pietà."

It is beyond the scope of this essay to examine in detail the music of the Duet, or even to refer to interesting aspects of its genesis.[9] But it is important to point out how articulations of the Aida theme interact with larger issues. Perhaps most obvious is its involvement with a cycle of dominant pedals that cuts across the first half of the scene. As we see from Example 8.9, the orchestral statement of Aida's theme, just before the Duet proper begins, is underpinned by a pedal G. After the Scena, which tonicizes A, Aida's theme returns a fourth higher, for the start of the *tempo d'attacco*. Then, as the verse form changes yet again and Amneris begins her assault on Aida, a further pedal is established, on F, another step in the cycle of fifths. This measured preparation finally unwinds as Amneris launches her first thunderbolt: she announces Radames's death, and the F pedal is emphatically released onto a B♭-minor triad. From then until the adagio, all is flux as we lurch from one diminished-chord crisis to the next.

An even more fundamental element of the articulation of the Duet involving the Aida theme is the textual and musical relationship established between the

---

8. Ricordi's production book (the *disposizione scenica*), which is the best indication we have of Verdi's and his collaborators' ideas on staging, is particularly revealing during this section, its gathering number of stage directions making clear that stage action should mirror the rapidly changing music and verse. The *disposizione scenica* is reproduced, in English translation, in Hans Busch, *Verdi's "Aida": The History of an Opera in Letters and Documents* (Minneapolis, [1978]), 558–618.

9. For further information, see Philip Gossett, "Verdi, Ghislanzoni, and *Aida*: The Uses of Convention," *Critical Inquiry* I, no. 2 (1974), 291–334, in particular 321–24; and Marcello Conati, "Aspetti di melodrammaturgia verdiana: a proposito di una sconosciuta versione del finale del duetto Aida-Amneris," *Studi verdiani* 3 (1985), 45–78.

CHART 8.1. Amneris-Aida Duet structure.

TRADITIONAL MODEL	AMNERIS-AIDA DUET, ACT II, SCENE 1
Scena (versi sciolti)	Scena (versi sciolti)
1. *Tempo d'attacco* (versi lirici)	*Tempo d'attacco* (versi lirici)
	(versi sciolti)
2. Adagio (versi lirici)	Adagio (versi lirici)
3. *Tempo di mezzo* (versi lirici)	
4. Cabaletta (versi lirici)	Cabaletta (versi lirici)

EXAMPLE 8.9. Amneris-Aida Duet, *Aida*, Act II, Scene 1.

beginning of the *tempo d'attacco* and the adagio. Both are dominated vocally by Aida and have texts that, if viewed from a certain perspective, are interestingly related. As we see from Chart 8.2, the two quatrains are set in identical verse forms (*doppio quinario*) and in spite of the transformation of lexical features—the greater directness of the second passage—each contains three main semantic elements. First there is a statement on the nature of love, in which the word *amore* is repeated in a prominent position. In the *tempo d'attacco*:

> Amore! amore!—gaudio . . . tormento . . .
> Soave ebbrezza—ansia crudel!

and in the adagio:

> È vero . . . io l'amo d'immenso amore
>
> . . . .
>
> Io vivo solo per questo amor . . .

Then comes an acknowledgment of Amneris's superior power and of the happiness this can bring her: the *tempo d'attacco*'s "Un tuo sorriso—mi schiude il ciel," and, with typically greater explicitness, the adagio's "Tu sei felice . . . tu sei possente." Finally, the all-important indicator of difference is a play on "I," on "you," and on "sorrow." The *tempo d'attacco* has "Ne' tuoi dolori—la vita io sento," while the adagio reverses the roles, transfers sorrow from "you" to "me": "Pietà ti prenda del mio dolore."

The musical setting of these passages continues the parallel. As we see from Example 8.10, the phrase structures are identical, while the change of tempo (allegro animato to adagio) and mode (F major to F minor) makes the necessary alteration of "affect." The mode change is particularly interesting: not only does it link with a series of mixtures through the duet, but it also serves to make manifest the modal mixtures hinted at in the Aida theme, in one sense releasing its tragic implications. More telling still is the way the opening phrases of the theme are absorbed into the central climax of "Pietà ti prenda." It is as if Aida's vocal statement of her love has finally been laid to rest, transmuted into tragedy and the acceptance of fate.

Small wonder that the theme's final appearance in the opera, near the beginning of Act III, is shadowy and unrealized, wisps of orchestral sound almost engulfed by the evocation of ambience. As Pierluigi Petrobelli has shown, the

---

CHART 8.2. *Tempo d'attacco* and adagio compared (Amneris-Aida Duet).

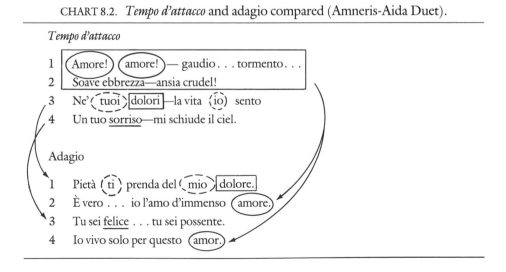

EXAMPLE 8.10. Musical setting of *tempo d'attacco* and adagio
compared, Amneris-Aida Duet.

opening moments of the act are characterized in the simplest possible manner, through a single pitch, G. A few moments before Aida appears, Ramfis and Amneris emerge from the background and attempt to revive something of the motivic world left in Act I, Scene 1. But their initiative is short-lived: soon the G sonority is reasserted and, in Petrobelli's telling phrase, "Amneris and Ramfis are 'absorbed' into the night, cold and impassive as is the chanting of the priests."[10] The orchestral Aida theme follows after some further moments of chanting. It also grows directly and literally from the characteristic sonority of the Act III Prelude, is restricted to a middle register, and is accompanied throughout by busy string figures that constantly remind us of the nocturnal, rustling atmosphere. As a final gesture of submission, it merges into the bass as Aida appears on stage. True, our heroine's struggle is not yet over, but from now on the primary adversary is Amonasro; the battle will be joined on different, perhaps even sterner terms.

∗   ∗   ∗

It is no accident that each occurrence of the Aida theme has occasioned new analytical directions. As we have seen, each statement has responded to the changing dramatic situation by engaging its surroundings with a new degree of complexity: from the relatively simple incursion of Act I, Scene 1; to the more

10. Pierluigi Petrobelli, "Music in the Theatre (à propos of *Aida,* Act III)," in James Redmond, ed., *Themes in Drama 3: Drama, Dance and Music* (Cambridge, England, 1981), 134.

unstable and personally revealing appearance in "Ritorna vincitor"; and finally to the many-layered confrontation of Act II, Scene 1. In this way, its "transmutation" into the adagio "Pietà ti prenda" and subsequent absorption into the ambience of the Act III Prelude become profoundly indicative of the fact that a new phase of Aida's progress is about to begin. My argument has centered on technical matters, in particular on the way the theme interacts with various tonal schemes and events. The central point is, however, a dramatic one. The changing status of Aida's theme is intimately bound to our changing perception of the heroine in the first half of the opera.

But there is, I think, a larger conclusion, one that involves both recurring themes and the smaller-scale motives considered earlier. We might remind ourselves, returning to Dahlhaus's image, that, however subtle and complex its interaction with surrounding events, the Aida theme does nevertheless recur largely intact, without significant internal development. It is in that sense a "building block." But the metaphor is too restricted, may even carry with it a suggestion of condescension, of an artistic purpose that is narrowly pragmatic or synthetic. The Verdi of *Aida* deserves something better.

The business of articulating musical drama through such manipulations, through the clash of systems and their imperatives, is one of the essential elements of Verdi's art. As I hope I have demonstrated, this art is, no less than Wagner's, one of "transition"; but, in spite of its rich vein of motivic working, passages such as the opening of Act I do not typically aspire to a condition of Wagnerian fluidity. The process is more aptly compared to seismic disturbance: large units, heavy with tension and the accumulation of years, make contact with one another, causing dramatic readjustments and, occasionally, even an alteration in the entire surrounding landscape. It is in this robust, violent, elemental context that Verdi's play of motives and recurring themes seems best approached and, perhaps, more readily appreciated.

Part 3

Tonality and Structure

Chapter 9

The Tonality of *Rigoletto*

MARTIN CHUSID

In an earlier essay, I proposed that D♭, the key of Monterone's curse (Act I, No. 2) and the key in which the opera ends, is the principal tonality of *Rigoletto*.[1] This paper develops that suggestion in more detail and supplements those remarks with a more comprehensive analysis of the opera's key structure. (See Charts 9.1 and 9.2.)

A glance at the charts shows the importance of D♭, and also of A♭, the opera's dominant. Other keys are categorized as "closely" or "moderately closely" related to these two tonalities (Chart 9.3) or as "more distant" (Chart 9.4). In Charts 9.1 and 9.2 these categories are shown in the second and third columns. Although for brevity's sake the words "or moderately" are omitted, the second column includes all the keys represented in Chart 9.3.

The hierarchy thus created may require some preliminary comment. It is based, first, on the usual assumption that keys constructed on scale degrees $\hat{1}$ to $\hat{6}$ are closely related to the tonic, as are the opposite modes of the tonic and dominant, here D♭ minor and A♭ minor. Second, keys closely related to A♭ (E♭ major and C minor) count as "moderately close" (and hence warrant inclusion in Chart 9.3) by virtue of their importance in the Prelude and Acts I and II, and because of their position, usually in close proximity to A♭, D♭, or F minor. The keys at the opposite mode to B♭ minor, F minor, and C minor (B♭, F, and C major) are designated as "moderately closely" related, and those on the lowered third, sixth, and seventh degrees of D♭ (F♭ [=E], B♭♭ [=A], and C♭ [=B]) are assumed to be "distantly" related. In this opera (and elsewhere), Verdi followed compositional practices dating back to the late eighteenth century in moving to

1. Martin Chusid, "Rigoletto and Monterone: A Study in Musical Dramaturgy," *Proceedings of the XI Congress of the International Musicological Society* (Copenhagen, 1974), I, 325–36. Reprinted in *Verdi: Bollettino dell'istituto di studi verdiani* IX (Parma, 1982), 1544–58. Page references are to the latter version.

CHART 9.1. Keys in *Rigoletto,* Act I.

NO. AND TITLE	CLOSELY RELATED KEYS	MORE DISTANT KEYS
No. 1, Prelude, 34 mm.	c [A♭: iii]	
	⊠ ↓	
No. 2, Introduzione		
Part 1: mm. 1–440	A♭ [A♭: I]	
Part 2: mm. 441–521		
m. 441	c [A♭: iii]	
m. 458	C [A♭: III]	
m. 478	f [A♭: vi/D♭: iii]	
	mod.	
m. 497	D♭ [D♭: I]	
m. 504		(D)
Stretta: mm. 522–57	d♭ [D♭: i]	
mm. 558–626	D♭ [D♭: I]	
No. 3, Duetto [R, S]	↓	
Introduction: mm. 1–13		
m. 1	f [D♭: iii]	
m. 11	((C)) ⊠	
Duet: mm. 14–69	F [D♭: III]	
No. 4, Scena e Duetto [R, G]	↓	
Scena: mm. 1–124		
m. 1	F [D♭: III]	
m. 12	((C)) ⊠	
m. 15	D♭ [D♭: I]	
	mod.	
m. 30	B♭ [D♭: VI]	
m. 41		(E)
m. 59	((C)) ⊠	
	f [D♭: iii/A♭: vi]	
m. 69	C [A♭: III]	
	mod.	
Andante: mm. 125–161	A♭ [A♭: I]	
Tempo di mezzo: mm. 162–242		
m. 162	a♭ [A♭: i]	
	mod.	
m. 184	D♭ [A♭: IV/D♭: I]	
m. 203		(A)
m. 229	e♭ [D♭: ii/A♭: v]	
Cabaletta: mm. 243–350	E♭ [D♭: II/A♭: V]	
No. 5, Scena e Duetto [G, D]	↓	
Scena: mm. 1–69		
m. 9		G; mod.; ((D))
Andantino: mm. 70–140	B♭ [D♭: VI/A♭: II]	
Tempo di mezzo: mm. 141–70		
m. 152	b♭ [D♭: vi]	
m. 160	d♭ [D♭: i]	
Cabaletta: mm. 171–248	D♭ [D♭: I]	
	↓	

CHART 9.1. *continued*.

No. 6, Aria [G]
    Scena: mm. 1–10   mod.
    Aria: mm. 11–85   E

No. 7, Finale 1⁰
    Part 1: mm. 1–59
        m. 4   ((C))   [X]
        m. 8   A♭ [D♭: V/A♭: I]
    Part 2: mm. 60–167
        m. 60   E♭ [D♭: II/A♭: V]
        m. 133   e♭ [D♭: ii/A♭: v]

(D♭) = tonicized chord of D♭
((E)) = sonority of E
 ↓   = tonal link between numbers
[X]   = recurring musical figure stressing the sonority of C ("Quel vecchio maledivami")
mod. = modulatory

CHART 9.2. Keys in *Rigoletto,* Acts II and III.

NO. AND TITLE	CLOSELY RELATED KEYS	MORE DISTANT KEYS

Act II

No. 8, Scena ed Aria [D]
    Prelude and Scena: mm. 1–56

m. 1		d [D: i]
m. 32		mod.
m. 47	D♭ [D♭: I]	
Adagio: mm. 57–88	G♭ [D♭: IV]	(= F♯ [D: III])
Tempo di mezzo: mm. 89–162		
m. 89	(G♭ [D♭: IV])	F♯ [D: III]
m. 106		A [D: V]
Cabaletta: mm. 163–260		D [D: I]

No. 9, Scena ed Aria [R]
    Scena: mm. 1–76

m. 1		e [D: ii/E: i]
m. 40		mod.
Aria		
Part 1: mm. 77–102	c [A♭: iii]	
Part 2: mm. 103–13	f [A♭: vi/D♭: iii]	
Part 3: mm. 114–30	D♭ [D♭: I]	

continued

CHART 9.2. *continued*.

NO. AND TITLE	CLOSELY RELATED KEYS	MORE DISTANT KEYS
No. 10, Scena e Duetto [R, G]	(Finale 2⁰)	
Scena: mm. 1–68		
m. 1	D♭ [D♭: I]	
m. 5	b♭ [D♭: vi]	
m. 21	f [D♭: iii/A♭: vi]	
m. 33	C [A♭: III]	
Andantino: mm. 69–166		
Part 1: mm. 69–119*		
mm. 69 and 90		e [D: ii]
mm. 86 and 100	C [A♭: III] ⟵⟶	
Part 2: mm. 120–36	f [A♭: vi/D♭: iii]	
Part 3: mm. 137–66	D♭ [D♭: I]	
Tempo di mezzo: mm. 167–94	c [A♭: iii]	
Cabaletta: mm. 195–283	A♭ [A♭: I]	
Act III		
No. 11, Scena e Canzone [D]		
Prelude: mm. 1–10		a ((E))
Scena: mm. 10–36		
m. 15	mod.	
m. 25	↓	((E))
Canzone: mm. 37–153		[B] [E: V]
No. 12, Quartetto [D, M, R, G]		
Part 1: mm. 1–48		E~c♯ [E: I~vi]
	(d♭ [D♭: i] =)	
Part 2: mm. 49–105	D♭ [D♭: I]	(= C♯ [E: VI])
Recit.: mm. 106–12	D♭ [D♭: I]	
No. 13, Scena, Terzetto [S, M, G], e Tempesta		
Scena: mm. 1–221		
m. 1		D [D: I]
m. 59		G [D: IV]
m. 80		[B] [D: VI/E: V]
m. 152		E [E: I]
m. 182		A [E: IV/D: V]
Terzetto: mm. 222–400		
mm. 222 and 288		d [D: i]
mm. 235 and 301		D [D: I]
m. 320		d [D: i]
m. 360		A [D: V]
		↓

CHART 9.2. *continued*.

No. 14, Scena e Duetto Finale [R, G]
  Scena: mm. 1–176
    m. 1   A [D: V/E: IV]
    m. 23   C [A♭: III]
    m. 40   mod.
    m. 78   B̲   [E: V]
    m. 115   mod.
    m. 125   ((E))
    m. 157   E♭ [A♭: V]
    m. 167   mod.
  Largo: mm. 177–230
    m. 177   d♭ [D♭: i]
    m. 193   D♭ [D♭: I]
    m. 217   d♭ [D♭: i]

---

    *Key signature and beginning of each strophe in E minor; final phrase of each strophe and last section in C major.

    (D♭)   = tonicized chord of D♭
    ((E))   = sonority of E
    ↓   = tonal link between numbers
    B̲   = recurring Canzone in B major ("La donna è mobile")
    mod.   = modulatory

CHART 9.3. Keys closely and moderately closely related to D♭ major and
A♭ major in *Rigoletto*.

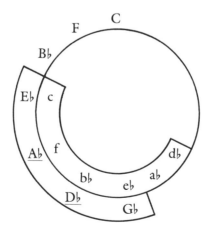

Enclosed keys are more closely related than those outside the enclosure.

CHART 9.4. More distant keys.

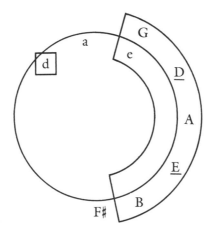

Enclosed keys are more closely related than those outside the enclosure.

the key of the opposite mode as a means of extending his range of related keys, and he usually did so directly from a key labeled here as "closely" related. In *Rigoletto,* for example, the Perigordino and "Voi congiuraste" from the Introduction (No. 2) are both in C major, and each follows a passage in C minor. Likewise, the F-major Duet for Rigoletto and Sparafucile (No. 3) has an extremely important introduction in F minor and a striking retransition in that key, and it borrows notes, chords, and even the tonicization of related areas from F minor.

Perhaps the assumption requiring most discussion is my initial one, that D♭ is the tonic. For one thing, *Rigoletto* does not start in D♭. However, five of the fourteen numbers in the opera end in that key. These include both the Introduction (No. 2) and the *Finale Ultimo* (No. 14), the Duet for Gilda and the Duke (No. 5), Rigoletto's scene in Act II (No. 9), and the Quartet in Act III (No. 12). All of these are substantial numbers and are positioned so that the listener is periodically reminded of the key. Two each are in Acts I and III, and the other is the central number of three in Act II. Moreover, two additional numbers have sections in D♭. In the scene before the first Duet for Rigoletto and Gilda (No. 4) a tonicized D♭ begins Rigoletto's outburst "O uomini! o natura," and in the *tempo di mezzo* a more lengthy passage in the same key begins with his "Culto, famiglia, la patria." The tonality also appears twice in their second Duet (No. 10): Rigoletto's "Piangi, piangi fanciulla" and Gilda's solo portion of the cabaletta, "O mio padre, qual gioia feroce." Finally, a D♭ chord is employed for the recitative "M'odi, ritorna a casa" following the Quartet. Appearing, then, in seven numbers and the recitative following No. 12, D♭ is by far the most frequently heard "color" in the opera.

The dominant, A♭, is heard significantly in four numbers, three of which have been mentioned previously: the Introduction (No. 2) and the Duets for Rigoletto and Gilda in Acts I and II (Nos. 4 and 10). It is also important in the Finale of Act I (No. 7). The placing in each instance is again noteworthy. The key of A♭ opens two crucial numbers, the Introduction and Finale to Act I, and closes the Finale to Act II with the cabaletta, "Sì, vendetta." In the first of the father-daughter Duets (No. 4) it is the key of the Andante ("Deh non parlare al misero"), begins the *tempo di mezzo* (Gilda's "Il nome vostro ditemi"), and is also heard importantly in the cabaletta "Ah! veglia, o donna" (mm. 259–74: this is not evident from the chart). We will have occasion to return to this last passage later.

Another observation about the overall key scheme seems in order. Verdi introduces areas distant to the A♭–D♭ axis only gradually in *Rigoletto*. There are relatively few in Act I, and although more appear in Act II, the emphasis is still on closely related areas. Only in Act III do the distant keys predominate. One simple reason for this is the presence of the storm in Act III: a physical disturbance that seems virtually to command (rather than invite) unusual tonal activity. But tonal distance may also symbolize dramatic distance (either geographic or temporal), and thus account for the distant key areas in Act III: Sparafucile's inn marks the most distant point from the Duke's court (the locale for the first part of Act I and all of Act II); and a month has elapsed between Act II and Act III, while there were only hours between the first two acts.

Most important, the dramatic progress justifies a wider range of tonal expression. In Act III Rigoletto has raised the stakes of the game considerably, from mockery and dishonor to murder.

So far the discussion has centered on one aspect of musical design (key relationships) rather than on the drama. This too is based on an assumption, namely, that the musical forces or tendencies inherent in major-minor tonality that operate in the instrumental music of the eighteenth and nineteenth centuries also operate in music for the theater. The successful composer of opera coordinates these forces of abstract musical design with the drama; or, more accurately, he exploits them in the service of the drama.

*   *   *

Most commentators on *Rigoletto* tend to overlook or minimize the importance of the first part of the Introduction, the section before Monterone's entrance. Yet this is one of the longest continuously unfolding passages in the opera (440 mm.). The tonal emphasis is on A♭ major. The Introduction begins with five separate themes played by the wind band backstage, and they are heard in four different keys (Chart 9.5). Each theme is important later in the Introduction, and with rare exceptions it returns in its original key.

Bar no.	1	9	17	25	42
CHART 9.5. The themes of the Introduction.					
Theme	B(anda) 1	B2	B3	B4	B5
Key	Ab	Eb	c	Ab	Db
In Ab:	I	V	iii	I	IV

In the earliest published score of the opera,[2] as well as in the new complete edition (*Works of Giuseppe Verdi,* Series I, Vol. XVII), this passage (mm. 1–56) precedes the designation "Scene 1," although the curtain has already risen.

The music is deliberately predictable, even banal, and is presumably intended to reflect the low moral climate of the Duke's court. In addition to sharing tempo and meter, each of Verdi's *banda* tunes is either eight bars long (B1–3) or sixteen (B4 and B5). Except for B4, each subdivides into equal, parallel units, with the second half identical to the first except for a more conclusive final cadence. (B4 is not really an exception. It is one of the two longer tunes, and Verdi merely carries the subdivision further: there are *two* eight-measure groupings, each subdivided as before in parallel fashion.) Additional similarities include openings on the third degree of the scale (B1–B5),[3] gavotte-like anacruses (B1–B4), and final perfect authentic cadences in which the melody moves from leading tone to tonic (B1, B3–B5). The cadence of B2 is somewhat different: the final figure, a scale descending from dominant to tonic, is adopted to begin B3.[4] As the cadences suggest, the harmony is relatively simple, and tonic pedals reduce the potential novelty of the two diminished chords present (m. 10, repeated at m. 14; and m. 42, repeated at m. 50).

I have spent some time describing these melodies because they recur so frequently in this part of the Introduction. How important they are to the musical fabric of this part, to the predominantly parlante texture, is evident from Chart 9.6. As the double bar in the score before m. 267 indicates, the first part of the Introduction may be further subdivided. Scenes 1–3 form a dramatic unit showing the decadent milieu of the Mantuan court and the Duke's interest in the as-yet-unnamed Gilda and the Countess Ceprano. We also learn of his contempt for the feelings and honor of the men with whom these women are linked. I have stressed elsewhere the importance of honor and fear of dishonor in *Rigoletto* and have pointed to its association with the sonority of C; I have also suggested an extension of the association from the two fathers, Rigoletto

2. The piano-vocal score published by Ricordi (Milan, 1851–1852), plate nos. j23071–23090, oblong format.

3. B2 begins with an ornamental slide, but the first significant pitch is G.

4. Compare mm. 16–17 (B2) with mm. 17–18 (B3). I am indebted to Andrew Porter for this observation.

CHART 9.6. Introduction, Part 1.

SCENE	THEME	BAR	KEY	TEXT [NOTES]
1	B1	57	A♭	None. [Band backstage.]
	B2	65	E♭	*Duke*: "Della mia bella incognita borghese / Toccare il fin dell'avventura io voglio." [*Parlante* texture.]
	B3	73	c	*Borsa*: "La sua dimora?" *Duke*: "In un remoto calle; / misterioso un uom v'entra ogni notte."
	B2	81	E♭	*Borsa*: "E sa colei chi sia l'amante suo?" *Duke*: "Lo ignora." *Borsa*: "Quante beltà! Mirate?" *Duke*: "Ma vince tutte di Cepran la sposa."
	Transition	97	V of A♭	*Borsa*: "Non v'oda il conte, o Duca . . . " [Pit orchestra.]
	(Ballata)	107	A♭	*Duke*: "Questa o quella . . . " [Pit orchestra; strophic aria.]
2	Minuet	193	A♭	*Duke*: "Partite! Crudele! . . . " [String orchestra onstage; *parlante* texture.]
3	repeated Cs	232	((C))	*Rig.*: "In testa che avete / Signor di Ceprano?" [Unaccompanied.]
	B2	234	E♭	*Rig.*: "[Cepra]no? Ei sbuffa! Vedete?" *Chorus*: "Che festa!"
	B3	242	c	*Rig.*: "Così non è sempre? . . . "
	repeated Cs'	250	((C))	*Rig.*: "Or della Contessa l'assedio egli avanza . . . " [Unaccompanied.]
	Perigordino	254	C	None. [String orchestra on stage; in the sketch, a different Perigordino in F.]
4	B1	267	A♭	None until m. 274, then *Mar.*: "Gran nuova! Gran nuova!" [Band; *parlante* texture.]
	B4	275	A♭	*Chorus* +: "Che avvenne? Parlate! . . . "
	B5	292	D♭	*Mar.*: "Il pazzo possiede." *Chorus*: "Infine." *Mar.*: "Un'amante! . . . "
5	B1	307	A♭	None.
	B2	311	E♭	*Duke*: "Ah più di Ceprano importuno non v'è! / La cara sua sposa è un angiol per me!"
	B3	319	c	*Rig.*: "Rapitela." *Duke*: "È detto; ma il farlo?" *Rig.*: "Stasera! . . . "
	(B3)	331	(E♭)	*Duke*: "Ah no!" *Rig.*: "Ebben . . . s'esiglia . . . "
	(B3)	336	(g)	*Rig.*: "Allora . . . la testa . . . "
	(B3)	339	(B♭)	*Cep.* (da sè): "Oh l'anima nera!" / *Duke*: "Che di'? questa testa!"
	Transition	343	mod.	*Rig.*: "È ben naturale . . . Che far di tal testa?" [Pit orchestra.]
	B2	351	E♭	*Cep.* (infuriato battendo la spada): "Marrano!" *Duke*: "Fermate! . . . " [Band.]
	B4	359	A♭	*Duke*: "Ah sempre tu spingi lo scherzo all'estremo" / *Cep.*: "Vendetta del pazzo . . . " *Rig.*: "Che coglier mi puote?" [Band backstage; string orchestra onstage; pit orchestra.]
	B6 (B4)	375	A♭	Repetition of text mm. 359–74.
	B7	384	mod.	Repetition of text mm. 359–74.

continued

CHART 9.6. *continued.*

SCENE	THEME	BAR	KEY	TEXT [NOTES]
	(B4)			
	B1	411	A♭	*Chorus+*: "Sì,vendetta" [to m. 418]; m. 415, *Duke* and *Rig.*: "Tutto è gioia, tutto è festa"
	Cadences	419	A♭	[Più vivo] *Tutti*: "Tutto è gioia, tutto è festa, / Tutto invitaci a godere! . . . "

(B3)	=	Thematic material derived from B3; B6 (B4), B7 (B4) = thematic material related to B4, especially rhythmically
((C))	=	Sonority of C (unaccompanied middle C's)
(E♭)	=	Tonicization of E♭
/	=	End of line in the libretto for the premiere (Venice, 1851)
mod.	=	Modulatory
Chorus +	=	male chorus (courtiers) and one or more of the comprimario parts (e.g., Borsa)

and Monterone, to Ceprano.[5] We see this clearly in Scene 3. After the Duke's flirtation with the Countess (Scene 2, after the Minuet), Rigoletto asks her husband, "In testa che avete, / Signor di Ceprano?" All but the last two notes are set to middle C's without accompaniment. Later in the scene Rigoletto describes the Duke's profligacy and concludes with "Or della Contessa l'assedio egli avanza, / E intanto il marito fremendo ne va." Again there are unaccompanied, repeated middle C's.

After Scene 4, in which Marullo's report that Rigoletto has hidden away a woman is set to themes B4 and B5—not heard since the wind band passage at the beginning of the Introduction, and with the same key progression as before, A♭ (mm. 275–91) to D♭ (mm. 292–307)—the climax and conclusion of this portion of the Introduction takes place during Scene 5. Rigoletto urges the Duke to seize the Countess "stasera" (theme B3, C minor), ridding himself of her husband by execution if necessary. When the infuriated Ceprano asks the other courtiers to join him in seeking vengeance, their response largely echoes his words: "Vendetta del pazzo . . . Contr'esso un rancore / Pei tristi suoi modi, di noi chi non ha? Vendetta! vendetta! Sì, a notte, sarà" (mm. 394–411). Their concluding words, "Sì, vendetta" (mm. 411–18) are set to the ritornello-like theme B1, a passage which constitutes the only completely texted statement of that theme. The music for the plotting is derived from the two themes in A♭, B1 and B4.

5. See "Rigoletto and Monterone," 1552. Within the broad term *sonority of C* are included the keys of C major and C minor, passages of tonicized C major or minor, and passages in which C is emphasized melodically or harmonically during a modulatory section or where the prevailing key is some other area such as F minor, A♭ major, or E♭ major in which the pitch or chord C is important.

It can hardly be a coincidence that in a later part of Act I, when the courtiers gather outside Rigoletto's house to carry out their plan, the key is again A♭ (Act I, No. 7, *Finale Primo,* mm. 8–59). There is another association of vengeance and the key of A♭: the cabaletta that ends Act II, Rigoletto's "Sì, vendetta." The jester's opening words are identical with those of the courtiers in mm. 411–18 of the Introduction, and this has, I think, special significance inasmuch as Verdi himself wrote them.[6] The composer's choice of text and key implicitly draws attention to the shared guilt of Rigoletto and the courtiers for similarly base actions, much as he and Piave—and Hugo before them—had done explicitly during the monologue following the scene with Sparafucile.

We might call these shared relationships tonal-dramatic threads or links. Since there are only a limited number of keys and a multitude of possible dramatic situations, it is not surprising that Verdi should use the key of A♭ in other dramatic settings as well. During the first of the three father-daughter Duets (Act I, No. 4), Rigoletto responds to Gilda's request to learn of her mother with "Deh non parlar al misero," the andante of the usual four-part duet structure, and it is in A♭. Later in the same number, during the cabaletta "Ah! veglia, o donna," Gilda, disturbed by her father's anguish and fears, tries to calm him. She does so with the same melody he has been singing, but now the key is A♭ rather than E♭.

> Quanto affetto! . . . quali cure!
> Non temete, padre mio.
> Lassù in cielo, presso Dio
> Veglia un angiol protettor!
> Da noi stoglie le sventure
> Di mia madre il priego santo;
> Non fia mai disvelto o franto
> Questo a voi diletto fior!

Whether consciously or not, Verdi has tonally linked the two passages relating to Gilda's mother. Commentators on *Rigoletto* tend to accept Gilda's constant reliance on divine intervention, including that prompted by her departed mother, without recognizing that there is no counterpart in *Le Roi s'amuse.* (In fact, during Act I of the play the anticlerical Hugo has Latour suggest to Francis that the unknown *bourgeoise* [Blanche] is probably "some sly priest's mistress."[7] Piave prudently removed this and other similar remarks: for example, the re-

---

6. In his letter to Piave of 20 January 1851, Verdi drafted the text of the cabaletta as follows: "*Rig.*: 'Sì vendetta, vendetta. . . . / Sol desia respira quest'alma / L'ora della punizione è giunta / E l'avrai dal tuo buffone— / Si vendetta vendetta. . . .' *Gilda*: 'Qual gioia feroce . . . / Respira vostr'alma / Perdonate perdonate . . . / Anche Dio perdonò sul patibolo . . . / (Gran Dio non ascoltatelo / Perché io l'amo ancora).' " (Cited from the Introduction to my edition of *Rigoletto, Works of Giuseppe Verdi,* Series I, XVII, xviii.)

7. *Le Roi s'amuse,* Act I, Scene 1, translated by Helen A. Gaubert in *Three Plays by Victor Hugo* (New York, 1964), 140.

sponse by Saltabadil to Triboulet's question "You brave the rack for this?" "Oh no," says the assassin, "we bribe the police.")[8] With Gilda, then, the character of Blanche has been changed to that of a more religious (more Italian?) young lady; her departed mother has been placed in heaven (certainly never suggested by Hugo); and the girl invokes divine power in each of the three Duets with Rigoletto. Changes in text from Verdi's draft of "Sì, vendetta" to the final version by Piave suggest that it was the librettist who led the way.[9]

* * *

One famous feature of Hugo's play is the extent to which it makes use of dramatic irony. In Hugo's own words,

> The more [Triboulet] speeds the contagion of debauchery and vice in town, the more he seeks to isolate and immure his daughter. He brings up his child in faith, innocence and modesty. His greatest fear is that she may fall into evil, for he knows, being himself wicked, all the wretchedness that is endured by evildoers. . . . This same King whom Triboulet urges to pitiless vice will be the ravisher of Triboulet's daughter. The buffoon will be struck by Providence precisely in the same manner as was M. de Saint-Vallier. And more, his daughter once seduced and ruined, he lays a trap for the King by which to avenge her; but it is his daughter who falls into it. Thus Triboulet has two pupils—the King and his daughter; the King, whom he has trained to vice, his daughter, whom he has reared for virtue. One will destroy the other. He intends Mme. Cossé to be carried off for the King; it is his daughter who is carried off. He wishes to kill the King, and so avenge his child; it is his daughter whom he slays.[10]

How does Verdi reflect irony by musical means? At least to some extent, he does so tonally: a key with one association appears in a related dramatic situation, but with precisely the opposite dramatic meaning.[11] For example, the very first words of the libretto are about Gilda: the Duke's remark to Borsa, "Della mia bella incognita borghese, toccare il fin dell'avventura voglio." The latter responds, "Di quella giovin che vedete al tempio?" The music is that of the second tune played by the offstage wind band, B2, and appears in E♭. When we hear that key again at the end of the first Duet for Rigoletto and Gilda, she is again the subject, as Rigoletto urges Giovanna, "Ah! veglia, o donna." So far we have a tonal-dramatic thread. But the point of the drama is that Gilda is *not* well-guarded, and the courtiers kidnap her to the music of their chorus "Zitti, zitti," which is also in E♭ (Act I, No. 7).

8. Ibid., Act II, Scene 1, 156.
9. Verdi's text is cited in footnote 6 above.
10. "Author's Preface," based on the Gaubert translation, 127–28.
11. *Tonal irony* is a term I first used in an unpublished paper, "Gilda's Fall," read at the first joint meeting of the American Institute for Verdi Studies and the Greater New York Chapter of the American Musicological Society, New York University, December 1976. The present paper is based in part on "Gilda's Fall."

Another example occurs when Gilda confesses to Giovanna her feelings for the young man who has been following her from church, the beginning of the Duet for Gilda and the Duke (Act I, No. 5, "Signor nè principe"). The key is G major, but there are a remarkable number of dominant harmonies and dominant pedal points in this passage: one or the other occupies twenty of the thirty measures concerned. Furthermore, twenty-four of the fifty melody notes between m. 9 and m. 38 of the Duet are on the pitch D—and they are not brief passing tones; this is a clear instance of an emphasis on the sonority of D. At the beginning of the next act the recitative, "Ella mi fu rapita," begins in D minor, and the cabaletta, "Possente amor," is in D major. Ostensibly the subject is Gilda, but the Duke constantly emphasizes "mi," "Io," and "mio." He is primarily concerned with himself:

> Possente amor mi chiama
> > Volar io deggio a lei;
> > Il serto mio darei
> > Per consolar quel cor.
> Ah sappia alfin chi l'ama,
> > Conosca alfin chi sono,
> > Apprenda che anco in trono
> > Ha degli schiavi amor.

Then, in the next scene, precisely at the moment when Rigoletto realizes that the abducted Gilda is locked in with the Duke, the music modulates to D minor.

RIG.:	Ah, ella è qui dunque! Ella è col Duca!	(modulating)
TUTTI:	Chi?	
RIG.:	La giovin che stanotte Al mio tetto rapiste . . . Ma la saprò riprender . . . Ella è là.[12]	(D minor)

D major next appears at the beginning of the storm-murder scene (Act III, No. 13), specifically during the recitative in which Rigoletto pays Sparafucile to murder the Duke. Up to and including this point we again have tonal-dramatic threads. The dramatic irony—and this is the most important example for the development of the plot—occurs at the close of the number. When Gilda sacrifices herself for the Duke, to music in D minor with passages in D major, in effect she replaces him both dramatically and tonally. The supreme irony of the

12. "Rigoletto and Monterone," 1556.

situation is that he is not even aware of her gesture. He blithely continues to sing "La donna è mobile" in B major, the key Verdi assigned to all three statements of the Canzone.

At this point it may be useful to trace the tonal-dramatic associations of another important tonal center in the opera: E. We first hear E major during Rigoletto's monologue "Pari siamo" (Act I, No. 4). After the key has been established (mm. 41–51), the solo flute plays a tender idea accompanied by sustained strings (mm. 52–55). Rigoletto then sings a variant of this phrase to the words "Ma in altr'uomo qui mi cangio" (mm. 55–57). By "qui" he is clearly referring to the home he has made for Gilda and, by extension, to Gilda herself; and his phrase foreshadows music that is quintessentially Gilda's, the opening phrase of her aria "Caro nome" (Ex. 9.1). The scoring for flute, the moderate tempo, and the *dolce* performance direction support the melodic-tonal connection. But while the music of the Duet unequivocally depicts the love between Rigoletto and Gilda, the dramatic setting and the text tell us that father and daughter are not closely in touch with each other's feelings. And this remains true throughout the opera. Gilda constantly asks more than Rigoletto is willing to tell her: she wants to visit the city—he won't permit it; she attempts to find out what worries him—he responds vaguely, in a disquieting manner; after her seduction, she begs her father to forgive the Duke—he refuses. And so on to the bitter end.

It is of course significant in this context that Gilda's "Caro nome" reveals aspects of her emotional life of which Rigoletto has no idea and that he can never accept when he eventually learns of them:

> Caro nome che il mio cor
>   Festi primo palpitar,
> Le delizie dell'amor
>   Mi dei sempre rammentar!
> Col pensier il mio desir
>   A te sempre volerà,
> E fin l'ultimo sospir,
>   Caro nome, tuo sarà.

The text of her only aria is a remarkable declaration of the intensity of Gilda's love; and the final couplet is prophetic. To her last breath she belongs to Gualtier Maldè, not to her father, and, what is perhaps even more important, not even to herself. In Act II, when she confesses to her father, "Tutte le feste al tempio," she begins each strophe in E minor, although endings are in C major. With the first words of Act III, Rigoletto asks his daughter, "E l'ami?" and she responds, "Sempre." Once again there is an emphasis on the sonority of E, although the actual key is that of the Prelude, A minor.[13] He tries to reason with

---

13. The continuity draft has a Prelude in E minor at this point.

EXAMPLE 9.1. "Ma in altr'uomo" and "Caro nome" compared.

her, finally asking, "E se tu certa fossi / Ch'ei ti tradisse, l'ameresti ancora?" Meanwhile the music has modulated toward G major (mm. 15–21). "Nol so . . . ma pur m'adora!" she answers, the music returning to E minor (mm. 21–23). Rigoletto jeers, "Egli? Ebben, osserva dunque!" and the strings recall the close of the Prelude, a Phrygian cadence on E (mm. 23–26). This is followed by a tonicization of E as the Duke enters (mm. 28–30), once more in disguise. The music shifts to B major as she recognizes him (mm. 30–31) and remains there for his Canzone, "La donna è mobile."

The initial section of the Quartet, which follows "La donna è mobile," returns to E major. Dramatically as well as musically this is one of the high points in the opera, for it is here that Gilda's illusions are destroyed once and for all. Specifically, her love for the Duke is trivialized. This is reflected musically on a number of levels, one of which is certainly by means of tonal irony. The key is that of "Caro nome," and indeed the harmonic progression of the first eighteen measures of the Quartet—measures that in large part return before the andante—is almost identical with the underlying harmonies of "Caro nome" (Chart 9.7). Furthermore, and this appears to confirm that the relationships are intentional, there is a close similarity between the accompaniment figures of the first violins in alternate measures of each number (Ex. 9.2). Observe the staccato repeated notes played above the staff, approached by a large leap from below, and consistently occupying the first half of the 4/4 measures. The flute and piccolo joining the violin for the descending trills in measure 8 of the Quartet also recall—even caricature—both the scoring and the constantly ornamented lines of "Caro nome" (Ex. 9.3). Played at the much faster tempo of the Quartet's allegro, the passage brilliantly reflects the superficiality of the Duke's and Maddalena's love-play.

For the remainder of the opera, Verdi associates the sonority of E with two dramatic situations. First is Maddalena's increasingly serious love for the Duke. After his second presentation of "La donna è mobile," she sings "È amabile invero cotal giovinotto" to the accompaniment of an E-major triad in the strings. A moment later—Gilda has returned to the scene in time to overhear this—she argues with her brother over the fate of the Duke: "Somiglia un Apollo quel

CHART 9.7. Harmonies of "Caro nome" and the Act III Quartet.

"Caro nome"	I	I	V	V$^{(7)}$	I	I	II^6	V^7	I	(V)–VII$^4_3$ of V–V–VII$^4_3$ of V
Quartet	I	I	V^7	V^7	I	I	II^6	V^7	I	V^7 of V

"Caro nome"	V–IV of V	V^7 of V	V^7	I	II♮$^6_3$–II^6	V^7	I
Quartet	V	V^7 of V	V^7	I	II^6	V^7	I

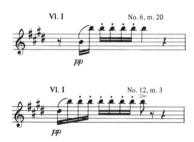

EXAMPLE 9.2. Repeated violin figures from "Caro nome" and the Act III Quartet.

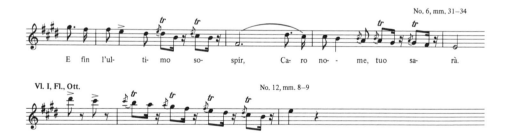

E fin l'ul- ti- mo so- spir, Ca- ro no - me, tuo sa- rà.

EXAMPLE 9.3. Melodies from "Caro nome" and the Act III Quartet.

giovine. Io l'amo . . . / Ei m'ama. Riposi, nè più l'uccidiamo." The passage is in E major.

The final appearances of E in the opera take place after the last statement of the Duke's "La donna è mobile," the statement that signals to Rigoletto that his plans for vengeance have miscarried (mm. 78–102 and 105–14). After the Duke's high, sustained B, there is a moment of disorientation. Rigoletto's confusion is depicted by a modulatory passage: B minor to G (oscillating from major to minor and back), followed by a diminished-seventh chord (mm. 115–23). After Rigoletto's frantic exclamations, "Mia figlia!" and "Dio!" (diminished seventh on the accented syllable), the second "mia figlia!" coincides with a passage stressing the sonority of E (mm. 125–34); despite his attempt to reason away what he sees ("Ah no! . . . è impossibil! per Verona è in via! / Fu vision!") the sonority helps to confirm the truth. Another modulatory passage follows, and as the music passes through E minor, Rigoletto once again calls "Mia figlia? Mia Gilda? oh mia figlia!" (mm. 147–51).

∗   ∗   ∗

The final arrangement of tonalities evolved gradually during the composition of *Rigoletto* (Chart 9.8). We have traces of four compositional stages, overlapping at times: sketch fragments, continuity draft, skeleton score (the initial stage of the autograph), and the final orchestrated version of the autograph.[14] With the assistance of the published facsimile of the *Rigoletto* continuity draft, the autograph, and the letters Verdi wrote to Piave, it is often possible to guess approximately when and (in some cases) even why the key changes were made.

The earliest ideas we have for the first part of the Introduction are two sketch fragments in A major (Chart 9.8, nos. 1 and 3). With the many open strings in that key, this would result in a relatively bright orchestral sound. The change to Ab may have been tied (at least to some extent) to the composer's decision to use the wind band rather than the orchestra for most of the party music. One might recall that in the comparable opening scene of *La traviata,* where it is the orchestra that begins the festivities, the key chosen was A major. When the

---

14. There are eleven sketch fragments for *Rigoletto,* all on bifolios containing material of the continuity draft. As is noted in the Introduction to the edition of *Rigoletto* cited in footnote 6 above, there probably existed, or still exist, other sketch fragments for the opera: none of the eleven, for example, relates to Act II, and it is inconceivable that Verdi drafted the entire act without writing down some preliminary thoughts, particularly in view of the problems he and Piave had met in the opening scene. Although some of the fragments were written down as the composer worked on the continuity draft (for example, the eleventh fragment is a slightly longer version of mm. 207–12 of the opera's Finale and was clearly sketched to help solve a specific problem), and one even postdated the continuity draft (the cadenza for "È il sol dell'anima," which is out of order and in the key of the final version, Bb), the majority seem to predate the specific portion of the continuity draft to which they relate.

The continuity draft is certainly the most important stage in the *Rigoletto* sketches, with material on all but the first folio, and Verdi considered it the basic compositional document. When he had written this version the composer considered the opera to be finished (see the letter to Piave of 5 February 1851, cited in the Introduction to the new edition, xx). For a more extended discussion of the continuity draft, see the Critical Notes to the new edition: II, 6–7.

The skeleton score was the next compositional stage, one in which, as Verdi described it, it was necessary "to set down neatly" ("mettere in netto") the music of the completed continuity draft. On music paper that was ultimately to become part of the completed full score the composer drew bar lines the entire length of the page and entered all the voice parts, together with their texts. Where there was no vocal part, he wrote out the principal instrumental line, usually the first violin. Occasionally instrumental bass parts were also present. Skeleton scores have not been extensively discussed in the musicological literature because they tend to be part of a disappearing phase. After the composer completes the orchestration, we see it only in the different-colored inks and in corrected passages or discarded pages.

CHART 9.8. Principal changes of key in the course of composition.

ACT/NO.	TITLE + SECTION	MM. (FINAL VERSION)	SKETCH FRAGMENTS	CONTINUITY DRAFT	AUTO-GRAPH
I/2	Introduction				
	1. *Banda* 1		A	Ab	Ab
	2. Perigordino			F	C
	3. Cpt. *Banda,* voices	360–65	A	Ab	Ab
	4. Monterone's curse	501–20		db	(D)*
				Db	Db
I/3	Duet				
	5. Introduction			No tonal link from No. 2	See pp. (=26–27)
	6. Rig. brooding on the curse			F	((C))**
I/4	Duet				
	7. Rig. brooding on the curse	12–14		F	((C))
	8. Rig. brooding on the curse	59–61		Db	((C))
I/5	Duet				
	9. Andantino			B	skeleton score: B; full score: Bb
	10. Cabaletta			Ab	Db
I/6	Aria				
	11. Introduction	1–10		Ab–F	Db–E
	12. Aria			F	E
I/7	Finale 1⁰				
	13. Part 1			F–Eb	[E]***
	14. Rig. brooding on the curse			Eb	((C))
II/10	Finale 2⁰				
	15. "Tutte le feste"—			f–Db	e–C
	"Piangi, piangi"—			f#	f
	"Solo per me l'infamia"			D	Db
III/11	Canzone				
	16. Prelude			e	((E))
	17. Canzone		E	B	B
III/14	Duet				
	18. Largo		Eb	Db	Db

*(D)   sustained D-major chord
**((C))   sonority of C
***[E]   link from No. 6 by way of the pitch B♮ (as dominant of E), the first note of No. 7

backstage band enters in *La traviata,* it does so in E♭ and remains in the flat keys. Both operas were, of course, written for the same instrumental ensembles at La Fenice.

There is evidence that during the second and third weeks of January 1851, after Piave had completed a draft of the newly finished libretto entitled *Rigoletto,* Verdi both composed the continuity draft for Act II and also put Act I into skeleton score.[15] It was at this stage that he altered the four passages in which Rigoletto broods on the curse (Chart 9.8, nos. 6, 7, 8, and 14) to stress the sonority of C. In this he may have been influenced by his decision to write "Cortigiani, vil razza dannata" (Act II, No. 9) and Monterone's second scene (Act II, *tempo di mezzo* of No. 10) in C minor. Because of this emphasis on middle C, the passages to the text "Quella porta, assassini, m'aprite" (No. 9, mm. 93–96) and in the scene with Monterone are particularly noteworthy.

Around the same time, Verdi composed a new Perigordino in C instead of the one in F indicated in the continuity draft. Did he do so to save the tonic F for Monterone's explosive "Novello insulto"? He also inserted the chord of D major into the curse (Chart 9.8, no. 4), in the process refashioning the passage in a more chromatic vein and, perhaps, referring to the Duke.

In its original form, the Duet for Rigoletto and Sparafucile (Act I, No. 3; Chart 9.8, no. 5) began with leaping octave C's in the bass, as in mm. 38–40 of the final version. This first version thus established a tonal break between the Introduction and the following scene, a break quite at variance with the dramatic situation: Rigoletto has just left the Duke's "Festa da Ballo" and Monterone's curse is still resonating in his mind. In the final version Verdi positioned a D♭ in the first clarinet as the uppermost pitch of the initial chord, thereby referring to the octave D♭'s ending the Introduction. In short, he created a tonal-harmonic analogue for the continuity between the two scenes. The opening chord, a half-diminished seventh,[16] is reminiscent of many similar chords in the preceding stretta (No. 2, mm. 542–45, 588, 592, 596, and 606–7). The fact that both the stretta and the splendidly evocative introduction to the Duet are in the minor mode also contributes to the strong sense of coherence across the separate sections.

The most far-reaching changes of key in Act I—for that matter, in the entire opera—begin with the Duke's "È il sol dell'anima" (No. 5) and continue through "Caro nome" (No. 6) to the first bars of the *Finale Primo* (No. 7: see nos. 9–13 of Chart 9.8). From evidence in the autograph, at both the beginning and the end of this long passage, it seems clear that Verdi executed a skeleton score of much of this music, one corresponding to the keys of the continuity draft. For instance: in the autograph a B-major version of "È il sol dell'anima"

---

15. See the Introduction to the new edition, xix, left-hand column.
16. That is, a chord with a diminished fifth and a minor seventh.

is visible beneath a layer of corrections; these corrections, to a large extent changes of accidentals, effect a transposition to B♭ major, the definitive key of the piece. In addition, the foliation of the Finale (No. 7) suggests that Verdi replaced the opening bars. It is conceivable that he did so to provide a new transition from the E-major final version of "Caro nome."[17] The timing of these changes can be determined with some accuracy. Verdi sent the skeleton score of Nos. 2–7 (all of Act I except the Prelude) and Nos. 11–13 (Act III without the final Duet) to Venice in the same package on 5 February; the version in this skeleton score was, then, decided upon before that date.[18]

The continuity draft for Act III reveals Verdi's continued rethinking of keys and overall tonal design. Only after he was well into this continuity draft of Act III did he decide on B major as the key for "La donna è mobile." The original sketch fragment (Chart 9.8, no. 17) was in E major. Since the Duke's Canzone is heard three times in the last act (Nos. 11, 13, and 14), Verdi evidently decided rather late in the process of composing the opera to save B for the last act, where it works so neatly as the dominant of the E-major section opening the Quartet (No. 12). But more than this: about the same time as the change in key for "La donna è mobile," Verdi drafted the Quartet. Since there are a number of significant musical relationships between the E-major section of the Quartet and "Caro nome," as we have seen, it is at least plausible that the composer altered the key of Gilda's aria from F to E after composing the Quartet, in order to make these relationships even clearer. He could have done so between 20 January, when he had finished the continuity draft of Act I, and 5 February, when he mailed the completed skeleton score of most of Act III, Nos. 11–13.

*　　*　　*

In summary: the overall key scheme of *Rigoletto* seems to show two primary compositional considerations. The first is basically musical, an essential tonal coherence and *tinta* for each act and for the whole work, manifesting itself first as an emphasis on keys related to A♭ (Acts I and II) and D♭ (throughout the opera). More distant keys, especially D, B, and E, are of lesser importance early in the opera but become gradually more significant in Act II and especially in Act III. But this tonal planning, this gradual shift in the spectrum of keys, is not an isolated or purely musical gesture. Verdi is careful to forge distinct associations between certain keys or sonorities and dramatic situations or emotions. Indeed, these associations are never rigid or mechanical; many keys (A♭ and E in particular) have more than one function. As musical symbols, they may well occur at the dictates of musical (rather than musico-dramatic) concerns. As for the key of D♭, associated early in the opera with Monterone's curse and later

17. See the Critical Notes to the new edition: II, 52.
18. See again the letter to Piave of 5 February 1851, cited in the Introduction to the new edition, xx.

with the working-out or tragic effects of that curse, it is of such importance to the overall key design and dramatic course of events that it might well be understood as a kind of tonic for the entire opera.

Both the changes Verdi made in the course of composition and the artful design of the final version suggest that such tonal symbolism was a critical aspect of his musico-dramatic thinking. Indeed, in the case of *Rigoletto,* one might even propose that the irony in *Le Roi s'amuse* has found a counterpoint in Verdi's ironies of tonal symbolism. This was Verdi's musical analogy for Hugo's barbed and cutting wit.

Chapter 10

Tonal Systems in *Aida,* Act III

DAVID LAWTON

In the third volume of his monumental study *The Operas of Verdi,* Julian Budden describes Act III of *Aida* as "among the most dramatic as well as the most atmospheric that Verdi ever wrote."[1] As evidence that the composer was aware of the uniqueness of the act's dramatic and musical shape, Budden cites a famous passage from Verdi's letter of 26 August 1871 to Tito Ricordi: "Tell your copyist that the entire third act, although it includes a choral scene, a *solo* scene for Aida, *a scene with her father,* another *scene with her lover,* and *a little trio and a finale,* forms but a single scene and therefore a single piece."[2] Referring to this letter, Philip Gossett comments: "Verdi conceived of the act as a series of formal numbers during its composition. . . . It is true that the third act has a remarkable unity, but it is hard to view it as a 'single piece,' and it is quite clear that Verdi did not so consider it while he was composing."[3] Gossett's analysis of the Aida-Radames Duet demonstrates the extent to which Verdi's musical imagination—even as late as 1871—was conditioned by the formal conventions that he had inherited from his predecessors. Two more recent studies have examined the third act with particular attention to the great Aida-Amonasro Duet. Pierluigi Petrobelli sees in the Duet a deliberate departure from the standard four-movement form as exemplified by the Aida-Radames Duet.[4] Harold Powers, by contrast, argues persuasively that the novelty of the Aida-

1. Julian Budden, *The Operas of Verdi* III (London, 1981), 244.
2. Hans Busch, *Verdi's "Aida": The History of an Opera in Letters and Documents* (Minneapolis, [1978]), 205.
3. Philip Gossett, "Verdi, Ghislanzoni, and *Aida*: The Uses of Convention," *Critical Inquiry* I, no. 2 (1974), 327.
4. Pierluigi Petrobelli, "Music in the Theatre (à propos of *Aida,* Act III)," in James Redmond, ed., *Themes in Drama 3: Drama, Dance and Music* (Cambridge, England, 1981), 133.

Amonasro Duet results, not from the rejection of formal conventions, but rather from what he calls "a radically modified evocation of the 'solita forma.' "[5]

Common to all these studies is the assumption that Act III of *Aida* presents a challenging intersection of the traditional, closed-form structure and some larger musical unity; and each analysis offers valuable insights both into the internal construction of individual numbers and into the continuity between such numbers—what Gossett appropriately calls "the blurring of the outlines."[6] Powers's contention that the *tempo d'attacco* of the Aida-Radames Duet starts out as if it were the *tempo di mezzo* of the Aida-Amonasro Duet offers a fine example of this blurring process.[7]

What the literature has not yet addressed sufficiently, however, is the degree of unity that many of us feel in this act. The purpose of the present study is to investigate some of the factors that contribute to this unity, in particular its tonal structure. The latter is especially significant because, in relying on the power of tonality to bind strongly contrasting scenes into a coherent whole, Verdi reached back to procedures that he had used successfully early in his career.

We might usefully distinguish between two contrasting methods through which Verdi approached the problem of the large-scale structure of an extended scene. One was to expand the dimensions of a single number to the proportions of an entire act. For example, Act III of the original, 1847 version of *Macbeth* can be regarded as an enormously expanded aria for Macbeth.[8] Verdi's other method was to cast an extended scene into distinct numbers linked together into a larger design by means of motivic relationships and tonal planning. The locus classicus of this procedure in early Verdi is surely the last act of *Rigoletto*. Although there are four separate numbers, the act as a whole is unified by a clear tonal structure supported by motivic and thematic cross-references.[9]

Verdi's solution to the problem of unity in Act III of *Aida* is of the *Rigoletto* type. The act divides into the five numbers listed by the composer in the letter quoted above. (Although there are no titles for the numbers in the autograph, they have been added to the Ricordi scores and will be used here for convenience.) Chart 10.1 summarizes the large form and structure of the act. The divi-

---

5. Harold S. Powers, " 'La solita forma' and 'The Uses of Convention,' " *Acta Musicologica* LIX (1987), 65–90.

6. Gossett, "The Uses of Convention," 327.

7. Powers, "La solita forma," 85–86.

8. After a choral Introduzione for the witches, an unusually long Scena extends from Macbeth's entrance up to that of the eight kings, from which point it is continually interrupted by *cantabile* phrases. Following the appearance of the last king (Banquo), the *cantabile* proper begins ("Oh mio terror! Dell'ultimo . . . "). The *tempo di mezzo* begins with Macbeth fainting, continues with the ballet and chorus of the sylphs who try to revive him, and ends with his return to consciousness. The cabaletta ("Vada in fiamme") completes this huge act-long aria. A detailed analysis of this act appears in my "Tonality and Drama in Verdi's Early Operas," diss. University of California, Berkeley, 1973, 97–104.

9. See my "Tonal Structure and Dramatic Action in *Rigoletto*," in *Verdi: Bollettino dell'istituto di studi verdiani* IX (Parma, 1982), 1559–81.

CHART 10.1. *Aida*, Act III, summary.

Cycle I

Set piece

[Introduzione—Preghiera—Coro]	[Scena e Romanza—Aida]	[Scena e Duetto—Aida-Amonasro]		

Formal subdivision

| | | *scena* | *tempo d'attacco* | *cantabile* |

Prevailing tonality

G major   F major   F minor   Db major   C minor   Db maj.-min

Cycle II

Set piece

[Scena e Duetto—Aida-Radames]		[Scena—Finale III]		

Formal subdivision

| *tempo d'attacco* | *cantabile* | *tempo di mezzo* | *cabaletta* | *terzetto* *finale* |

Prevailing tonality

C major   G minor   modulatory   F major   Db maj.-min. D minor

sion into movements of the two central Duets follows that of Powers in the article quoted earlier.[10] Solid vertical lines indicate the boundaries of numbers; dotted lines the boundaries of movements within numbers. Only the most important, most firmly established key areas appear on the table.

I. THE DOUBLE-CYCLE CONSTRUCTION

As we see from Chart 10.1, the overall tonal plan reveals the operation of what I have called elsewhere a *double cycle*: a distinctive tonal plan (through a number or across numbers) that is repeated in order to unify musically a larger scene complex or to underline a parallel between two dramatic situations.[11] Here a motion from G major or minor through F major to D♭ major/minor occurs twice, articulating a large structure that cuts across the formal division into separate numbers. Double cycles are not unique to *Aida*; Verdi had used them from the beginning of his career. In his early operas he frequently reinforced the relationships between the beginnings and/or endings of cycles by means of clear thematic, motivic, or textural associations on the foreground level. In view of the complexity of Verdi's mature style, it is not surprising that the musical relationships between the two cycles in Act III of *Aida* are more subtle and elusive. Perhaps it is as well to begin at a level where the correspondences are most readily apparent—that is, with the relationships between the final key-pair in the double cycle.

The clearest indication of the operation of a double cycle is a musical parallel between the end of the Aida-Amonasro Duet—while Amonasro withdraws to observe Aida and Radames—and the end of the terzetto section of the Finale—while Amonasro attempts to drag Radames away (cf. 306/2/1–3 with 343/1/3–2/3).[12] Both passages are in D♭ minor and in common time. It is true that, on first hearing, the differences between them may seem more pronounced than the similarities. The tempo of the first is much slower than that of the second; the character of the first is grief-ridden and resigned, while that of the second, though also tinged with grief, is full of urgency; the first seems to be winding down from a crisis, whereas the second builds up to one. Nevertheless, several details establish a powerful aural link between the two passages. Most important is the similarity of the vocal writing, often an important associative device in Verdi. In both cases Amonasro has three short utterances on the same re-

10. Powers, "La solita forma," 85.

11. The term is further defined, and an example from *Nabucco* is given, in David Lawton and David Rosen, "Verdi's Non-Definitive Revisions: The Early Operas," in *Atti del 3º congresso internazionale di studi verdiani* (Parma, 1974), 216–19.

12. Page/system/measure numbers refer to the Ricordi full orchestral score, "Nuova Edizione Riveduta e Corretta," pl. no. P.R. 153. In cases where there is only one system, references will be to the page and the measure only.

peated D♭. This is supported by other common features: the scoring (strings in the first, and strings and a solo horn in the second); a moving bass line in the lower strings against an ostinato pattern in the violins; and prominent flat sixths in the bass line.

Significantly, there is a clear dramatic parallel analogous to the musical one: in both cases Amonasro has just achieved an important objective. In the first, he has convinced Aida to wrest the vital military secret from Radames; in the second, he has learned that secret through Radames's betrayal. Amonasro's two triumphs bring about corresponding reactions from Aida and Radames. Aida has betrayed her love for Radames for the sake of her father and her country; Radames has betrayed his country for the sake of his love for Aida. That Verdi himself saw the parallel between the emotional states of Aida and Radames is clear from a letter to Antonio Ghislanzoni of 28 September 1870:

> I have always been of the opinion that *cabalettas* should be used when the situation demands it. Those in the two duets are not demanded by the situation; and the one in the duet between father and daughter, especially, seems out of place to me. In such a state of fear and moral depression, Aida cannot and must not sing a *cabaletta*. In the outline there are two extremely dramatic points, both true and good for the actor, which are not well realized in the poetry. The first: after Amonasro has said *Sei la schiava dei Faraoni*, Aida can only speak in broken phrases. The other: when Amonasro says to Radames *il Re d'Etiopia*, Radames must hold and control the scene, almost by himself, with strange, mad, highly agitated words.[13]

It is surely significant that Verdi set these two ending points of the cycles in the same key: D♭ major/minor, the tonal goal of each.

The relationship between the beginnings of the cycles, the G-major Introduzione and the G-minor cantabile of the Aida-Radames Duet, seems at first even more obvious. The tempi of the two excerpts are nearly equivalent: ♩ = 76 for the Introduzione, and ♩ = 84 for the *cantabile*. Both passages set out to evoke natural landscapes—the first, the moonlit Nile; the second, the Ethiopian forests, and in each case Verdi creates an exotic atmosphere through the use of modal inflections that mildly obscure the tonality, and through delicate orchestral textures in which solo woodwinds predominate (flute in the Introduzione; three flutes and oboe in the Duet). However, although the general effect of the two pieces is similar enough to establish an audible relationship, their inner workings are quite different.

Petrobelli has pointed out that the entire opening scene, the Introduzione, is built around the "static persistence of just one pitch, [G]."[14] The importance of single sonorities in Verdi has been noted elsewhere by Petrobelli (with refer-

---

13. Busch, *Verdi's "Aida,"* 69.
14. Petrobelli, "Music in the Theatre," 134.

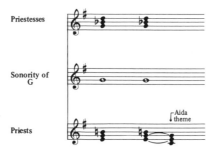

EXAMPLE 10.1. Inversional balance around G.

ence to *Il trovatore*) and by Martin Chusid (with reference to *Rigoletto*).[15] What
is especially interesting here is that G gradually changes its tonal function and,
in spite of its "static persistence," ultimately generates the tonal motion that
leads to the next stable key area in the cycle, the F major of Aida's romanza.
Example 10.1 shows how the sonority of G serves as a center of inversion. The
triads arranged above and below the central G are vertical summaries of the content of the chanting of the priestesses and priests (the G-minor and the E-minor
triad, respectively). In the absence of any key-defining harmonic progressions,
the chords implied by the chants create an ambiguity of mode (major or minor?) and key (G major/minor or E minor?). The sonority G is common to all
three triads; and the balancing of the G-minor and E-minor triads around it
requires one more element for stability: a C-major triad.

Verdi does not supply this C-major harmony immediately. First he clarifies
the G-major tonality in the short scene between Ramfis and Amneris with two
unequivocal cadences, one on the dominant, the other on the tonic of G major
(see 268/1/5 and 269/1/1). The opening material (the G pedal and the offstage
chanting) then returns and, as Petrobelli puts it, "Amneris and Ramfis are 'absorbed' into the night, cold and impassive as is the chanting of the priests."[16]
Immediately afterward (271/1/1–4/2), the orchestra plays the Aida theme in C
major, establishing the C root required for inversional balance around G. This
harmony soon proves unstable itself and is eventually absorbed into the F major
of Aida's romanza.

The G-minor *cantabile* of the Aida-Radames Duet also plays with tonal ambiguity, though of a different sort. The oboe solo (316/3/1–317/1/5), though
colored with exotic chromatic alterations, implies G minor clearly enough, even

15. Cf. Pierluigi Petrobelli, "Per un'esegesi della struttura drammatica del 'Trovatore,' " in *Atti del 3° congresso internazionale di studi verdiani*, 387–400; and Martin Chusid, "Rigoletto and Monterone: A Study in
Musical Dramaturgy," in *Verdi: Bollettino dell'istituto di studi verdiani* IX, 1544–58.

16. Petrobelli, "Music in the Theatre," 134.

though the ends of both phrases are only half-cadences. The possibility of a B♭-major tonal center, raised at the entry of the three flutes (317/2/1–4) is temporarily dispelled by a strong cadence in G minor at the end of Aida's stanza (318/2/2). Radames's stanza does, in fact, move into the relative major and cadence there (319/2/3), and the condensed reprise of the oboe melody at this point has a new harmonic context: the same notes that had implied G minor before are now heard in the key of B♭ major. The reentry of the three flutes (319/2/4–320/1/3) appears to confirm the new key, but the continuation of Aida's stanza closes, as before, in the tonic, G minor (321/2/1). Ultimately, the *cantabile* does end in the relative major—but the *tempo di mezzo* touches briefly on G minor before setting up the key of the cabaletta, F major (322–24).

It is, incidentally, perfectly consistent with Verdi's earlier practice that, having established firm yet subtle relationships between the beginning and ending sections of a double cycle, he would allow the central portions to be relatively independent, or even sharply contrasting in style.[17] The present cycle is a good case in point, as it would be hard to imagine a greater contrast between the two central, F-major sections: between the delicate, evocative sonority of Aida's romanza and the flashy, conventional tone of the Aida-Radames cabaletta, a piece that disturbed Verdi's friends and foes alike.[18]

Before leaving the question of the double-cycle construction, we should point out that there are two key areas in Cycle II that do not fit the G–F–D♭ pattern outlined in Chart 10.1: C major at the beginning of the Aida-Radames Duet, and D minor at the end of the act. The latter, introduced suddenly by a half-step shift upward at Amneris's entrance (344), is easily explained. Amneris's appearance is an important turning point in the action, confounding the lovers' decision to escape together and assuring Radames's destruction: it seems entirely appropriate that these final moments should abandon the tonal orbit that has dominated the act until then.

The C-major area is more difficult to account for satisfactorily. Motivically and tonally it serves as a pivot between Cycles I and II: as Powers has observed, the orchestral motive that heralds Radames's approach and then becomes his opening phrase "Pur ti riveggo, mia dolce Aida" (307) is a transformation of the beginning of Amonasro's "Rivedrai le foreste imbalsamate" from the D♭

---

17. Interestingly enough, there is a strong connection between Aida's F-major Romanza in Cycle I and the G-minor *cantabile* of the Aida-Radames Duet in Cycle II, especially at the beginnings of the pieces (cf. 272/1/3–273/4/3 with 316/2/2–317/3/1). In both cases strong cadential preparation gives way to a weak resolution by the solo oboe; in the continuation the plaintive tones of the oboe, tinged with exotic chromatic inflections, are set against declamatory murmuring on a single low pitch for Aida. Following these introductory sections, each of the formal adagio movements features the orchestral sonority of three flutes and solo clarinet with pizzicato strings. Significantly, the texts of both pieces express Aida's longing for Ethiopia, her homeland. Thus Verdi has drawn a musical parallel between two pieces that do not occupy temporally or tonally equivalent positions in their respective cycles. See also the conclusion of this essay.

18. See Busch, *Verdi's "Aida,"* 295 and 299.

section of Cycle I (see orchestral score, page 281).[19] In the first half of this *tempo d'attacco,* Radames sings the music of the "Pur ti riveggo" phrase five times in the key of C major. The phrase is not heard again until the coda of the F-major cabaletta, where Aida and Radames sing it twice in octaves: the first time in A♭, and the second—right before the final F-major cadence—in C (330/5–332/1). The C-major version picks up the C-major statements from the *tempo d'attacco* and resolves them into F major. The A♭ version is a dominant signal for D♭, the final key of the cycle. The relationship of the two versions to the main keys of the cycle can be expressed as a ratio: C:F = A♭:D♭. It thus appears that the C-major *tempo d'attacco* serves, in some sense, as dominant preparation for the F-major cabaletta.[20]

II. THE INNER COHERENCE OF EACH CYCLE

Having located the principal key areas of the two cycles and described the connections between them, we might now turn our attention to those aspects which serve to unify each cycle internally. Foremost among them is the establishment of what might be termed a harmonic *tinta*. Each cycle has its own distinctive *tinta,* but the harmonic procedures that characterize them are to some extent shared by the two cycles.

In Cycle I this *tinta* is characterized in part by the frequent use of major-minor mixtures, particularly between a major tonic and its parallel minor, and by an ambiguity between a major tonic and its relative minor. The equivalence of a major key and its parallel minor, or a major key and its relative minor, is of course common to harmonic procedures in much late-nineteenth-century music; there is no a priori reason to assign it any special significance. However, its use in Cycle I is so prominent and so carefully integrated into the tonal structure of each of the principal key areas that it may almost be said to assume the function of a harmonic motive.

The ambiguity between G major and minor and between G major and E minor has already been noted in Example 10.1. In the Aida theme, which provides the linking C-major harmony between the G major of the Introduzione and the F major of the romanza, the vacillations in the theme between C major and C minor in the middle and between C major and A minor at the end are features that are familiar from the theme's first presentation in the Preludio to the opera. Aida's F-major romanza borrows from the parallel minor as an interruption of the large cadential progression (see 274/2/2–275/2/1); inflections from the rel-

19. Powers, "La solita forma," 86.

20. Here the motivic connection provides a strong aural link between the two areas. Also, the C-major–E-minor ambiguity in the *tempo d'attacco* recalls an analogous ambiguity between F major and A minor in Aida's Romanza, Cycle I. (See also further remarks at the conclusion of this essay.)

ative minor (D minor) are important both in the refrain preceding the romanza and in the structural cadence of the romanza itself. The D♭ area of the cycle has two parts: the beginning of the *tempo d'attacco,* and the *cantabile* of the Aida-Amonasro Duet.[21] The first strongly tonicizes the relative minor (B♭ minor); the second is built on the alternation of D♭ minor (when Aida is singing) and D♭ major (when Amonasro is singing).

Important as modal mixture may be to the *tinta* of Cycle I, the use of harmonic interruptions—deceptive cadences, interrupted cadences, and delayed resolutions—is even more wide-reaching and significant. Indeed, interruptions are the very substance of the harmonic processes in the transitions between the cycle's principal key areas. The model for interrupted or delayed cadences is established in the short scene between Ramfis and Amneris (268/2/3–269/1/1). The tonicizations of VI (268/2/3–4 and 268/3/4) are integrated into the G-major cadences, resolving the ambiguity created earlier by the chanting of the priests. The chromatic passing tones E♭ and B♭ (268/2/5) have a similar integrative function with respect to the major-minor mixtures. Together with the augmentation of the harmonic rhythm from quarter-notes to half-notes (268/2/4), these chromatic passing tones delay the resolution of the cadential $^6_4$ chord until the downbeat of 268/3/1. The completion of the cadence is then left to Amneris, who makes use of the same motive ("io pregherò") with which Ramfis had ended ("a lei è noto").

Harmonic interruptions of a more complex nature are found in the transition between the end of the G-major Introduzione and the beginning of the F-major romanza. In the large, the harmonic motion, G–C–F, is simple and direct; on the foreground level, however, the space between C and F is elaborated by a series of interlocking interruptions whose resolutions are postponed until well into the romanza itself. The deceptive cadence at the end of the C-major Aida theme prevents closure in that key. The harmony that replaces the expected tonic—V of VI—is itself a dominant that requires resolution. This is denied by a second interruption at "Io tremo," the D-minor harmony that controls the next nine measures (271/5/1–272/2/1). The last phrase of the Scena, Aida's "e pace forse—e pace forse e oblio" (272/2/2–4) does finally take care of the V of C left hanging at the end of the Aida theme, by resolving it into a C chord that now functions clearly as V of F.[22] The refrain of the romanza (273/1/1–273/3/4) alludes to the other two pieces of unfinished business, the "unexplained" D-minor harmony and the unresolved V of A. The local sense of A minor at the

21. Of great significance in the linking of the two D♭ areas is the parallel between the recitative that precedes the first (279/2/1–280/4/5) and that which prepares Amonasro's C-minor outburst "Su dunque!" (289/2/3–291/4). The latter is a transformation of the former, a "replay" that preserves the essential tonal, harmonic, and motivic features of the original model. Since the C-minor allegro eventually returns to D♭, the two recitatives occupy corresponding positions in the respective approaches to the two D♭ areas.

22. The second and third measures recall the Ramfis-Amneris cadence mentioned earlier (268/2/3–268/3/1) and anticipate the cadence at the end of the Scena of the Aida-Amonasro Duet (280/4/4–5).

end of the second phrase of the refrain and the beginning of the romanza resolves the suspended V of A. The powerful F-major cadence at the end of the first strophe (275/2/1–5) then pulls all the loose threads together with a capsule summary that integrates the D and A roots into the principal tonality of F (see the prominent D-minor chord in 275/2/3, and the A-major triad, interpolated between the cadential $^6_4$ and the V^7 in 275/2/4).

The Scena of the Aida-Amonasro Duet (279/2/1–280/4/5) is the transition between the F and D♭ areas of Cycle I. This is the most difficult passage we have examined so far; it elaborates the old model of the deceptive cadence and establishes a new one that will become increasingly important in Cycle II. It will require closer analysis than we have applied so far.

Example 10.2 is a three-layer reduction of 279/1/1–283/2/2, moving from the foreground to the basic structure. Example 10.2*c* shows that the overall sense of the Scena is an interrupted I$^6_4$–V cadential progression in F major/minor. The space between the cadential $^6_4$ and the resolving $^5_3$ is elaborated by motions in the top voice and the bass that establish the parallel minor mode. Especially significant is the use of the minor subdominant right before the return of the cadential $^6_4$ chord; this recalls not only the interruption of the cadential progression in the F-major section of the romanza (274/2/2), but also the D-minor interruption ("Io tremo"—also with a local subdominant function) following the Aida theme in the Scena of the romanza (271/5/1–272/2/1). Two interesting details are shown in Example 10.2*b*: one is that the interruption unfolds in two stages, the first controlled by the E♭ root that supports the passing tone B♭ in the upper voice, and the second by the F root that sets in after the chromatic passing tone B♮. These two stages are so clearly related harmonically that the second can be heard as a transposed variation of the first (see the brackets, marked "model" and "variation" in the Example). Another important detail is the pivotal function of the chromatic passing tone B♮ between the two stages. It enters first as a neighbor-note—notated in the example as C♭—to the diatonic passing tone B♭ and is then reinterpreted as a chromatic passing tone—notated as B♮—before continuing on to the structural fifth, C.

Example 10.2*a* illustrates the foreground detail of the passage. The succession of parallel sixths in the E♭-minor section, marked "model," is a new feature that will play an increasingly important role in the scene. They are "Amonasro gestures," carrying a clear association with the Ethiopian King in the pursuit of his objectives.

The detail after the key change in Example 10.2*a* reveals that the new key, D♭, is also introduced as an interruption. The *tempo d'attacco* begins on the dominant of the new key, leaving incomplete the F-minor cadential progression at the end of the Scena. The treatment of the dominant harmony in the cadential progression, at Amonasro's line "Tutto tu avrai," is familiar from two parallel passages earlier in the cycle: the G-major cadence on 268/2/5–268/3/1, and the F-major cadence on 272/2/3–4.

EXAMPLE 10.2. Three-layer reduction of 279/1/1–283/2/2.

Turning to Cycle II, we find that the harmonic *tinta* lies in a tonal model in the transitions between the key areas of the cycle. The model first appears in the C-major *tempo d'attacco* of the Aida-Radames Duet, where it is used to prepare the E-minor tonality of Radames's "Nel fiero anelito" (see 309/2/2–311/1/1).

The passage begins in C major ("Gli Dei m'ascoltano"); Aida's reply moves immediately toward E minor, but a deceptive cadence postpones the arrival of the new key. After a cadence on G (locally V of C), "Amonasro gestures" (parallel sixths) lead to a second cadence in E minor, which is now completed.

Verdi uses a variant of this model at the approach to the G-minor *cantabile* (314/1/1–316/3/1). The C-minor motive of Amneris's jealousy pivots to become the subdominant of G minor. A deceptive cadence at Aida's "tu nol potresti" denies tonal closure; "Amonasro gestures" then conclude with a second cadence, in which the G-minor tonality is finally secured by the oboe solo at the beginning of the *cantabile*.

The transition between the G-minor and F-major areas transforms the model somewhat, but it is still recognizable. The transition between the F-major and Db-major/minor areas varies the model even further, but the derivation is still clear to the ear. Examples 10.3 and 10.4—reductions of the two transitions—will facilitate comparison.

The first passage (323/1/1–325/4; Ex. 10.3) makes a fleeting glance back at G minor, but then shifts abruptly to F minor. After a deceptive cadence on VI (Db), "Amonasro gestures" appear in a modified form, now as a rising line of

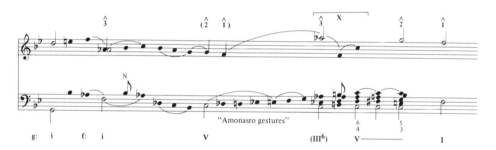

EXAMPLE 10.3. Transition from G minor to F major.

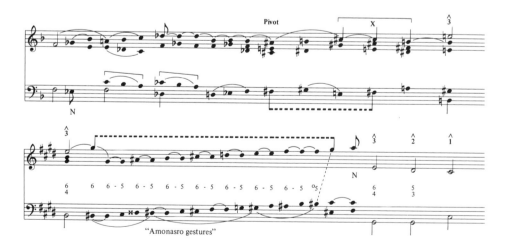

EXAMPLE 10.4. Transition from F major to C♯ (= Db) major/minor.

the voice parts doubled in unison by the orchestra, without the usual harmonization in parallel sixths. The line culminates on a high A♭, the structural third of the F-minor cadential progression; the harmonic support for this note is not I$^6_4$, but, rather, III^6, a chord that nevertheless has the correct bass note, C. After an intervening chromatic passing chord, the cadential $^6_4$ does appear, and resolves to V. The scoring of this cadential passage is particularly distinctive and will be heard again at a nearly analogous point in the transition to D♭ (see the passages marked X in Examples 10.3 and 10.4).

In the second passage (333/2–337/2; Ex. 10.4), the first eight measures following the close of the F-major cabaletta can be heard locally as an elaboration of B♭ minor (333/3–334/2/2). An enharmonic change in the upper voice from B♭ to A♯ (334/2/3)—perhaps recalling the C♭/B♮ pivot in the comparable approach to D♭ in Cycle I—leads to expectations of a cadence in B major. Amonasro's line "Ivi saranno i miei" closes melodically on B, but the harmonic support in the orchestra renders the cadence deceptive, with V$^4_2$ of IV substituting for the expected B-major tonic. The substitute harmony moves on to an E-major $^6_4$ chord underneath E, the structural third in the forthcoming C♯-minor (D♭-minor) cadence. The harmonization of the *Kopfton* $\hat{3}$ with a III$^6_4$ chord recalls the substitution of III^6 for I$^6_4$ in the approach to the F-major cabaletta (see Ex. 10.3). This time, the "Amonasro gestures" take the form of a chain of $\hat{6}$–$\hat{5}$ progressions that cadence into the D♭ minor of the Terzetto, the final goal of the cycle.

III. CONCLUSION

The tonal articulation of *Aida*, Act III, into a double cycle provides a structure that is in tension with the formal design—a tension analogous, perhaps, to that between the two-part structure and three-part form of a Classical sonata-allegro movement. As was Verdi's usual procedure, the beginnings and endings of the cycles are related through common features on the surface of the music. Each cycle is unified by its own harmonic *tinta,* and in both, the identifying characteristics of that *tinta* find their clearest expression in the transitions between the principal key areas. The *tinta* of Cycle II is, furthermore, clearly derived from the harmonic interruptions of Cycle I, with the interpolation of "Amonasro gestures" already foreshadowed there.

The succession of keys G–F–D♭ is an unusual one. Is it merely a key scheme, a pattern imposed by the composer to create an orderly design, or is there a *functional* relationship between the blocks? The connection between the G and F areas in each cycle is certainly functional, but that between the F and D♭ is much less satisfactorily accounted for in such terms. What about the final key of each cycle, D♭? Although it seems to be the goal of each cycle, it would be risky to suggest that this key should be regarded as the tonic for the entire act.

The problem hinges on this question of functionality. To what extent are we justified in positing a functional relationship between two key areas that are widely separated in time? Surely more than mere tonal correspondence is necessary to support such a relationship. In arguing that the C-major *tempo d'attacco* of the Aida-Radames Duet serves, "in some sense," as dominant preparation for the F-major cabaletta, we took into account not only a clear motivic connection but also a harmonic ambiguity that had precedents in Cycle I. Similarly, the ends of the cycles were heard as parallel because of certain clearly audible analogies. Even the two D♭ areas in Cycle I were equated—despite a powerful intervening C-minor passage—on the basis of motivic and harmonic similarities between the respective approaches to the two areas.

But the problem of functionality has, of course, a larger focus: it lies at the heart of the relationship between tonal structure and dramatic action—something largely (and deliberately) avoided in the present study. In the context of a style as fluid and complex as that of late Verdi, one must be extremely careful about attaching dramatic labels to particular keys, chords, or sonorities. Too often such attempts fail to take into account the larger tonal context. If two passages in the same key are to be heard in an associative context, there must be convincing evidence on the foreground; even more, the two areas must be functionally equivalent. For example, it is always hazardous to equate one passage that functions as a dominant with another that functions as a tonic, no matter what the dramatic parallel. Moreover, in Verdi's late works, important tonal articulations do not always coincide with the completion of dramatic actions, even when they are analogous. Indeed, much of the present study has concerned itself with noncongruence; we noted, for example, that Verdi established much stronger foreground connections between the F-major and G-minor areas than between the two F-major areas in the double cycle.

Verdi's late style involves a complex and subtle interaction of what Petrobelli has termed "systems," each of which operates "according to its own nature and laws."[23] Petrobelli lists "dramatic action, verbal organization, and music,"[24] and the musical parameter is capable of division into numerous subcategories: formal conventions, motivic relationships, and tonal structure, to name a few. Analytical studies of Verdi's mature style are in their infancy. Before we can address the question of the interaction between the systems, we must first unlock the secrets of a musical language which, in spite of its emotional immediacy, has only recently begun to yield to analysis.

23. Petrobelli, "Music in the Theatre," 129.
24. Ibid., 129.

Chapter 11

Schenker and the Norns

PATRICK MCCRELESS

We have become accustomed to considering Schenker and Wagner as representatives of diametrically opposed points of view. Schenker, for all the originality of his theory, is often regarded as reactionary; the theory is accompanied by cries for a restoration of musical ideals embodied in eighteenth- and nineteenth-century German instrumental music. Wagner, on the other hand, is conventionally seen as the innovator, the revolutionary who merged poetry, drama, and music into a single art form. This appraisal is, as far as it goes, unexceptionable. It is borne out by Schenker's late writings (wherein the calls-to-arms became strident), by his critical comments concerning Wagner, and by his refusal to consider Wagner's works as worthy of analytical attention.

If we can, however, put aside the ideological differences between theorist and composer and concentrate instead on their beliefs about how music should "work," we discover more common ground than might be expected. Schenker's opinions are not hard to find; he purveyed the ideology, unblushing, in the polemic that accompanied his analyses. Wagner's ideas about musical art found expression in his letters, in his writings, in autobiography, and, finally, in daily conversation with Cosima, reported dutifully in her two thick diaries. Yet ideology is not merely expressed in prose. Schenker's graphic analyses—in effect wordless musical artifacts in their own right—communicate an interpretation of music and a conviction about its nature no less marked than that expressed in his writing. This is, of course, one secret of Schenker's attractiveness. The graphic analyses interpret music by means of musical signs; they communicate in the same medium as their object of study.

But the composition of a musical work is itself, in some sense, also a commentary on the phenomenon *music* cast in musical form. We can extend the idea to Wagner. Are Wagner's scores in some sense commentaries on musical issues such as tonality or form? Do the scores as musical artifacts express beliefs about the nature of music, beliefs that are accessible? If, for instance, our experience of Wagner's scores convinces us of their musical integrity or unity, we may wish to impute to Wagner certain aesthetic convictions: insistence on the autonomy of the musical work or the organic wholeness of a self-sustaining musical structure.[1] In the end, these must be our beliefs, not (necessarily) Wagner's; but if we deal in generalities such as organicism, the gap between Wagner's music—as we perceive it—and Schenker's theory shrinks perceptibly.

When we set Schenker's analytical precepts against the details of Wagner's scores, we nonetheless expect sparks to fly. The differences between Schenker's explicit notions of coherence and an implicit aesthetic of "unity" expressed in Wagner's scores may be brought into relief in a twofold interpretation of a single Wagnerian scene: the Norns' Scene that opens *Götterdämmerung*. The first analysis adopts a more or less ad hoc method for which no detailed theoretical framework can be adduced but that has consistently proved appropriate and fruitful in my analysis of Wagner's works.[2] This ad hoc analysis addresses the scene in terms of the structure and meaning of the text and in terms of the formal, tonal, and motivic construction of the music, both in and of itself and in association with the text. In contrast, the second analysis is based on concepts and methodology derived from Schenkerian theory. This approach implies that our analyses of late-nineteenth-century chromatic music are in a broad sense Schenkerian. Yet at the same time it may also suggest that in this music linear phenomena per se do not achieve the status that Schenker claimed for them in the music of an earlier time. In the Norns' Scene, certain linear phenomena are still operative; they articulate a long stretch of music. But the musical gestures that shape the scene are above all *harmonic* and, what is more, lie outside the realm of diatonic tonality.

I. TEXTUAL, FORMAL, TONAL ANALYSIS

The Rope of Time

If the Norns' Scene is about anything, it is about time. It is the only scene in the *Ring* that encompasses within a narrative not only the story of the entire cycle (from the theft of the gold to the destruction of Valhalla), but time before the theft of the gold as well.[3] The central visual symbol of the scene, the golden

---

1. Ruth A. Solie gives a valuable historical perspective on the metaphor of organicism in "The Living Work: Organicism and Musical Analysis," *19th-Century Music* IV (1980–1981), 147–56.

2. Although not formulated in comparable detail, Robert Bailey's analytical model for Wagner's operas is indispensable. See especially "The Structure of the *Ring* and Its Evolution," *19th-Century Music* I (1977–1978), 48–61. His analysis (59–61) of the Prologue and Act I of *Götterdämmerung* provides the starting point for the present study.

ct II of *Die Walküre* also encompasses the entire time span
iled prophecy of "the end of the gods," while the earlier

rope that is spun by the Norns, is a symbol of time; the rather sullen, sinuous music that accompanies the winding of the rope evokes the linear passage of time from moment to moment.

Yet we can experience the full impact of the image of the cord, just as we can experience time itself, only if we understand its division into discrete parts. How the scene is thus divided is shown in Example 11.1. As Alfred Lorenz observed, the scene involves three parts—that is, three progressively shorter rounds of speeches for the three Norns, culminating in the breaking of the rope at the end of the Third Norn's third speech.[4] Lorenz's view of the passage works perfectly well: a three-part scene, with three subdivisions in each part, for three Norns. However, in such an analysis it is easy to overlook crucial differences between the final round (Round III in the Example) and the initial two. The first two sections are narrative and, thus, outside the time frame of the scene itself. The final round begins as a history of Alberich, but the narrative is quickly overwhelmed by the real time of the present, and by disaster, as the rope begins to tear and finally breaks.

Round I, Round II

The first two parts of the scene share a common symbol, the Weltesche (the mythic ash tree that stands at the center of the world). The Weltesche is the locus through which the Norns view the two characters, Wotan and Loge, whose histories they sing. In the first narrative the Norns stand outside real time. They tell the story of Wotan, from his initial violation of natural order— he breaks a branch from the Weltesche—to the flames that engulf him and his fortress, flames fed by the Weltesche's dead limbs. In the second cycle the Norns tell Loge's story, and they give us Loge both as a god and as fire, the fire that purges Wotan's transgression. Each of these two rounds is divided into three sections, one for each Norn. In both, the older Norns (First and Second) take the story from distant to recent past, while the youngest (Third) carries it into the future, to the end of the world and the end of the opera.

Intertwined with these two big sections in narrative time are smaller passages that lie outside the narrative: the Norns awaken from their ruminations and comment on their surroundings. These are like the refrains of epic poetry, re-curring texts that lie outside the time of the story. The first begins with a question, asked at the opening of each narrative round: is the light on the cliff the coming of dawn, or is it Loge as the *Feuerzauber*?

> FIRST: Welch' Licht leuchtet dort?
> SECOND: Dämmert der Tag schon auf?
> THIRD: Loges Heer
>   lodert feurig um den Fels.
>   Noch ist's Nacht.

---

4. Alfred Lorenz, *Das Geheimnis der Form bei Richard Wagner* I (Berlin, 1924).

Or, to open the second round:

> FIRST: Dämmert der Tag?
> Oder leuchtet die Lohe?

The second group of refrains recurs at the end of each Norn's speech in all three rounds; each Norn casts the rope to her sister and asks for information:

> FIRST: Singe, Schwester,
> dir werf ich's zu:
> Weisst du, wie das wird?

In the third round, the gesture is reduced to the question alone: "Weisst du was aus ihm wird," "Weisst du was daraus wird?"

Round III, Which Is Different

Lorenz's third round begins, like the others, as a narrative (the history of Alberich), but is engulfed by present time; in a sense the Norns are frightened out of their storytelling dream by the catastrophe of the tearing rope. The singularity of this third round is signaled at its beginning, as the question ("Welch' Licht leuchtet dort?") is replaced by an answer: "Die Nacht weicht." The third round drifts away from the central symbol of the first two, the Weltesche. But, most important, while in the first two rounds the Norns can see and understand the implications of what they see—what has happened, how this determines what will happen—in the third round they are blinded by the vision of Alberich's "wüstes Gesicht." The narrative collides with the present as the Second Norn tells of the Curse; the Curse itself "gnaws at the strands" of the rope. At the last moment, they see only one thing—the rope that frays and breaks in their hands.

The final section, then, plays a double role: as a climactic third round similar in design to the first two, and as a counterpart to the textual "refrains," the non-narrative interruptions that focus on both present time and the rope itself.

Music for the Golden Rope

It is perhaps ironic that Wagner employs such a strictly symmetrical musical form as the vehicle for unfolding the image of the golden rope. Yet compositionally he strikes an imaginative balance between continuity and articulation, between undifferentiated and differentiated time. He achieves continuity by weaving the sinuous, winding motive heard in the opening of the scene—music derived from the arpeggiated motive that symbolized the undisturbed state of the Rhine at the beginning of *Das Rheingold*—into and out of the texture. Its continual appearance, disappearance, and reappearance give the illusion that it

Introduction mm. 1–49		Round I: The Wotan Narrative mm. 49–189			Trans. mm. 190–94	Round II: The Loge Narrative mm. 195–247			Trans. mm. 248–58	Round III: Alberich mm. 259–317			
Orchestral	Vocal	First Norn	Second Norn	Third Norn	Second Norn	First Norn	Second Norn	Third Norn	Second Norn	First Norn	Second Norn	Third Norn	All
eb	eb	E eb eb	c		eb	F [Fb]	[f#] [c]	V of eb	[G]	[eb]	[eb]	[b]	[b]
RS	RS RS¹	RS RS¹	RS RS¹	RS	RS RS¹				RS¹	RS¹			
		RW	RW	RW		RW	RW		RW	RW	RW		

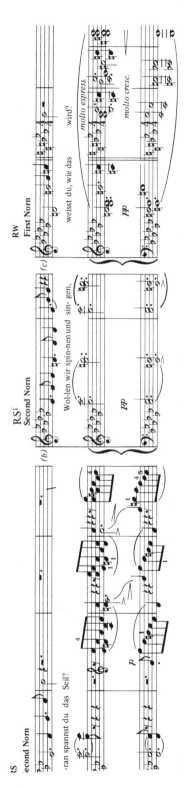

EXAMPLE 11.1. *Götterdämmerung*, Norns' Scene, formal and tonal structure.

is there all the time: like the rope of time it symbolizes, it is continuous. At the same time, the recurrences of this sinuous music are far from random, for Wagner in fact uses it as the central articulative refrain in the scene.

The sinuous arpeggio music is one part of a complicated, interwoven collection of musical refrains that recur through the entire scene (see Ex. 11.1). We can identify three more or less distinct ideas. The first is a pair of alternating triads, one major and one augmented, in dotted half-notes: a kind of narcotic spinning-song (RS[1] in the Example). These triads begin the famous "Zauberschlaf" motive from *Die Walküre* (Wotan's "Im festen Schlaf / verschließ ich dich") and appear here in association with the text variations on "wollen wir spinnen und singen" (as in m. 38, 3/1/4)[5] and "Singe, Schwester, dir werf ich's zu" (m. 147, 8/4/1).

The second refrain idea is the sinuous arpeggio itself, recurring in association with texts referring to the "Seil" and in close proximity to the spinning-song refrain ("So gut und schlimm es geh; / schling ich das Seil, und singe," mm. 43–47, 3/2–3/3/4; or "muß mir die Tanne / taugen zu fesseln das Seil," mm. 103–4, 6/3/4–4/1). This refrain is labeled RS in the Example.[6]

The third refrain idea is the main theme of the "Todesverkündigung" (*Walküre*, Act II, Scene 4). As in the "Todesverkündigung," it is associated here with the asking of a question about the future: "Weisst du wie das wird?" It recurs, with the question, through all three rounds (RW in the Example).

The refrains, like the image of the rope, weave in and out of the scene and, like the rope, gradually weaken and dissolve. The three together mark the ends of the three individual speeches in the first round; during the Wotan Narrative the effect of structure, of a symmetrical and stately dividing-off, is at its strongest. In the second and third rounds, only the "Todesverkündigung" music divides the speeches from one another; the narcotic chords of the spinning song are banished from the interior of each round and circle in a slower orbit to divide Rounds II and III.

The refrains are, then, truly the music for the golden rope. They work as rhetorical devices associated not only with the questions, with the words *spinnen, singen, schlingen, Seil,* but with the stage actions suggested by these words, as each Norn casts the rope to the next. The stage action itself articulates time in the theater. The object, the rope, the thread of time that binds the story, is con-

---

5. In the ensuing discussion, (00/0/0) refers to the page number, system, and measure number within the system in the widely available vocal score arranged by Karl Klindworth and published in the United States by G. Schirmer.

6. The ordering of the three refrains may seem counter-intuitive, since the musical passages in Example 11.1 illustrating refrains RS and RS[1] are reversed with respect to their ordering in the music itself. Refrain RS is shown first in the example because it occurs in the orchestra at the very beginning of the scene, and because it is the most important and most extensively used of the three refrains. However, it occurs with the appropriate alliterative text only after refrain RS[1] is heard with text; hence the reversal of order.

Lorenz also identifies three refrains in the scene, which he classifies as a "refrain-form." Although his three refrains are not precisely the ones noted here, his interpretation of their structural function is similar.

tinuous. The passing of the rope, the passing of the story, is a visual gesture that divides the continuous time into briefer, comprehensible slices.

Other Symmetries

The scene is articulated by other musical means, ranging from the simplest to the most complex. To give one classic instance: the First Norn, the eldest, who tells of the past, has the lowest tessitura; the Second Norn, the narrator of the present, is a mezzo; the Third Norn, who envisages the future, is often sung by a high soprano (often one who aspires to the role of Brünnhilde). In the first two narratives, the music of the First Norn is primarily in 6/4 meter, that of the Second primarily in 3/4, that of the Third in 4/4. Furthermore, of course, the orchestral fabric accompanying each Norn invokes thematic material appropriate to the dramatic topic: Valhalla, in the First Norn's first solo; the bass dotted figure associated with Wotan's spear and the treaties engraved on it, in the Second Norn's first solo; the solemn, martial music of the Immolation, in the Third Norn's first solo; and so on through the Loge Narrative and Round III, the denouement.

Of E♭ and B

Certain key areas also play a role in articulating the time of the scene. Basically, the scene turns on a shift from E♭ minor toward a B minor only hinted at in the final moments (this shift is also represented in Example 11.1). Both keys have associative connections that go back to *Das Rheingold*: E♭ minor echoes the E♭ major of the *Rheingold* "Vorspiel" and the undisturbed state of the world, while B minor is linked to Alberich's Curse and to his kingdom. In a vague sense, the shift from E♭ minor at the opening of the Norns' Scene toward the implied B minor of its close presages both dramatic events to come and their corresponding tonal symbolism: both the B cadence at the end of *Götterdämmerung*, Act I, and the (illusory) triumph of Alberich's (Hagen's) mischief.

Of the two tonal colors, E♭ minor and B minor, E♭ minor is far more important. While E♭ major at the beginning of *Das Rheingold* suggested the natural state of the Rhine, in its minor mode it now alludes to another symbol of nature, the Weltesche. E♭ is the primary tonal center of the scene, for it is established solidly both in the orchestral and vocal introductions, as well as in the opening monologue of the First Norn (see Ex. 11.1). E♭—in both major and minor modes—is the tonal thread of continuity analogous to the thematic continuity of the arpeggiated opening melodic material. Allusions to both modes of E♭, as key and chord, weave in and out of the texture, usually in association with the arpeggiated motive, providing the illusion that E♭—as a kind of icon— is always there, and supplying the background through which both the narratives and the drama of the Norns' golden ⌐⌐⌐⌐ ⌐⌐ ⌐⌐⌐⌐⌐ ⌐⌐⌐ ⌐⌐ ⌐

hinted at in the conclusion of the first round and the beginning of the second (mm. 190–97, 11/3/1–11/4/4). After this, the tonality disappears (as does the sinuous arpeggiated music with which it is linked) until the last moments of Round II: the cadential gesture at the climax of the Third Norn's speech ("den wirft der Gott / in der Weltesche / zuhauf geschichtete Scheite").

This cadence at the end of the second round is a nodal point in the scene and is worth lingering over. In a single climactic moment, the Third Norn reaches her highest note in the scene (b♭²). At the same moment, she reforges the connection between the image of the Weltesche and E♭ minor, by arpeggiating the triad on that word: a direct echo of the First Norn's "An der Weltesche wob ich einst" (m. 50, 3/4/3), the opening words of the first narrative round. The Third Norn, having prophesied the events that devolve from the despoiling of the mythic tree, refers to this symbol one last time.

The cadence for "den wirft der Gott in der Weltesche zuhauf geschichtete Scheite" turns toward E♭ minor without arriving at the tonic chord; it is a half-cadence. The incompleteness of the cadence, the uncertain status of the key, may be seen as allegorical. The questions the Norns have posed (what is the light?) have not been answered; the fate of the rope is still uncertain. The third round, the denouement, brings the answers, but it brings no tonic E♭. Hints of the chord E♭ float back into the third round, for example at "Die Nacht weicht" (m. 259, 16/1/2); the key signature for E♭ holds sway from "Ein wüstes Gesicht" (m. 265, 16/3/2) to "ragt mir des Niblungen Ring" (m. 276, 17/2/3)—but E♭ in either mode is not represented as a tonic. Rather, E♭ is subsumed, exists only as the memory of the First Norn's E♭-minor song, while the broader purpose of the third round is to twist the end of the scene toward a B minor itself presented only by allusion. Put another way, as E♭ crops up in the denouement, it creates no closure in the conventional sense; it is juxtaposed, weakened from the status of key to chord *en passant,* with B minor as the tonal end-point of the scene.

Shapes Made by Keys

Against the tonal background of the E♭-minor opening and the final twist toward B minor, Rounds I and II are heavily marked by divisions created by tonal means. Example 11.1 also shows the essence of this structuring-by-key. In Round I, the First Norn has what is in effect a closed ternary piece in E♭, with a contrasting section in E. The Second Norn has a similarly closed piece in C, a key suggested by its frequent connection with Wotan's vision of world redemption through Siegfried's sword. The music of the Third Norn, however, does not involve a closed tonal structure in any sense, but, rather, moves linearly through a complex chromatic sequence finally to circle back to the music of the minor signature.

Round II abandons the associative tonal references of Round I and instead builds on an abstract tonal relationship there prefigured. In Round I the music of the First Norn moved from E♭ to E and back. In Round II, this ascent of a half-step is continued: the First Norn begins on E♭ and then progresses quickly to F♭, F, and (by the end of her refrain) F♯, in such a way that she establishes each key but cadentially articulates none of them. Picking up from the First Norn, the Second Norn begins in F♯, only to move for the remainder of her speech into music that suggests, again without fully articulating, C, the same key that she had in Round I. The Third Norn continues in the same chromatic vein she had in Round I, so that neither her music nor that of her sisters in Round II reveals a closed tonal structure. Rather, the ascent by semitone begun in Round I is continued through F♯ before disintegrating into a linear-chromatic maze. The Third Norn's music moves *toward* E♭ and brings us to the climactic half-cadence aimed at that key ("in der Weltesche zuhauf geschichtete Scheite"). The structural refrain at "Schwinget, Schwestern, das Seil!" (m. 255, 15/4/1) begins with a G-major triad, which may be regarded as the end point of that motion in semitones in Round II; this triad, along with the melodic focus on B, is the first indication that the tonal focus will soon turn away from E♭ toward B minor.

Looking back over the scene, we can see that it achieves an impressive synthesis, both as abstract music and as a tonal structure with associative connections. As is shown in Example 11.1, the structural motion from E♭ minor to B minor is accomplished in two ways. First, the more local downward motion of a minor third within both Rounds I and II, from E♭ minor to C, is echoed in the diminished fourth, E♭ to B, that spans the scene's opening and end. Second, the upward motion of a semitone in Round I, E♭ to E, is continued through F, F♯, and G in Round II, and this G moves on to B, so that the tonal dynamic of the scene so far turns on the augmented triad E♭–G–B. Weaving its way through the scene is E♭ minor, the tonal symbol of the golden rope of time. Allusions to E♭, as pitch, chord, key, continually return in the refrains, and E♭ minor eventually articulates the end of the first two narrative sections by means of its structural dominant, at the climactic conclusion of the Third Norn's music in Round II. Furthermore, not only E♭ and B are intertwined as symbols in the drama: the tonal centers of Round I, E♭, C, and E, are all associative keys in the *Ring*. But what about the F, F♯, and G of Round II? Although these keys do not have literal referential connections, they do have their source in the drama. That dramatic basis concerns, not the keys themselves, but the particular way they progress—that is, stepwise by semitone. This is a type of progression associated throughout the *Ring* with Loge, who is, of course, the subject of Round II. Accordingly, Wagner has it both ways: the tonal plan makes sense as an abstract musical design, yet at the same time it is buttressed at every turn by a symbolic connection to the drama.

II. WAGNER AND SCHENKER

What about Schenker?

What, now, does such a tonal plan have to do with Schenker? Not much, we are forced to answer; Schenker would certainly have had nothing to do with it. Since Schenker's sine qua non for a coherent tonal piece is the prolongation of a tonic triad, the Norns' Scene falls at the first fence. Yet, if we distill the essence of his system, we can observe similarities between his explicitly stated theories and the implicit musical principles operating in the Norns' Scene. The parallels between Schenker's ideas and Wagner's music can be understood, appropriately enough, on three levels. The first is a deep level of abstraction, in which we can note conceptual parallels, but must admit that the vast gap that separates the diatonic music approved by Schenker and the chromatic music composed by Wagner prohibits any precise correspondences. The second is an intermediate level in which, with a minimum of readjustment, insights about diatonic music are transferable to Wagner's music. The third is a final level, in which Schenker's analytic methods and his graphic technique seem fruitful as devices for an exegesis of the scene.

At the first level, most fundamental, of course, is the very idea that music must be "organic": a metaphor that suggests not only a certain standard of relationship between the parts and the whole, but also the possibility, and even the desirability, of finding adequate terms and symbols to describe such relationships. Also fundamental is a concept of structural levels: the tonal plan presented in Example 11.1 would be impossible were we unable to differentiate between tonal phenomena that control the whole structure and those that take place on the surface. Finally, Schenker was deeply concerned with the unfolding of music in time. Although we may criticize him for seeming to ignore this aspect in his later work, his earlier essays betray a continual sensitivity to how musical events unfold in their compositional order. In our analysis of the Norns' Scene, Example 11.1 represents the tonal structure of the scene in chronological time: the large-scale progression is from E♭ minor toward B minor; the other keys must occur in a fixed progression in order to make tonal sense.

At the second level of parallels between Schenker's thought and the Norns' Scene, our insights become more specific. A closer look at certain aspects of the music will not only clarify passages in the scene that we have hitherto passed over—particularly, the difficult chromatic music of the Third Norn—but will also show that Schenker's concepts and analytical techniques may serve Wagner's music more convincingly as we approach the musical surface. At this level, two processes are crucial in the unfolding of the scene: first, the role of the pitch F♭ or E in the development of the tonal structure; and second, the function of the seventh chord F–A♭–C♭–E♭. Both become clearer when seen through a Schenkerian lens.

The process involving the pitch E in the Norns' Scene concerns a phenomenon central to Schenker's theory: the expansion of a chromatic detail early in a piece and its functions at progressively higher structural levels. The F♭ in measure 2 is the first chromatic pitch in *Götterdämmerung*. When we first hear the F♭, it is merely a passing tone between E♭ and G♭. But in measure 4, briefly, and at "Welch' Licht leuchtet dort" (m. 28, 2/3/1), it becomes the seventh of the dominant seventh of C♭, and it is in this guise that it serves as the harmonic preparation—that is, a V of V—for the tonicization of E in the First Norn's music of Round I (mm. 64–67, 5/1/1–4). In both cases the F♭ is a dissonance: a passing tone in the first case, a seventh in the second. A further, complementary aspect of its growth involves its gradual acquisition of status as a consonance. The first instance of its consonant use is measure 10, where F♭ is the third of the D♭-minor triad; a second and more important instance occurs on the final word of "dämmert der Tag schon auf?" (m. 31, 2/4/1), where F♭ becomes the root of a major triad. Having thus been a third and a root of foreground triads early in the piece, the next step for it is to be expanded to become the root of a triad that controls a large-scale tonal area, and that is precisely what happens when the F♭, respelled as E, becomes the tonal center for the middle section of the First Norn's music in Round I. This motion, up a semitone from E♭ to E, will set up the ascending tonicizations in Round II, after the allusion to E♭ between the first two rounds (mm. 190–95, 11/3/1–11/4/2). The First Norn in Round II begins with the same F♭ triad as at measure 31 (2/4/1) and then progresses through triads on F, F♯, and, eventually, G. In this way a single chromatic pitch, the first of the piece, serves as a clue to the tonal structure of the entire section.

Schenker and F♭

The expansion of the pitch F♭/E is, at the most fundamental level, Schenkerian, for it concerns the transferral of an element of the musical surface to higher levels. However, a comparison of our example with one of Schenker's own analyses of a diatonic tonal composition (one, indeed, that reminds us of the Norns' Scene) can show us precisely how the process described here differs from that described by Schenker. The work in question is Chopin's Etude in E♭ Minor, Op. 10, No. 6. The two works are in the same key, of course; more strikingly, the Etude also involves the expansion of a chromatic detail and plays with the pitches E♭–F♭. In the Etude the pitch F♭ is introduced as a passing tone, in an inner voice of measure 4; it becomes the root of an F♭-major triad in measure 7; and later, respelled as E major, it is expanded into a full-fledged tonicization that governs a large part of the middle section of the ternary form. Schenker's multilevel analytical sketch of the Etude is shown in Example 11.2. His explanation of the tonal motion to E (which is, he notes, F♭ enharmonically respelled)

EXAMPLE 11.2. Heinrich Schenker's analytical sketch of Chopin, Op. 10, No. 6 (from *Das Meisterwerk in der Musik* I [Vienna, 1925], 148).

is characteristic in that he attributes a logical, indeed, a compositional priority to the voice-leading. For him the middle section of the ternary form arises from the large-scale neighboring motion $\hat{5}-\hat{6}-\hat{5}$, or B♭–C♭–B♭, in such a way that the striking tonicization of E results from the progression through ♭II in the harmonization of melodic scale degree $\hat{6}$.[7]

In the Norns' Scene, of course, we find similar voice-leading, in particular, a melodic emphasis on the fifth scale degree and motion from that tone to the neighbor a semitone above. It is, however, much more difficult to claim that Wagner's tonal structure is actually rooted in voice-leading. The evidence is to the contrary, suggesting that voice-leading is secondary to harmonic function. The initial harmonic progression in the Norns' Scene involves a $\hat{5}-\hat{6}$ neighbor-

7. Heinrich Schenker, *Das Meisterwerk in der Musik* I (Vienna, 1925), 148–49.

tone in the top voice, and in a linearly minded analysis we could expand this neighbor-note to incorporate, at a higher level, the C♭ of measure 31 (2/4/1) and the B of measures 64–67 (5/1/1–4). But we could hardly consider voice-leading to be the ultimate source of the tonal structure. The latter is best defined as an assemblage of tonalities that are symbols for dramatic elements, tonalities either briefly cited or convincingly tonicized, lined up into patterns of rising half-steps and falling thirds. Furthermore, what happens in the Chopin Etude is more linear than harmonic; we perceive the linear process as more important than the harmonic one—so, at least, it might be argued. In the Norns' Scene there is much less possibility for disagreement. Voice-leading is compatible with, but not the determinant of, the tonal structure.

The Third Norn and a Certain Chord

A similar, fundamentally "harmonic," idea is unfolded during the strange music for the Third Norn. Her speeches turn the tonal color of each round in new directions, and her music ultimately turns E♭ minor toward B minor.

A single, peculiar seventh chord, F–A♭–C♭–E♭, is the point around which the turn is made. This chord, spaced in this way, is a familiar sound in the *Ring*. It is born of the Ring motive in *Rheingold* (Wellgunde, "Wer aus dem Rheingold schüfe den Ring," outlining F♯–A–C–E); the chord is the verticalization of the motive and all those born of it (the Curse, "Heilig ist mein Herd," etc.), a kind of pure harmonic essence of danger and disaster.

In the Norns' Scene the chord first appears during the instrumental prologue, in association with the sinuous arpeggiated material (m. 21, 2/1/4). As the scene progresses, the chord becomes a recurring harmonic motive that can take on many thematic-melodic disguises. It accompanies the first words sung, "Welch' Licht leuchtet dort?" and (a few measures later) "Woran spannst du das Seil?" (m. 40, 3/2/1); its characteristic sound saturates the recurrences of the arpeggiated material, the music for the rope of time. The refrains abound with citations of the chord (cf. m. 103, 6/3/4; m. 146, 8/3/4; mm. 192–94, 11/3/3–4/1).

But, within the first two narratives, the chord is given to the Third Norn alone. In Round I, she sees a vision of the Weltesche's branches, heaped up around Valhalla, waiting for the torch, "Gehau'ner Scheite / hohe Schicht . . . ." The F–A♭–C♭–E♭ chord sounded at this moment is blended into the solemn martial music that will later open Brünnhilde's Immolation speech. The chord in the Third Norn's speech is transposed through an ascending sequence, from bass F to A♭ to C♭; the sequence linearizes the pitches of the initial chord on F.

In the second round, this peculiar chord is again reserved exclusively for the Third Norn. She begins her second prophecy of disaster with the "Immolation" music of her first, transposed up a semitone. (Her first prophecy transposed the chord on F through F–A♭–C♭ in the bass; this second prophecy begins with the chord F♯ and progresses upward through A and C.) But when the sequence continues, the pattern is broken; it is not F♯–A–C–E but F♯–A–C–E♭ that is outlined by the transpositions of the chord. The sounding of this "wrong" note—E♭—and the E♭-minor chord built on it mark the critical moment of the Third Norn's speech, her highest note, her arpeggiation of the E♭ triad, her vision of the world's end: Wotan's igniting of the wood with his burning spear.

The Meaning of the Chord

What purpose is served by the manipulations of this chord? The chord itself—by the time we hear it in *Götterdämmerung*—is heavily laden with dramatic associations. Musical allusions and associations also seem to spring from its recurrences in the Norns' Scene. For instance, the E♭–F♭ (or E) relationship discussed above (see "What about Schenker?" and "Schenker and F♭") is mirrored in the two most important transpositions of the chord, F–A♭–C♭–E♭ and F♯–A–C–E. The E♭–E locus is played upon once more in Third Norn's second narrative, when her "Immolation" music is transposed upward on F♯–A–C, then E♭ (not E).

In a certain sense, it is the chord that mediates between the E♭-minor idea of the scene's opening and the twist toward B minor at its end. What happens to E♭ minor after the First Norn's first song? In effect, it recedes. But the Third Norn's climactic notes at the monumental half-cadence of her second speech ("in der Weltesche zuhauf geschichtete Scheite") wrench the harmonic fabric very close to a tonic cadence in E♭ minor, without stating the tonic chord. This cadence, half-finished, pointing at E♭ minor, looms over the third round. But the tension wound up in it is never fully played out. Where is the chord of resolution? What can we make of those E♭ pitches and chords in the third round? The brief allusion to the chord E♭ (mm. 259–61, 16/1/2–16/2/1) is made *en passant*; E♭ here is one of the chain of triads in the "Zauberschlaf" motive. This is no "resolution" of the faraway dominant cast up by the Third Norn's big cadence. The tonality of E♭ minor has gone for good; in its place, the peculiar chord F–A♭–C♭–E♭ intervenes to twist the scene's end to B minor.

In Round III, the chord is no longer the exclusive property of the Third Norn; it reappears as the First Norn sees Alberich's "wüstes Gesicht" and is here tied to the Ring motive that had given it birth. When the chord is lodged within this motive, it becomes an explicit allusion to the disaster the Ring's forging will bring. In this form, it saturates the music of Round III, thundering out as the Curse (on F♯–A–C–E) precisely as the golden rope breaks: "Straffer sei es gestreckt . . . Es riss!"

The quotation of the Curse is also an allusion, finally, to B minor. But the third round's swift transposition of the chord from F–A♭–C♭–E♭ (sees "aus Noth und Neid," mm. 274–75, 17/2/1–2) to F♯–A–C–E (see "nagt meiner

Fäden Geflecht," m. 279, 17/3/2) turns the harmonic color from flat to sharp. In an abstract and ethereal way, it also turns the story from E♭ minor to B minor, for a chord that could once function as diatonic II^7 in E♭ minor (see m. 192, 11/3/3) is transposed and, in the last seconds of the denouement, becomes part of a harmonic gesture toward the dominant of B minor. The transposition, and the change of function assigned to the Third Norn's peculiar chord, come together to create the B-minor twist at the scene's end.

The Third Norn, Who Is Different

A crucial function of the Third Norn's music is now apparent. Not only do both her solos serve as the high points of the first two narrative sections, but they also prepare the climactic end of the scene, the breaking of the rope. The Third Norn, the youngest of the three sisters, is distinct not only in foretelling the future rather than retelling the past; she is also given a different kind of tonal language, more chromatic and less tonally focused. This new language, first heard in Rounds I and II, returns toward the end of Round III; and its particular vein of chromaticism, its concentration on a single chord (F–A♭–C♭–E♭ and its transposition) supplies, as we have seen, the means by which the scene is turned from E♭ minor to B minor.

The Third Norn's chromatic music is thus woven into the fabric of both the abstract musical and the dramatic-musical designs that control the scene: the half-step ascent of the crucial seventh chords is a shadow of the E♭–E motion of Round I and, on a more general level, echoes the ascending semitone transpositions in the scene. Both the seventh chord on F and that on F♯ (like the diatonic triads and the keys for which they stand) symbolize particular aspects of the drama. More speculatively, we might even suggest that although the winding first refrain does not return literally at the end of the scene, it does, in a sense, return after all: as a characteristic chord, now transformed, given a more menacing tune—the Curse—and a more malevolent key—B minor.

Schenker Would Not Have Liked the Third Norn

It goes without saying that our analytical conclusions go far beyond Schenker's norms. Not only are they more harmonic than linear, they also deal with keys in a chromatic-relational rather than a diatonic-prolongational sense, and elevate a seventh chord—a necessarily dissonant element in Schenkerian terms—to a central background function. Yet, viewed from a somewhat less literal perspective, we are led to the same kinds of judgments as Schenker: to hear stepwise connections between events widely separated in musical time; to develop, first intuitively, then cognitively, ways of separating elements that are structural in the most comprehensive sense from those that are local in effect. And, perhaps most significant, we have an example of a particular process identified by Schenker himself: the higher-level expansion of chromatic detail.

A Graphic Analysis

The third and final level of the relation between Schenker's theory and Wagner's music—discussion of which was threatened above—involves linear analysis of the foreground of the Norns' Scene and yields the sketch given in Example 11.3, which is offered in the above-mentioned spirit of "wordless musical artifacts" that "interpret music by means of musical signs."

A few explanatory words, however, are necessary. At the "deepest structural level" (upper system, Ex. 11.3) the scene reveals a striking consistency in melodic use of the fifth scale degree: B♭ as the fifth of E♭ in the Introduction and the music of the First Norn in Round I; B as the fifth of E in the inner section of the First Norn's first solo; and C and C♯ as the fifth of F and F♯, respectively, in Round II. More important, the First and Second Norns' solos in Round I are bona fide, fully Schenkerian tonal pieces in virtually every sense: they prolong a tonic triad; they focus melodic activity around a particular member of this triad (the fifth, B♭, in the First Norn's first solo; the third, E♭, in the Second Norn's first solo); and they achieve closure by means of a structural linear descent from this tone to the tonic, concluding with the obligatory V–I cadence. In this sense, the Norns' Scene, like many other passages in Wagner's later operas, preserves Schenkerian, diatonic linear principles in closed stretches of the musical surface, while abandoning such principles at higher levels.

There is another sense in which Schenkerian principles are preserved. When the language changes in the music of the Third Norn, it loses its tonal-prolongational character while maintaining its linear character. It no longer prolongs tonal scale degrees but is free to use directional linear motion as a way of attaining a climax, with no need to relate all the supporting harmonies to a prolongational center—although one might argue that the difference is simply that the prolongational "center" becomes dissonant, that is, a seventh chord. Such freedom allows, for example, the Third Norn's climactic words "Der ewig'en Götter Ende / dämmert ewig da auf"—words derived from the very title of the opera—to be set to music that progresses from C♯ (or, enharmonically, D♭, the key of Valhalla, and of the end of *Götterdämmerung* as well as of the *Ring* as a whole) to E♭ (the key of the Rhine, of the beginning of *Götterdämmerung*, and the beginning of the *Ring*), all in the space of three measures (mm. 177–79, 10/4/1–3). Here and elsewhere in his later operas, stepwise lines are a way Wagner preserves coherence, while gaining a maximum saturation of associative keys. These moments are generally the musical realizations of nodal points in the poems—points where the density of symbol and meaning calls for as much musical cross-reference as possible.

Finally, even at the deepest structural level, the Norns' Scene seems to be linear in some Schenkerian sense. The analytical sketch shows a single, *Urlinie*-like line spanning the entire scene. Whether such a line is aurally perceptible, and whether it is analytically defensible, I leave as open questions; I only note that,

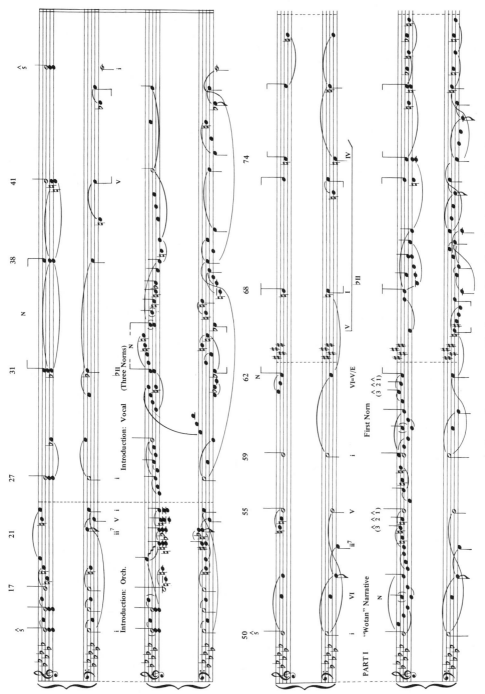

EXAMPLE 11.3. *Götterdämmerung*, Prologue, Part I, voice-leading sketch.

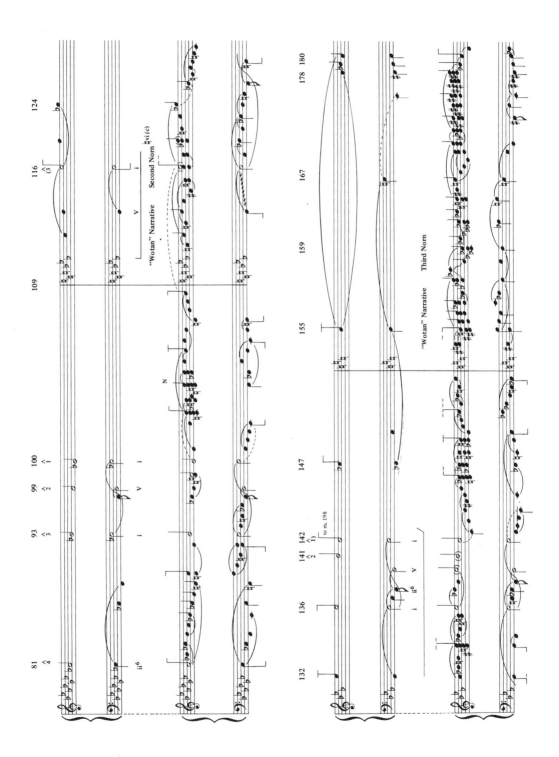

EXAMPLE 11.3 *continued.*

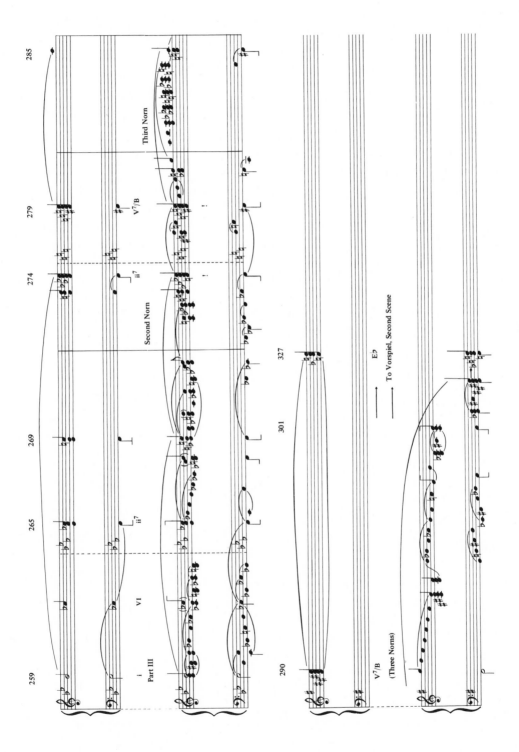

given Wagner's music, Schenker's system, and necessity as the mother of invention, it is analytically obtainable. Certainly a number of aspects of the piece argue for some sort of linear continuity: the Schenkerian prolongations in the music of the First and Second Norns in Round I; the clear ascending stepwise line in the orchestral music accompanying the Third Norn in all her solos; the linear ascent in measures 194–238 (11/4/1–14/3/1) of Round II—Cb, C, C♯, D, Eb, E, F♯; and the unmistakable $\hat{3}$–$\hat{2}$ half-cadence at the end of the Third Norn's music in Round II—a cadence that threatens to make a real Schenkerian piece out of the whole scene. This moment gives every impression of being a classic background interruption; we would hardly be surprised to hear the Eb-minor triad and the music of measure 1 follow immediately in its wake. And in a sense it *is* an interruption, although separated from the return of Eb by a transition and a refrain; for, as we have seen, the First Norn "begins again" at the opening of the final section. This section is in essence a consequent to the antecedent that began with the first words of the scene, "Welch' Licht leuchtet dort?" and that concludes with the Third Norn's half-cadence or, in Schenkerian terms, interruption.[8] That the consequent gives an answer that is shocking (in the dramatic sense) to the Norns and (in a musical one) to Schenker only serves to emphasize the virtuosity with which Wagner has combined traditional tonal language with a language of his own.

POSTSCRIPT: AN ALLEGORY

We began our analysis by remarking how the Prologue divides musical time while seeming to make it continuous. We might conclude by viewing the scene as an allegory, told by the stage directions, acted out by the music. Early in the scene, just before the beginning of her music in Round I, the First Norn "unwinds a golden rope from herself and ties one end of it to a branch of the fir tree."[9] At the end of her music, she throws it to the Second Norn, who "winds the rope thrown to her round a projecting rock at the entrance of the cave." When the rope is passed to the Third Norn, however, she is seen simply "catching the rope and throwing the end behind her"; it remains unattached. At the conclusion of her music, at the end of Round I, she throws the rope back to the Second Norn, who throws it back to the First. At the beginning of Round II, the First Norn "loosens the rope from the bough and fastens it on another." At the end of her short section she again throws the rope to the Second Norn, who again winds it around the rock. But when the Third Norn receives the rope for the second time, she again fails to attach it. Instead, after her climactic final

8. Lorenz, *Das Geheimnis der Form,* 233 notes that the cadence on the dominant at measure 249 (15/3/1) makes a structural conclusion in Eb impossible. He does not, of course, invoke Schenker's concept of interruption.

9. All citations of Wagner's stage directions are from the English translation in the Schirmer vocal score.

words, she throws it back to the Second Norn, who throws it back to the First. Thus far, clearly enough, the winding or not winding of the rope around the rock can serve as a symbol of the tonal language used in each Norn's music: the tonal-prolongational music—music able, as it were, to be tied around a single tonal center—is the music of what we might call the Schenkerian Norns. This is contrasted with the more linear-chromatic music of the Third Norn. But it is only in the third round that the consistency of the stage actions as symbols of tonal language becomes fully clear. The First Norn, beginning with an echo, *en passant,* of E♭, fastens the rope again. Fourteen measures later, droning on the pitch E♭, the Second Norn "with busy haste winds the rope round the jagged rock at the cave's mouth." Between her initial words and her throwing of the rope to the Third Norn for the last time, the music moves inexorably from the flat color of the F–A♭–C♭–E♭ chord to the preparation for B minor. At the climax, the Third Norn, having hastily caught it for the last time, "pulls hard at the rope," which breaks exactly at the moment that the F♯ pedal appears in the bass, signifying the arrival at B minor.

While the allegory demands no extensive interpretation, three points are worth considering. First, the Third Norn's musical language changes in a way that parallels both the text and the stage action: whereas the first two Norns narrate the past, she prophesies the future; whereas they fasten the rope, she does not; whereas their music can prolong a tonal center, hers cannot. Second, the rope of time, articulated in the variety of dramatic and musical ways we have seen, can cope with the Third Norn and her music no better than Schenker can; it is with her music that the rope breaks.

Finally, perhaps the most telling symbol of all, it is the Third, chromatic-language Norn, rather than the Schenkerian First and Second Norns, who is given the classic tonal interruption. It is she who "interrupts" the dramatic gesture, who throws the rope back to her sisters. It is she who forces us to understand both musical languages in the scene: the diatonic and the chromatic. It is she whose tremendous half-cadence at the end of Round II suggests that neither for her, nor for the main characters of the *Ring,* nor for Wagner will there be a satisfactory return to that natural state of E♭ they once knew. And for us, living in a different time, more than a hundred years after the death of Wagner and more than fifty years after the death of Schenker, it is the Third Norn who best ties together the musical strands of the scene itself, and the musical strands that link the work of Richard Wagner and Heinrich Schenker.

Index

Note: Individual operas discussed at length are listed as separate entries; otherwise operas are listed under their composers.

Designer: Janet Wood
Compositor: A-R Editions, Inc.
Text: 11/13 Galliard
Display: Galliard
Printer: Malloy Lithographing
Binder: John H. Dekker & Sons